RESEARCH AND THEORY TO FOSTER CHANGE IN THE FACE OF GRAND HEALTH CARE CHALLENGES

ADVANCES IN HEALTH CARE MANAGEMENT

Series Editor: Jennifer Hefner

Associate Editors: Dori A. Cross and Patrick D. Shay

Recent Volumes:

ADVANCES IN HEALTH CARE MANAGEMENT
VOLUME 22

RESEARCH AND THEORY TO FOSTER CHANGE IN THE FACE OF GRAND HEALTH CARE CHALLENGES

EDITED BY

JENNIFER L. HEFNER
Ohio State University, USA

DORI A. CROSS
University of Minnesota, USA

AND

PATRICK D. SHAY
Trinity University, USA

United Kingdom – North America – Japan
India – Malaysia – China

Emerald Publishing Limited
Emerald Publishing, Floor 5, Northspring, 21-23 Wellington Street, Leeds LS1 4DL

First edition 2024

British Library Cataloguing in Publication Data
A catalogue record for this book is available from the British Library

ISBN: 978-1-83797-656-0 (Print)
ISBN: 978-1-83797-655-3 (Online)
ISBN: 978-1-83797-657-7 (Epub)

ISSN: 1474-8231 (Series)

Printed and bound by CPI Group (UK) Ltd, Croydon, CR0 4YY

INVESTOR IN PEOPLE

CONTENTS

ABOUT THE EDITORS

Jennifer L. Hefner is an Associate Professor in the Division of Health Management and Policy, The College of Public Health, Ohio State University, USA.

Dori A. Cross is an Assistant Professor in the Division of Health Policy and Management, School of Public Health, University of Minnesota, USA.

Patrick D. Shay is an Associate Professor in the Department of Health Care Administration at Trinity University, USA.

ABOUT THE CONTRIBUTORS

Casey Canfield is Assistant Professor in Engineering Management and Systems Engineering at Missouri S&T. She has an Engineering & Public Policy PhD from Carnegie Mellon University and Engineering: Systems BS from Olin College. Her research quantifies the human part of complex systems to improve decision-making in infrastructure transitions.

Nathan W. Carroll is Associate Professor of Healthcare Administration at Virginia Commonwealth University. His research focuses on understanding the financial incentives healthcare organizations face, and how organizations are responding to those incentives.

Ganisher Davlyatov, The University of Oklahoma Health Sciences Center, Department of Health Administration and Policy.

Akbar Ghiasi, University of the Incarnate Word, H-E-B School of Business and Administration.

Rachel Gifford is Assistant Professor of Healthcare Management and Organization Studies at Maastricht University. She holds a PhD in Organizational Behavior from University of Groningen. Her research interests include the organization of care delivery and healthcare professionals, organizational adaptation and the evolution of professional work in health care.

Mark Govers is Associate Professor in Organisation and Management at Maastricht University's Care and Public Health Research Institute (CAPHRI). He holds a PhD on the intersection between business information technology and organization development. His interests include socio-technical systems thinking, and digital developments and entrepreneurial behavior.

Jyotsna Gutta is Policy Analyst in the Center for Health Policy in the Department of Health Policy & Management at the Indiana University Richard M. Fairbanks School of Public Health in Indianapolis.

Larry R. Hearld, The University of Alabama at Birmingham, School of Health Professions, Department of Health Services Administration.

Anne M. Hewitt is Professor and Chair for the Department of Interprofessional Health Sciences and Health Administration and a Professor at Seton Hall University. She is primary editor of *Population Health Management: Strategies,*

Tools, Applications and Outcomes and author of the upcoming text, *Population Health: Practical Skills for Future Health Professionals.*

Tory H. Hogan, The Ohio State University, College of Public Health, Division of Health Services Management and Policy.

Saleema A. Karim, Associate Professor of Healthcare Administration at Virginia Commonwealth University. Her research focuses on hospital financial sustainability, disparities, geographic variation, and HVBP and HRRP reimbursement.

Clair Reynolds Kueny, Associate Professor at Missouri S&T, received her MS and PhD in Industrial-Organizational Psychology from Saint Louis University. Her research related to applying organizational theory to healthcare delivery has been published in outlets including *Occupational Health Science*, *Journal of Clinical Oncology*, and *Journal of Interprofessional Education & Practice*.

Lisa Kutschera is rotation coordinator for the Medical Residency Program for the IU School of Medicine located on the Indianapolis Campus. Lisa is also the parent of a son with Autism.

Shoou-Yih D. Lee is the inaugural Martha and Wickliffe Lyne Professor of Health Administration at Virginia Commonwealth University. He is an organizational sociologist and health services researcher whose research seeks to improve health care delivery through critical examination of factors that drive organizational as well as individual decisions and behaviors.

Robert Wheech Maldonado, The University of Alabama at Birmingham, School of Health Professions, Department of Health Services Administration.

Arnold Milstein, Stanford University School of Medicine, is the Director of the Clinical Excellence Research Center at Stanford University. The Center discovers and disseminates innovations in clinical process and bedside applications of machine intelligence that lower the cost of high-quality health care.

Ingrid Mur-Veeman was Associate Professor in Organisation and Management at Maastricht University in Maastricht, the Netherlands. She played an initiating role in conceptualizing the RPB concept within the organizational DNA theory. She passed away in 2016.

Zhanna Novikov, UTHealth Houston, School of Public Health and Stanford University School of Medicine, is interdisciplinary researcher who applies organizational theory and behavior models to explore how individuals and teams in health care can innovate and improve care-safety. She's an affiliate of Stanford University's Clinical Excellence Research Center.

Alex Price is Assistant Professor in Radiation Oncology at Case Western Reserve SoM. He is currently pursuing his PhD in Systems Engineering from Missouri S&T. He has an MS in Medical Physics from Duke University. His research interests are healthcare systems modeling and novel approaches to radiation oncology.

Minakshi Raj is Assistant Professor at the University of Illinois Urbana Champaign. Her research focuses on identifying organizational and policy approaches to integrating family caregivers of older adults into the health care system with an emphasis on culturally diverse caregivers.

Shu-Fang Shih is Assistant Professor of Healthcare Administration at Virginia Commonwealth University. Her research provides empirical evidence that supports the design and implementation of human-centered, technology-driven, and integrated health and social care models to improve population health and promote health equity.

Sara J. Singer, Stanford University School of Medicine and Graduate School of Business, is Associate Director of the Clinical Excellence Research Center at Stanford university. Her research in health care management and policy focuses on how organizational leadership and culture impact efforts to implement health delivery innovations, integrate patient care, improve safety and reliability of health care organizations, and promote a culture of health.

Elveta D. Smith is Associate Professor in the Master of Healthcare Administration program at the University of North Carolina at Wilmington. After 20 years in hospital administration, she now teaches future healthcare leaders.

Sarah M. Stelzner focuses on developing programs in Community Pediatrics (e.g., the Anne E. Dyson Community Pediatrics Training Initiative, and the Our Kids Our Community Advanced Training) to improve the skills and competencies of primary care pediatricians. She provides team-based care including care conferencing to underserved populations.

Jeff Szychowski, The University of Alabama at Birmingham, School of Public Health Department of Biostatistics.

Arno van Raak is a Sociologist. He has worked at Maastricht University as an Associate Professor until 2023. His research particularly concerns integrated care, care supply chains, and interorganizational networks of care providers. Among his publications is the book entitled "Integrated Care in Europe" (2003).

Daan Westra is Assistant Professor of Healthcare Management at Maastricht University's Care and Public Health Research Institute (CAPHRI). His research focuses on the structures of and collaborative processes within interorganizational networks in the healthcare sector and across the healthcare and social services sectors.

Valerie A. Yeager is Professor and MPH Concentration Lead for the Department of Health Policy & Management at the Indiana University Richard M. Fairbanks School of Public Health in Indianapolis. Her research broadly examines the intersection and interaction of public health and health care.

LIST OF REVIEWERS

Mona Al-Amin	Suffolk University, USA
Nathan W. Carroll	University of Alabama at Birmingham, USA
Elveta Denise Smith	University of North Carolina in Wilmington, USA
Matt DePuccio	Rush University, USA
Bram Fleuren	Maastricht University, Netherlands
Greg Gascon	Ohio State University and Ohio Health, USA
Rachel Gifford	Maastricht University, Netherlands
Mark Govers	Maastricht University, Netherlands
Megan E. Gregory	The Ohio State University, USA
Anne M. Hewitt	Seton Hall University, USA
Tory Hogan	Ohio State University, USA
Clair Reynolds Kueny	Missouri University of Science & Technology, USA
Sarah R. MacEwan	The Ohio State University, USA
Zhanna Novikov	UTHealth Houston, USA
Minakshi Raj	University of Illinois, USA
Cynthia Sieck	Dayton Children's Hospital, USA
Lena Stevens	Nationwide Children's Hospital, USA
Maike Tietschert	Erasmus University, Netherlands
Dan Walker	The Ohio State University, USA
Daan Westra	Maastricht University, Netherlands
Valerie A. Yeager	Indiana University Richard M. Fairbanks School of Public Health, USA

PREFACE

We are pleased to share Volume 22 of *Advances in Health Care Management (AHCM): Research and Theory to Foster Change in the Face of Grand Health Care Challenges*. The past few volumes have focused on identifying and setting a research agenda for grand health care challenges (see Preface, Vol. 20, Hefner & Nembhard 2021). Through informed commentaries from prominent scholars in health care management, Volume 21 (Shortell et al., 2022) highlighted the current opportunities and challenges of: health system digitization; diversity, equity, and inclusion; COVID-19; performance improvement; network governance; inter-sector alliances; alterative payment models; and social determinants of health. A common theme across the chapters in Volume 21 was discussion of the organizational change needed to address these challenges.

Many have recognized that healthcare organizations today face the certainty of change as they confront varied grand challenges, all occurring in a broader landscape that scholars describe as radically and rapidly transforming at an unprecedented and accelerating pace (Amis & Greenwood, 2021; Dempsey et al., 2022). Such an environment is characterized by "exacerbated levels of uncertainty," with people seeing and valuing their work differently as a result (Amis & Greenwood, 2021, p. 585; Wright et al., 2023). As healthcare leaders work to navigate the continual questions surrounding radical change and heightened uncertainty, they require an understanding of effective approaches to organizational change, yet what scholars know about change management continues to evolve.

Management models designed to understand and respond to organizational change have proliferated in the past several decades, with some of the most widely recognized models of change management now common elements in business administration and health administration education, such as Lewin's (1947) three-step model, Kotter's (1996) eight-step approach to change, or the ADKAR model for change (Hiatt, 2006). However, scholars are increasingly questioning commonly held views within the change management literature and the models they have shaped, finding empirically that no single model is a universally supported or clearly preferred approach to change management (Phillips & Klein, 2023). For example, they challenge the belief that the vast majority of changes result in failure, instead suggesting that change can yield both successes and failures simultaneously while also calling for a deeper examination and clarification of what we mean when we talk about change success or failure (By, 2020; Hughes, 2022; Suddaby & Foster, 2017). Numerous works have pushed against the assumption that successful organizational change results primarily from the behaviors, characteristics, or strategies of an individual acting as a change agent in a position of authority, instead highlighting that change leadership can be provided from numerous sources, with intentional collaboration and effective configuration of coordinated change efforts mattering more than the specific sources of leadership functions (Cummings et al., 2016; Ford et al., 2021; Karasvirta & Teerikangas, 2022).

These and other developments in change management scholarship increasingly point to the value of approaches to change management that embrace complex adaptive systems thinking. The rational, standardized, and reductionist approaches to change management that were commonly employed throughout the 20th century are increasingly recognized as inadequate to address the emergent, complex, and wicked problems faced by today's health care delivery system. Transformational change is required and, as systems themselves, organizations must embrace systems thinking in order to realize effective transformation (Beer, 2021; Bryson et al., 2021; Waddock, 2020). A systems view challenges us to focus beyond a single variable or fragment of the system within change; instead, it recognizes the system's interconnected elements and purposes, making sense of it in ways that develop a new understanding of potential transformations, and promoting collective engagement among change agents to identify key leverage points producing sizable effects and long-term solutions (Gersick, 2020; Uhl-Bien, 2021; Waddock, 2020). However, the adoption of systems thinking in and of itself presents a significant challenge to organizations today, particularly among those subject to "short-term pressures for performance" and a general "reluctance to confront inconvenient and complicated truths that might expose deeper systemic barriers" (Beer, 2021, p. 16). In light of this, some may ask: Are today's healthcare organizations up for the challenge? To that question, we find the chapters collected for this volume provide reason for optimism.

In an environment characterized by ambiguity and uncertainty, effective change management can also be seen in the collaboration, coordination, and complementarity practiced among distributed sources of change leadership (Dempsey et al., 2022; Errida & Lotfi, 2021; Ford et al., 2021; Phillips & Klein, 2023). Scholars call for approaches to change management that emphasize the power of empathy, that recognize the importance of taken-for-granted social factors underlying processes of change, that promote the involvement of varied participants, and that foster an openness to engage deeply beyond surface-level changes, such as design thinking (Hvidsten et al., 2023) and leadership-as-practice (Raelin, 2022). Such approaches encourage levels of adaptation, improvisation, and creative problem solving that are commonly aligned with both systems thinking and design thinking (Shay, 2023), leading to more effective navigation of change in the midst of complexity (Hvidsten et al., 2023). Furthermore, the mindsets that connects systems thinking and human-centered approaches to problem solving such as design thinking – including collaboration, curiosity, mindfulness, resilience, recognition of interconnections, and an appreciation for diverse perspectives (Mugadza & Marcus, 2019; Shay, 2023; Shrier et al., 2020) – not only serve as drivers of effective change management, but they also emerge consistently in this volume's chapters as critical approaches to addressing health care's grand challenges.

Therefore, this year's volume examines how health care organizations position for, and pursue, successful sustained change. We organize the chapters into four complementary sections, each a mix of theoretical and empirical contributions to guide organizations in an environment of ever-evolving challenges.

Our first section focuses on persistent drivers of environmental uncertainty to which health care organizations must be responsive. Chapter 1, by Gifford and colleagues, offers a theory-building reflection on the changing ways in which health care organizations must understand and build capacity to thrive in a state of persistent, deep uncertainty. Using a framework that contrasts approaches to buffer against environmental change with efforts to actually incite and be on the leading edge of evolving expectations, authors propose the need for organizations to remain adaptive and – where possible – create potential futures rather than engaging in avoidant, controlling approaches to change. This chapter concludes with advice to organizations on how to move toward an "Adapt and Create" approach using systems thinking and the notion of temporal work – that is, encouraging individuals and teams to break the inertia of path dependency by challenging the linkages between "what was/is done" with what could or should be done.

The subsequent two chapters offer additional tools to organizations seeking to build resilience in the face of persistent environmental uncertainty. Chapter 2, by Reynolds, Price, and Canfield, focuses on the challenge of health care organizations needing to provide timely and accessible services in rural communities. Authors detail a simulation-based approach to model the feasibility and impact of proposed organizational changes as one way to assess readiness and guide subsequent change management efforts. They illustrate via case study how this approach was used to help guide design and implementation considerations for a mobile radiation oncology unit in a rural community. In Chapter 3, authors Hogan et al. detail a theory-driven empirical analysis focused on culture change in nursing homes – that is, highly regulated health care environments plagued by chronic under-resourcing. With the uncertainties caused by such persistent financial constraint, authors seek to identify the types of change management activity that are feasible in this environment and associated with these organizations moving toward a culture of more person-centered care. They find that knowledge management (i.e., the seeking and use of information relevant to guiding organizational functioning) is associated with culture change, and that this relationship is moderated by leadership and measures of staffing ability. These findings offer insights to health care leaders looking to build adaptive systems that support organizational readiness for change despite chronic resource limitations.

The second section of this volume focuses on the mechanisms of change – how leaders within organizations frame and execute change. Chapter 4, by Govers et al., offer a theoretical consideration of why organizational change often fails, using a framework that suggests that leaders too often attempt to change routines without first modifying the underlying principles and beliefs of organizational work. Using an analogy of organizational DNA to detail how principles, beliefs, and routines bind together an organization's core technical capabilities and social capital, they use an exemplar case to showcase specific aspects of leadership intentionality and action that foster deep successful change. However, successful change also depends on characteristics of the innovation itself, and of the individuals leading the effort. In Chapter 5, Novikov, Singer, and Milstein, use a national survey of clinicians to assess how these characteristics are associated with use of artificial intelligence and other forms of innovation diffusion. Authors investigate how individuals' job aspects associated with connectivity (i.e., professional purview, supervisory responsibility, tenure with an organization) increase knowledge and awareness of innovation such that they are more likely to use and spread care delivery innovations. A key part of this knowledge and awareness building is its association with higher perception of value of new innovations, which may build personal interest in engagement as well as these individuals' ability to facilitate diffusion within their network. Chapter 6, by Tietschert et al., explores the association between management practices and safety culture after implementation of the Safe Surgery Checklist. They use longitudinal survey data from the checklist implementation at 42 general acute care hospitals in a leading hospital network. Their findings suggest that the changes in safety culture encouraged by implementation of the Safe Surgery Checklist are significantly related to changes in management practices, highlighting structured checklist implementation as an avenue for hospital administrators to enhance safety culture in their organizations.

The third section of this volume investigates organizational preparedness and response in the face of acute crisis. In Chapter 7, Carroll et al. investigate the extent to which hospital finances were impacted in Washington state due to the Covid-19 pandemic. They find a significant hit to operating margins across all hospitals for 2020 and 2021, with hospitals that treat vulnerable patients being most affected (i.e., safety-net and critical access hospitals). Both revenues and expenses were adversely impacted by the pandemic. This analysis calls into question what organizations can be doing now to buffer against the financial vulnerability caused by such extended acute disruption. A detailed commentary by Dr Smith in Chapter 8 highlights the cyclical nature of organizational attention to preparedness over the past 20 years, and the threat of complacency that sets in between spikes of large-scale crises. This chapter describes post-event recommendations issued after each recent global epidemic, and finds a lack of depth or substance in the guidance given to organizations to support sustained preparedness alongside normal operations.

The fourth and final section of the volume highlights key ways in which sociopolitical and demographic shifts are encouraging organizations to reconsider what preparedness means outside of acute crisis. In Chapter 9, Hewitt interrogates limitations of outdated paradigms we hold about health systems and health care delivery. The author details an updated "co-production of health" framework that better reflects the boundary-spanning interorganizational and inter-sector ways that health and value are created for patients and communities. This chapter offers important suggestions for future research that refines and tests this model as a useful way to design and execute transformative organizational change. Chapter 10, by Yeager and colleagues, offers a thoughtful examination of one way in which a large health system embraced a community-partnered approach to care delivery. This study qualitatively explores efforts to enhance case conferencing for children with complex needs by using parent liaisons to facilitate connection with community resources and social support. Indeed, having these boundary-spanning agents helped organizations offer patients more holistic services that reduced stress for clinicians as well as family members. Authors offer insights into the necessary coordination structures and policy-based payment changes that would help sustain this model of care. Finally, in Chapter 11, Dr Minakshi Raj offers a commentary piece that draws attention to family caregivers as a critical but under-recognized partner in the co-production of health. She details the problems of a fragmented policy landscape and a lack of enabling factors (e.g., time, awareness, connectivity) that allow for meaningful engagement of caregivers. Using a coproduction of health paradigm, organizational leaders should be thinking strategically about how to proactively integrate caregivers as boundary-spanning and value-generating members of the care team.

Jennifer L. Hefner, PhD, MPH, Ohio State University
Dori A. Cross, PhD, University of Minnesota
Patrick D. Shay, PhD, MS, Trinity University

REFERENCES

Amis, J. M., & Greenwood, R. (2021). Organisational change in a (post-) pandemic world: Rediscovering interests and values. *Journal of Management Studies, 58*(2), 582–586.

Beer, M. (2021). Reflections: Towards a normative and actionable theory of planned organizational change and development. *Journal of Change Management, 21*(1), 14–29.

Bryson, J. M., Barberg, B., Crosby, B. C., & Patton, M. Q. (2021). Leading social transformations: Creating public value and advancing the common good. *Journal of Change Management, 21*(2), 180–202.

By, R. T. (2020). Organizational change and leadership: Out of the quagmire. *Journal of Change Management, 20*(1), 1–6.

Cummings, S., Bridgman, T., & Brown, K. G. (2016). Unfreezing change as three steps: Rethinking Kurt Lewin's legacy for change management. *Human Relations, 69*(1), 33–60.

Dempsey, M., Geitner, L., Brennan, A., & McAvoy, J. (2022). A review of the success and failure factors for change management. *IEEE Engineering Management Review, 50*(1), 85–93.

Errida, A., & Lotfi, B. (2021). The determinants of organizational change management success: Literature review and case study. *International Journal of Engineering Business Management, 13*, 1–15.

Ford, J., Ford, L., & Polin, B. (2021). Leadership in the implementation of change: Functions, sources, and requisite variety. *Journal of Change Management, 21*(1), 87–119.

Gersick, C. (2020). Reflections on revolutionary change. *Journal of Change Management, 20*(1), 7–23.

Hiatt, J. M. (2006). *ADKAR: A model for change in business, government and our community*. Prosci, Inc.

Hughes, M. (2022). Reflections: How studying organizational change lost its way. *Journal of Change Management, 22*(1), 8–25.

Hvidsten, A., Rai, R. S., & By, R. T. (2023). Design(erly) thinking: Supporting organizational change and leadership. *Journal of Change Management, 23*(1), 1–11.

Karasvirta, S., & Teerikangas, S. (2022). Change organizations in planned change – A closer look. *Journal of Change Management, 22*(2), 163–201.

Kotter, J. P. (1996). *Leading change*. Harvard Business Press.

Lewin, K. (1947). Frontiers in group dynamics: Concept, method and reality in social science; equilibrium and social change. *Human Relations, 1*(1), 5–41.

Mugadza, G., & Marcus, R. (2019). A systems thinking and design thinking approach to leadership. *Expert Journal of Business and Management, 7*(1), 1–10.

Phillips, J., & Klein, J. D. (2023). Change management: From theory to practice. *TechTrends, 67*, 189–197.

Raelin, J. (2022). What can leadership-as-practice contribute to OD? *Journal of Change Management, 22*(1), 26–39.

Shay, P. D. (2023). Leadership matters – for healthcare's present and future. In C. F. Dye (Ed.), *Leadership in healthcare: Essential values and skills* (4th ed., pp. 389–412). Health Administration Press.

Shortell, S. M., Burns, L. R., & Hefner, J. L. (Eds.). (2022). *Responding to the grand challenges in health care via organizational innovation: Needed advances in management research*. Emerald Publishing Limited.

Shrier, L. A., Burke, P. J., Jonestrask, C., & Katz-Wise, S. L. (2020). Applying systems thinking and human-centered design to development of intervention implementation strategies: An example from adolescent health research. *Journal of Public Health Research, 9*(1746), 376–380.

Suddaby, R., & Foster, W. M. (2017). History and organizational change. *Journal of Management, 43*(1), 19–38.

Uhl-Bien, M. (2021). Complexity leadership and followership: Changed leadership in a changed world. *Journal of Change Management, 21*(2), 144–162.

Waddock, S. (2020). Thinking transformational system change. *Journal of Change Management, 20*(3), 189–201.

Wright, A. L., Irving, G., Zafar, A., & Reay, T. (2023). The role of space and place in organizational and institutional change: A systematic review of the literature. *Journal of Management Studies, 60*(4), 991–1026.

SECTION 1

PERSISTENT DRIVERS OF ENVIRONMENTAL UNCERTAINTY

CHAPTER 1

BACK TO THE FUTURE: WHAT HEALTHCARE ORGANIZATIONS NEED TO THRIVE IN THE FACE OF PERSISTENT ENVIRONMENTAL UNCERTAINTY

Rachel Gifford, Arno van Raak, Mark Govers and Daan Westra

Maastricht University, The Netherlands

ABSTRACT

While uncertainty has always been a feature of the healthcare environment, its pace and scope are rapidly increasing, fueled by myriad factors such as technological advancements, the threat and frequency of disruptive events, global economic developments, and increasing complexity. Contemporary healthcare organizations thus persistently face what is known as "deep uncertainty," which obscures their ability to predict outcomes of strategic action and decision-making, presenting them with novel challenges and threatening their survival. Persistent, deep uncertainty challenges us to revisit and reconsider how we think about uncertainty and the strategic actions needed by organizations to thrive under these circumstances. Simply put, how can healthcare organizations thrive in the face of deeply uncertain environments? We argue that healthcare organizations need to employ both adaptive and creative strategic approaches in order to effectively meet patients' needs and capture value in the long-term future. The chapter concludes by offering two ways organizations can build the dynamic capabilities needed to employ such approaches.

Research and Theory to Foster Change in the Face of Grand Health Care Challenges
Advances in Health Care Management, Volume 22, 3–27
Copyright © 2024 Rachel Gifford, Arno van Raak, Mark Govers and Daan Westra
Published under exclusive licence by Emerald Publishing Limited
ISSN: 1474-8231/doi:10.1108/S1474-823120240000022001

Keywords: Healthcare organizations; environmental uncertainty; strategic management; grand challenges; organizational adaptation; future studies

INTRODUCTION

The pace and scope of uncertainty facing today's organizations is rapidly increasing (Teece et al., 2016). While uncertainty has always been a feature of the healthcare environment, both the threat of (OECD, 2023) and the frequency of severe environmental disturbances is growing (Mithani, 2020), creating persistent and sustained environmental uncertainty that yields novel challenges for healthcare organizations (Issel et al., 2023). For example, the early 2020s have been marked by a global pandemic, political turmoil, and social unrest (Barrett, 2022), and the outbreak of war with severe global and economic consequences (OECD, 2023). These punctuated events occur in addition to more gradual but deeply impactful crises – or "grand challenges" – that healthcare organizations face, such as achieving the quadruple aim (Hefner & Nembhard, 2021) or mitigating healthcare's climate footprint and the impact of climate change on populations' healthcare needs (Hensher & McGain, 2020; Karliner et al., 2020). These challenges furthermore interact with one another in complex and unpredictable ways, perpetuating their scope and impact (Hefner & Nembhard, 2021). It can thus be argued that today's organizations face what Teece and colleagues (2016) label persistent, "deep uncertainty," where complexity is high and outcomes are not easily predictable. In such environments, the ability of organizations and managers to comprehend or assess all the outcomes of the many decisions they must make is significantly diminished (Alvarez et al., 2018), presenting healthcare organizations with novel challenges and requiring a new understanding of how organizations can thrive in the face of deep uncertainty.

In light of recent events, there have been calls in the general management literature for more attention to how organizations respond to environmental uncertainty (Alvarez et al., 2018; George et al., 2016) as well as the importance of taking into account the increased frequency and life-threatening nature of environmental threats (Mithani, 2020). Some scholars assert that organizational and management researchers tend to neglect environmental uncertainty as a central concept in organization theory (Alvarez et al., 2018), and more specifically, the contingent relationship between perceived uncertainty within the environment and strategic decision-making processes (e.g., López-Gamero et al., 2011). Alvarez and colleagues (2018) suggest this is because environmental uncertainty has "fallen out of favor" in many disciplines (p. 169), with scholars focusing instead on other aspects of the environment such as stakeholder expectations or regulations (López-Gamero et al., 2011). However, the shift to persistent, deep uncertainty challenges us to revisit and reconsider how we think about uncertainty and the strategic approaches organizations need to effectively deal with it (c.f., Fergnani, 2022; Griffin & Grote, 2020; Rindova & Courtney, 2020). The extant literature comprises primarily two lines of thinking about how organizations can deal with uncertainty: (1) adapting to uncertainty; and, (2) preventing or controlling uncertainty. However, given its persistence in the current environment, trying to prevent or control uncertainty has become untenable. We argue that in such an environment, healthcare organizations not only need to learn to cope with and adapt to uncertainty but should also become more proactive (Schilke et al., 2018) and search for opportunities to exploit their uncertain surroundings. For example, while scholars have been quick to point out the turmoil resulting from global crises like the COVID-19 pandemic, we note how such situations of high uncertainty have inspired rapid, large-scale change and innovation, such as the expansion of eHealth (Hollander & Carr, 2020) and improved interorganizational networks during COVID-19 (Gifford et al., 2022). Therefore, we need a more thorough consideration of how organizations can cope with and adapt to uncertainty, as well as how they might embrace and use uncertainty as the means to thrive, creating new ways of organizing and new innovations.

In this chapter, we question how healthcare delivery organizations (HCOs) can thrive in uncertain environments, bounding our scope specifically to HCOs that provide care delivery services such as hospitals, nursing homes, and primary care practices, among others. We conceptualize *thriving* in this context as organizations that are able to achieve their goals and create value despite persistently uncertain conditions. We unpack this question by focusing on which strategic approaches organizations can – and should – adopt in the face of uncertainty as well as identifying the underlying capabilities that HCOs need in order to employ these approaches. In doing so, we take up the calls for management scholars to "take uncertainty seriously" (Alvarez et al., 2018, p. 169), offering insights into how HCOs can go beyond merely trying to survive in uncertain environments (e.g., weathering external shocks but potentially sacrificing goals or failing to create value), and instead thrive in the face of uncertainty by achieving goals and generating new opportunities to create value (Mithani, 2020).

We first offer a review of existing theory to conceptualize uncertainty and consider what strategic approaches organizations should employ when we classify uncertainty as a given environmental feature. While we recognize that healthcare management scholars have examined the concept of uncertainty widely, we refer specifically to the application of strategic management to HCOs in the context of uncertainty, identifying that as an area still ripe for further exploration (c.f., Agwunobi & Osborne, 2016). Thus, we review the rich body of literature in strategic management to support the conceptualization of the environment as persistently uncertain, allowing us to focus on the strategic responses of HCOs to persistent and dynamic uncertainty. Using the insights gleaned from our initial review, we draw upon strategic management literature to propose what specific capabilities are needed for organizations to move toward and employ these approaches. Lastly, we identify ways in which HCOs can thrive in the face of persistent uncertainty. We posit that the difference between simply maintaining organizational continuity in spite of external changes (i.e., surviving) versus capitalizing on the environment to improve, expand, or pivot the organization to create more value (i.e., thriving) may be the key to not only short-term survival but long-term success and innovation within the field.

BACKGROUND: UNCERTAINTY

In this chapter, we focus on environmental uncertainty. This type of uncertainty is classified as external or exogenous uncertainty, as it exists beyond and independently of individuals (Griffin & Grote, 2020). As Kreiser and Marino (2002) point out in their historical analysis, environmental uncertainty has been explored in the literature for almost a century, beginning with Barnard's *The Functions of the Executive* (1938). As a result, there have been several conceptualizations of environmental uncertainty, and the concept has suffered from conceptual ambiguity (Kreiser & Marino, 2002) and insufficient understanding (Milliken, 1987). While it is beyond the scope of this chapter to offer a full review of classical perspectives on environmental uncertainty, in our focus on strategic approaches in response to uncertainty, we subscribe generally to the notion of uncertainty as a lack of information about the external environment (Duncan, 1972; Lawrence & Lorsch, 1967; Milliken, 1987). In this regard, Duncan's (1972) conceptualization of environmental uncertainty offers a useful starting point.

Duncan (1972) explicated three key components of uncertainty that are directly relevant for strategic decision-making: (1) lack of information regarding the environmental factors associated with a specific decision, (2) not knowing the outcome of a specific decision in terms of how much the organization would lose if the decision were incorrect, and (3) inability to assign probabilities with any degree of confidence with regard to how environmental factors are going to affect the success or failure of the decision unit in performing its function. In this view, environmental uncertainty makes it difficult for organizations to predict or anticipate the future directions of the external environment within which they are situated (Kafetzopoulos et al., 2019) due to a lack of complete information. This aligns with later reviews of environmental uncertainty as cited by organization theorists (Milliken, 1987), which leads us to a comprehensive definition of environmental uncertainty as "a state of the environment in which organizations and decision makers are faced with a lack of information about current and future events which significantly impacts their ability to assign probabilities to both the occurrence of future events and potential outcomes of decision making." This definition highlights both the complexity of strategic decision-making and the need for the development of dynamic capabilities in order to better sense and seize opportunities and threats in the environment (Teece et al., 1997, 2016).

Scholars have studied uncertainty by examining the environment (i.e., considering uncertainty as an objective feature of that environment) as well as by examining perceptions of the environment (i.e., considering uncertainty as a psychological state). An emphasis on uncertainty as a psychological state gained traction in the 1970s (Downey & Slocum, 1975), which was contrasted by scholars who emphasized the objective features of the environment (López-Gamero et al., 2011). In the present study, we conceptualize environmental uncertainty as an objective state in the current environment that requires organizations to adapt their strategic approaches. We certainly acknowledge the core argument in work that focuses on perceived uncertainty (Downey & Slocum, 1975); namely, that in organizations' reactions to uncertainty, individuals' perceptions matter, such as in their sensemaking trajectories and when deciding whether to enact a certain strategy. However, we do not take the view of scholars who suggest that decision-makers' perceptions of uncertainty is what matters most (Dill, 1958; Downey et al., 1975; Duncan, 1972; Lawrence & Lorsch, 1967). Rather, we align with the notion of environmental uncertainty as an objective state and environment "in which the relevant factors for decision making are in a constant state of change" (Downey & Slocum, 1975, p. 573), which complicates the decision-making process for organizations. We suggest that, when viewing environmental uncertainty in this way, focus should be directed on the *capabilities* needed by managers and organizations to both ensure organizational survival and thrive in such an environment, rather than on assessing individuals' perceptions and processing of information.

Uncertainty as a Given Environmental Feature

The prevalence and importance of environmental uncertainty for organizations has been clearly identified over decades of organization theory literature. Classical theorists such as Thompson (1967) and Milliken (1987) put forward the notion that uncertainty is "the fundamental problem with which top-level organizational administrators must cope" (Thompson, 1967, p. 159). Recent work has extended this sentiment, recognizing the fundamental nature of uncertainty for all levels of the organization. For example, Teece (2018) has recently highlighted that the capabilities firms need to flourish relate to addressing the "prevailing degree of uncertainty" (p. 360). In contrast to Duncan (1972) and other classical theorists who position uncertainty as an ephemeral construct, suggesting that uncertain environments are temporary and sparse, we argue that, in the modern era, uncertainty is constant – particularly in the healthcare environment (c.f., Mithani, 2020).

While organizations have always faced some level of environmental uncertainty, the frequency of disruptive events or "surprises" is increasing (Mithani, 2020; Teece et al., 2016). Additionally, beyond the prevalence and probability of disruptive shocks, the environment itself has become increasingly uncertain, with increasing social unrest (Barrett, 2022), polarization, and politicization that present HCOs with "unique and unprecedented challenges" (Issel et al., 2023, p. 1). The general environment of HCOs is also influenced by "international forces such as world peace, global economy, and national conditions such as the demographic profile of the population, price inflation and unemployment rates" (Begun & Kaissi, 2004, p. 32).

The general environment not only provides context for HCOs but also influences their task environment, which has a more direct impact on organizational behavior and success (Ginter et al., 2018). This task environment includes resources (e.g., financial, physical, human), patients, suppliers, and regulatory and market conditions (Begun & Kaissi, 2004; Dill, 1958). For example, the Russian invasion of Ukraine in 2022 and its escalation of the Russo-Ukrainian war sparked a global economic downturn and energy crisis which resulted in increasingly constrained resources and drove supply costs up, creating more precarious and difficult market conditions in the healthcare sector. Similarly, due to what has been dubbed the "great resignation," HCOs face increasing uncertainty around the supply of their key resource: staff (Gifford et al., 2023). While HCOs have always faced uncertainty and have had to cope with environmental shocks, the likelihood of disruptive events increases as the general environment becomes increasingly unstable (Mithani, 2020). The increased probability and occurrence of shocks makes the environment deeply uncertain as "surprises and black swans become the norm" (Teece et al., 2016, p. 15), requiring new types of management and organizational capabilities.

Taking uncertainty as a given environmental feature does not imply that the nature or type of uncertainty is static. In fact, the reality that organizations face several types of uncertainty and that the level and type of uncertainty that is prominent is ever changing is what makes the environment so persistently uncertain, complicating organizational responses. Drawing upon Milliken's (1987) work, and based upon the definition of environmental uncertainty as previously introduced (Duncan, 1972), there are three types of uncertainty that affect organizations: state uncertainty, effect uncertainty, and response uncertainty. State uncertainty – referring to the unpredictability of the state of the environment – is most closely related to other conceptualizations of environmental uncertainty. Examples of state uncertainty include general shifts in the external environment, such as changing demographics, or potential regulatory actions that may significantly alter the state of the external environment in which organizations are embedded.

Effect uncertainty pertains to the inability to predict the effects of environmental shifts on the organization. For example, at a certain point, HCOs knew that COVID-19 was going to impact them, but due to the unknown nature of the disease, its pathology, and its treatment, there was high uncertainty regarding the effects it would have for organizations and the healthcare system (Begun & Jiang, 2020).

Drawing upon the same example of the COVID-19 pandemic, we can also see a clear illustration of the third type of uncertainty: response uncertainty. Response uncertainty refers to a lack of information or knowledge about how to respond, or an inability to predict the probable outcomes of a certain action (Milliken, 1987). As Milliken (1987) describes, this uncertainty often accompanies the need to act in response to an event that poses a threat or opportunity. During the COVID-19 pandemic, HCOs needed to take action without clear knowledge of the repercussions of their choices. Empirical work by Gifford and colleagues (2022) has shown that the responses to the pandemic varied between HCOs as well as over time within a single HCO. While it is important to recognize these different types of uncertainty, it is their intermingling, coexistence, and dynamic evolution (rather than their individual characteristics) that creates a persistently uncertain environment and requires organizations to alter their strategic approaches to enable them to effectively face all types of uncertainty.

Persisting Uncertainty in Health Care

In the Uncertainty as a Given Environmental Feature section, we conceptualized uncertainty as a given environmental feature for modern day organizations.

While, we thus consider environmental uncertainty as persistent, the type and sources of uncertainty that organizations face are not static, but are dynamic and ever-changing. How organizations are affected by and can respond to such uncertainty will vary across sectors, depending upon key features of their task environment. From existing literature, we identify four aspects which we believe make the task environment persistently uncertain for contemporary HCOs: (1) increased complexity amid resource constraints, (2) increasing interconnected-ness, (3) threat of shock, and (4) rapid digital/technological developments. In this section, we briefly describe these four factors and their contribution to persistent uncertainty in health care.

First, as has been pointed out by numerous scholars (e.g., Figueroa et al., 2019; Nembhard et al., 2020) healthcare systems face an aging population with increasing spread and complexity of disease (e.g., chronic disease and multimorbidities), requiring a shift in care delivery processes toward new and unknown futures. The increasing resource scarcity within the healthcare sector (e.g., budgetary constraints, staff shortages) and regulatory pressures to create more value (i.e., increase quality while reducing costs) not only accentuate the necessity of these shifts but also make them less likely and more uncertain. For example, many preventative and necessary health system changes require staff time and resources and upfront financial investments to make long-term gains, such as investing in population health (Morgan & James, 2022). However, buy-in from funders can be difficult to ascertain, and resource scarcity such as staff shortages and budgetary constraints deplete the slack resources of these organizations, making it less likely that they are able to make the necessary investments and changes (Bentley & Kehoe, 2020). As Lopez-Gamero and colleagues (2011) found in their study of the environmental management industry, conditions of scarcity make it more challenging for organizations and managers to establish processes that support prevention, and thus to influence the environment in which they operate. They argue that cooperation is a means in which to exert more control over scare resources and secure them (López-Gamero et al., 2011). However, as Pffefer and Salancik (1978) argued from a resource dependency view, when organizations become increasingly interconnected, the environment becomes more uncertain and unstable (Dess & Beard, 1984). While interconnec-tedness is thus needed to cope with the complexity of care delivery and resource constraints, the increased interconnectedness of HCOs can also be seen as inducing more uncertainty and instability into the environment (Pffefer & Salancik, 1978), increasing effect uncertainty (Milliken, 1987). Consequently, we identify increasing interconnectedness as a second source of persistent uncertainty in the healthcare sector.

Almost 20 years ago, Begun and Kaissi (2004) suggested that interconnec-tedness between elements in the healthcare environment played a key role in influencing the amount of uncertainty facing HCOs. At the time, they rated interconnectedness between elements as moderate, focusing more on the linking pins between elements rather than on organizations. However, over the last 20 years, HCOs themselves have become more interconnected. In fact, in health care, interconnectedness between organizations has been increasingly pushed and called for in both the literature and in policy efforts (Burns et al., 2022) as a result of increasing health system burdens and the need to improve value (Porter, 2010). As described by Hearld and Westra (2022), we see an emergence of networks, interorganizational collaborations, and joint efforts in health care. While this is to some degree required to improve the value of service delivery, recent work by Peeters and colleagues (2023) suggests that the institutionalization of this approach limits its value. The resulting interconnectedness does, however, make the environment of HCOs more complex and uncertain.

Third, the broader environment in which we live has become increasingly prone to destabilization, whether it be as the result of natural disasters, attacks, epidemics, or financial disasters. As a result, scholars have recently called attention to the persistent threat of health system shocks facing today's healthcare systems (Hefner & Nembhard, 2021; Mayo et al., 2021; Mithani, 2020), heightening both state and response uncertainty (Milliken, 1987). Where crises occur or disaster strikes, even when not directly a public health crisis or event, the healthcare system remains prone to fluctuations in demand, resource availability, and the need for adaptability. For example, the World Health Organization (WHO) and European health observatory detailed how the financial crisis of 2008 can be constituted as a health system shock, defined as "an unexpected occurrence originating outside the health system that has a large negative effect on the availability of health system resources or a large positive effect on the demand for health services" (Mladovsky et al., 2012, p. v). While in the past, such shocks occurred as singular events with ripple effects, in the current climate we see an increase of interconnected crises occurring with multiple sources of destabilization and threats, exacerbating the surrounding uncertainty and increasing the likelihood of shocks (Hefner & Nembhard, 2021).

Lastly, the rapid digitalization and technological advancements of modern society lead to increased opportunity but also induce a level of uncertainty into the broader environment in which HCOs operate. Breakthroughs in artificial intelligence (AI) and other technologies have the potential to support HCOs in facing their most persistent challenges, such as the workforce shortage, or to provide more accurate diagnoses for patients. While their heavily institutionalized nature has rendered HCOs relatively slow to adopt such technologies (e.g., Ferlie et al., 2005), the increasing pace of these developments and breakthroughs is likely to change the face of medicine, HCOs, and care delivery as we know it, inducing effect uncertainty. Such technological advancements also require restructuring, and they may come quickly and with unintended consequences for which HCOs cannot predict with any certainty. We believe that the involvement of big technology firms in the sector, as the acquisition of One Medical by Amazon signals, for example, or the integration of AI chatbots such as ChatGPT into clinical practice, can significantly amplify such uncertainty for HCOs.

STRATEGIC RESPONSES TO UNCERTAINTY

This chapter is primarily concerned with how HCOs can thrive under conditions of uncertainty. The emphasis on the organizational and environmental interface is therefore inherently on the strategic approach that organizational boards, leaders, and managers take in the face of deep uncertainty. Contending with an uncertain future is indeed a core challenge for strategy makers (Kaplan & Orlikowski, 2013). Knight (1921) argued that uncertainty arose when it became impossible for decision-makers to predict possible outcomes or the probability of the outcomes of their decision-making. Given the prevalence of this form of uncertainty in modern times, we see an emergence of literature focusing particularly on strategic decision-making under conditions of environmental uncertainty. Drawing upon this recent scholarship (e.g., Alvarez et al., 2018) and coupling it with a comprehensive review of the classical literature, we identify three broad categories of responses that HCOs can have toward uncertainty: Control (avoid), Adapt (react), and Create (project). While in practice, HCOs may incorporate multiple responses; for conceptual clarity, we posit these as distinct and prototypical strategies. Table 1.1 provides an overview of these strategies and associated organizational actions.

Control

Many organization theorists traditionally focused on the importance of eliminating and avoiding strategies in order to cope with uncertainty and assert a sense of control over the environment (March & Simon, 1958; Pffefer & Salancik, 1978; Thompson, 1967). At a strategic level, a Control strategy infers a static approach with a focus on defending existing structures, processes, and positions against environmental shifts. The goal of such responses is to buffer the organization from external shifts and protect the status quo as much as possible by eliminating sources of uncertainty. This aligns with what Miles et al. (1978) may classify as a Defender or Reactor strategy, whereby organizations try to avoid uncertainty. The Control approach can still be seen today in organizational life, as organizations and managers work to build in structures, protocols, and standardized

Table 1.1. Strategic Approaches to Uncertainty.

Strategies	Control	Adapt	Create
Response to change	Avoid	React	Project
Temporality	Past	Present	Future
Aim	Protect status quo	Stability and survival in the short-term	Competitive edge and long-term sustainability
Principles	Uncertainty should be avoided as much as possible	We must respond to uncertainty	We should leverage uncertainty for change
Actions	Use organizational structures and routines to buffer against change	Reconfigure organizational structures and routines in response to with environment	Seize opportunities to create new processes, structure, and products in order to sustain the organization into the future
Motivation	Buffer against environmental change	Maintain equilibrium with environmental change	Incite and join environmental change

processes as the means to eliminate or buffer the organization from uncertainty. However, it has been recognized that those organizations who adopt such a positioning are likely to fail or "perish" (Miles et al., 1978).

Adapt

Adaptation has been hailed as a key factor for organizational success in dynamic environments (Agwunobi & Osborne, 2016; Teece et al., 2016). Organizations that engage in an Adapt approach respond to environmental uncertainty and external cues in a more flexible way. They take in information from the environment and adapt the organization in response to ongoing events. Although the engagement with the external environment makes this approach more active and dynamic than controlling, Adapting can best be seen as a reactive strategy. That is, its main goal is to achieve equilibrium with the existing environment, adapting as needed to maintain survival as the environment shifts. This strategy aligns best with Miles et al.'s (1978) Analyzer strategy, whereby organizations are not proactively working to shape the environment around them but rather are taking in information about what is occurring, reacting based on environmental cues.

Create

Organizations that want to create competitive advantage or ensure future success and performance are often encouraged to not only confront but to *embrace* uncertainty. While adaptation strategies encourage organizations to respond actively to uncertainty, they remain a reactive approach, responding to what is already happening or has happened, which limits the ability of the organization to better position itself for the future. Going beyond responding to the existing environment requires organizations to become more proactive and project future realities in order to create opportunities for growth in the market and for the organization itself. A Create approach can concern influencing the conditions of the current environment where organizations already operate (i.e., shaping), or more radically, stepping outside of the existing paradigm to create a new environment with new conditions (i.e., disrupting). This aligns with the Prospector strategy of Miles et al. (1978) typology, whereby organizations are sitting at the forefront of innovation and advancement, working to not only shape but disrupt the status quo. The idea from business resonates here that those that are not thinking to the future and disrupting current practice will eventually fall behind.

Bounding Our Scope: Healthcare Organizations

While healthcare management scholars have applied a variety of insights from management in the healthcare field (c.f., Mayo et al., 2021; Reay et al., 2021) and have helped to advance our understanding of the environment in which HCOs operate (c.f., Yeager et al., 2014), our understanding of how HCOs can thrive in uncertain environments remains in many ways ripe for further development (Agwunobi & Osborne, 2016). First, previous studies have worked to show how the environment influences decision-making in HCOs (Menachemi & Collum, 2011).

However, our understanding of what types of strategies HCOs should pursue at a macro level to best adapt and respond to environmental conditions remains limited. For example, many studies examining strategic decision-making in health care focus on particular strategies as they relate to a specific topic, such as the implementation of new technologies (Kazley & Ozcan, 2007; Menachemi & Collum, 2011) or human resource management (Schneider et al., 2021). While these studies offer important insights, they tend to consider the impact of particular environmental conditions such as competition and location (Kazley & Ozcan, 2007; Schneider et al., 2021), rather than assessing the state of the environment as a whole. This leaves a gap in our understanding of the types of strategies HCOs employ and how they respond to environmental uncertainty more generally, which is important to assess given the significance of HCOs' adaptive capacity in the modern era (Gifford et al., 2022; Pablo et al., 2007).

Secondly, when applying concepts from strategic management more broadly, we must take care to contextualize them within the healthcare sector. The majority of strategic management literature focuses on firms that operate in different industries, where profit and competitive advantage are core attributes and desired outcomes. In these industries, the market also plays a key role, and there is a level of risk that organizations are able, and expected to take. For example, breakthrough innovations in the tech sector, such as the creation of ChatGPT, have produced societal advancements and may support efficiency gains (Li et al., 2023), but they require investors willing to take risks in financing the next technological breakthrough (c.f., Chowdhury, 2023). Such organizations require and embrace a certain level of risk as part of the price of innovation that ultimately leads to competitive advantage. Although HCOs are still expected to strive for good financial performance, and in some cases have a profit motive, they operate in a specific regulatory and policy context that may limit the strategic options and choices they have (Helmig et al., 2014). Despite the recognition that organizations should become more flexible in uncertain environments (Child, 1972), HCOs operate in a highly regulated and institutionalized context, which slows innovation and change, makes HCOs more rigid (Reay et al., 2021), and creates barriers to adopting an Adapt or Create approach for these organizations. Therefore, processes of adaptation and more radical prospects of moving toward new futures will likely entail some level of deinstitutionalization. Furthermore, we suggest that given the institutional constraints on, and ethical responsibility of, HCOs in the healthcare sector, not all organizations will be able to adopt a pure Create strategy. Rather, we suggest that most HCOs will need to be adaptive at their core to ensure the continuity and stability of care delivery, while also actively engaging in actions to influence, shape, and ultimately create the environment around them for the longevity of healthcare delivery.

PROPOSED STRATEGIES TO EMBRACE UNCERTAINTY

As stated by Courtney and colleagues (1997), "Under uncertainty, traditional approaches to strategic planning can be downright dangerous" (p. 2). With the notion that uncertainty is a given for HCOs presently and in the future, it becomes imperative to unpack the strategic approaches necessary for HCOs to thrive in the face of uncertainty. In the following sections, we highlight the need for HCOs to shift toward Adapt and Create strategies to support organizational decision-making. Importantly, we highlight the need for organizations to move from reactive toward proactive approaches in order to cope with dynamic uncertainty; that is, from Control to Adapt, and from Adapt to Create. We then detail the capabilities needed by organizations to make these transitions.

From Controlling to Adapting

With contemporary organizations existing in what Snowden and Boone (2007) refer to as "the realm of unknown unknowns," there is an increased need for flexibility and adaptability of organizations and organizational leaders. As they point out, "Leaders who try to impose order in a complex context will fail, but those who set the stage, step back a bit, allow patterns to emerge, and determine which ones are desirable will succeed" (Snowden & Boone, 2007, p. 5). This highlights the notion that trying to mitigate or control uncertainty is not an effective strategy, and conversely can become critically counterproductive. In healthcare, reducing uncertainty and variability has become a focal point, particularly in the care delivery trajectories of patients (Issel, 2019). However, the overemphasis on standardization and protocols can also undermine the adaptive approach needed to deliver the most effective care (Cutrer & Ehrenfeld, 2017; Issel, 2019) and can institutionalize processes in a way which leads to organizational rigidity (Andersson & Gadolin, 2020). Therefore, in the current environment, we argue that organizations can no longer operate from a strategic approach of Control, trying to mitigate uncertainty; they must instead recognize uncertainty as a regular feature of the environment and engage in Adapt behaviors to cope with environmental shifts. As Bourgeois (1985) suggests, for managers and organizations in dynamic environments, such as health care, attempts to reduce or avoid uncertainty may have negative consequences for organizations and organizational performance.

While organization theorists in the 1960s focused on the importance of eliminating and avoiding uncertainty, in subsequent years scholars began to recognize that in turbulent environments this advice is futile and can in fact harm organizational efforts or lead to dysfunction (Bourgeois, 1985). Strategically, this calls for organizations to move toward Adapt approaches, whereby they can embrace uncertainty to become more dynamic and flexible in order to maintain balance with – and create opportunities in – the external environment. Earlier scholarship also hinted at the importance of embracing uncertainty for competitive advantage. For example, Miles et al. (1978) identified that so-called "Prospector organizations embrace uncertainty by exploring previously unexplored areas of the market or task environment. In doing so, they outperformed organizations they identified as Defenders and Reactors, which seek to avoid uncertainty and only react to the environment (Miles et al., 1978). This leads us to believe that Adapt strategies support organizations to better withstand environmental disruptions, minimizing the impact on organizational performance.

Based on the preceding arguments, we derive the following proposition:

P1: Healthcare organizations that adopt Adapt strategies will be better equipped than those that adopt Control strategies to respond to environmental shifts.

From Adapting to Creating

Where uncertainty is high and there is "novel and unpredictable" change occurring, as occurred during the COVID-19 pandemic, decision-makers must overcome previous ways of thinking (Rindova & Martins, 2021). While the COVID-19 pandemic has forced HCOs to adapt in various ways (e.g., Gifford et al., 2022; Hollander & Carr, 2020), adapting alone is not enough to safeguard their sustainability in the future. Scholars have recently argued that it is essential that organizations become more proactive to generate new knowledge and enact new strategies (Fontana & Gerrard, 2004; Rindova & Courtney, 2020, p. 791). As Rindova and Courtney (2020) argue, strategy making under conditions of high uncertainty require the creation of new knowledge and active reshaping of the present. This line of thinking points to the need for organizations to remain adaptive at their core while also building an emphasis on creative and proactive approaches. Proactive, prospective work and sensemaking by actors can support organizations to go beyond finding balance with the environment, additionally finding ways to thrive in conditions of uncertainty; for example, by sensing emergent opportunities and subsequently redefining organizational goals. This echoes other calls and recent emphasis on such work, which stresses the need for organizations to move beyond shaping and instead move toward *creating* possible futures (Fergnani, 2022). Here we see a turn in the literature toward a focus on temporal work and on organizations as proactive, rather than reactive, participants in the organizational-environmental interface.

Based on the preceding *arguments*, we derive the following proposition:

P2: Healthcare organizations that adopt Create strategies will be more successful than those that adopt Control or Adapt strategies in redefining and meeting (new) organizational goals amid environmental uncertainty, making them more resilient in responding to environmental shifts.

ORGANIZATIONAL CAPABILITIES AMID UNCERTAINTY

We utilize the capabilities literature to offer insights on how organizations and their leaders may make the necessary shifts from Control strategies toward Adapt and Create strategies. According to this literature, organizations can draw upon "ordinary" and "dynamic" capabilities. Ordinary capabilities can be seen as an organization's core business or "best practices" (Teece, 2014, p. 330) that allow them to "do things right" (Teece, 2014, p. 331). Embedded within administrative, operational, and governance functions, such capabilities offer organizations efficiency but do not allow firms to gain long-term advantage or secure performance in the long run as they are not targeted at maintaining equilibrium with a shifting and competitive market. Dynamic capabilities, on the other hand, have been conceptualized as higher-order capabilities that "involve a combination of organizational routines and entrepreneurial leadership/management" (Teece, 2014, p. 338) and allow organizations to capture competitive advantage. Importantly, dynamic capabilities are what offer organizations the ability to respond to change, capture opportunities, ensure good performance, and gain competitive advantage. These capabilities thus allow organizations to "do the right things." However, they do not operate alone. As Teece (2014) argues, to improve performance, dynamic capabilities must be both accompanied by and congruent with a good strategy (c.f., Teece et al., 2016).

Defined by Teece and colleagues (2016), "dynamic capabilities are what enable organizations to integrate, build, and reconfigure internal and external resources to address and shape rapidly changing business environments" (p. 7). Three categories of dynamic capabilities are generally distinguished: sensing, seizing, and transforming. Sensing concerns the ability to identify, develop, and assess opportunities and threats in the environment as they relate to patient needs. Seizing is the capacity to mobilize resources to meet these needs, responding to opportunities or threats and ultimately "capturing value" by doing so (Teece et al., 2016, p. 18). Lastly, transforming regards a process of continual renewal whereby the organization is renewing their existing base of dynamic capabilities or building new ones. It also concerns an ability to build a culture of learning within the organization to become more dynamic and gain advantage.

In the context of health care, organizations may not use dynamic capabilities to gain competitive advantage per se, but they can nevertheless benefit from developing them. For example, HCOs may develop better sensing capabilities to find opportunities to redesign parts of healthcare delivery that can deliver better value to patients, seizing capabilities to generate new ways of doing things, unstick from old routines, and transform to develop learning organizations, including unlearning. A primary care organization we have encountered in our research, for example, sensed both the latent needs of patients in its service area as well as the growing worries of its purchasers regarding the increased expenditures for these patient groups. Subsequently, it was able to seize this as an opportunity to develop a new way of organizing several primary care practices in the region (i.e., in so-called Plus Practices). Based on an ongoing evaluation process, it learned that the new approach delivered more value to patients at lower costs to insurers. The organization has now transformed all practices in the region to this novel way of working.

The above example illustrates that developing dynamic capabilities enables HCOs to create new ways of working. Such a Create strategy can transform healthcare delivery in a way that "unsticks" organizations from the past so that they can move the field forward toward reaching system goals, such as the Quadruple Aim, and work for sustainability of care despite the rapidly changing environment. As previous scholars have recognized, dynamic capabilities enable organizations to engage in institutional change by empowering actors to engage in institutionalization and deinstitutionalization practices (Dixon et al., 2010). This is an important aspect of dynamic capabilities for the healthcare field that is highly institutionalized in order to break path dependency and forge new ways forward to protect sustainability of care delivery in a changing environment.

Based on the preceding arguments, we derive the following proposition:

> *P3*: The higher the degree of dynamic capabilities a healthcare organization possesses, the higher the likelihood that it adopts a Create strategy.

Ambidexterity

Ambidexterity is a concept that is closely intertwined with the dynamic capabilities literature and can be seen as a part of the dynamic capabilities framework (O'Reilly & Tushman, 2013). While it is not in the scope of this chapter to provide a full review of this relationship, literature has contended that ambidexterity can be considered as a distinct concept but acts as a complement to organizations' sensing, seizing, and transforming capabilities. While dynamic capabilities allow organizations to maintain equilibrium with a dynamic and rapidly changing environment, ambidexterity is what allows organizations to gain competitive advantage by managing a balance between exploration and exploitation. Primarily, ambidexterity concerns striking the optimal balance of explorative (e.g., searching for and creating new knowledge, products, processes, and competencies) and exploitative (e.g., using existing resources, competencies, and knowledge) activities to respond to and manage environmental change (O'Reilly & Tushman, 2004). In other words, it refers to organizations' ability to simultaneously enact create strategies, in which they explore new ways of working, and Adapt strategies, in which they improve the existing way of working.

The primary care organization to which we alluded previously (i.e., "Plus Practices") is a prime example of such an ambidextrous approach. That is, it decided to explore the new way of working in several of its practices. These were the practices that self-identified as being innovative and constituted approximately 10% of all the practices affiliated with the organization. In those practices, the primary care organization experimented and evaluated over the course of several years to develop and refine their new approach. They facilitated these practices by providing required data, hosting collaborative innovation sessions, negotiating with insurers, and explicating their vision for the future. During this period, they worked with the other 90% of the affiliated practices in "business as usual." In doing so, the organization had to take on two different roles and performance measures with both groups of practices. This meant that they simultaneously required the capabilities to do both: balancing a Create strategy in 10% of their practices and an Adapt strategy in the other 90%. Thus, the organization needed to be, and benefited from being, ambidextrous.

In the current framework, we see ambidexterity as a critical ability for organizations to be able to balance Adapt and Create strategies. In regards to these approaches, exploration can be seen as necessary to Create and exploitation to Adapt, whereby both are necessary in some capacity for organizations' survival and competitive advancement in the current environment.

Based on *the* preceding arguments, we derive the following proposition:

P4: Healthcare organizations that have ambidextrous capabilities are better able to deploy Adapt and Create strategies simultaneously and are therefore more successful than organizations lacking ambidextrous capabilities in meeting both organizational goals and health system aims.

THE (UN)CERTAIN FUTURE

In the remaining sections, we outline two ways for HCOs to build the necessary capabilities to support a move toward Adapt and Create approaches in order to thrive under conditions of uncertainty. First, HCOs can engage in future work (e.g., temporal work), which includes recognition that there is no transforming without sensing. Second, HCOs can adopt systems thinking, recognizing the importance and interdependence of all levels in the organization, and embedding capabilities throughout via "trickle-down strategizing."

Future Work

In recent years, scholars have taken up the call to consider the role of temporality and its importance for organizational life and strategic management (Bansal et al., 2022; Kaplan & Orlikowski, 2013). In particular, scholars have recognized that in order to cope with the volatile, uncertain, complex, and ambiguous (VUCA) environment and the "wicked problems" or "grand challenges" facing them, organizations must become more future oriented (Whyte et al., 2022). Management research and organizational studies more broadly have been criticized for overlooking how organizations and their members can engage with the future (Wenzel, 2022; Wenzel et al., 2020). As a result, scholars have introduced the concept of "futures studies" (Fergnani, 2022), highlighting the importance of creating imagined futures or "future making" (Whyte et al., 2022). Within this work, we see a similar trend as we have outlined in the shift to the organizational responses to uncertainty, whereby there is a shift from more reactive (i.e., present-day focused) to more proactive (i.e., future-oriented) organizational approaches. The necessity of this shift is underscored by the reality that in the current state of deep uncertainty in which organizations operate, the future is "unknowable" but should also be created.

It is important to note that the work on future studies faces some criticism, particularly as our interests lie in contributing to practical and real-time actions HCOs can take. For example, Wenzel (2022) has criticized the tendency in the work on future studies to overstate the capacity of actors to manage the future, setting unrealistic expectations about how organizations can "manage the future" (p. 846). Importantly, Wenzel (2022) points out that the trend toward future making or future studies aims to control the future (Wenzel et al., 2020), which goes against the very idea that strategies of command and control are no longer viable in the current context. Therefore, while we suggest that a future orientation is essential for managers and HCOs to thrive in conditions of uncertainty, we recognize that there are inherent uncertainties within the current environment that makes knowing or predicting the future impossible. We do believe that drawing attention to certain future-making practices can be a useful step forward for HCOs and actors to expand their abilities to make decisions and strategize with an eye toward the future. For example, the literature on prospective sensemaking highlights the importance of individuals considering the future impact of current action or inaction (Gephart et al., 2010; Hernes & Maitlis, 2012). Gioia and colleagues (1994) describe prospective sensemaking as "the conscious and intentional consideration of the probable future impact of certain actions, and especially non-actions, on the meaning construction processes of themselves and others" (p. 378). While we draw upon the notion of environmental certainty as creating a sense of "unknowing," consideration of the potential future impact of current decisions prompts individuals to develop a future-oriented cognitive frame that can support a temporal shift or temporal work toward the creation of imagined futures.

One way to embed a future-oriented perspective within HCOs is through the encouragement and engagement of individuals' temporal work. Temporal work requires individuals to reconsider the linkages between their conceptions and constructions of time, in particular the past, present, and future constructions. It thus involves not just prospecting an imagined future, but "rethinking the past and reconsidering present concerns" (Kaplan & Orlikowski, 2013, p. 966). Defined by Bansel and colleagues (2022), temporal work is "any individual, collective, or organizational effort to influence, sustain, or redirect the temporal assumptions or patterns that shape strategic action (p. 7). It is in this collective process of aligning past, present, and future that sustainable strategies can be crafted (Bansal et al., 2022) to help the organization break from the status quo (Kaplan & Orlikowski, 2013). In particular, we believe that the work for HCOs in coping with the dynamically uncertain environment involves the temporal work of moving toward imagined futures, breaking the normal linkages of path dependency based on past assumptions in order to reconsider both current realities and future needs (Andersson & Gadolin, 2020). For example, considering how to reorganize care delivery for an acute patient should not be based on what was done in the past, but rather based on a collective imagining of the future which demands a reconsideration of what individuals perceive as possible and valuable (Rindova & Martins, 2021). The creation of such "futurescapes" helps open up perceptions of what is possible and can build support for new, imagined futures (Rindova & Martins, 2021). We believe that such work will allow HCOs to become more dynamic and build the capabilities necessary to withstand disruptions and seek out new futures. For example, temporal work can support the building of sensing capabilities that can motivate the reconfiguration of existing resources toward an imagined future, helping them seize opportunities to capture value. It will also encourage organizations to engage in constant transformation by reconsidering the linkages between past practice, current reality, and imagined futures.

Ways to Support Organizational Members in Temporal Work

The importance and promise of imagining new ways of doing things is significant, especially for HCOs that are currently stuck between recognizing the need to change and the regulatory and institutional forces that make such change feel impossible (Andersson & Gadolin, 2020). The inertia of healthcare cannot be overstated; even with impactful forces such as the COVID-19 crisis, the status quo largely prevails and remains hard to shift. We believe this is largely due to a lack of imagination, which can be seen to partially be driven by a fear of failure that is pervasive throughout the healthcare system at large. This fear of failure is positive in one perspective, because it derives from a sense of duty toward patients and society; however, it also risks stifling creativity and imagination. To ease fears of the risks taken by doing things differently, organizations can simultaneously imagine desired and undesired futures (Alimadadi et al., 2022). Envisioning undesirable futures can accelerate planning and taking of action to avoid imagined scenarios (Alimadadi et al., 2022). Leaders of HCOs should be engaging in the visioning of potential undesirable futures based on the existing status quo in order to leverage healthcare's more cautious nature and prompt the urgency needed for both imagining new futures and strategizing on how to create them. Additionally, to support a shift toward creation, as well as both learning and unlearning from the past, management can be encouraged internally to speak up about ideas, and this should be extended for staff at all levels. Imagining new futures requires recognition of current realities and past mistakes in order to avoid repeating the past. However, it also requires psychological safety to encourage organizational members to "dream big" and speak up about new ways of doing things. Psychological safety is "a shared belief held by members of a team that the team is safe for interpersonal risk taking" (Edmondson, 1999, p. 350), and it can support individuals to both voice concerns (Edmondson, 1996) and put forward new, bold ideas that can support the imagining of new futures.

Based on the preceding arguments, we derive the *following* proposition:

P5: Healthcare organizations that engage in future work are more capable of deploying Create strategies.

Applying Systems Thinking and Management

As argued in recent studies as well as calls for scholarly work on uncertainty, organizations' responses to uncertainty or the development of organizational capabilities to thrive under conditions of uncertainty require input and involvement at all levels of the organization. In particular, the work on corporate foresight emphasizes the importance of all levels of the organization and provides a solid base from which to consider how organizations can create scenarios and imagine possible futures in order to gain competitive advantage (Fergnani, 2022). We believe this opens the door for incorporation of systems thinking, whereby organizational decision-makers recognize the interdependency of their actions, behaviors, and approaches with that of all other subunits or layers of the organization. Further, as mentioned by Rindova and Courtney (2020), "Uncertain situations involve new and unpredictable interactions with unknown consequences, including unpredictable competitive interactions" (p. 791). This points in particular to the utility of complexity science, which conceptualizes HCOs as complex adaptive systems (CASs) operating in uncertain and unpredictable environments (Begun & Jiang, 2020). The CAS perspective is useful for HCOs given its emphasis on relationships between organizations and their environments, and it is based on the underlying notion that the future is "relatively unknowable" (Begun et al., 2003, p. 13). CASs are constantly seeking to find balance and adapt to the environment, sending the signal to organizations that flexibility rather than static approaches is key and that adaptation is a necessary and natural part of organizational life.

Importantly, CAS highlights the importance of trying to recognize, respect, and acknowledge the complex web of interdependencies when enacting changes or pushing for new ways forward (Khan et al., 2018). Failing to account for the interdependency between system components is likely to lead to strategic failure and result in wasted resources, thereby perpetuating the problem of resource constraints. When thinking about the interdependencies between organizational members and components, it also becomes clear that it is essential for everyone to be aware of and working toward the same goal or aim, including strategic goals. Therefore, in order for strategic actions to be successfully employed, recognition of interdependencies is required not only at the top levels of management but throughout the entire organization. The interactions and interdependencies within the organizational system itself are of course only one aspect to consider. When adopting a systems approach, organizations are urged to consider the scope of interactions across the broader system. For example, when a HCO adopts a new structure or pursues a disruptive strategy, such as eliminating certain disciplines from hospital care or vertically integrating healthcare delivery services with purchasing, this has ripple effects for the broader organizational field and health system (e.g., via isomorphic pressures, competitor behavior, etc.). Failure to engage in systems thinking when pursuing strategy can lead to dispersed challenges, such as pushing constraints downstream. For example, many healthcare systems have been pursuing a strategy of moving care out of hospitals and toward primary care and preventive services. However, failure to consider the long-term effects or appropriately reconfigure resources has meant that the same problems have now fallen downstream to other healthcare providers such as general practitioners (GPs). Reports of GPs feeling overloaded, overworked, and burnt out (Picquendar et al., 2019) as well as increasing shortages of primary care professionals (Howley, 2022) risk exacerbating health system challenges. A lack of systems thinking can thus undermine the formation of viable strategy and strategic action, while adopting this approach can support leaders to find important leverage points for change and sense opportunities for growth.

Ways to Build Systems Thinking in the Organization
When thinking about ways organizations can become more adaptive, we believe that a CAS perspective is a useful starting point for organizations and their members. In particular, recognizing that conventional means of management such as command-and-control do not function to support system performance

(Khan et al., 2018) can help organizational leaders and management begin to consider how to approach strategic change. This not only relates to considerations of how to transform an organization but also how to become more agile by ensuring involvement and compliance of organizational members at large with reconfigurations and adaptations (for example, moving from top-down or command-and-control mechanisms toward focusing on incentivizing the right behavior toward adaptability and gaining value for patients) (Rouse, 2008). Organizations must incentivize their members and subsystems in ways that promote achievement of strategic aims and activities along the way. In general, the first step requires a shift in mindset or culture, whereby organizational members recognize interdependencies between parts and the importance of flexibility. This can support in seizing and transforming the organization, and consequently it may require beginning with an unlearning process (e.g., siloed thinking and organizing).

Based on the preceding arguments, we derive the following proposition:

P6: Healthcare organizations that employ systems thinking are more capable of deploying Adapt strategies.

A Model of Strategic Responses to Environmental Uncertainty

Following the above propositions, and in line with our conceptualizations of environmental uncertainty and organizational strategic responses, we present a conceptual model which visualizes the proposed relationships between the nature of environmental uncertainty, organizations' strategic responses, and the associated need for and capacity of organizational dynamic capabilities (see Fig. 1.1). In this model, we connect the conceptualization of environmental uncertainty – represented

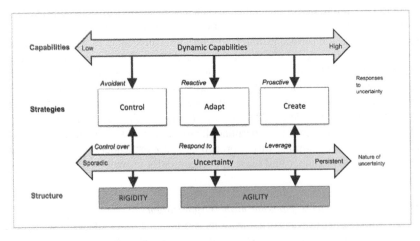

Fig. 1.1. Strategy Amid Environmental Uncertainty.

as a spectrum from more sporadic (as conceptualized in previous literature) to persistent (as conceptualized in this chapter) – with organizational strategies. We argue that persistently uncertain environments necessitate Adapt and/or Create strategies, thereby requiring a higher level of dynamic capabilities to employ. We furthermore suggest a bidirectional relationship between organizational strategies and structure; for example, more agile organizations will be better suited to pursue Adapt and/or Create strategies, and organizations that pursue Adapt and/or Create strategies will become more agile. We further specify how different conceptualizations of environmental uncertainty dictate organizational perceptions of, and responses to, uncertainty. For example, in conceptualizing the environment as sporadically uncertain, uncertainty becomes perceived as event-based (i.e., always attached to an event, rather than a feature of the environment) and something to be controlled and avoided. However, in conceptualizing uncertainty as persistent, it becomes something to be leveraged and triggers proactive responses. We call on future research to further develop the ideas put forward in this chapter by testing its propositions empirically. Studies across different settings (e.g., country contexts, health system types, and diverse healthcare organizations) are particularly warranted in order to further contextualize the model and add important boundary conditions.

CONCLUSION: WHERE TO GO FROM HERE?

We welcome scholars to use this chapter as a basis for reconceptualizing environmental uncertainty and reconsidering strategy in the current organizational environment. We have laid out several propositions that can support scholars in designing future empirical work, but there certainly remains room for more conceptual development in the relationship between uncertainty, temporal work, and strategy making. Practically speaking, we believe that by beginning to "take uncertainty for granted," HCOs can begin to move toward adaptation and creation in a way that can support health system aims, ensuring sustainability. Given the urgency of health system reform and the increasing complexity and dynamism of the environment, HCOs need to shift away from the status quo and move toward new imagined futures. However, considering the importance of healthcare as a public good, it is essential that organizations continue to focus on sustainability and maintaining an equilibrium with the environment, while also engaging in Create strategies. HCOs should implement adaptability at the core of their organizational strategy, which will allow them to become more agile and responsive to environmental shifts. Simultaneously, organizational members must begin looking farther into the future, imagining both desirable and undesirable scenarios to motivate more radical change and even the creation of a new way forward.

REFERENCES

Agwunobi, A., & Osborne, P. (2016). Dynamic capabilities and healthcare: A framework for enhancing the competitive advantage of hospitals. *California Management Review, 58*(4), 141–161.

Alimadadi, S., Davies, A., & Tell, F. (2022). A palace fit for the future: Desirability in temporal work. *Strategic Organization, 20*(1), 20–50.

Alvarez, S., Afuah, A., & Gibson, C. (2018). Editors' comments: Should management theories take uncertainty seriously? *Academy of Management Review, 43*(2), 169–172.

Andersson, T., & Gadolin, C. (2020). Understanding institutional work through social interaction in highly institutionalized settings: Lessons from public healthcare organizations. *Scandinavian Journal of Management, 36*(2), 101107.

Bansal, P., Reinecke, J., Suddaby, R., & Langley, A. (2022). Temporal work: The strategic organization of time. *Strategic Organization, 20*(1), 6–19.

Barnard, C. I. (1938). *The functions of the executive*. Harvard University Press.

Barrett, M. P. (2022). *Reported Social Unrest Index: March 2022 update*. International Monetary Fund.

Begun, J. W., & Jiang, H. J. (2020). Health care management during Covid-19: Insights from complexity science. *NEJM Catalyst Innovations in Care Delivery, 1*(5).

Begun, J. W., & Kaissi, A. A. (2004). Uncertainty in health care environments: Myth or reality? *Health Care Management Review, 29*(1), 31–39.

Begun, J. W., Zimmerman, B., & Dooley, K. (2003). Health care organizations as complex adaptive systems. *Advances in health care organization theory, 253*, 253–288.

Bentley, F. S., & Kehoe, R. R. (2020). Give them some slack—They're trying to change! The benefits of excess cash, excess employees, and increased human capital in the strategic change context. *Academy of Management Journal, 63*(1), 181–204.

Bourgeois, L. J., III. (1985). Strategic goals, perceived uncertainty, and economic performance in volatile environments. *Academy of Management Journal, 28*(3), 548–573.

Burns, L. R., Nembhard, I. M., & Shortell, S. M. (2022). Integrating network theory into the study of integrated healthcare. *Social Science & Medicine, 296*, 114664.

Child, J. (1972). Organizational structure, environment and performance: The role of strategic choice. *Sociology, 6*(1), 1–22.

Chowdhury, H. (2023). ChatGPT cost a fortune to make with OpenAI's losses growing to $540 million last year, report says. *Business insider*. https://www.businessinsider.com/openai-2022-losses-hit-540-million-as-chatgpt-costs-soared-2023-5?international=true&r=US&IR=T

Courtney, H., Kirkland, J., & Viguerie, P. (1997). Strategy under uncertainty. *Harvard Business Review, 75*(6), 67–79.

Cutrer, W. B., & Ehrenfeld, J. M. (2017). Protocolization, standardization and the need for adaptive expertise in our medical systems. *Journal of Medical Systems, 41*(12), 1–2.

Dess, G. G., & Beard, D. W. (1984). Dimensions of organizational task environments. *Administrative Science Quarterly*, 52–73.

Dill, W. R. (1958). Environment as an influence on managerial autonomy. *Administrative Science Quarterly*, 409–443.

Dixon, S. E., Meyer, K. E., & Day, M. (2010). Stages of organizational transformation in transition economies: A dynamic capabilities approach. *Journal of Management Studies, 47*(3), 416–436.

Downey, H. K., Hellriegel, D., & Slocum, J. W., Jr. (1975). Environmental uncertainty: The construct and its application. *Administrative Science Quarterly*, 613–629.

Downey, H. K., & Slocum, J. W. (1975). Uncertainty: Measures, research, and sources of variation. *Academy of Management Journal, 18*(3), 562–578.

Duncan, R. B. (1972). Characteristics of organizational environments and perceived environmental uncertainty. *Administrative Science Quarterly*, 313–327.

Edmondson, A. C. (1996). Learning from mistakes is easier said than done: Group and organizational influences on the detection and correction of human error. *The Journal of Applied Behavioral Science, 32*(1), 5–28.

Edmondson, A. (1999). Psychological safety and learning behavior in work teams. *Administrative Science Quarterly, 44*(2), 350–383.

Fergnani, A. (2022). Corporate foresight: A new frontier for strategy and management. *Academy of Management Perspectives, 36*(2), 820–844.

Ferlie, E., Fitzgerald, L., Wood, M., & Hawkins, C. (2005). The nonspread of innovations: The mediating role of professionals. *Academy of Management Journal, 48*(1), 117–134.

Figueroa, C. A., Harrison, R., Chauhan, A., & Meyer, L. (2019). Priorities and challenges for health leadership and workforce management globally: A rapid review. *BMC Health Services Research, 19*(1), 1–11.

Fontana, G., & Gerrard, B. (2004). A Post Keynesian theory of decision making under uncertainty. *Journal of Economic Psychology, 25*(5), 619–637.

George, G., Howard-Grenville, J., Joshi, A., & Tihanyi, L. (2016). Understanding and tackling societal grand challenges through management research. *Academy of Management Journal, 59*(6), 1880–1895.

Gephart, R., Topal, Ç., & Zhang, Z. (2010). Future-oriented sensemaking: Temporalities and institutional legitimation. In *Process sensemaking and organizing*. Oxford University Press.

Gifford, R., Fleuren, B., van de Baan, F., Ruwaard, D., Poesen, L., Zijlstra, F., & Westra, D. (2022). To uncertainty and beyond: Identifying the capabilities needed by hospitals to function in dynamic environments. *Medical Care Research and Review, 79*(4), 549–561.

Gifford, R., van de Baan, F., Westra, D., Ruwaard, D., & Fleuren, B. (2023). Through the looking glass: Confronting health care management's biggest challenges in the wake of a crisis. *Health Care Management Review, 48*(2), 185–196.

Ginter, P., Duncan, W. J., & Swayne, L. E. (2018). *The strategic management of health care organizations*. John Wiley & Sons.

Gioia, D. A., Thomas, J. B., Clark, S. M., & Chittipeddi, K. (1994). Symbolism and strategic change in academia: The dynamics of sensemaking and influence. *Organization Science, 5*(3), 363–383.

Griffin, M. A., & Grote, G. (2020). When is more uncertainty better? A model of uncertainty regulation and effectiveness. *Academy of Management Review, 45*(4), 745–765.

Hearld, L. R., & Westra, D. (2022). Charting a course: A research agenda for studying the governance of health care networks. *Responding to the Grand Challenges in Health Care via Organizational Innovation, 21*, 111–132.

Hefner, J. L., & Nembhard, I. M. (Eds.). (2021). *The contributions of health care management to grand health care challenges*. Emerald Publishing Limited.

Helmig, B., Hinz, V., & Ingerfurth, S. (2014). Extending Miles & Snow's strategy choice typology to the German hospital sector. *Health Policy, 118*(3), 363–376.

Hensher, M., & McGain, F. (2020). Health care sustainability metrics: Building a safer, low-carbon health system: Commentary examines how to build a safer, low-carbon health system. *Health Affairs, 39*(12), 2080–2087.

Hernes, T., & Maitlis, S. (Eds.). (2012). *Process, sensemaking, and organizing*. Oxford University Press.

Hollander, J. E., & Carr, B. G. (2020). Virtually perfect? Telemedicine for COVID-19. *New England Journal of Medicine, 382*(18), 1679–1681.

Howley, E. (2022). The U.S. Physician shortage is only going to get worse. Here are potential solutions. https://time.com/6199666/physician-shortage-challenges-solutions/

Issel, L. M. (2019). Paradoxes of practice guidelines, professional expertise, and patient centeredness: The medical care triangle. *Medical Care Research and Review, 76*(4), 359–385.

Issel, L. M., Rathert, C., & Hearld, L. (2023). Strategy research in a polarized and politicized environment. *Health Care Management Review, 48*(2), 109.

Kafetzopoulos, D., Psomas, E., & Skalkos, D. (2019). Innovation dimensions and business performance under environmental uncertainty. *European Journal of Innovation Management*. https://doi.org/10.1108/EJIM-07-2019-0197

Kaplan, S., & Orlikowski, W. J. (2013). Temporal work in strategy making. *Organization Science, 24*(4), 965–995.

Karliner, J., Slotterback, S., Boyd, R., Ashby, B., Steele, K., & Wang, J. (2020). Health care's climate footprint: The health sector contribution and opportunities for action. *The European Journal of Public Health, 30*(Suppl. 5), 165–843.

Kazley, A. S., & Ozcan, Y. A. (2007). Organizational and environmental determinants of hospital EMR adoption: A national study. *Journal of Medical Systems, 31*, 375–384.

Khan, S., Vandermorris, A., Shepherd, J., Begun, J. W., Lanham, H. J., Uhl-Bien, M., & Berta, W. (2018). Embracing uncertainty, managing complexity: Applying complexity thinking principles to transformation efforts in healthcare systems. *BMC Health Services Research, 18*(1), 1–8.

Knight, F. H. (1921). *Risk, uncertainty and profit.* Hougthon Mifflin company.

Kreiser, P., & Marino, L. (2002). Analyzing the historical development of the environmental uncertainty construct. *Management Decision.* https://doi.org/10.1108/00251740210441090

Lawrence, P. R., & Lorsch, J. W. (1967). Differentiation and integration in complex organizations. *Administrative Science Quarterly*, 1–47.

Li, R., Kumar, A., & Chen, J. H. (2023). How chatbots and large language model artificial intelligence systems will reshape modern medicine: Fountain of creativity or Pandora's box? *JAMA Internal Medicine.* https://doi.org/10.1001/jamainternmed.2023.1835

López-Gamero, M. D., Molina-Azorín, J. F., & Claver-Cortés, E. (2011). Environmental uncertainty and environmental management perception: A multiple case study. *Journal of Business Research, 64*(4), 427–435.

March, J. G., & Simon, H. A. (1958). *Organizations.* Wiley.

Mayo, A. T., Myers, C. G., & Sutcliffe, K. M. (2021). Organizational science and health care. *The Academy of Management Annals, 15*(2), 537–576.

Menachemi, N., & Collum, T. H. (2011). Benefits and drawbacks of electronic health record systems. *Risk Management and Healthcare Policy*, 47–55.

Miles, R. E., Snow, C. C., Meyer, A. D., & Coleman, H. J., Jr. (1978). Organizational strategy, structure, and process. *Academy of Management Review, 3*(3), 546–562.

Milliken, F. J. (1987). Three types of perceived uncertainty about the environment: State, effect, and response uncertainty. *Academy of Management Review, 12*(1), 133–143.

Mithani, M. A. (2020). Adaptation in the face of the new normal. *Academy of Management Perspectives, 34*(4), 508–530.

Mladovsky, P., Srivastava, D., Cylus, J., Karanikolos, M., Evetovits, T., Thomson, S., & McKee, M. (2012). *Health policy responses to the financial crisis in Europe: Policy summary 5.* World Health Organization.

Morgan, D., & James, C. (2022). *Investing in health systems to protect society and boost the economy: Priority investments and order-of-magnitude cost estimates.* https://doi.org/10.1787/d0aa9188-en

Nembhard, I. M., Burns, L. R., & Shortell, S. M. (2020). Responding to Covid-19: Lessons from management research. *NEJM Catalyst Innovations in Care Delivery, 1*(2).

O'Reilly, C. A., & Tushman, M. L. (2004). The ambidextrous organization. *Harvard Business Review, 82*(4), 74–83.

O'Reilly, C. A., & Tushman, M. L. (2013). Organizational ambidexterity: Past, present, and future. *Academy of Management Perspectives, 27*(4), 324–338.

OECD. (2023). *OECD Economic Outlook, Interim Report March 2023: A Fragile Recovery.* OECD Publishing. https://doi.org/10.1787/d14d49eb-en

Pablo, A. L., Reay, T., Dewald, J. R., & Casebeer, A. L. (2007). Identifying, enabling and managing dynamic capabilities in the public sector. *Journal of Management Studies, 44*(5), 687–708.

Peeters, R., Westra, D., van Raak, A. J. A., & Ruwaard, D. (2023). Getting our hopes up: How actors perceive network effectiveness and why it matters. *Social Science & Medicine, 325.* https://doi.org/10.1016/j.socscimed.2023.115911

Pffefer, J., & Salancik, G. (1978). *The external control of organizations: A resource dependence perspective.* Pitman Press.

Picquendar, G., Guedon, A., Moulinet, F., & Schuers, M. (2019). Influence of medical shortage on GP burnout: A cross-sectional study. *Family Practice, 36*(3), 291–296.

Porter, M. E. (2010). What is value in health care. *New England Journal of Medicine, 363*(26), 2477–2481.

Reay, T., Goodrick, E., & D'Aunno, T. (2021). *Health care research and organization theory.* Cambridge University Press.

Rindova, V., & Courtney, H. (2020). To shape or adapt: Knowledge problems, epistemologies, and strategic postures under Knightian uncertainty. *Academy of Management Review, 45*(4), 787–807.

Rindova, V. P., & Martins, L. L. (2021). Shaping possibilities: A design science approach to developing novel strategies. *Academy of Management Review, 46*(4), 800–822.

Rouse, W. B. (2008). Health care as a complex adaptive system: Implications for design and management. *Bridge-Washington-National Academy of Engineering-, 38*(1), 17.

Schilke, O., Hu, S., & Helfat, C. E. (2018). Quo vadis, dynamic capabilities? A content-analytic review of the current state of knowledge and recommendations for future research. *Academy of Management Annals, 12*(1), 390–439.

Schneider, A. M., Oppel, E. M., & Winter, V. (2021). Explaining variations in hospitals' use of strategic human resource management: How environmental and organizational factors matter. *Health Care Management Review, 46*(1), 2–11.

Snowden, D. J., & Boone, M. E. (2007). A leader's framework for decision making. *Harvard Business Review, 85*(11), 68.

Teece, D. J. (2014). The foundations of enterprise performance: Dynamic and ordinary capabilities in an (economic) theory of firms. *Academy of Management Perspectives, 28*(4), 328–352.

Teece, D. J. (2018). Dynamic capabilities as (workable) management systems theory. *Journal of Management and Organization, 24*(3), 359–368.

Teece, D., Peteraf, M., & Leih, S. (2016). Dynamic capabilities and organizational agility: Risk, uncertainty, and strategy in the innovation economy. *California Management Review, 58*(4), 13–35.

Teece, D. J., Pisano, G., & Shuen, A. (1997). Dynamic capabilities and strategic management. *Strategic Management Journal, 18*(7), 509–533.

Thompson, J. D. (1967). *Organizations in action.* McGraw-Hill.

Wenzel, M. (2022). Taking the future more seriously: From corporate foresight to "future-making". *Academy of Management Perspectives, 36*(2), 845–850.

Wenzel, M., Krämer, H., Koch, J., & Reckwitz, A. (2020). Future and organization studies: On the rediscovery of a problematic temporal category in organizations. *Organization Studies, 41*(10), 1441–1455.

Whyte, J., Comi, A., & Mosca, L. (2022). Making futures that matter: Future making, online working and organizing remotely. *Organization Theory, 3*(1). https://doi.org/10.1177/2631787 7211069138

Yeager, V. A., Menachemi, N., Savage, G. T., Ginter, P. M., Sen, B. P., & Beitsch, L. M. (2014). Using resource dependency theory to measure the environment in health care organizational studies. *Health Care Management Review, 39*(1), 50–65.

CHAPTER 2

MEASURE TWICE, CHANGE ONCE: USING SIMULATION TO SUPPORT CHANGE MANAGEMENT IN RURAL HEALTHCARE DELIVERY

Clair Reynolds Kueny[a], Alex Price[b] and Casey Canfield[a]

[a]Missouri University of Science & Technology, USA
[b]Case Western Reserve University, USA

ABSTRACT

Barriers to adequate healthcare in rural areas remain a grand challenge for local healthcare systems. In addition to patients' travel burdens, lack of health insurance, and lower health literacy, rural healthcare systems also experience significant resource shortages, as well as issues with recruitment and retention of healthcare providers, particularly specialists. These factors combined result in complex change management-focused challenges for rural healthcare systems. Change management initiatives are often resource intensive, and in rural health organizations already strapped for resources, it may be particularly risky to embark on change initiatives. One way to address these change management concerns is by leveraging socio-technical simulation models to estimate techno-economic feasibility (e.g., is it technologically feasible, and is it economical?) as well as socio-utility feasibility (e.g., how will the changes be utilized?). We present a framework for how healthcare systems can integrate modeling and simulation techniques from systems engineering into a change management process. Modeling and simulation are particularly useful for investigating the amount of uncertainty about potential outcomes, guiding decision-making that considers different scenarios, and validating theories to determine if they accurately reflect real-life processes. The results of these simulations can be integrated into critical change management recommendations related to developing readiness for change and addressing resistance to

Research and Theory to Foster Change in the Face of Grand Health Care Challenges
Advances in Health Care Management, Volume 22, 29–53
Copyright © 2024 Clair Reynolds Kueny, Alex Price and Casey Canfield
Published under exclusive licence by Emerald Publishing Limited
ISSN: 1474-8231/doi:10.1108/S1474-823120240000022002

change. As part of our integration, we present a case study showcasing how simulation modeling has been used to determine feasibility and potential resistance to change considerations for implementing a mobile radiation oncology unit. Recommendations and implications are discussed.

Keywords: Rural healthcare; change management; simulation modeling; systems thinking; radiation oncology; case study

INTRODUCTION

Approximately 46 million US residents live in rural areas (defined as counties with populations less than 50,000, particularly those with noncore central communities or metropolitan areas with populations larger than 50,000; USDA Economic Research Service, 2019), representing 14% of the US population. Rural communities are consistently more sparsely populated and farther away from services such as healthcare (Dobis et al., 2021). Over 130 rural hospitals closed between 2010 and 2021, with 14% of those closures in 2020 (American Hospital Association, 2022). When rural hospitals close, there is a measurable drop in primary care physicians, not just surgical specialists (Germack et al., 2019). In addition, rural areas struggle to recruit and retain doctors. Ultimately, it is often economically infeasible to build specialized healthcare centers closer to rural patient populations. These ripple effects can limit economic development and quality of life, creating feedback loops that increase disparities between urban and rural communities. These disparities are even higher when considering rural counties with majority Black or Indigenous populations (Henning-Smith et al., 2019). These grand challenges are experienced at multiple levels within the system, including rural patients, rural healthcare providers, and rural healthcare organizations.

Rural Patients' Grand Challenges

Rural patients tend to be more reluctant to seek healthcare treatment due to access, financial, and cultural barriers (Douthit et al., 2015). For example, for cancer treatment, rural residents are 1.6 times more likely to have unstaged disease (i.e., incomplete diagnosis), which negatively impacts treatment decisions, and are less likely to receive treatment compared to urban patients (Johnson et al., 2014). In large part, this is because rural residents are less likely to receive specialized treatments due to the high travel burden required for daily visits to a distant facility for treatment. In general, limited geographic outreach in rural areas because of the costly facilities needed for treatment delivery, lack of specialized treatment care teams, and time-consuming operations result in more rural patients having unstaged disease and thus not receiving necessary treatment.

People within rural communities also tend of have higher poverty rates and poorer insurance coverage. Consequently, rural patients face a higher financial burden associated with receiving care. Disproportionately, more rural counties are termed "persistently poor," meaning that at least 20% of the population is living below the poverty line over four consecutive US Census measurements. This includes 15% of rural (or nonmetro) counties and 4% of urban (or metro) counties. Persistently poor counties tend to have higher population declines and higher mortality rates (Dobis et al., 2021). Although the number of uninsured has decreased over time (largely due to the Affordable Care Act), rural communities still tend to have higher uninsured rates. Rural residents often have fewer insurance options because smaller employers may not be able to provide coverage. As a result, Medicaid covers almost 25% of nonelderly rural residents (Foutz et al., 2017).

In response to negative interactions with healthcare systems and other health stigmas, many rural residents are disinclined to trust their healthcare systems or utilize care (Rural Health Information Hub, 2022a). It is common for doctors living in rural areas to be overburdened and/or underpaid, which may negatively affect continuing education or introduction of new techniques, resulting in many residents receiving poor or inadequate care (Douthit et al., 2015). Additionally, in small communities, doctors are part of the social network, and individuals may be embarrassed to discuss medical issues with someone they perceive as a friend or neighbor (Brems et al., 2006). There may be stigma against receiving medical treatment, particularly in the context of mental health (Douthit et al., 2015). Rural residents may turn to other more trusted institutions, such as religious institutions, to provide support during chronic healthcare crises (Pham et al., 2020). Furthermore, lower health literacy rates and access to health information among rural patients may contribute to lower likelihood of patients seeking screening services as well as access to healthcare specialists (Chen et al., 2019), particularly when combined with the other hurdles mentioned (lack of insurance coverage, transportation, geographic hurdles, etc.). The lack of understanding related to managing one's health combined with significant difficulty to access care contribute to these very real rural grand challenges for patients (Rural Health Information Hub, 2022a).

Rural Healthcare Provider's Grand Challenges

Over the past decade, rural communities have experienced significant decreases in medical specialists when compared to metropolitan communities (Machado et al., 2021). This lack of replenishment in the physician workforce results in a higher workload for physicians already present within the rural healthcare facility as rural populations are not declining at the same rate (Skinner et al., 2019). Additionally, there is lower reimbursement on average across rural patients due to the higher likelihood of this population being uninsured or using Medicaid/ Medicare which have a lower reimbursement rate compared to private insurers (Meit et al., 2014; Waibel & Perry, 2022). As such, healthcare providers in rural communities are potentially faced with a higher workload and lower reimbursement for the same work as colleagues in suburban or urban settings. Additionally, rural healthcare providers often are not able to specialize their care (e.g., an oncologist choosing to focus only on breast cancer patients) and instead must treat any and all types of patient illnesses (e.g., all types of cancer), resulting in more complex workloads and greater cognitive loads throughout a given day (Kueny et al., 2020). Further, many providers are active members in their small, rural communities, meaning that often they know their patients beyond the patient–provider relationship (e.g., they belong to the same church, their children play on the same teams, etc.), creating even greater emotional labor for rural healthcare providers (Kueny et al., 2020). These challenges can further exacerbate provider retention challenges.

Specialist healthcare providers can potentially supplement care to rural or regional facilities with telemedicine; however, the technological gap between rural and suburban/urban communities is significant when looking at access to broadband (Kryszkiewicz et al., 2022; Waibel & Perry, 2022). Further, many treatments cannot happen via telehealth (e.g., radiation treatment for cancer), and thus, this is not a viable solution to address all rural healthcare challenges. To help mitigate some of these challenges, specialty providers can look to coordinate care in a compressed timeframe for rural patients at specialty or high-volume centers. However, that coordination can often be challenging where patients and providers (of varying specialties) do not understand the importance of certain procedures or tests and their timing. Additionally, as mentioned, there is potential hesitation and lack of desire for patients to travel for care in the first place (Waibel & Perry, 2022).

Rural Healthcare Organization's Grand Challenges

While healthcare organizations broadly are facing numerous grand challenges, particularly since the introduction of the coronavirus, rural healthcare organizations continue to have more substantial issues than suburban or even urban/inner-city counterparts. We define rural healthcare organizations as organizations responsible for healthcare delivery in a rural area (as defined earlier), particularly addressing the healthcare needs of rural patients, typically short-term, general acute care. Often these organizations are critical access hospitals, sole community hospitals, and/or small regional clinic systems (NC Rural Health Research Program, 2022; Rural Health Information Hub, 2022b).

Providing healthcare in rural areas in and of itself is a grand challenge due to the culmination of patient and provider issues mentioned as well as broader system/institutional issues. For example, as mentioned, rural healthcare organizations face some of the largest detriments in recruitment and retention of healthcare providers/employees (Machado et al., 2021; Moore et al., 2022). Additionally, the demographics of the patient population make it challenging to provide care, in particular, as patients have low health literacy rates (exacerbating the complexity of their health needs), low income/lack of health insurance/Medicaid or Medicare reliance (resulting in significant systemic budget/billing issues), and significant transportation barriers as a result of lack of public transportation and resources (resulting in systemic scheduling problems and missed appointments) (Dobis et al., 2021; Kueny et al., 2020; Rosko, 2020). All of this is further exacerbated by financial challenges as rural healthcare organizations face the conundrum of low-density population (i.e., lower volume of billable hours) with higher overhead/operational costs due to location (Rosko, 2020). Rapid changes to reimbursement models and health informatics/electronic recordkeeping further threaten already lean budgets and personnel systems (Litwin, 2022). As a result, rural healthcare organizations are closing at an increasingly rapid rate (NC Rural Health Research Program, 2022; Rural Health Information Hub, 2022b), further exacerbating the problems of access to care for rural patients.

With these rural healthcare organization issues in mind, including the system inputs of challenges associated with rural patients and rural healthcare providers, it can be advantageous for rural healthcare organizations to explore new ways to bring and provide care to their rural communities. However, there needs to be great care and planning before implementation to avoid ill-advised financial and change-focused decision-making that could in fact further compromise access to healthcare in a rural setting. Thus, we present an integration of systems engineering, change management theory, and a model case study to provide possible solutions on how these grand challenges in rural healthcare might be addressed.

How Grand Challenges Contribute to Change Management Challenges

There are a number of models associated with (planned) organizational change processes (e.g., Cummings & Worley, 2015; Kotter, 2012; Senge, 2006) and other models associated with community-focused change (e.g., Brown & Wyatt, 2009; IAP2, 2018; Leach & Katcher, 2014). While they all have their unique approaches to addressing planned change processes, they all also follow similar guidelines overall, just utilizing slightly different vocabulary. Notably, Stouten et al. (2018) provide an integrated framework for successfully planned organizational change, which we use for the basis of planned change management to organize how grand challenges faced across rural patients, rural healthcare providers, and rural healthcare organizations further enhance change management challenges. We do combine a few of their steps to more succinctly address the overall process. Finally, while there are other types of organizational change processes, including unplanned or emergent change (e.g., see Burnes, 2013), we focus specifically on planned change processes directed at addressing specific challenges in the organizational system. Moving forward, where we refer to organizational change and change management, we specifically mean *planned* change. Broadly, these planned change management models consider the following steps/components:

- Assessing the opportunity/problem motivating the change;
- Select and support a guiding change coalition;
- Formulate and communicate a clear, compelling vision of the change;
- Mobilize energy for change and empower others to act, including through knowledge development;
- Sustain and monitor momentum through short-term wins and reinforcement of change.

Assessing the Opportunity/Problem Motivating the Change

While there is some debate whether urgency is an appropriate motivator for organizational change (Stouten et al., 2018), rural healthcare organizations and providers alike appear to be acutely aware of the threats and challenges facing rural healthcare (e.g., Levit et al., 2020; Rural Health Information Hub, 2022b), and that change must occur if these institutions will continue to survive. However, there still appear to be challenges impacting developing an action for change, or a readiness for change. Readiness for change is defined as not only a belief that change is needed (i.e., overcoming complacency) but also a belief that change is achievable and there is a commitment to engage in the change process (Cummings & Worley, 2015). For example, patients' distrust of providers could contribute to an uncertainty or unwillingness to participate in new treatments or new care delivery approaches. Additionally, considering the pressure, stressors, and burnout rural healthcare professionals already face (Kueny et al., 2020), they likely struggle to find the capacity to whole-heartedly support more initiatives, more work, and the potential for new roles or responsibilities to bring about change. Finally, as mentioned, rural healthcare organizations are strapped for monetary/tangible/physical resources, as well as human capital resources. Thus, the readiness to contribute and redirect resources to a change process or new strategic direction can seem particularly daunting. As such, while rural healthcare organizations likely do not deny that there are opportunities for change, it can still seem overwhelming to commit to and prepare for a new process or strategy. Furthermore, as discussed below in formulating a vision (as well as the politics surrounding rural healthcare organizations – see Select and Support a Guiding Coalition section on guiding coalition), there are so many challenges that need to be addressed with planned change, that it is often difficult to decide which problem(s) to tackle above others.

Select and Support a Guiding Coalition

The challenges associated with creating a readiness for change also feed into a rural healthcare organization's ability to build political support (create a coalition) to facilitate the change. Notably, because of rural health organizations' roles in supporting public health, much of this guiding coalition discussion necessitates a discussion of political and economic environmental influences on building the coalition in the first place. Research shows that since the Great Recession, rural healthcare systems/institutions and rural public health has been underinvested in terms of public and government-led programs (Leider et al., 2020). Thus, literally, there has been a lack of governmental programming and political support in external environment systems to generate initiatives in rural health. That is a particularly significant hurdle. But additionally, in communities where health stigmas are still strong (Leider et al., 2020) and resources are strapped, it can be challenging to convince groups, organizations, and individuals to take the lead and serve as change agents for significant change processes (Stouten et al., 2018). Finally, as with any change process, there will be individuals who stand to gain but also individuals who may lose because of new processes (Cummings & Worley, 2015). For example, as small rural healthcare organizations approach closure, large (usually [sub]urban) healthcare institutions often swoop in to purchase and "save" the rural location. This tends to rock communities who are used to and comfortable with their local system and feel threatened by large institutions coming in to change things (e.g., La France et al., 2022). Research also suggests that mergers and acquisitions within healthcare systems can create "us versus them" cultures among the healthcare professionals (Majumdar et al., 2022). Additionally, when these large acquisitions or affiliations occur, it can threaten primary care provided in the rural community (La France et al., 2022; O'Hanlon et al., 2019), further enhancing distrust among rural patients and their healthcare providers. Thus, the composition of a guiding coalition to motivate change in a rural healthcare organization will play a significant but delicate role and should be developed with these challenges in mind.

Formulating and Communicating a Clear, Compelling Vision

One of the greatest challenges for rural healthcare organizations is knowing where to start and what to focus on. There are so many areas of rural healthcare that require attention (as noted in our Introduction section) that knowing which should be the priority and the focal point of the change vision for the rural healthcare organization is difficult to determine. On top of that, creating and communicating an effective vision is one of the most critical but delicate and easily incorrectly implemented components of a change management plan. For example, Kotter (2012) states "In some ways, it's easier to describe visions that don't help produce needed change than those that do" (p. 79). As mentioned, with the overwhelming challenges rural healthcare providers face, and often having direct integration in their communities, they are likely to have strong views on where their rural healthcare organization should focus its resources. It may turn out that that a healthcare provider will not support a certain vision or direction, particularly if they do not believe it will directly address what they perceive are the most critical issues (e.g., Stouten et al., 2018).

Mobilize Energy for Change and Empower Others to Act

For a change process to be effective, there must be purposeful transition management efforts in place and efforts to get relevant actors actually engaged in the process (Cummings & Worley, 2015). Examples of managing the change transition include activity planning such as creating roadmaps of new directions forward and plans to get there, continuing to engage commitment for the change, readying managers for change, and ensuring structures do not hinder change (e.g., IT systems that do not align with new processes, payment models that inhibit new patient care delivery structures, etc.; Kotter, 2012; Stouten et al., 2018). However, many of these systems and structural issues are beyond a rural healthcare organization's control, let alone a provider's control. For example, insurance payment models (private or Medicare/Medicaid) are not within the scope of the organization's control, and systemic social challenges such as lower patient health literacy rates, limited access to broadband for telemedicine, etc., go well beyond a single rural healthcare organization or provider's capability to influence for change management purposes. These limitations can make it difficult to empower rural providers and employees to actively engage in and commit to a change process even if they wish to (e.g., Stouten et al., 2018), as removing some of these obstacles may be almost impossible.

Sustain and Monitor Momentum Through Short-Term Wins and Reinforcement

Finally, change management models recommend that organizations help generate short-term wins during the change process to sustain momentum and reinforce that the change is moving the organization in the right direction (Kotter, 2012; Stouten et al., 2018). Example strategies to support change transitions include ensuring continued access to resources, providing new resources as issues/needs arise, providing opportunities for personnel to experience personal wins, developing new individual skills, and reinforcing new behaviors (Cummings & Worley, 2015). Additionally, short-term wins provide evidence that while there are challenges, the sacrifices have been worth it, allow for continued refinement of the vision, and undermine straggling change resisters (Kotter, 2012). However, with the seemingly constant revolving door of rural healthcare providers and changing personnel (due to retention challenges), and limited resources throughout rural organizations and rural communities, it can be hard to maintain momentum. An ability to agilely anticipate new resource needs, to find and provide these new resources to support the change and combat criticism, and to justify even more sacrifice in already lean systems may seem an insurmountable problem for rural healthcare organizations trying to survive while also advance the patient care they can provide. This can often result in abandoned or incomplete change processes (Stouten et al., 2018).

While describing the combined challenges of rural healthcare and change management may read as if these are somewhat hopeless efforts, we believe that there are ways to help rural healthcare organizations overcome these seemingly insurmountable problems. Specifically, we propose utilization and integration of systems engineering modeling to help rural healthcare organizations identify what, where, when, and how to implement critical change processes to improve rural healthcare provider and rural patient experiences.

Using Systems Engineering to Advance Rural Healthcare Change Management

One strategy for rural healthcare organizations to overcome these challenges is to conceptualize both the problems and solutions within a system. *Systems* are made up of interrelated parts within a whole that has a function or purpose. In some cases, this complexity between the parts and the whole can be framed as a *system-of-systems* (also called SoS) characterized by autonomy, belonging, connectivity, diversity, and emergence. An SoS, rather than subsystems, has high independence between systems (high autonomy), decentralization (low belonging), multiple connections between systems in a network structure (high connectivity), more diversity in the types of parts (high diversity), and are less predictable (high emergence) (Gorod et al., 2008). As a result, *systems thinking* involves recognizing how system structure influences and constrains system behavior (Meadows, 2008). Systems thinking has been applied to a wide range of socio-technical problems characterized by high complexity and uncertainty, such as safety (Leveson, 2011), energy efficiency (Chai & Yeo, 2012), climate change (Berry et al., 2018), and healthcare (Clarkson et al., 2018). In these cases, introducing an intervention or change can add risk and potentially lead to negative outcomes or disruptions.

Modeling and simulation are particularly useful techniques for developing and testing potential interventions that may have nonlinear and nonobvious impacts within a system. These tools can be used by practitioners to develop a vision or change strategy and estimate outcomes that can be shared with other stakeholders to increase buy-in. There are two modeling approaches that we find particularly useful in the context of change management, (1) Monte Carlo and (2) agent-based modeling (ABM). Monte Carlo simulation is one of the most common strategies for understanding the impact of uncertainty for decision-making (Morgan & Henrion, 1990). In a Monte Carlo simulation, each input is assigned a known probability distribution. In each iteration of the simulation, values for each input are sampled from these distributions and an outcome is calculated. Via thousands of iterations, a distribution for the outcome is estimated. This is particularly useful when modeling high impact, low probability events which are rare but can influence the distribution of potential outcomes such as high-cost healthcare delivery strategies. It is also useful in scenarios where there is limited linearity between cause and effect, which is often present within healthcare systems (de Savigny & Adam, 2009). Different strategies can be compared in terms of the average (or expected) outcome as well as best-case versus worst-case scenarios. This can support risk management efforts. For example, it may be preferable to choose a more expensive strategy to minimize chances of a worst-case scenario outcome.

In the context of change management, Monte Carlo simulation can support efforts to develop a vision that is robust to potential negative scenarios. For example, if a rural health organization is considering implementing a new telemedicine program, they could use Monte Carlo simulation to estimate the probability that it will be cost-effective, given uncertainty (i.e., distributions) for input parameters related to the percentage of patients with insurance, percentage of patients with access to the internet, and type of care required. Additionally, this simulation approach can be used to evaluate differing telemedicine software or medical specialties to understand the impact before purchasing and widespread implementation. In fact, this approach has been applied in the context of reducing phishing risk (Canfield & Fischhoff, 2018), choosing energy portfolios (Vithayasrichareon & MacGill, 2012), and health risk assessment (Khoshakhlagh et al., 2022).

Next, agent-based modeling (ABM) is a bottom-up simulation approach that is particularly effective for modeling the impact of human behavior. In ABM, there are no high-level governing equations determining the outcome (unlike

Monte Carlo models). Instead, decision rules are specified for how individual agents (such as patients and physicians) interact with each other as well as the environment. Each agent is initialized with different values and has different interactions, which influences behavior. As a result, ABM is useful for modeling heterogeneous populations and nonlinear interactions (Marshall et al., 2015, 2020). For example, ABM has been used to model solar adoption (Rai & Robinson, 2015), spread of COVID-19 in the presence of various mitigation efforts (Shastry et al., 2022), and strategies for protecting privacy in digital trade (Potluri et al., 2020).

In the context of change management, ABM is useful for incorporating a better behavioral model in the development of a vision, as well as to develop a better understanding of how key actors are likely to act within the new direction. Continuing the example of a new telemedicine program, a rural health organization could incorporate uncertainty related to patient satisfaction with receiving care via telemedicine and the role of referral networks (both from medical practitioners and friends/family). Rural health organizations could also evaluate different implementation approaches of telemedicine to ensure high patient satisfaction and referral patterns – this would help solidify the compelling vision further as the rural healthcare organization would be able to more clearly communicate the likely positive impact on patients and care potential. In fact, ABM is particularly useful for evaluating the impact of new processes on sub-populations, predicting reinforcing feedback loops, and comparing the outcomes for a wide range of interventions, and an agent-based model can be framed as a virtual testbed when initialized and validated with real-world data (Silverman et al., 2015). For example, within healthcare, ABM has been used to simulate the implementation of whole genome sequencing for nonsmall cell lung cancer within the Netherlands, which included 78 hospitals, 7 molecular tumor boards, 1 whole genome sequencing center, and over 5,000 patients per year. Their findings suggest that insufficient capacity for genome sequencing and referral patterns had the greatest impact on timeliness of further treatment options (van de Ven et al., 2022).

Since the 1990s, there has been a movement within systems engineering toward using model-based systems engineering (MBSE), which is a holistic approach for designing complex systems. This approach involves creating a single model in the design process to coordinate across team perspectives. This central repository avoids errors driven by inconsistent assumptions, supports system inter-connectivity, and reduces the amount of time spent writing and reviewing reports. As a result, it is possible to effectively design and analyze implications for complex systems (Madni & Sievers, 2018). In some cases, the single model in MBSE is characterized as a "digital twin" which fully reflects an existing object or system based on real-time data to support decision-making. This is consistent with the concept of using ABM as a type of virtual testbed, although an agent-based model would typically have less fidelity than a true digital twin. For example, NASA has shifted toward using MBSE via a digital twin for developing new spacecraft (Holladay et al., 2019; Madni et al., 2021).

Within healthcare, modeling and simulation techniques can be used to predict potential outcomes that can occur in a change management process without devoting resources to a full-blown implementation. This is consistent with efforts to leverage implementation science to increase the uptake of evidence-based practices (Bauer et al., 2015; Bauer & Kirchner, 2020). For example, it is possible to initialize a simulation for a new healthcare delivery process to get tailored predictions, particularly related to patient usage and provider uptake, as well as understanding the financial and systemic impact on the rural healthcare organization considering implementation. To explain this further, we provide a case study below using Monte Carlo simulations and ABM to evaluate the introduction of a mobile radiation oncology unit. After reviewing the case study, we provide a theoretical integration of systems engineering to improve change management as well as broader practical implications for this marriage beyond rural healthcare.

Case Study – Implementation of Mobile Radiation Oncology Unit

Oncological care is a specialty care that suffers from disparities based on geographical location. For example, 70% of counties within the United States do not have a medical oncologist, and 36% of rural patients state that they have to travel too far for their care compared to 19% of nonrural patients (Charlton et al., 2015). In towns of less than 2,500 individuals, almost one half of the cancer patients needed to travel more than 60 minutes to get to a radiotherapy center, which is problematic considering that roughly 50% of cancer diagnoses receive a radiation treatment (Kenamond et al., 2022). Patients with limited access to travel and housing while traveling to distant locations with radiotherapy centers are less likely to receive treatment (Charlton et al., 2015). In addition, radiotherapy facilities are also limited from widespread implementation in rural communities because radiation oncology machines (linear accelerators or linacs) require radiation protecting infrastructure and auxiliary technology that can be cost-prohibitive for many rural healthcare systems, especially if the expected patient volume is low. Thus, rural patient access to radiation oncology is a prime example of the culmination of grand challenges in rural healthcare in which change is needed but, because of the type of care, change could also be particularly costly and success uncertain for a rural healthcare organization to implement.

Notably, vendors have been developing linacs (Halcyon, Varian Medical Systems, Palo Alto, CA) for low-resource settings that are cheaper, smaller in physical footprint, simpler in capabilities, and robust to potential failure modes. Due to these more compact and self-shielding linacs, a mobile radiation oncology unit has been proposed to bring specialty care to rural patients (Chamberlain et al., 2020). In this scenario, the compact linac would be mounted within a tractor trailer that can relocate on a weekly basis to a new location. At each location, a building structure that protects all relevant individuals from additional radiation from the mobile system will be necessary to meet regulatory requirements. With these considerations in mind, there is a sizable capital investment (in the realm of multiple millions of US dollars) required by an owning healthcare organization to implement a mobile radiation oncology unit. Additionally, there are no existing systems similar to the one proposed here, thus limiting precedence and experience to draw from during implementation. As such, this rural healthcare delivery problem is an ideal scenario to test a comprehensive systems modeling approach, with a human-centered focus, to understand how this system may function in practicality, particularly from a planned change perspective, and whether this change in a healthcare delivery process is likely to be effective.

We propose a three-step method of systems modeling for healthcare implementation. The first step is to simulate the economic and technical aspects of the system using Monte Carlo simulation. Secondly, targeted interviews and surveys with all key stakeholders, including patients and physicians, are needed to measure how individuals might behave within the system. This step is necessary because healthcare systems are socio-technical systems where human decision-making and interaction have significant impacts on the operation of a system. Finally, the third step requires performing ABM, incorporating information learned in the first two steps to model and simulate the system deployment in scenarios to predict what the real-life outcomes may be.

For our case study focused on providing mobile radiation oncology in rural communities, we model a mobile radiation oncology system in both northern and southern Missouri as part of a Monte Carlo simulation, to understand the impacts of the new healthcare delivery process in different areas with varying patient volumes and disease types (see Fig. 2.1 for the simulation structure). Only five fraction treatment regimens for breast, lung, and rectal disease sites were considered. These data were extracted from the Cancer Incidence Missouri Information for Community Assessment website from the Missouri Department of Health and Senior Services (Missouri Cancer Registry & Research Center, 2020). A probability-based approach, appropriate for Monte Carlo simulation, was used for many of the independent variables such as patient type, insurance type, cost of all equipment, cost of linac housing structures, and all time-based activities including transit and setup time for the mobile linac (see Price et al., 2022 for more details).

When comparing the northern versus southern regions, the northern region had fewer patients and thus lower revenue when compared to the southern region. Using sensitivity analysis, the number of lung patients had the highest impact in change on the overall cost to the system, followed by insurance type, and the other types of cancer patients. The cost of the equipment and structures had a lower impact on the overall cost of the system. In a break-even analysis (see Fig. 2.2), the interplay between disease type and insurance types had different break-even points depending on the region, again underscoring the importance of evaluating the scenarios present within scope that may be different depending on location of implementation. Based on this Monte Carlo modeling, a rural healthcare organization could conclude that a mobile radiation oncology may be cost-effective, and thus a worthwhile change to pursue – but the guiding coalition

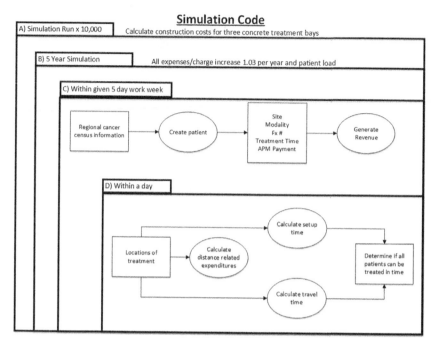

Fig. 2.1. The Simulation Workflow for a Mobile Radiation Oncology System Illustrating the Sublevel Iterations Needed to Run the Monte Carlo System. Fx is the number of fractions; APM is the alternative payment model. *Source:* Figure reprinted from Price et al. (2022).

chosen to lead the change needs to include both patients and referring physicians, who all need to buy into the new system.

For the second phase, we recommend utilization of the Theory of Planned Behavior (TPB) to guide study design and behavior modeling to understand what might impact key stakeholder change-focused behaviors, including readiness and resistance to changes in care delivery. For our case study, we focused on patient intentions to utilize a mobile radiation oncology unit. TPB, as an example of a reasoned action approach theory, has frequently been utilized to better understand health-focused behaviors, intentions to engage in health-focused behaviors among patients, and the impact of perceptions of contextual influences (e.g., possible outcomes of the behavior, what others will think, and perceived control in one's environment) on those intentions (Ajzen et al., 2007). Additionally, it has been recommended in the change management literature as a key theory to understand how to influence individual behavior as the building blocks for change momentum (Stouten et al., 2018). By utilizing this theory to model factors that may influence patients to engage or not engage in a particular health-focused behavior, we can help healthcare decision-makers understand how system-focused interventions may impact individual healthcare decision-making before the intervention has occurred.

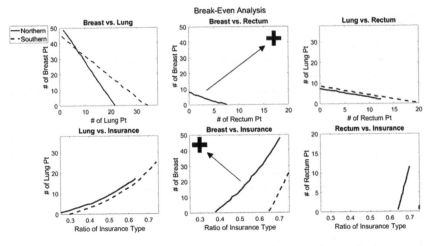

Fig. 2.2.   Break-Even Analysis for All 6 Scenarios Investigated. In the top row, the area point to the top right indicates increasing profit. In the bottom row, the arrow pointing to the top left indicates the direction of increasing profit. Each line within the graph represents the line at which a positive profit is made based on varied parameter on the x- and y-axis. Below that line, or in the direction opposite of the arrow, represents loss in profit. For example, in the breast versus insurance pane, as the rate in Medicare/Medicaid patient population increases, there is an increase in the number of breast patients that need to be seen to generate a profit. An insurance ratio of 0.25 means that the clinical makeup for the patient population would be 75% private insurers and 25% Medicare/Medicaid based. *Source:* Figure reprinted from Price et al. (2022).

TPB is also one of the most relied upon individual-behavior modeling approaches in ABM (Scalco et al., 2018).

According to TPB, intentions to engage in a behavior are influenced by attitudes about the behavior (e.g., whether the behavior will result in positive or negative outcomes) and likelihood of achieving those positive/negative outcomes by engaging in the behavior, social norms (e.g., what relevant important others think about the individual engaging in the behavior), and perceived control, including opportunities and resources available to engage in the behavior (Ajzen, 1991). In terms of our case study, a qualitative pilot study based on 14 interviews identified which factors impact patient and physician decision-making with respect to receiving and referring, respectively, radiation treatment on a mobile truck. Key influences on whether patients would utilize radiation treatment on a mobile truck (i.e., behavior intentions) included the recommendation of the referring physician (i.e., norm beliefs), prior experience (and resulting outcomes) with radiation treatment and/or mobile diagnostic imaging (e.g., mobile mammography; i.e., attitude beliefs), and proximity to home (i.e., behavioral control beliefs), among others.

Following recommendations on TPB research design and ABM, the qualitative trends identified in the pilot study should then be validated and quantified via a survey administered among a larger, more representative sample to measure factors that will likely influence stakeholder intentions to embrace the new process/change, in this case patient intentions to utilize mobile radiation oncology. Specifically, as shown in Fig. 2.3, physician intentions will likely have a strong influence on patient intentions for two separate reasons. First, in the pilot data, patients stated that a physician factored into their decision to receive their cancer care for both location of current treatment and hypothetical choice of mobile radiation treatments. Second, there is corroborating research that suggests that physician recommendations, based both on clinical guidelines and physician preference, overpower patient preferences for the type of treatment received for prostate cancer, which can range from surveillance to active treatment (e.g., radiation therapy) (Scherr et al., 2017). As such, from an ABM perspective, it is critical to model both patient intentions to utilize the new healthcare delivery approach – but also physician intentions to refer this particular treatment. This more realistically captures the social-technical system complexities in understanding individuals' likelihood of utilizing a new healthcare delivery system. In the context of change management, this survey data collection informs who needs to be included in the coalition, but also who is needed to endorse and champion the change to take advantage of existing social networks. Without physician support, a mobile radiation oncology system is unlikely to be successful, even if popular among patients. The survey data clarifies how big of an obstacle physician support could be.

Notably, ABM can model multiple interconnected factors that impact how a new healthcare delivery system (e.g., a mobile radiation oncology system) is implemented to estimate its overall success. As represented in Fig. 2.4, specific to our case study on mobile radiation oncology, this model includes multiple feedback loops, multiple types of physician agents (i.e., medical, radiation, and surgical oncologists), and varying cause and effects. Ultimately, the overall

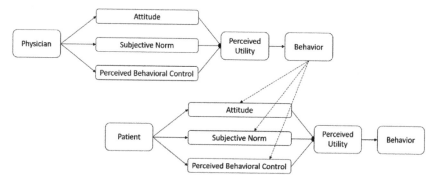

Fig. 2.3. Theory of Planned Behavior Diagrams for Physician/Patient Interaction.

success of the mobile radiation system is determined based on two primary factors, (1) reliability and (2) patient satisfaction. Both physicians and patients are only going to continue to participate in the mobile radiation system if there is both high reliability and patient satisfaction. However, this varies across individuals who may be more or less predisposed to prefer the mobile system (i.e., intent as modeled in Fig. 2.4).

When interacting with this system, patients are most likely to first see a medical oncologist, who refers the patients to a radiation oncologist. As such, the overall success of the mobile radiation system will likely influence the radiation oncologist's attitude toward referring a patient treatment on a mobile unit. However, multiple other factors can interact with referral patterns and patient preferences. For example, if a medical oncologist's patients have low patient satisfaction or suboptimal treatment outcomes, the referral pattern may change (at a specified probability) away from radiation oncologists who use mobile radiation oncology. In contrast, patients who had a positive experience with the mobile radiation oncology system may increase other patients' preferences for treatment on a mobile radiation system via social norms or attitudes. This in turn may impact a radiation oncologist's intent to refer subsequent patients for mobile radiation oncology. This example and Fig. 2.4 convey how modeling and simulation approaches can capture the complexities within a system, particularly

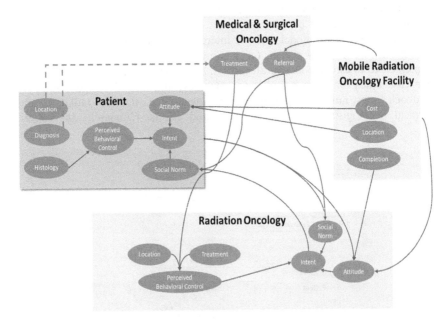

Fig. 2.4. Influence Map of Individual Interactions Within a Mobile Radiation Oncology System. Dashed lines represent influencer variables where as solid lines represent factors that dictate treatment choice.

in terms of understanding nonlinear behavioral and technical system interactions, and help key stakeholders understand emergence of readiness and resistance to new processes during change implementation.

Specifically, performing sensitivity analyses in the context of ABM and techno-economic feasibility modeling approaches supports efforts to identify key variables, understand break-even points, and conduct bounding analysis. For example, patient flow rates and patient volumes impact feasibility outcomes due to a limit in patient uptake within the system. There is a minimum number of patients that need to be served for the system to function from an economic perspective. However, many factors influence whether a patient chooses to participate in the mobile radiation system. The ABM simulation, which directly models patient intentions based on survey input, provides a more realistic "what-if" playground for key stakeholders to explore various scenarios.

Our systems modeling methodology using human-centered agent-based modeling aids in change management strategies because it is focused on the human agents, their interactions within the system, and among themselves, which largely drives how healthcare systems function and how change will ultimately be implemented. This human-centered focus can capture and simulate many of the qualitative forces that drive change-management that are otherwise difficult to measure. Because ABM is developed on the individual level, we can adjust various parameters, whether it be a patient agent's attitude toward mobile radiation or a physician agent's perceived control to use new medical interventions, to understand different scenarios, as well as areas of readiness and/or resistance to change. This can help inform a number of different approaches to implement change for a certain scenario, including where and how to address concerns related to change and how to build upon those concerns in order to inform change. These approaches can also change during the course of actual implementation and can be fed back into the model to refine expectations as the implementation becomes more mature.

In addition, these modeling and simulation techniques can support dialogue and communication among stakeholders throughout the change management process. For example, it may be valuable to enlist a guiding change coalition to develop the assumptions utilized in the simulation model to ensure a common understanding of change progression. That common understanding may support the evaluation of alternatives and build consensus around a path forward. As the change is implemented, progress can be measured against the simulation to identify any unexpected challenges and identify short-term wins.

Importantly, this is a low-cost methodology, which is critical for rural healthcare organizations, where resources may be limited. While this approach does require targeted surveys, market analysis, and software development, this is much less than a multimillion-dollar (USD) investment in a new healthcare delivery system (e.g., a mobile radiation oncology system) that may not be economically viable, thus costing the healthcare organization more in the long term. This methodology can help healthcare organizations understand the impacts of decision-making during change management that would otherwise be difficult to predict without the actual change occurring.

DISCUSSION AND IMPLICATIONS

Overall, we propose that more purposeful integration of systems engineering into change management processes can further advance change management theory as well as address other grand challenges in healthcare – not just limited to rural healthcare grand challenges. For example, referring back to the main steps in a change management process (i.e., assessing opportunities/problems to motivate change, select, and support a guiding coalition, formulating and communicating a compelling vision, mobilizing energy for change and empower others, and sustaining momentum through short-term wins), we have identified the following ways systems engineering can be utilized at each step (see also Fig. 2.5).

First, simulations, particularly Monte Carlo techno-economic feasibility simulations, can be used to help identify opportunities for change by quantifying problems or pitfalls that can happen if issues in the current system are not addressed. Additionally, as noted previously, one of the greatest challenges in change management for rural healthcare organizations (but arguably across healthcare broadly) is knowing what issues to tackle first. Simulations can help provide data-driven information about where the biggest threats or weaknesses may exist if different urgent challenges are left unaddressed – essentially, where will the healthcare organization suffer the most if this particular challenge is not addressed? Or, from a positive perspective, what area of change for an organization could result in the greatest benefit (e.g., greatest number of patients cared for) or boost if addressed? This can help key stakeholders understand the motivation for change. Furthermore, Monte Carlo simulations can help identify technological and economic feasibility for different change initiatives, including identifying boundary conditions of changes processes (i.e., identify at what points a new process/change initiative would no longer be technologically or economically feasible). This simulation data will help inform clearer directions and tangible inputs that can directly shape the vision formulation and communication strategies.

Second, once ABM is incorporated, these modeled systems can help identify where political support is needed and/or who could be well-suited to include as part of a change-focused guiding coalition. For example, by factoring in individual perceptions and motivational factors, change leaders can identify different, representative perspectives of the change issues at hand and can identify possible ways those perspectives will guide the change process (i.e., because those human-driven interactions are modeled as part of the system simulation). For example, in our case study, initial ABM suggests the need to directly model physician influence on patient utilization of a new healthcare delivery process – suggesting that a guiding coalition would require incorporating active dialogue from both parties.

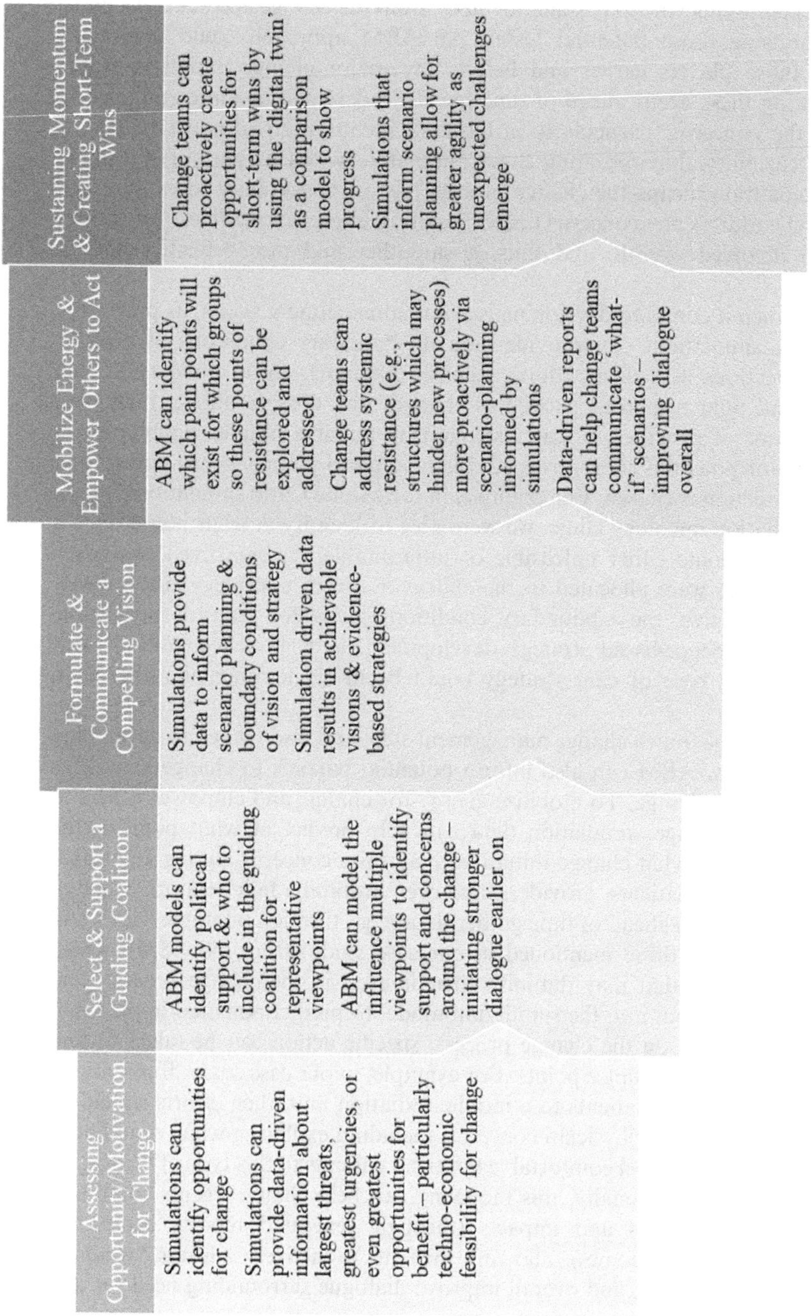

Assessing Opportunity/Motivation for Change	Select & Support a Guiding Coalition	Formulate & Communicate a Compelling Vision	Mobilize Energy & Empower Others to Act	Sustaining Momentum & Creating Short-Term Wins
Simulations can identify opportunities for change Simulations can provide data-driven information about largest threats, greatest urgencies, or even greatest opportunities for benefit – particularly techno-economic feasibility for change	ABM models can identify political support & who to include in the guiding coalition for representative viewpoints ABM can model the influence multiple viewpoints to identify support and concerns around the change – initiating stronger dialogue earlier on	Simulations provide data to inform scenario planning & boundary conditions of vision and strategy Simulation driven data results in achievable visions & evidence-based strategies	ABM can identify which pain points will exist for which groups so these points of resistance can be explored and addressed Change teams can address systemic resistance (e.g., structures which may hinder new processes) more proactively via scenario-planning informed by simulations Data-driven reports can help change teams communicate 'what-if' scenarios – improving dialogue overall	Change teams can proactively create opportunities for short-term wins by using the 'digital twin' as a comparison model to show progress Simulations that inform scenario planning allow for greater agility as unexpected challenges emerge

Fig. 2.5. Integrated Change Management Process Informed by Systems Engineering Simulation Modeling.

Often, one of the largest considerations in effective change management includes identifying who may stand to "lose" from the change and acknowledging and addressing those potential losses. An ABM approach could potentially identify those players earlier and before any major change initiatives begin. Anticipating these needs ahead of time means leaders will be more equipped to address the concerns, particularly in terms of identifying real issues related to change feasibility. Incorporating these alternative views as part of the initial guiding coalition means the change process has an opportunity to explore and proactively address any concerns raised, resulting in greater readiness for change from all involved overall, and thus, a smoother and more effective change process.

Next, when it comes to developing and communicating a vision, as previously mentioned, simulations can provide data on boundary conditions of possible change directions as well as inform scenario planning. In an industry of thin margins and tight resources, as well as changes that directly impact individual lives in terms of provision of care, recognizing possible pitfalls, boundaries of scope, and/or potential alternatives (through scenario planning) can ensure that the right direction is chosen. For example, in the Monte Carlo simulations for the mobile radiation oncology clinic, we were able to identify at what points such a plan would become either unfeasible or unprofitable via breakeven analysis – before resources were allocated to the endeavor. From a strategy/vision development perspective, these boundary conditions allow for realistic, achievable visions and evidence-based strategy development, as well as recognition of at what point this type of care strategy could be more detrimental rather than beneficial.

In terms of the fourth change management step, and also related to developing political support, ABM can also inform potential barriers to change as well as mobilization for change. To mobilize energy for change and empower others to believe in the change, simulation data can help predict at what point in the change process or what change initiatives may raise concerns among key stakeholders, including patients, providers, and even hospital administrators. If initial diagnostic processes ahead of time gather data (e.g., through pilot interviews and surveys, similar to those mentioned in our case study) from individuals about possible deterrents that may diminish their interest in the change process, and that data are then put into the simulation model to predict potential impact that resistance will have on the change process, specific action can be taken to find solutions for those resistance points. For example, in our case study, if physicians are less likely to refer patients to a mobile radiation unit, then efforts should be taken to address those physician concerns, including exploring what would need to change for them to feel comfortable referring patients to this type of healthcare delivery system. Additionally, this modeling can help change agents communicate different scenarios and impacts (through generated reports comparing different predicted outcomes), allowing them to proactively address "what if" questions and concerns, and overall improve dialogue surrounding need for and optimization of the change.

In terms of technical feasibility and managing the transition, the scenario-planning and feasibility modeling will have already addressed potential systems or structures that may hinder or run counter to the change efforts. For example, payment models can be included and manipulated as part of the technical systems that may impact the change process and different scenarios can be run to determine how and possible at what point this critical healthcare structure could influence the change process. Having this knowledge ahead of time allows the team to incorporate these limitations into their change plan so that when implementation begins it is realistic and proactive in how it works with or around these structures. This ensures systems are ready for change as well as individuals.

Finally, this anticipation and proactive planning to address potential road-blocks or systems/structures that may hinder change means that the change process and the change team are already more equipped to create the short-term wins necessary to sustain momentum in the change process. As mentioned previously, short-term wins indicate to those involved with and impacted by the change process that things are moving in the right direction, even when there are bumps along the way. When simulation modeling is used, boundary conditions can be identified and data-driven, informed scenario-planning can take place, and all of this ensures the change process is able to agilely anticipate different resource needs as the change progresses. Additionally, because this modeling serves as a "digital twin," it allows the guiding coalition to compare real-time advances to projected realistic models in order to show progression, which is one of the best ways to identify short-term wins. In the fast-paced, high-risk industry of healthcare and with patients' lives as the ultimate outcome of healthcare change processes, responsible, evidence-based change processes are critical – as is provider buy-in (particularly in terms of ensuring provider retention). The simulation modeling recommendations we provide can strengthen every part of the change process from initial identification of the most appropriate change to implement, through realistic and responsible vision development, to ultimate buy-in and commitment to the change through sustained momentum. This integration of change management theory informed by systems engineering via modeling and simulation can help ensure a more strategic and well-informed change process.

CONCLUSION

The grand challenges facing rural healthcare systems, ranging from patient, provider, and organizational challenges, have been well-documented. However, to combat these challenges, changes in care delivery must occur (e.g., Levit et al., 2020). Change is not easy, and it can be costly – two substantial threats against already lean systems with few resources and patients with unique needs. Essentially, change management for rural healthcare organizations is a grand challenge in and of itself. We believe this integration of systems modeling along with well-known planned change management processes can help rural healthcare organizations (and really any healthcare organization) more effectively and efficiently identify opportunities and scenario-plan for change while minimizing the potential risk to the organization. Certainly, healthcare organizations may have to consider some resource investment (e.g., the necessary software, identifying individuals with the right skills to analyze the simulations, etc.), but these costs result in a significant return on investment if the simulations provide evidence-based directions on how to move a change process forward most effectively. In an industry where change must happen for its continued survival, these investments and data-driven strategies may help rural healthcare organizations and their providers and patients thrive instead of simply survive.

REFERENCES

Ajzen, I. (1991). The theory of planned behavior. *Organizational Behavior and Human Decision Processes, 50*, 179–211.

Ajzen, I., Albarracin, D., & Hornik, R. (2007). *Prediction and change of health behavior: Applied the reasoned action approach*. Psychology Press.

American Hospital Association. (2022, September). *Rural hospital closures threaten access: Solutions to preserve care in local communities*. American Hospital Association Guides & Reports. https://www.aha.org/2022-09-07-rural-hospital-closures-threaten-access

Bauer, M. S., Damschroder, L., Hagedorn, H., Smith, J., & Kilbourne, A. M. (2015). An introduction to implementation science for the non-specialist. *BMC Psychology, 3*(1), 1–12. https://doi.org/10.1186/S40359-015-0089-9

Bauer, M. S., & Kirchner, J. A. (2020). Implementation science: What is it and why should I care? *Psychiatry Research, 283*. https://doi.org/10.1016/j.psychres.2019.04.025

Berry, H. L., Waite, T. D., Dear, K. B. G., Capon, A. G., & Murray, V. (2018). The case for systems thinking about climate change and mental health. *Nature Climate Change, 8*(4), 282–290. https://doi.org/10.1038/s41558-018-0102-4

Brems, C., Johnson, M. E., Warner, T. D., & Roberts, L. W. (2006). Barriers to healthcare as reported by rural and urban interprofessional providers. *Journal of Interprofessional Care, 20*(2), 105e18.

Brown, T., & Wyatt, J. (2009). Design thinking for social innovation. *Stanford Social Innovation Review, 8*(1), 31–35. https://doi.org/10.48558/58Z7-3J85

Burnes, B. (2013). A critical review of organization development. In H. S. Leonard, R. Lewis, A. M. Freedman, & J. Passmore (Eds.), *The Wiley-Blackwell handbook of the psychology of leadership, change, and organizational development* (pp. 381–404). Wiley-Blackwell.

Canfield, C. I., & Fischhoff, B. (2018). Setting priorities in behavioral interventions: An application to reducing phishing risk. *Risk Analysis, 38*(4), 826–838. https://doi.org/10.1111/risa.12917

Chai, K. H., & Yeo, C. (2012). Overcoming energy efficiency barriers through systems approach-A conceptual framework. *Energy Policy, 46*, 460–472. https://doi.org/10.1016/j.enpol.2012.04.012

Chamberlain, D., Murphy, B., & Freeman, H. (2020). *Mobile radiation oncology coach system with internal and/or external shielding for same*. United States Patent Application Publication. https://doi.org/10.1037/0033-3204.38.4.365

Charlton, M., Schlicting, J., Chioreso, C., Ward, M., & Vikas, P. (2015). Challenges of rural cancer care in the United States. *Oncology, 29*, 633–640. PMID: 26384798.

Chen, X., Orom, H., Hay, J. L., Waters, E. A., Schofield, E., Li, Y., & Kiviniemi, M. T. (2019). Differences in rural and urban health information access and use. *The Journal of Rural Health, 35*, 405–417. https://doi.org/10.1111/jrh.12335

Clarkson, J., Dean, J., Ward, J., Komashie, A., & Bashford, T. (2018). A systems approach to healthcare: From thinking to practice. *Future Healthcare Journal, 5*(3), 151–155. https://doi.org/10.7861/futurehosp.5-3-151

Cummings, T. G., & Worley, C. G. (2015). *Organization development & change* (10th ed.). Cengage Learning.

de Savigny, D., & Adam, T. (2009). *Systems thinking for health systems strengthening*. World Health Organization.

Dobis, E. A., Krumel, T. P., Cromartie, J., Conley, K. L., Sanders, A., & Ortiz, R. (2021). *Rural America at a glance: 2021 edition* (No. 1962-2021-3215). U.S. Department of Agriculture: Economic Research Service.

Douthit, N., Kiv, S., Dwolatzky, T., & Biswas, S. (2015). Exposing some important barriers to health care access in the rural USA. *Public Health, 129*(6), 611–620. https://doi.org/10.1016/j.puhe.2015.04.001

Foutz, J., Artiga, S., & Garfield, F. (2017, April). *The role of Medicaid in rural America.* The Kaiser Family Foundation. https://www.kff.org/medicaid/issue-brief/the-role-of-medicaid-in-rural-america/

Germack, H. D., Kandrack, R., & Martsolf, G. R. (2019). When rural hospitals close, the physician workforce goes. *Health Affairs, 38*(12), 2086–2094. https://doi.org/10.1377/hlthaff.2019.00916

Gorod, A., Sauser, B., & Boardman, J. (2008). System-of-systems engineering management: A review of modern history and a path forward. *IEEE Systems Journal, 2*(4), 484–499. https://doi.org/10.1109/JSYST.2008.2007163

Henning-Smith, C. E., Hernandez, A. M., Hardeman, R. R., Ramirez, M. R., & Kozhimannil, K. B. (2019). Rural counties with majority black or indigenous populations suffer the highest rates of premature death in the US. *Health Affairs, 38*(12), 2019–2026. https://doi.org/10.1377/hlthaff.2019.00847

Holladay, J. B., Knizhnik, J., Weiland, K. J., Stein, A., Sanders, T., & Schwindt, P. (2019). MBSE infusion and modernization initiative (MIAMI): "Hot" benefits for real NASA applications. In *IEEE Aerospace Conference Proceedings*, 2019, March. https://doi.org/10.1109/AERO.2019.8741795

International Association for Public Participation - 2. (2018). *IAP2 Spectrum of public participation.* IAP2 International Federation.

Johnson, A. M., Hines, R. B., Johnson, J. A., & Bayakly, A. R. (2014). Treatment and survival disparities in lung cancer: The effect of social environment and place of residence. *Lung Cancer.* https://doi.org/10.1016/j.lungcan.2014.01.008

Kenamond, M. C., Mourad, W. F., Randall, M. E., & Kaushal, A. (2022). No oncology patient left behind: Challenges and solutions in rural radiation oncology. *The Lancet Regional Health – Americas, 13*, 100289. https://doi.org/10.1016/j.lana.2022.100289

Khoshakhlagh, A. H., Chuang, K. J., & Kumar, P. (2022). Health risk assessment of exposure to ambient formaldehyde in carpet manufacturing industries. *Environmental Science and Pollution Research*, 1–12.

Kotter, J. P. (2012). *Leading change.* Harvard Business Review Press.

Kryszkiewicz, P., Canfield, C., Bhada, S. V., & Wyglinski, A. M. (2022). A systems approach for solving inter-policy gaps in dynamic spectrum access-based wireless rural broadband networks. *IEEE Access, 10*, 25165–25174. https://doi.org/10.1109/ACCESS.2022.3156106

Kueny, C. A. R., Majumdar, D., & Spencer, C. (2020). A qualitative assessment of the impact of the rural setting on healthcare professionals' work experiences. *Occupational Health Science, 4.* https://doi.org/10.1007/s41542-020-00061-6

La France, A., Batt, R., & Appelbaum, E. (2022). Hospital ownership and financial stability: A matched case comparison of nonprofit health system and a private equity-owned health system. In J. L. Hefner & I. M. Nembhard (Eds.), *Advances in health care management: The contributions of health care management to grand health care challenges* (Vol. 20, pp. 173–220). Emerald Publishing Ltd.

Leach, M., & Katcher, R. (2014). OD practitioners as agents of social change. In B. B. Jones & M. Brazzel (Eds.), *The NTL handbook of organization development and change: Principles, practices, and perspectives* (pp. 581–604). Center for Creative Leadership.

Leider, J. P., Meit, M., McCullough, J., Remick, B., Dekker, D., Alfonso, N., & Bishai, D. (2020). The state of rural public health: Enduring needs in a new decade. *American Journal of Public Health, 110*, 1283–1290. https://doi.org/10.2105/AJPH.2020.305728

Leveson, N. G. (2011). *Engineering a safer world: Systems thinking applied to safety.* MIT Press.

Levit, L. A., Byatt, L., Lyss, A. P., Paskett, E. D., Levit, K., Kirkwood, K., Schenkel, C., & Schilsky, R. L. (2020). Closing the rural cancer care gap: Three institutional approaches. *JCO Oncology Practice, 16*, 422–430. https://doi.org/10.1200/OP.20.00174

Litwin, A. S. (2022). Technological change and frontline care deliver work: Toward the quadruple aim. In J. L. Hefner & I. M. Nembhard (Eds.), *Advances in health care management: The contributions of health care management to grand health care challenges* (Vol. 20, pp. 99–142). Emerald Publishing Ltd.

Machado, S. R., Jayawardana, S., Mossialos, E., & Vaduganathan, M. (2021). Physician density by specialty type in urban and rural counties in the US, 2010 to 2017. *JAMA Network Open, 4*(1), e2033994. https://doi.org/10.1001/jamanetworkopen.2020.33994

Madni, A. M., Erwin, D., & Madni, C. C. (2021). Digital twin-enabled MBSE testbed for prototyping and evaluating aerospace systems: Lessons learned. *IEEE Aerospace Conference Proceedings.* https://doi.org/10.1109/AERO50100.2021.9438439

Madni, A. M., & Sievers, M. (2018). Model-based systems engineering: Motivation, current status, and research opportunities. *Systems Engineering, 21*(3), 172–190. https://doi.org/10.1002/sys.21438

Majumdar, D., Kueny, C. R., & Anderson, M. (2022). Impact of merging into a comprehensive cancer center on health care teams and subsequent team-member and patient experiences. *JCO Oncology Practice.* http://ascopubs.org/doi/full/10.1200/OP.22.00280

Marshall, D. A., Burgos-Liz, L., IJzerman, M., Crown, W., Padula, W. V., Wong, P. K., Pasupathy, K. S., Higashi, M. K., Osgood, N. D., & ISPOR Emerging Good Practices Task Force. (2015). Selecting dynamic simulation modeling method for health care delivery research – Part 2: Report of the ISPOR dynamic simulation modeling emerging good practices task force. *Value in Health, 18*, 147–160. https://doi.org/10.1016/j.jval.2015.01.006

Marshall, D. A., Grazziotin, L. R., Regier, D. A., Wordsworth, S., Buchanan, J., Phillips, K., & IJzerman, M. (2020). Addressing challenges of economic evaluation in precision medicine using dynamic simulation modeling. *Value in Health, 23*, 566–573. https://doi.org/10.1016/j.jval.2020.01.016

Meadows, D. H. (2008). *Thinking in systems: A primer.* Chelsea Green Publishing.

Meit, M., Knudson, A., Gilber, T., Tzy-Chyi Yu, A., Tanenbaum, E., Ormson, E., TenBroeck, S., Bayne, A., Popat, S., & NORC Walsh Center for Rural Health, and Analysis. (2014). *The 2014 update of the rural-urban chartbook.* Rural Health Reform Policy Research Center. http://www.ruralhealthresearch.org/

Missouri Cancer Registry & Research Center. (2020). *Missouri cancer registry.* University of Missouri, School of Medicine. https://medicine.missouri.edu/centers-institutes-labs/cancer-registry-research-center

Moore, H., Dishman, L., & Fick, J. (2022). The challenge of employee retention in medical practices across the United States: An exploratory investigation into the relationship between operational succession planning and employee turnover. In J. L. Hefner & I. M. Nembhard (Eds.), *Advances in health care management: The contributions of health care management to grand health care challenges* (Vol. 20, pp. 45–76). Emerald Publishing Ltd.

Morgan, M. G., & Henrion, M. (1990). *Uncertainty: A guide to dealing with uncertainty in quantitative risk and policy analysis.* Cambridge University Press.

NC Rural Health Research Program. (2022, December). *Rural hospital closures database.* The Cecil G. Sheps Center for Health Services Research. https://www.shepscenter.unc.edu/programs-projects/rural-health/rural-hospital-closures/

O'Hanlon, C., Kranz, A., DeYoreo, M., Mahmud, A., Damberg, C. L., & Timbie, J. (2019). Access, quality, and financial performance of rural hospitals following health system affiliations. *Health Affairs, 38.* https://doi.org/10.1377/hlthaff.2019.00918

Pham, T. V., Beasley, C. M., Gagliardi, J. P., Koenig, H. G., & Stanifer, J. W. (2020). Spirituality, coping, and resilience among rural residents living with chronic kidney disease. *Journal of Religion and Health, 59*(6), 2951–2968.

Potluri, S. R., Sridhar, V., & Rao, S. (2020). Effects of data localization on digital trade: An agent-based modeling approach. *Telecommunications Policy, 44*(9). https://doi.org/10.1016/j.telpol.2020.102022

Price, A. P., Canfield, C., Hugo, G. D., Kavanaugh, J. A., Henke, L. E., Laugeman, E., Samson, P., Reynolds-Kueny, C., & Cudney, E. A. (2022). Techno-economic feasibility analysis of a fully mobile radiation oncology system using Monte Carlos simulation. *JCO Global Oncology, 8*, e2100284. https://doi.org/10.1200%2FGO.21.00284

Rai, V., & Robinson, S. A. (2015). Agent-based modeling of energy technology adoption: Empirical integration of social, behavioral, economic, and environmental factors. *Environmental Modelling & Software, 70*, 163–177. https://doi.org/10.1016/j.envsoft.2015.04.014

Rosko, M. D. (2020). Profitability of rural hospitals: An analysis of government payment policies. In J. L. Hefner & M. Al-Amin (Eds.), *Advances in health care management: Transforming health care: A focus on consumerism and profitability* (Vol. 19, pp. 25–42). Emerald Publishing Ltd.

Rural Health Information Hub. (2022a, November). Health access in rural communities. https://www.ruralhealthinfo.org/topics/healthcare-access

Rural Health Information Hub. (2022b, February). Rural hospitals. https://www.ruralhealthinfo.org/topics/hospitals

Scalco, A., Ceschi, A., & Sartori, R. (2018). Application of psychological theories in agent-based modeling: The case of the Theory of Planned Behavior. *Nonlinear Dynamics, Psychology, and Life Sciences, 22*, 15–33.

Scherr, K. A., Fagerlin, A., Hofer, T., Scherer, L. D., Holmes-Rovner, M., Williamson, L. D., Kahn, V. C., Montgomery, J. S., Greene, K. L., Zhang, B., & Ubel, P. A. (2017). Physician recommendations trump patient preferences in prostate cancer treatment decisions. *Medical Decision Making: An International Journal of the Society for Medical Decision Making, 37*(1), 56–69. https://doi.org/10.1177/0272989X16662841

Senge, P. M. (2006). *The fifth discipline: The art & practice of the learning organization.* Doubleday.

Shastry, V., Reeves, D. C., Willems, N., & Rai, V. (2022). Policy and behavioral response to shock events: An agent-based model of the effectiveness and equity of policy design features. *PLoS One, 17*(1), e0262172. https://doi.org/10.1371/journal.pone.0262172

Silverman, B. G., Hanrahan, N., Bharathy, G., Gordon, K., & Johnson, D. (2015). A systems approach to healthcare: Agent-based modeling, community mental health, and population well-being. *Artificial Intelligence in Medicine, 63*(2), 61–71. https://doi.org/10.1016/j.artmed.2014.08.006

Skinner, L., Staiger, D. O., Auerbach, D. I., & Buerhaus, P. I. (2019). Implications of an aging rural physician workforce. *New England Journal of Medicine, 381*, 299–301. https://doi.org/10.1056/NEJMp1900808

Stouten, J., Rousseau, D. M., & De Cremer, D. (2018). Successful organizational change: Integrating the management practice and scholarly literatures. *The Academy of Management Annals, 12*, 752–788. https://doi.org/10.5465/annals.2016.0095

USDA Economic Research Service. (2019). *What is rural?* United States Department of Agriculture. https://www.ers.usda.gov/topics/rural-economy-population/rural-classifications/what-is-rural/

van de Ven, M., IJzerman, M., Retel, V., van Harten, W., & Koffijberg, H. (2022). Developing a dynamic simulation model to support the nationwide implementation of whole genome sequencing in lung cancer. *BMC Medical Research Methodology, 22*, 83. https://doi.org/10.1186/s12874-022-01571-3

Vithayasrichareon, P., & MacGill, I. F. (2012). A Monte Carlo based decision-support tool for assessing generation portfolios in future carbon constrained electricity industries. *Energy Policy, 41*, 374–392. https://doi.org/10.1016/j.enpol.2011.10.060

Waibel, K. H., & Perry, T. T. (2022). Telehealth and allergy services in rural and regional locations that lack specialty services. *Journal of Allergy and Clinical Immunology: In Practice, 10*, 2507–2513. https://doi.org/10.1016/j.jaip.2022.06.025

CHAPTER 3

EXAMINING KNOWLEDGE MANAGEMENT AND THE CULTURE CHANGE MOVEMENT IN LONG-TERM CARE: A STUDY OF HIGH-MEDICAID-CENSUS NURSING HOMES

Tory H. Hogan[a], Larry R. Hearld[b], Ganisher Davlyatov[c], Akbar Ghiasi[d], Jeff Szychowski[e] and Robert Weech-Maldonado[f]

[a]*The Ohio State University, USA*
[b]*The University of Alabama at Birmingham, USA*
[c]*The University of Oklahoma Health Sciences Center, USA*
[d]*University of the Incarnate Word, USA*
[e]*The University of Alabama at Birmingham, School of Public Health Department of Biostatistics, USA*
[f]*The University of Alabama at Birmingham, School of Health Professions, Department of Health Services Administration, USA*

ABSTRACT

High-quality nursing home (NH) care has long been a challenge within the United States. For decades, policymakers at the state and federal levels have adopted and implemented regulations to target critical components of NH care outcomes. Simultaneously, our delivery system continues to change the role of NHs in patient care. For example, more acute patients are cared for in NHs,

Research and Theory to Foster Change in the Face of Grand Health Care Challenges
Advances in Health Care Management, Volume 22, 55–74
Copyright © 2024 Tory H. Hogan, Larry R. Hearld, Ganisher Davlyatov, Akbar Ghiasi, Jeff Szychowski and Robert Weech-Maldonado
Published under exclusive licence by Emerald Publishing Limited
ISSN: 1474-8231/doi:10.1108/S1474-823120240000022003

and the Center for Medicare and Medicaid Services (CMS) has implemented value payment programs targeting NH settings. As a part of these growing pressures from the broader healthcare delivery system, the culture-change movement *has emerged among NHs over the past two decades, prompting NHs to embody more person-centered care as well as promote settings which resemble someone's home, as opposed to institutionalized healthcare settings.*

Researchers have linked culture change to high-quality outcomes and the ability to adapt and respond to the ever-changing pressures brought on by changes in our regulatory and delivery system. Making enduring culture change within organizations has long been a challenge and focus in NHs. Despite research suggesting that culture-change initiatives that promote greater resident-centered care are associated with several desirable patient outcomes, their adoption and implementation by NHs are resource intensive, and research has shown that NHs with high percentages of low-income residents are especially challenged to adopt these initiatives.

This chapter takes a novel approach to examine factors that impact the adoption of culture-change initiatives by assessing knowledge management and the role of knowledge management activities in promoting the adoption of innovative care delivery models among under-resourced NHs throughout the United States. Using primary data from a survey of NH administrators, we conducted logistic regression models to assess the relationship between knowledge management and the adoption of a culture-change initiative as well as whether these relationships were moderated by leadership and staffing stability. Our study found that NHs were more likely to adopt a culture-change initiative when they had more robust knowledge management activities. Moreover, knowledge management activities were particularly effective at promoting adoption in NHs that struggle with leadership and nursing staff instability. Our findings support the notion that knowledge management activities can help NHs acquire and mobilize informational resources to support the adoption of care delivery innovations, thus highlighting opportunities to more effectively target efforts to stimulate the adoption and spread of these initiatives.

Funding: The Agency for Healthcare Research and Quality.

Keywords: High Medicaid nursing homes; culture-change initiatives; knowledge management; adoption of innovations; knowledge management, innovation adoption, nursing homes, long-term care, culture change

INTRODUCTION

In 2001, the Institute of Medicine identified person-centered care as one of six key areas to focus on to improve health care in the 21st century (IOM, 2001). Broadly speaking, person-centered care describes care which is responsive to the multidimensional needs, values, and preferences of a patient (IOM, 2001). It is also increasingly recognized as an aspirational goal for healthcare systems (Berenson et al., 2008; Davis et al., 2005; Epstein & Street, 2011). One of the clearest manifestations of the promotion of person-centered care is the emergence and growing adoption of culture-change initiatives as part of the nursing home (NH) industry's "culture-change movement" (Koren, 2010; White-Chu et al., 2009; Zimmerman et al., 2014), defined as the reorientation of an NH's culture to promote more person-centered care that resembles a homelike setting more so than an institution (Koren, 2010).

The *culture-change movement* began as a grassroots movement in the 1980s, becoming formalized in 1997 as a result of the inaugural meeting of the NH Pioneers. Throughout the late 1990s and early 2000s, a series of initiatives led by the Centers for Medicaid and Medicare Services (CMS), state agencies, consumer advocates, and trade associations established that the ideal NH would include: a homelike atmosphere; resident-directed care; close relationships between residents, caregivers, and staff; staff empowerment; collaborative decision-making; and quality improvement processes (Koren, 2010).

The following describe the key elements of the *culture-change movement* as described by White-Chu and colleagues (2009):

(1) *Workforce Redesign:* The shift from hierarchical organizational structures, where management follows a top-down approach and work is directed by a chain of command, to a flatter organizational structure, where self-directed work teams manage residents and care processes.

(2) *Person-Centered Individualized Care:* Direct-care staff adopt person-centered approaches to caregiving. For example, using resident input to redesign the bath or meal time approach can facilitate a more homelike experience for residents. Person-centered care is also supported by the assignment of the same frontline staff to each resident to support a meaningful personal relationship between residents and staff.

(3) *Resident Choice:* Supporting relationships and experiences where residents have privacy, autonomy, and power over their day-to-day experiences as well as how NH staff approach the care they provide. Enabling residents to dictate their sleeping and eating schedules, their food selection, and their activities supports a more homelike experience for NH residents.

To date, empirical evidence of the outcomes of culture-change initiatives identified during the *culture-change movement* is mixed (Rahman & Schnelle, 2008; Shier et al., 2014). However, there is some research suggesting culture-change initiatives are associated with a number of desirable outcomes, including fewer health-related deficiency citations (Grabowski et al., 2014b) and better psychosocial outcomes (Hill et al., 2011; Kane et al., 2007).

Despite these benefits, NHs' implementation of the *culture-change movement* has been largely incremental: while the majority of NHs report that they have implemented at least some of its elements, only a minority of NHs report adopting all elements (Miller et al., 2013). Studies examining the adoption of culture-change initiatives and NH characteristics have found that NHs with high percentages of Medicaid residents – subsequently referred to as "high-Medicaid-census NHs" – are especially challenged to adopt these initiatives (Chisholm et al., 2018; Grabowski et al., 2014a; Miller et al., 2013). One explanation for this finding is that Medicaid reimbursement for NHs is generally lower than private payer reimbursement, and consequently, this results in the organization being more resource constrained. As a result, the adoption of innovations may be limited. Such challenges have led some to question whether the *culture-change movement* will be widely adopted or if it will widen the quality gulf between high-Medicaid-census NHs, which tend to be in the poorest areas and are more likely to serve Black residents, and NHs that serve a more resource-rich resident base (Grabowski et al., 2014a). To prevent this from happening, it is important to identify ways to support the adoption and implementation of culture-change initiatives in these lower resourced NHs.

Knowledge management (KM) – defined as the process of creating or locating knowledge and managing the dissemination of knowledge within and between organizations (Bennett & Gabriel, 1999; Nonaka, 1994) – has been shown to be an important factor in promoting innovation (Darroch, 2005; Darroch & McNaughton, 2002; Lundvall & Nielsen, 2007). For high-Medicaid-census NHs, more robust KM activities may be especially beneficial in mitigating resource disadvantages and helping them acquire and utilize the requisite information needed to pursue innovations such as culture-change initiatives. In this chapter, we examine this possibility by investigating the relationship between KM activities of high-Medicaid-census NHs throughout the United States and the adoption of culture-change initiatives. To be clear, our focus is not upon the general phenomenon of culture change within organizations but instead the specific initiatives aligned with the *culture-change movement* in NHs, as previously described.

Our study contributes to an understanding of innovation adoption and the *culture-change movement* to promote person-centered care in NHs, examining the role of KM and the adoption of culture-change initiatives within high-Medicaid-census NHs. Its findings build upon the extant research in several ways. First, the results of this study provide valuable insights into how innovations are adopted within healthcare organizations that serve lower socioeconomic communities and communities with higher populations that have struggled to gain access to high-quality care. Since 2020, many healthcare delivery organizations have committed to addressing health equity as a part of their mission (Williams et al., 2022). However, moving beyond the identification of disparities in health outcomes and access to care has been a challenge, as organizations struggle to understand how they can better serve populations in communities receiving inequitable care. In the context of understanding innovation adoption and KM, organizations providing care for poor and minoritized communities often face financial barriers and human resource limitations (Mor et al., 2004b), making it difficult to support KM activities needed to enable the implementation of new, evidence-based practices.

Additionally, the findings from our study suggest that KM activities can support the adoption of innovations which are critical to providing high-quality care to the aging population. Despite some research on KM activities in hospitals

(Gowen et al., 2009; McFadden et al., 2014; Myllärniemi et al., 2012), very little research has extended this work to innovation adoption within NHs. Thus, this study provides some baseline insights into the prevalence of these activities in these organizations. Likewise, a number of studies have examined the prevalence of culture-change initiatives and factors associated with their adoption (Koren, 2010; White-Chu et al., 2009; Zimmerman et al., 2014), but we are aware of no studies that have investigated whether KM activities may support their adoption above and beyond the factors that have been previously identified as important. Therefore, findings from this study have important implications for advocates of *culture-change* initiatives who are interested in understanding ways to continue their dissemination throughout the NH industry.

Moreover, the examination of these relationships among under-resourced NHs will extend our understanding of ways these organizations can support the adoption of innovations among organizations who serve underinsured or underserviced populations such as the Medicaid-enrolled aging population. Additionally, our findings also identify and contribute to a broader understanding of the implementation of person-centered care for the aging population. The findings are likely to be of interest to NH providers, residents, families, and policymakers who are interested in supporting lower resourced NHs.

Thus, we examine the intersection of two grand healthcare challenges in this chapter: (1) *innovation adoption* within lower resourced healthcare organizations that provide care to minoritized populations and individuals of lower socioeconomic status and (2) the *culture-change movement* to improve person-centered care within NHs, referred to subsequently as the adoption of "culture-change initiatives." We begin with our conceptual framework, exploring concepts from the KM literature to develop hypotheses relating to the adoption of culture-change initiatives in NHs.

CONCEPTUAL FRAMEWORK

The knowledge-based view (KBV) of the firm is an organizational learning theory that helps explain how firms can achieve competitive advantage (Grant, 1996). According to this theory, knowledge is one of the key resources used to gain competitive advantage because knowledge-based resources are socially complex and generally difficult to imitate (Grant, 1996). For example, knowledge accrued over time about how to effectively and efficiently coordinate care with local hospitals may be difficult to replicate in the short-term, providing an NH with a unique advantage over other NHs lacking such knowledge. Thus, organizations may be able to generate a sustainable competitive advantage by cultivating heterogeneous knowledge resources (Grant, 1996; Kogut & Zander, 1992). The ability to do so, however, is predicated on an organization's ability to implement practices that can harness these knowledge resources.

The widespread innovation adoption and dissemination of evidence-based practices is a challenge for healthcare delivery organizations across the care continuum. At the heart of understanding the adoption and implementation of new, evidence-based practices is understanding how knowledge is disseminated within and across organizations, or simply put, what activities support the adoption of innovation. Such activities are examined in the study of knowledge management, describing how knowledge is created, organized, shared, stored, and used within and across organizations. Generally speaking, organizations must devote resources, either in the form of human capital or physical assets, to facilitate KM activities.

KM has been conceptualized as consisting of three dimensions: (1). knowledge acquisition, (2). knowledge dissemination, and (3). knowledge responsiveness (Darroch, 2003; Orzano et al., 2008). Knowledge acquisition pertains to the processes used to locate, create, or discover knowledge, including activities such as systematically assessing resident and employee needs and the use of competitive market surveys to develop products and services. Knowledge dissemination pertains to how knowledge is distributed and applied throughout the organization, including activities such as the use of residents' electronic health records that are easily accessible to caregivers while providing care. Knowledge responsiveness relates to the way the organization utilizes knowledge and includes activities such as how quickly the organization responds to resident/family complaints and the time required to implement changes related to new information.

More robust KM practices can play an important role in fostering innovation, such as culture-change initiatives, by an organization (Choi & Lee, 2002; Nonaka, 1994; Sheng et al., 2013; Zack et al., 2009). This is because more robust KM practices can help generate or acquire more diverse yet comprehensive information that is accessible to more organizational members in a more timely fashion. Likewise, more extensive KM processes enable organizations to combine information in novel and timely ways to learn from their history and adopt changes (Nonaka, 1994; Nonaka & Von Krogh, 2009). Consequently, we hypothesize that:

H1. More robust knowledge management practices will be associated with a greater likelihood of adopting person-centered, culture-change initiatives.

H1a. More robust knowledge management practices within the dimensions of knowledge acquisition and will be associated with a greater likelihood of adopting person-centered, culture-change initiatives.

H1b. More robust knowledge management practices within the dimensions of knowledge dissemination and will be associated with a greater likelihood of adopting person-centered, culture-change initiatives.

H1c. More robust knowledge management practices within the dimensions of knowledge responsiveness and will be associated with a greater likelihood of adopting person-centered, culture-change initiatives.

In NHs, culture-change initiatives emphasize person-centered relationships with residents, whereby staff bring their personal knowledge of residents into the caregiving process (Misiorski, 2003). It is perhaps not surprising, then, that turnover among NHs' nursing staff and leaders can undermine the adoption of culture-change initiatives (Grabowski et al., 2014a; Scalzi et al., 2006). We submit that the ability of KM practices to support the adoption of innovations may be particularly important for organizations that lack stability in leadership and staffing. This is because much organizational knowledge is tacit (Nonaka, 1994; Nonaka & Von Krogh, 2009), and within healthcare organizations, knowledge exists beyond published, peer reviewed articles and exists in the form of working knowledge of experts in the field or within an organization (Wyatt, 2001). The communication patterns of team-based care and collaborative care approaches – as well as nonformal problem-solving efforts and discussions which occur between clinicians – support the existence and reliance of tacit knowledge within healthcare organizations (Panahi et al., 2016). To the extent some of this tacit knowledge can be encoded into more explicit organizational routines (i.e., KM practices), they may compensate for leader and nursing staff turnover in NHs. Therefore, we hypothesize that:

> *H2.* The positive relationship between knowledge management practices and adoption of a culture-change initiative will be stronger among NHs with shorter tenured leadership.

Additionally, KM may help NHs protect themselves from knowledge attrition. For example, NHs that have high KM activities may engage in the proactive management of transitions between employees during times of employee turnover. KM activities also have the potential to guard against the loss of organization-specific information when employees leave by supporting the sharing of such information when turnover occurs (Aymen et al., 2019). KM activities can promote the recognition of employees as critical to the overall knowledge within the firm, ensuring that when employees depart, there are processes in place to support them sharing their knowledge with other employees. Such processes may also support the ability for NHs to enable the ongoing implementation of culture-change initiatives. Therefore, we hypothesize that:

> *H3.* The positive relationship between knowledge management practices and the adoption of a culture-change initiative will be stronger among NHs with higher levels of nurse turnover.

METHODS

Datasets and Study Sample. Our study was approved by the (institution blinded for review purposes)'s Institutional Review Board (Protocol #: 140828005). From November 2017 to March 2018, we collected primary survey data of NH administrators (i.e., Executive Directors/CEOs) through a combination of mailed and online surveys. More specifically, to ensure a higher response rate, we followed a modified approach to Dillman's (1978) Total Design Method. Each survey was mailed to individual NH administrators with a cover letter explaining the purpose of the survey, providing information about the incentive payment ($25), and including a link to the online version of the survey. A postcard reminder was mailed to nonrespondents two weeks after the initial mailing, followed by a second round of postcard reminders at 6 weeks and phone call reminders at 8 weeks. Finally, a third mailing was conducted for those who had not returned the survey within 10 weeks. The NH sample frame consisted of 1,050 facilities. These facilities were identified using Mor et al.'s (2004a) criteria for lower tier facilities, a term that describes NHs serving mainly residents insured through Medicaid that, as a result, have very limited resources. In following this definition, our sample included NHs with 85% or higher Medicaid census with less than 10% of private pay and less than 8% supported by Medicare. There were 393 responses by NH administrators, yielding a response rate of 37%. A comparison of survey respondents and nonrespondents is provided in Table 3.1.

Secondary datasets included Brown University's Long-term Care (LTC Focus) data, the CMS's Medicare Cost Reports and NH Compare, and the Health Resources and Services Administration's (HRSA) Area Health Resource File (AHRF), all of which were used to control for organizational and environmental characteristics of the NHs. LTC Focus provides data on facility characteristics, staffing, and operations. Medicare Cost Reports is a public access dataset that captures cost report information for all CMS-certified NHs accepting Medicare residents. NH Compare data provide information on NH star ratings based on measures of NHs' performance on health inspections, staffing, and quality. Finally, AHRF contains data on socioeconomic and demographic characteristics of markets where NHs are located.

Dependent variable. Respondents were asked to indicate whether their NH had a formal connection to a culture-change initiative. *Culture change* was defined within the survey as, "initiatives that attempt to transform nursing homes from healthcare institutions to person-centered home offering long-term care services. Key elements of *culture-change* nursing homes include resident direction, homelike atmosphere, close relationships, staff empowerment, collaborative decision-making, and quality improvement processes" (Grabowski et al., 2014b; Koren, 2010). Respondents were also asked to indicate which specific initiative (e.g., Eden Alternative, Green House, Pioneer Network) was used. The number of respondents for each initiative, however, was generally small and prohibited stable statistical modeling. Therefore, our dependent variable was a dichotomous indicator of whether an NH had adopted a culture-change initiative of any type (1 = NH has adopted a culture-change initiative, 0 = NH had not adopted a culture-change initiative).

Independent variables. Our primary independent variable was the degree of KM activities utilized by an NH. We constructed a composite index by averaging across 17 items (Cronbach's alpha = 0.904; Table 3.2) validated for use in healthcare organizations by Gowen et al. (2009). All items were measured on a 5-point scale (1 = strongly disagree; 5 = strongly agree).

Although the resource-based view (RBV) of the firm recognizes the important role of knowledge for achieving a competitive advantage, proponents of the KBV argue that the resource-based perspective does not go far enough. Specifically, the RBV treats knowledge as a generic resource rather than having special characteristics. It, therefore, does not distinguish between different types of knowledge-based capabilities (Conner, 1991). Therefore, we also assessed whether adoption varied as a function of three subdimensions of KM: knowledge acquisition (6 items), knowledge dissemination (6 items), and knowledge responsiveness (5 items). Goodness of fit statistics from our confirmatory factor analysis supported the use of these three subdimensions (RMSEA = 0.057, CFI

Table 3.1. Nursing Home Characteristics (Respondents vs Nonrespondents).

Variable	Respondents	Non-Respondents	T-test/Chi²
	$N = 365$	$N = 1,531$	
Overall *culture change* (N/Percent)			
0 (Did not adopt)	229 (62.74%)	–	–
1 (Adopted)	136 (37.26%)	–	–
Knowledge Management		–	–
Acquisition (M/SD)	3.62 (0.85)		
Dissemination (M/SD)	3.39 (0.88)	–	–
Responsiveness (M/SD)	4.54 (0.64)	–	–
Overall Knowledge management (M/SD)	3.81 (0.67)	–	–
Nursing Home Administrator (NHA)'s Long-Term Care Experience (years) (M/SD)	19.62 (11.36)	–	–
Leadership (NHA) Stability (years) (M/SD)	8.13 (8.97)	–	–
Nurse Stability (%) (M/SD)	82.59 (18.15)		
Organizational structure			
Profit status			$p = 0.001$
For-profit	242 (70.35%)	1,019 (78.75%)	
Not-for-profit	102 (29.65%)	275 (21.25%)	
Ownership			$p = 0.001$
Hospital-owned	290 (83.33%)		
Not hospital-owned	58 (16.67%)		
Chain affiliation			$p = 0.002$
Chain affiliated	140 (40.70%)	651 (50.30%)	
Independent	204 (59.30%)	643 (49.70%)	
Total Beds (M/SD)	101.05 (85.04)	112.16 (74.97)	$p = 0.02$
Organizational operations/performance			
Occupancy Rate (M/SD)	84.27 (15.41)	81.86 (15.62)	$p = 0.01$
Percentage of Medicaid Residents (M/SD)	89.12 (7.03)	88.03 (6.76)	$p = 0.01$
Percentage of Medicare Residents (M/SD)	4.25 (4.49)	5.21 (4.48)	$p < 0.001$
Star rating (N/%)			$p = 0.02$
1	43 (13.56%)	220 (14.37%)	
2	66 (20.82%)	381 (24.89%)	
3	56 (17.67%)	326 (21.29%)	
4	70 (22.08%)	324 (21.16%)	
5	82 (25.87%)	280 (18.29%)	
Total margin (M/SD)	−3.43 (34.36)	−0.51 (12.88)	$p = 0.02$
Organizational staffing			
Direct Care Staff Hours Per Resident Day (M/SD)	3.62 (1.51)	3.45 (1.35)	$p = 0.07$
Ratio of RNs to all nurses (M/SD)	0.31 (0.21)	0.30 (0.20)	$p = 0.45$
Community/Market Characteristics			
Percentage of County Residents Over 65	11.22 (22.59)	14.31 (25.36)	$p = 0.04$
Herfindahl–Hirschman Index (M/SD)	0.26 (0.31)	0.20 (0.27)	$p = 0.01$
Location (N/%)			$p = 0.77$
0 (Rural)	20 (5.75%)	62 (4.79%)	$p = 0.47$
1 (Urban)	328 (94.25%)	1,232 (95.21%)	

Table 3.2. Factor Analysis Results for the Knowledge Management Scale.

Items (1 Strongly Disagree....... 5 Strongly Agree)	Acquisition	Dissemination	Responsiveness
We survey employees regularly to assess their attitudes to their work.	**0.51**	0.27	0.14
Managers frequently try to find out employees' true feelings about their jobs.	**0.51**	0.23	0.30
We have regular staff appraisals in which we discuss the needs of our employees.	**0.52**	0.37	0.19
Employees are encouraged to attend training seminars and/or conferences.	**0.48**	0.17	0.35
We have regular meetings with employees.	**0.49**	0.19	0.34
Employees are encouraged to undertake university or technical courses.	**0.48**	0.32	0.19
Our marketing people frequently spend time discussing residents' future needs with people in technical departments.	0.25	**0.58**	0.11
When people in our organization need information about marketing issues, they know exactly who to ask.	0.12	**0.61**	0.25
There are regular meetings between departments to discuss market trends and developments.	0.17	**0.60**	0.16
We keep a database of resident information that is easy to access.[a]	0.31	0.17	0.33
Information about resident satisfaction is disseminated to all levels of our organization on a regular basis.	0.37	**0.45**	0.29
We often record internal best practices.	0.38	**0.52**	0.26
When we find our residents are unhappy with the quality of our services, we act immediately.	0.10	0.09	**0.81**
We usually respond to changes in our residents' service needs.	0.12	0.09	**0.85**
When we find that a resident would like us to modify a service, the departments involved make a concerted effort to do so.	0.12	0.19	**0.78**
We are quick to respond to resident complaints.	0.12	0.09	**0.84**
We are quick to respond to concerns raised by employees.	0.28	0.24	**0.65**
Cronbach's alpha	0.78	0.77	0.90
Goodness of fit	Root squared error of approximation (RMSEA) = 0.057 Comparative fit index (CFI) = 0.947 Tucker-Lewis index (TLI) = 0.937		

[a]Item dropped from further analysis because it did not load uniquely on a single domain.

= 0.947, TLI = 0.937). Similar to the overall KM index, we created these sub-dimension indices by calculating the average of the items where the factor loadings were greater than 0.40 (Kline, 1994).

Moderating variables. Two variables were included in the analysis to test the potential moderating effects of leadership and staff stability (*H2* and *H3*). Leadership stability was measured as the number of years the NH administrator had been in their current position, which was obtained in the primary survey data of NH administrators. Nursing staff stability was operationalized as annual retention and calculated in two steps. First, we calculated turnover as the average percentage of registered nurses, licensed practical nurses, and certified nursing assistants who voluntarily quit the NH in the past year. We then deducted the turnover from 100% to quantify stability. We adopted this approach so that both moderating variables could be interpreted similarly (i.e., higher values representing greater stability). These variables were included as control variables in the primary analysis.

Control Variables. We controlled for a number of organizational and external environment characteristics associated with the adoption of culture-change initiatives (Chisholm et al., 2018; Grabowski et al., 2014a; Scalzi et al., 2006). These variables were categorized as organizational structure, organizational operations/performance, organizational staffing, and external environment characteristics. Organizational structure variables included profit status (1 = for-profit, 0 = not-for-profit), ownership (1 = hospital-owned, 0 = not hospital-owned), chain affiliation (1 = chain-affiliated, 0 = not chain-affiliated), and size (number of NH beds). Organizational operations/performance variables included occupancy (% of total beds occupied by residents), percentage of residents covered by Medicaid, percentage of residents covered by Medicare, overall CMS star quality rating (ranging from 1 to 5 stars), and total margin (calculated as total revenues minus total expenses, divided by total revenues). Organizational staffing variables included staffing intensity (number of direct care hours per paid day), nurse skill mix (ratio of registered nurses [RNs] to RNs and licensed practical nurses [LPNs]), and the NH administrator's years of experience in the long-term care industry. County-level market characteristics included the percentage of county residents over the age of 65, the level of competition between NHs (calculated as the Herfindahl–Hirchman Index, using the number of beds as a measure of market share, then squaring the number of beds in a market and summing the results), and whether the NH was located in a rural or urban county (based on Rural–Urban Continuum Codes; 1 = urban [codes 1–7], 0 = rural [codes 8–9]). Finally, we used state-level fixed effects to account for interstate differences.

Analysis. We used two separate logistic regression models to assess the relationship between KM and the adoption of a culture-change initiative: one for overall KM activities and a second model for the three separate dimensions of KM activities. Results of these models are reported as average marginal effects (AME), where a one-unit higher level of KM activity corresponded with an AME unit greater or lesser probability of adopting a culture-change initiative. These models were then re-estimated to include multiplicative interaction terms between KM activities and the leadership and staff stability variables. Prior to re-estimating the models, the multiplicative interaction term covariates were mean centered to facilitate interpretation. Our presentation of results from these models focused on whether the interactions were significant at different values of each constituent interaction term (i.e., pick-a-point approach). In this analysis, we used 0–25 years for leadership stability and 0–100% for nursing staff retention because these were the ranges of actual values in the dataset.

We again reported these as AME to facilitate interpretation. For example, the interpretation of an interaction term between overall KM activities and leadership stability would be: Among NHs with administrators who had been in their position 5 years, a one-unit higher level of overall KM activities was associated with a (insert AME) greater or lesser probability of adopting a culture-change initiative. Stata 15 was used for the statistical analysis (StataCorp, 2017). Statistical significance was evaluated at a 0.05 or smaller alpha level.

RESULTS

Sample Descriptives. As shown in Table 3.1, when compared to survey non-respondents, NHs in our study tended to have a lower mean number of beds (101.05 for respondents vs 112.16 for nonrespondents), have a higher percentage of Medicaid (89.12% vs 88.03%) but smaller percentage of Medicare beneficiaries (4.25% vs 5.21%), have a higher average occupancy rate (84.27% vs 81.86%), have higher quality (25.87% vs 18.29% with 5-star ratings), be located in communities with a lower percentage of residents over the age of 65 (11.22% vs 14.3%), and be in less competitive markets (0.26 HHI vs 0.20 HHI), compared to survey nonrespondents. We attempted to mitigate the external validity challenges presented by these differences by including these characteristics as control variables in our regression models.

NH respondents reported an average of 3.81 overall KM activities (standard deviation = 0.67, range = 1–5). Among the KM subdomains, NH respondents reported the highest level for responsiveness activities (mean = 4.54, standard deviation = 0.64), followed by acquisition activities (mean = 3.62, standard deviation = 0.859) and dissemination (mean = 3.39, standard deviation = 0.89). A little over one-third (37.26%, *n* = 136) of the responding NHs reported adopting a culture-change initiative.

Logistic Regression Results. Controlling for other organizational and environmental factors, the probability of adopting a culture-change initiative was 0.12 higher for NHs reporting a one-unit higher level of KM activities (AME = 0.12, 95% CI = 0.01, 0.22; Table 3.3). This can be interpreted as one-unit higher level of overall KM activities was associated with a 0.12 greater probability of adopting a culture-change initiative. Among the individual dimensions of KM, there was no significant independent relationship with culture-change initiative adoption.

The number of years an NH administrator was in their current position was the only control variable that was significantly associated with the adoption of a culture-change initiative. In this case, the probability of adopting a culture-change initiative was 0.01 lower for NHs with an administrator that had been in their current position for an additional year (AME = −0.01, 95% CI = −0.02, −0.003). This can be interpreted as a one-year increase in the tenure of an NH administrator was associated with a 0.01 lower probability of adopting a culture change initiative.

Interaction Results – NH Administrator Years in Current Position. To assess the possibility that the association between KM activities and the adoption of a culture-change initiative may vary based on NH administrator tenure, the AMEs were estimated at different values of NH administrator tenure (e.g., 0 years, 10

Table 3.3. Logistic Regression Results of the Relationship Between Knowledge Management and Participation in Culture-change Initiatives.

	ME (95% CI)[a]	ME (95% CI)[a]
Knowledge management		
Overall	0.12 (0.01, 0.22)*	
Acquisition	–	0.08 (−0.03, 0.20)
Dissemination	–	0.05 (−0.05, 0.15)
Responsiveness	–	−0.05 (−0.18, 0.08)
Organizational structure		
For-profit (1 = yes)	−0.06 (−0.24, 0.11)	−0.06 (−0.23, 0.11)
Hospital-owned (1 = yes)	−0.03 (−0.22, 0.16)	−0.04 (−0.23, 0.15)
Chain affiliated (1 = yes)	−0.02 (−0.18, 0.15)	−0.02 (−0.18, 0.15)
Number of beds	−0.001 (−0.002, 0.001)	0.001 (−0.001, 0.001)
Organizational operations/performance		
Occupancy	0.001 (−0.01, 0.01)	0.001 (−0.004, 0.01)
% Medicaid	−0.001 (−0.01, 0.01)	−0.001 (−0.01, 0.01)
% Medicare	0.003 (−0.02, 0.02)	0.003 (−0.02, 0.02)
Quality/star rating	0.04 (−0.03, 0.12)	0.04 (−0.03, 0.12)
Total margin	−0.01 (−0.02, 0.005)	0.01 (−0.05, 0.06)
Organizational staffing		
Direct care staff hours per resident day	0.02 (−0.07, 0.10)	0.02 (−0.07, 0.10)
Ratio of RNs to all nurses	0.03 (−0.45, 0.52)	0.03 (−0.45, 0.51)
Nursing staff retention	0.005 (−0.01, 0.001)	0.005 (−0.01, 0.01)
NH administrator years of long-term care experience	0.003 (−0.004, 0.01)	0.002 (−0.004, 0.01)
NH administrator years of in current position	−0.01 (−0.02, −0.003)*	−0.01 (−0.02, −0.01)*
Community controls		
Percentage of county residents over the age of 65	0.001 (−0.001, 0.001)	0.001 (−0.001, 0.001)
Herfindahl–Hirschman Index	0.08 (−0.20, 0.36)	0.09 (−0.19, 0.38)
Location (1 = Urban)	−0.18 (−0.58, 0.23)	−0.21 (−0.63, 0.20)
N	194	194

[a]Models include state-level fixed effects to account for differences in state-level policy.
*$p < 0.05$, **$p < 0.01$, ***$p < 0.001$.

years, 25 years; Table 3.4). KM activities were associated with a greater likelihood of adopting a culture-change initiative for NHs where the administrator had been in their position fewer years. For example, among NHs with administrators who had been in their position 0–1 years, a one-unit higher level of overall KM activities was associated with a 0.20 greater probability of adopting a culture-change initiative. However, this relationship declined in magnitude as the number of years increased, and the interaction was no longer significant by the time administrators had been in their position 10 years or more. There were no significant moderating relationships for the individual dimensions of KM and NH administrator tenure.

Table 3.4. Average Marginal Effects.

	Overall KM	Acquisition KM	Dissemination KM	Responsiveness KM
NH administrator years in current position				
0	0.20 (0.07, 0.34)**	0.07 (−0.09, 0.23)	0.10 (−0.03, 0.22)	0.01 (−0.18, 0.19)
5	0.15 (0.04, 0.26)**	0.10 (−0.02, 0.22)	0.05 (−0.06, 0.15)	−0.04 (−0.18, 0.11)
10	0.09 (−0.002, 0.19)	0.12 (−0.01, 0.25)	0.01 (−0.12, 0.12)	−0.07 (−0.20, 0.06)
15	0.04 (−0.06, 0.15)	0.13 (−0.02, 0.29)	−0.04 (−0.19, 0.12)	−0.09 (−0.23, 0.05)
20	−0.001 (−0.12, 0.11)	0.13 (−0.05, 0.31)	−0.06 (−0.24, 0.11)	−0.11 (−0.26, 0.05)
25	−0.03 (−0.16, 0.09)	0.13 (−0.07, 0.32)	−0.08 (−0.27, 0.10)	−0.11 (−0.28, 0.06)
Nursing staff retention				
0	0.26 (−0.11, 0.62)	0.12 (−0.24, 0.47)	0.13 (−0.09, 0.35)	−0.02 (−0.39, 0.36)
20	0.25 (−0.04, 0.54)	0.12 (−0.21, 0.44)	0.12 (−0.08, 0.33)	−0.02 (−0.37, 0.33)
40	0.23 (0.01, 0.46)*	0.12 (−0.16, 0.40)	0.11 (−0.08, 0.30)	−0.04 (−0.34, 0.27)
60	0.20 (0.04, 0.36)*	0.12 (−0.09, 0.33)	0.10 (−0.06, 0.25)	−0.05 (−0.28, 0.17)
80	0.13 (0.02, 0.24)*	0.10 (−0.03, 0.23)	0.06 (−0.05, 0.17)	−0.07 (−0.21, 0.06)
100	0.02 (−0.16, 0.20)	0.07 (−0.10, 0.23)	−0.001 (−0.15, 0.15)	−0.09 (−0.35, 0.16)

$*p < 0.05; **p < 0.01; ***p < 0.001.$

Interaction Results – Nursing Staff Stability. Similar to NH administrator tenure, to assess whether the association between KM activities and the adoption of a culture-change initiative varied based on nursing staff stability, the AMEs were estimated at different values of nursing staff retention (e.g., 0%, 20%, 60%; Table 3.4). Higher levels of overall KM activities were significantly associated with greater adoption of culture-change initiatives at intermediate levels of nurse retention. For example, for NHs with 40% nursing staff retention, a one-unit higher level of KM activity was associated with a 0.23 greater probability of adopting a culture-change initiative (AME = 0.23, 95% CI = 0.01, 0.46). The interactive relationship was smaller at higher levels of retention; for example, for NHs with 80% nursing staff retention, a one-unit higher level of KM activity was associated with a 0.13 greater probability of adopting a culture-change initiative (AME = 0.13, 95% CI = 0.02, 0.24). There were no significant moderating relationships for the individual dimensions of KM and nursing staff retention.

DISCUSSION

The purpose of this study was to examine whether and under what conditions KM activities may support or hinder the adoption of care delivery innovations among lower resourced NHs (i.e., those with high percentages of Medicaid residents). The study findings generally support the hypothesis that more KM activities are associated with a greater likelihood of adopting culture-change initiatives. These findings are consistent with arguments that KM activities support the adoption of innovations (Darroch, 2005; Darroch & McNaughton, 2002; Lundvall & Nielsen, 2007). They extend previous research conducted in hospitals that has found more robust KM activities associated with better quality of care (McFadden et al., 2014; Stock et al., 2010). Empirically establishing that similar relationships exist in NHs – particularly those that may be resource challenged – is important for understanding ways to support the dissemination of evidence-based innovations in an organizational population that may face challenges associated with operating in low-resourced environments and providing care for underserved populations. Similarly, to the extent innovations such as culture-change initiatives can improve resident experience and quality of care, a better understanding of how to promote adoption among these NHs may be important for addressing income-related disparities in care (Konetzka & Werner, 2009; Mor et al., 2004b). It is also notable, however, that different types of KM activities were not independently associated with the adoption of culture-change initiatives. This finding, along with the fact that the overall level of KM activities was significantly associated with adoption, suggests that these activities may work holistically to support the adoption of innovations such as culture-change initiatives. Our findings may also support the notion that KM may function within a system or rely on systems to support KM. Each type of KM activity may not be able to independently move the needle on supporting the implementation of innovations in healthcare organizations, but when functioning within a system of KM, each different activity can support the complex processes which occur during innovation adoption and implementation.

Our findings also suggest that more KM activities in an NH may be particularly effective at supporting the adoption of culture-change initiatives when NH administrators are relatively new to their position. One explanation for this finding pertains to the type of work done by NH administrators and the ability of KM activities to make this knowledge available for later use. More specifically, we submit that NH administrators engage in a high degree of tacit knowledge work on a day-to-day basis. For example, NH administrators are often responsible for developing and executing organizational strategy – activities for which an explicit "playbook" does not exist. More KM activities may reflect a more effective approach to encoding tacit information into organizational routines that can compensate for instability in leadership (Kimble, 2013). When these sorts of approaches to encoding tacit knowledge occur, there may be the potential for such knowledge systems to spill over and facilitate other initiatives of changes in an organization. In other words, more robust KM systems can provide a stable source of information to support new initiatives like culture change even while the tacit knowledge possessed by leaders is exiting the organization. In contrast, NHs that experience relatively little change in leadership may have less need for such systems as the knowledge is retained in the organization, albeit more tacitly in the minds of leaders.

With respect to nursing staff retention, KM activities in NHs were more effective at supporting the adoption of culture-change initiatives at facilities with intermediate-to-high levels of nurse staff retention, but not at low levels as hypothesized. Thus, rather than compensating for nursing staff turnover, it appears that KM activities are most effective when there is a certain level of nursing staff stability. Similar to leadership instability, one explanation for this finding relates to the type of work that nursing staff engage in on a day-to-day basis. Task performance for nursing staff tends to rely more heavily on explicit knowledge that is more easily codified for later retrieval and utilization with robust KM systems (e.g., care processes, admission/transfer protocols). That is, more robust KM systems help NHs "take advantage" of stable nursing staff by leveraging their knowledge in pursuit of a culture-change initiative. It is also possible, however, that more robust KM activities were not associated with greater adoption at low levels of retention (i.e., high nurse turnover) because the replacement of nursing staff under such extreme circumstances is practically all-consuming, requiring time and other resources that cannot be overcome with any amount of KM activities.

Regardless of the underlying explanation, these findings collectively highlight important differences in the leadership and staffing conditions where more robust KM activities may stimulate the adoption of culture-change initiatives. Specifically, KM activities appear to compensate for leader instability and accentuate nursing staff stability. Such distinctions are important for understanding ways to mitigate the potentially derailing effects of leadership and staff turnover when pursuing new innovations in care.

It is also notable that, in contrast to other studies (Grabowski et al., 2014a; Miller et al., 2013; Zimmerman et al., 2014), many of our control variables reflecting more stable, structural characteristics of NHs and the external environment were not significantly associated with culture-change adoption. One potential explanation for this divergence from previous research is that these factors may not provide the same support or impetus for adoption among lower resourced NHs providing care for Medicaid beneficiaries as they do among NHs with a more lucrative payer mix. Another possibility is that internal processes such as KM activities (and other management activities) may mediate the impact of these factors on NH adoption of culture-change initiatives (Gowen et al., 2009; McFadden et al., 2014; Stock et al., 2010). For example, it is plausible that NHs that are hospital-owned or chain-affiliated may have access to more abundant and diverse resources that may enable more robust KM activities, which in turn may help support the adoption of culture-change initiatives. To the extent previous studies omitted these types of internal processes in their analysis, more distal external and structural factors may have appeared to be direct correlates of culture-change adoption. If true, our findings highlight the importance of researchers, practitioners, and policymakers paying more attention to the complex interplay between external forces, relatively stable organizational attributes, and internal processes when trying to stimulate and support the adoption of innovations in NHs.

Limitations. The study's findings should be interpreted in light of several limitations. First, the analysis was cross-sectional, and we cannot make definitive causal claims about the study relationships. For example, it is conceivable that the adoption of a culture-change initiative would result in an NH implementing more KM activities. Second, our focus in this study was on high-Medicaid-census NHs, and the findings may not generalize to NHs with a different payer mix. While our analysis controlled for some notable organizational and community differences between our sample of NHs and those that were better resourced, these efforts were only as effective as the data and variables available to us. To the extent these efforts did not adequately address these differences, findings and recommendations from our study should be generalized to other NHs with caution. Third, the data used in our analysis were based on surveys completed by one person at each facility: the NH administrator. Therefore, it was not possible to corroborate the accuracy or reliability of these responses with other data (e.g., establish interrater reliability with survey responses from another NH member). Moreover, for measures like leadership stability, a focus on a single administrator's response does reflect the fact that many healthcare delivery organizations, including NHs, rely on pluralistic leadership structures (Chreim & MacNaughton, 2016; Leach et al., 2021). Consequently, it is conceivable that the respondents to our survey may have reported a short tenure in their role even though other members of the leadership team had longer tenures (and vice versa).

CONCLUSIONS

Within this chapter, we examined and addressed two grand healthcare challenges: (1) *innovation adoption* within lower resourced healthcare organizations that provide care to minoritized populations and individuals of lower socioeconomic status and (2) the implementation of *person-centered care for the aging* strategies in healthcare delivery organizations through the examination of the role of KM and culture-change initiatives within NHs with high percentages of Medicaid residents. Such NHs are especially challenged to adopt culture-change initiatives, which are aimed at advancing the organization's ability to provide person-centered care for the aging population. This chapter advanced our understanding of how KM activities may help high-Medicaid-census NHs acquire and mobilize informational resources in ways that can support the adoption of these initiatives and potentially bridge this gulf.

One of our most notable findings was that when examining KM activities holistically, there was a significant relationship between KM activities and the adoption of culture-change initiatives, yet when examined individually, the unique KM activities were not independently associated with culture-change initiatives. Within the broader context of the grand healthcare challenge of innovation adoption within healthcare organizations, these findings support the notion that organizations can harness knowledge as a key resource to gain an advantage and improve their outcomes. Additionally, as previously described in the conceptual framework, the KBV of a firm describes knowledge-based resources as socially complex and difficult-to-imitate resources that require organizations to implement practices to harness them. Our findings may suggest that when organizations are considering KM and how to harness such resources to gain a competitive advantage or improve an organization's outcome, KM must be implemented holistically as opposed to selecting specific types of KM activities over others. Without the acknowledgement that KM may rely on a sense of synergy to support innovation, the organization may not be able to reap the anticipated benefits as described in the KBV of the firm. Such activities may be particularly important for NHs that struggle with leadership and nursing staff instability.

Collectively, these findings highlight a number of opportunities for practitioners and policymakers to more effectively target their efforts to stimulate the adoption and spread of these initiatives. High-Medicaid-census NHs face barriers to implementing innovations in care, not just culture-change initiatives, and our study's results support the notion that KM activities can be incorporated into the innovation implementation process within such facilities. Systematically enabling KM activities can support organizations which otherwise do not have resources to facilitate innovation adoption. Additionally, we anticipate that the wide-scale implementation of culture-change initiatives will continue to be a challenge for NHs. The findings from this study support the inclusion of KM activities to advance NHs' provision of person-centered care to the aging population.

REFERENCES

Aymen, R. A., Alhamzah, A., & Bilal, E. (2019). A multi-level study of influence knowledge management small and medium enterprises. *Polish Journal of Management Studies, 19*(1), 21–31.

Bennett, R., & Gabriel, H. (1999). Organisational factors and knowledge management in large marketing departments: An empirical study. *Journal of Knowledge Management, 3*, 212–225.

Berenson, R. A., Hammons, T., Gans, D. N., Zuckerman, S., Merrell, K., Underwood, W. S., & Williams, A. F. (2008). A house is not a home: Keeping patients at the center of practice redesign. *Health Affairs, 27*, 1219–1230.

Chisholm, L., Zhang, N. J., Hyer, K., Pradhan, R., Unruh, L., & Lin, F.-C. (2018). Culture-change in nursing homes: What is the role of nursing home resources? *Inquiry: The Journal of Health Care Organization, Provision, and Financing, 55*, 0046958018787043.

Choi, B., & Lee, H. (2002). Knowledge management strategy and its link to knowledge creation process. *Expert Systems with Applications, 23*, 173–187.

Chreim, S., & Macnaughton, K. (2016). Distributed leadership in health care teams. *Health Care Management Review, 41*(3), 200–212.

Conner, K. R. (1991). A historical comparison of resource-based theory and five schools of thought within industrial organization economics: Do we have a new theory of the firm? *Journal of Management, 17*, 121–154.

Darroch, J. (2003). Developing a measure of knowledge management behaviors and practices. *Journal of Knowledge Management, 7*, 41–54.

Darroch, J. (2005). Knowledge management, innovation and firm performance. *Journal of Knowledge Management, 9*, 101–115.

Darroch, J., & Mcnaughton, R. (2002). Examining the link between knowledge management practices and types of innovation. *Journal of Intellectual Capital, 3*, 210–222.

Davis, K., Schoenbaum, S. C., & Audet, A.-M. (2005). A 2020 vision of patient-centered primary care. *Journal of General Internal Medicine, 20*, 953–957.

Dillman, D. A. (1978). *Mail and telephone surveys: The total design method* (Vol. 19, p. 375). Wiley.

Epstein, R. M., & Street, R. L. (2011). The values and value of patient-centered care. *The Annals of Family Medicine, 9*, 100–103.

Gowen, C. R., III, Henagan, S. C., & Mcfadden, K. L. (2009). Knowledge management as a mediator for the efficacy of transformational leadership and quality management initiatives in US health care. *Health Care Management Review, 34*, 129–140.

Grabowski, D. C., Elliot, A., Leitzell, B., Cohen, L. W., & Zimmerman, S. (2014a). Who are the innovators? Nursing homes implementing culture-change. *The Gerontologist, 54*, S65–S75.

Grabowski, D. C., O'Malley, A. J., Afendulis, C. C., Caudry, D. J., Elliot, A., & Zimmerman, S. (2014b). Culture-change and nursing home quality of care. *The Gerontologist, 54*, S35–S45.

Grant, R. M. (1996). Toward a knowledge-based theory of the firm. *Strategic Management Journal, 17*, 109–122.

Hill, N. L., Kolanowski, A. M., Milone-Nuzzo, P., & Yevchak, A. (2011). Culture-change models and resident health outcomes in long-term care. *Journal of Nursing Scholarship, 43*, 30–40.

IOM (Institute of Medicine). (2001). *Crossing the quality chasm: A new health system for the 21st century*. National Academy Press.

Kane, R. A., Lum, T. Y., Cutler, L. J., Degenholtz, H. B., & Yu, T. C. (2007). Resident outcomes in small-house nursing homes: A longitudinal evaluation of the initial green house program. *Journal of the American Geriatrics Society, 55*, 832–839.

Kimble, C. (2013). Knowledge management, codification and tacit knowledge. *Information Research, 18*(2).

Kline, P. (1994). *An easy guide to factor analysis*. Routledge.

Kogut, B., & Zander, U. (1992). Knowledge of the firm, combinative capabilities, and the replication of technology. *Organization Science, 3*, 383–397.

Konetzka, R. T., & Werner, R. M. (2009). Disparities in long-term care: Building equity into market-based reforms. *Medical Care Research and Review, 66*, 491–521.

Koren, M. J. (2010). Person-centered care for nursing home residents: The culture-change movement. *Health Affairs, 29*, 312–317.

Leach, L., Hastings, B., Schwarz, G., Watson, B., Bouckenooghe, D., Seoane, L., & Hewett, D. (2021). Distributed leadership in healthcare: Leadership dyads and the promise of improved hospital outcomes. *Leadership in Health Services, 34*(4), 353–374.

Lundvall, B.-Å., & Nielsen, P. (2007). Knowledge management and innovation performance. *International Journal of Manpower, 28*, 207–223.

Mcfadden, K. L., Lee, J. Y., Gowen, C. R., III, & Sharp, B. M. (2014). Linking quality improvement practices to knowledge management capabilities. *Quality Management Journal, 21*, 42–58.

Miller, S. C., Looze, J., Shield, R., Clark, M. A., Lepore, M., Tyler, D., Sterns, S., & Mor, V. (2013). Culture-change practice in US nursing homes: Prevalence and variation by state Medicaid reimbursement policies. *The Gerontologist, 54*, 434–445.

Misiorski, S. (2003). Pioneering culture-change. *Journal of Nursing Homes and Long Term Care Management, 52*, 24.

Mor, V., Zinn, J., Angelelli, J., Teno, J. M., & Miller, S. C. (2004a). Driven to tiers: Socioeconomic and racial disparities in the quality of nursing home care. *The Milbank Quarterly, 82*, 227–256.

Mor, V., Zinn, J., Angelelli, J., Teno, J. M., & Miller, S. C. (2004b). Driven to tiers: Socioeconomic and racial disparities in the quality of nursing home care. *The Milbank Quarterly, 82*, 227–256.

Myllärniemi, J., Laihonen, H., Karppinen, H., & Seppänen, K. (2012). Knowledge management practices in healthcare services. *Measuring Business Excellence, 16*, 54–65.

Nonaka, I. (1994). A dynamic theory of organizational knowledge creation. *Organization Science, 5*, 14–37.

Nonaka, I., & von Krogh, G. (2009). Perspective—Tacit knowledge and knowledge conversion: Controversy and advancement in organizational knowledge creation theory. *Organization Science, 20*, 635–652.

Orzano, A. J., Mcinerney, C. R., Tallia, A. F., Scharf, D., & Crabtree, B. F. (2008). Family medicine practice performance and knowledge management. *Health Care Management Review, 33*, 21–28.

Panahi, S., Watson, J., & Partridge, H. (2016). Conceptualising social media support for tacit knowledge sharing: Physicians' perspectives and experiences. *Journal of Knowledge Management, 20*(2), 344–363.

Rahman, A. N., & Schnelle, J. F. (2008). The nursing home culture-changemovement: Recent past, present, and future directions for research. *The Gerontologist, 48*, 142–148.

Scalzi, C. C., Evans, L. K., Barstow, A., & Hostvedt, K. (2006). Barriers and enablers to changing organizational culture in nursing homes. *Journal of Nursing Administration Quarterly, 30*, 368–372.

Sheng, M. L., Chang, S.-Y., Teo, T., & Lin, Y.-F. (2013). Knowledge barriers, knowledge transfer, and innovation competitive advantage in healthcare settings. *Management Decision, 51*, 461–478.

Shier, V., Khodyakov, D., Cohen, L. W., Zimmerman, S., & Saliba, D. (2014). What does the evidence really say about *culture-change* in nursing homes? *The Gerontologist, 54,* S6–S16.

STATACORP. (2017). Stata statistical software: Release 15. In LLC, S. (Ed.), StataCorp LLC.

Stock, G. N., Mcfadden, K. L., & Gowen, C. R., III (2010). Organizational culture, knowledge management, and patient safety in US hospitals. *Quality Management Journal, 17,* 7–26.

White-Chu, E. F., Graves, W. J., Godfrey, S. M., Bonner, A., & Sloane, P. (2009). Beyond the medical model: The *culture-change* revolution in long-term care. *Journal of the American Medical Directors Association, 10,* 370–378.

Williams, J. H., Silvera, G. A., & Lemak, C. H. (2022). Learning through diversity: Creating a virtuous cycle of health equity in health care organizations. *Responding to the Grand Challenges in Health Care via Organizational Innovation Advances in Health Care Management, 21,* 167–189.

Wyatt, J. C. (2001). 10. Management of explicit and tacit knowledge. *Journal of the Royal Society of Medicine, 94*(1), 6–9.

Zack, M., Mckeen, J., & Singh, S. (2009). Knowledge management and organizational performance: An exploratory analysis. *Journal of Knowledge Management, 13,* 392–409.

Zimmerman, S., Shier, V., & Saliba, D. (2014). Transforming nursing home culture: Evidence for practice and policy. *The Gerontologist, 54,* S1–S5.

SECTION 2

MECHANISMS OF CHANGE – HOW LEADERS WITHIN ORGANIZATIONS FRAME AND EXECUTE CHANGE

CHAPTER 4

TOWARD A THEORY OF ORGANIZATIONAL DNA: ROUTINES, PRINCIPLES, AND BELIEFS (RPBS) FOR SUCCESSFUL AND SUSTAINABLE ORGANIZATIONAL CHANGE

Mark Govers[a], Rachel Gifford[a], Daan Westra[a] and Ingrid Mur-Veeman[b]

[a]Maastricht University, The Netherlands
[b]Ohio State University, USA

ABSTRACT

Organizational change is a key mechanism to ensure the sustainability of healthcare systems. However, healthcare organizations are persistently difficult to change, and literature is riddled with examples of failed change endeavors. In this chapter, we attempt to unravel the underlying causes for failed organizational change. We distinguish three types of change with different levels of depth that require different change approaches. Transformations *are the deepest forms of change where beliefs and principles need to be modified to successfully influence routines.* Renewals *are deep forms of change where principles need to be modified to successfully influence routines.* Improvements *are shallow forms of change where only modifications at the level of routines are needed. Using deoxyribonucleic acid (DNA) as our metaphor, we propose a theory of "organizational DNA" to understand organizations and these three types of organizational changes. We posit that organizations are made up of a double helix consisting of a so-called "social string," which contains the "soft" interaction or communication*

Research and Theory to Foster Change in the Face of Grand Health Care Challenges
Advances in Health Care Management, Volume 22, 77–95
Copyright © 2024 Mark Govers, Rachel Gifford, Daan Westra and Ingrid Mur-Veeman
Published under exclusive licence by Emerald Publishing Limited
ISSN: 1474-8231/doi:10.1108/S1474-823120240000022004

among the organization's members, and a so-called "technical string," which contains "hard" organizational aspects such as structure and technology. Ladders of organizational nucleotides (i.e., Routines, Principles, and Beliefs) connect this double helix in various combinations. Together, the double helix and accompanying nucleotides make up the DNA of an organization. Without knowledge of the architecture of organizational DNA and whether a change addresses beliefs, principles, and/or routines, we believe that organizational change is constrained and based on luck rather than change management expertise. Following this metaphor, we show that organizational change fails when it attempts to change one part of the DNA (e.g., routines) in a way that renders it incompatible with the connecting components (e.g., principles and beliefs). We discuss how the theory can be applied in practice using an exemplar case.

Keywords: Socio-technical systems theory; organizational change; organizational DNA; routines, principles and beliefs; improvement, renewal and transformation; organizational failure and success

INTRODUCTION

Contemporary healthcare sectors across the globe face what are often referred to as "grand challenges" (George, 2014) or "wicked problems" (Rittel & Webber, 1973). Achieving the quadruple aim, labor shortages, and crises such as the recent COVID-19 pandemic are typical examples of these challenges (Fleuren et al., 2021; Litwin, 2021; Moore et al., 2021). Such large, persistent, and highly complex issues threaten the stability and sustainability of healthcare systems across the globe (OECD, 2018). Healthcare managers, and by extension healthcare management scholars, are believed to play a significant role in tackling these challenges, for example, through caring for vulnerable populations, maintaining the healthcare workforce, and implementing changes that enable healthcare organizations to address these challenges (Fleuren et al., 2021; Litwin, 2021; Moore et al., 2021).

One main assumption underlies these potential solutions – namely, that healthcare organizations are able to change their ways in their attempt to solve or address the problems society faces, preferably rapidly and sustainably. In fact, Mayo et al. (2021) point out that healthcare is an industry in which change never stops (p. 545). Yet, despite the high level of experience with change in healthcare, numerous examples of failed organizational changes can be found in the news, organizational reports, and academic literature (e.g., Nembhard et al., 2009). For example, studies have shown that clinicians often fail to adopt clinical guidelines that are meant to support their decisions about the most appropriate and effective care in specific circumstances (Cabana et al., 1999). Similarly, promising telehealth solutions fail to be adopted or scaled up (Standing et al., 2016). Hospital mergers result in long and laborious integration attempts that ultimately fail to reach their intended quality improvements (Gaynor et al., 2015). Overall, despite concerted efforts, dedicated resources, and urgent need for change, failed change remains a persistent problem.

Why does this happen? We argue that if we believe that successful change is a predominant route toward keeping healthcare systems sustainable and accessible for future generations, it is essential to know more about the underlying structure of organizational change before we attempt to impose it on people in an organization. In the healthcare management literature on organizational change, the fundamental question of the causes and reasons for the failure of change is often overlooked, and when it is asked, it is not answered satisfactorily (Mayo et al., 2021). Therefore, this chapter offers a new perspective on the question of the causes and reasons for failed organizational change, seeking a different answer to this question. More specifically, we use a socio-technical systems (STS) perspective to understand organizational change failure. Using this perspective, it is our key proposition that the causes and reasons for failed organizational change are as deeply hidden as they are anchored in, what we call, organizational deoxyribonucleic acid (DNA). Our theory proposes that changes in organizations differ in depth, depending on what part of the organizational DNA structure they target. In our theory, we distinguish three types of change:

(1) *Transformations* are the deepest forms of change, where beliefs and principles need to be modified to successfully influence routines. For example: introducing disruptive digital technologies, like artificial intelligence (AI), that will not only change the way professionals and patients collaborate but also the nature and impact of interactions and relationships within the larger society (e.g., Govers & van Amelsvoort, 2023).
(2) *Renewals* are deep forms of change, where principles need to be modified to successfully influence routines. For example: changing from a silo-based organization to a team-based healthcare organization (e.g., Will et al., 2019).
(3) *Improvements* are shallow forms of change, where only changes at the level of routines are needed. For example: implementing a training program for nurses to improve quality standards and adherence.

From our theoretical perspective, transformations and renewals can only be successful and sustainable if the organizational DNA is altered systematically, as we consider such profound changes to represent genetic manipulations of organizational DNA. We posit that the grand challenges the healthcare industry faces (Hefner & Nembhard, 2021) require successful transformations and renewals, but without knowledge of the architecture of organizational DNA and whether a change addresses beliefs, principles, and/or routines, we believe that organizational change is constrained and based on luck rather than change management expertise.

In what follows, we develop a theory of organizational DNA which helps to explain the nature of organizations and the functioning of organizational change. We describe the core components of the theory – namely, the double helix consisting of the so-called social and technical DNA strings of the organization as well as the connecting nucleotides: Routines, Principles, and Beliefs (RPBs). As we explain, the two strings and connecting nucleotides give insights into an organization's DNA and, with it, open the door to a systematic and replicable set of solutions for implementing and sustaining transformations, renewals, and improvements in healthcare organizations.

DNA AS AN ORGANIZATIONAL METAPHOR

Like Morgan (2006), we employ a metaphor of DNA to understand organizations in more depth. The DNA (deoxyribonucleic acid) architecture, established by Watson and Crick (1953), contains the genetic code to build and maintain an organism. Just like a computer runs on operating software, DNA contains the instructions that ensure an organism is built and runs smoothly. The DNA architecture is a double helix twisted on itself (i.e., its two strings) and interconnected by ladders (i.e., connecting nucleotides), as shown in Fig. 4.1.

Using DNA as a metaphor to understand organizations has been previously explored in the 1980s and 1990s (e.g., Hannan & Freeman, 1989; Nelson & Winter, 1982), but appeared in previous attempts to be too complicated to be useful. To take up this work and make the metaphor useful, we do not literally translate the clinical DNA theory to organizations. Instead, we focus on the basic structure of DNA to reveal and understand basic organizational architecture, processes, and changes. In doing so, we view the core of basic organizational architecture as something that consists of two strings (i.e., social and technical),

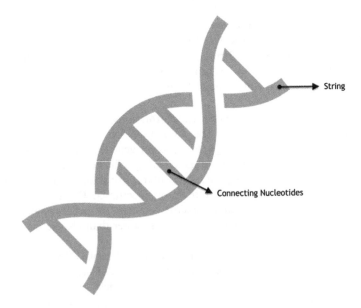

Fig. 4.1. Double Helix Architecture of Deoxyribonucleic Acid (DNA).

with differently patterned connections in between them (i.e., RPBs). Relating the diversity of humanity to organizations' infinite array of actions and structures, the DNA metaphor provides us with the insight that seemingly infinite variation can be rooted back to the same architecture of the double helix.

With the DNA metaphor, we stand in the tradition of ecological organizational thinking from a system theoretical perspective (c.f., Barnett, 1990; Hannan & Freeman, 1989; Hannan et al., 2007; Morgan, 2006). Within this tradition, we take an STS perspective that was originally developed by the British Tavistock Institute of Human Relations (e.g., Emery, 1959; Trist & Bamforth, 1951; Trist et al., 1963). It was used and further developed by a number of scientists and practitioners (e.g., Cherns, 1987; Davis, 1975; De Sitter et al., 1997; Galbraith, 1973; Mohr & Van Amelsvoort, 2015; Pava, 1983; Vriens & Achterbergh, 2011). For this chapter, the STS perspective has two important assumptions: (1) Every organization is built on two basic aspects – the social and the technical systems; and (2) All organizational behavior is based on RPBs.

THE THEORY OF ORGANIZATIONAL DNA: RPBS

First, like the two helical strings of the DNA structure, organizations also consist of two inseparable strings: social ("soft") and technical ("hard"). These strings are present in any organization, regardless of size, nature, or focus. The *social string* refers to the dynamic, meaningful interaction or communication between the members of the organization, which is at the heart of any organization (Luhmann, 1995). Without interaction or communication, nothing can be done in the context of the common organizational tasks, such as formulating a strategy, making operational decisions, or controlling task execution (Achterbergh & Vriens, 2010). The social string combines different organizational aspects such as people and culture (Kuipers et al., 2020). The *technical string* refers to the infrastructure or architecture of the organization (Achterbergh & Vriens, 2010; Beer, 1985). The infrastructure is an inevitable condition of the organization for functioning and survival. Without it, organizational interactions or communications (Luhmann, 1995) would end up in chaos, thus preventing primary activities, coordination, control, policy, and decision-making from running smoothly (c.f., Beer, 1985). The technical string combines different organizational aspects such as structure and technology (c.f., Achterbergh & Vriens, 2010; Beer, 1985).

The dichotomy of social and technical strings echoes key underlying arguments from institutional theory – specifically, that organizations often face conflicting demands from technical and institutional environments as they strive to both maintain their technical core while gaining legitimacy from the institutional environment (c.f., Alexander & D'Aunno, 1990, 2003; DiMaggio & Powell, 1983; Meyer & Rowan, 1977; Scott, 1987; Scott & Meyer, 1994; Zucker, 1987). Within the technical environment, organizations are influenced by the logic of technical rationality, which favors performance and efficiency, whereas the institutional environment promotes institutional norms and beliefs, valuing legitimacy and adherence to social rules or expectations even in the absence of rational explanation. Institutional theorists contend that rather than solely pursuing strategic changes to realize improved efficiency or effectiveness, organizations adopt structures or behaviors to be seen as legitimate by the institutional environment and thereby ensure their stability and survival.

Although further differentiations between the two strings likely exist, all differentiated aspects can always be rooted back to either the social or technical string. In practice, organizational change always targets either social aspects and/or technical aspects of the organization. However, the interaction between the two is complex and essential, yet it is often ignored in hopes that manipulating one will result in a desired outcome by positively inducing change in the other (e.g., change a technical system, improve interprofessional interactions). For example, a hospital may change the organizational structure (technical string) by creating multidisciplinary units (technical string) in hopes of promoting better interprofessional relationships (social string).

Just as DNA contains the instructions for cells to function, the social and technical strings within an organization contain the instructions for it to function and evolve. Thus, organizations are behavioral systems, and as such, they show their behavior in varying internal and external interactions (Luhmann, 1995). For instance, they produce products and services in different ways: efficiently, effectively, qualitatively, and sustainably, or not. Similarly, just as the genetic architecture of DNA shapes variation across individuals and species, the organizational architecture of the social and technical strings shapes variation across organizations. Organizations can have, for instance, an underlying machine architecture or, in opposite, a brain architecture (Morgan, 2006). The organizational architecture sets the basis for how the social and technical strings are interconnected.

The following propositions can be derived from the above considerations:

P1. Organizations, like living systems, have an underlying architecture of organizational DNA, with two interconnected strings.

P2. The two interconnected strings of the organizational DNA, the double helix, consist of the social string and the technical string.

P3. The social and technical strings contain the instructions for the organization to function.

To understand organizations and the change processes taking place within them, it is crucial to have a profound understanding of the architecture behind the social and technical strings. Working from the DNA metaphor, organizational change can be seen as a form of genetic manipulation. Without knowledge of the underlying organizational DNA architecture, we believe change is constrained and based more on luck than change management expertise. Therefore, we must examine the intertwinement of the socio-technical system, which raises the following question: What connects the social ("soft") and the technical ("hard") strings of an organization? The connecting factor is likely to be deeply embedded within organizational aspects, hidden from view, but will also reflect the essence of the socio-technical system as a whole. If we know what intertwines the social and technical strings, we can identify both what should be changed and how to effectively realize such change within organizations.

Our fourth and fifth propositions center on these connections between the social and technical strings, which we identify as RPBs. Collectively, they function as the core of our theory of organizational DNA, leading us to propose:

P4. The interconnections between the social and technical strings are three-fold: RPBs.

P5. RPBs reflect the underlying architecture of organizational DNA.

Hence, we further explore RPBs as the figurative nucleotides interconnecting the social and technical DNA strings of the organization. First, we begin with Routines, for which we posit:

P6. Routines are actions, which are automatically driven.

Routines are visible and tangible, as they are explicitly articulated (Feldman & Pentland, 2003). For instance, upon entering a patient's room, a clinician sanitizes their hands and identifies themselves to the patient. When administering medication, they follow specific routines, which are often explicated in protocols. After the visit, they put a note in the patient's medical file. These routine behaviors are often forced by measures (e.g., concerning speed, quality, and cost) which guide people to adopt organizational routines. As Goldratt (1985) stated: "Tell me how you measure me and I will tell you how I will behave" (p. 26). When people are measured to behave in a specific way (e.g., begin work at 8 a.m.), they develop the corresponding routine to enact that behavior. Yet, as Nembhard et al. (2009) show, it is precisely these routines within healthcare organizations – for example, related to leadership and performance management – that predispose them to a failure to change. Over time, routines may become deeply embedded within the organizational culture and become endowed with institutional values, thereby making change or adaptation difficult (Howard-Grenville, 2005). It is such institutionalized routines that are typically targeted in the implementation of science studies within the healthcare industry. As Mayo et al. (2021) point out, this body of literature focuses both on social as well as technical routines. In fact, the extent to which routines need to change within an organization is considered a key organizational factor as to why changes are not adopted, spread, scaled-up, or even pursued (Greenhalgh et al., 2017).

We continue from our examination of routines to explore principles, beginning with the following proposition:

P7. Principles represent the organizational, managerial, and professional logic for a routine.

Drawing on the established literature around institutional logics and their application in the healthcare industry (c.f. Reay et al., 2021), we consider principles as the logical basis that routines are built on. They are typically less visible and tangible than routines, as they are often more implicitly assumed than explicitly articulated. However, sometimes they are explicitly formulated and communicated, such as, "In this hospital, we should deliver patient-friendly care." Similarly, they can be formally (yet broadly) articulated in an organization's mission statement or legal entity (e.g., as a for-profit organization). Drawing upon the earlier example of clinicians adopting the routine of making notes in patient files after a patient visit, we may infer that the principle underlying such a routine is that "patient care should be promptly documented," or if medical records are accessible to patients, "patients should be well informed about the care they received." Similarly, the routine of introducing oneself to the patient might be driven by the underlying principle that, "in this organization, clinicians' encounters with patients are to be made as comfortable for the patient as possible."

Progressing from principles to beliefs, we suggest that applied principles evolve from the institutionalized beliefs that people within the organization hold regarding organizations, management, and professionalism. Therefore, we state the following proposition:

P8. Beliefs are reasons why a principle should be applied.

Drawing again from the institutional theory literature commonly applied in the healthcare industry (c.f. Reay et al., 2021), we define a belief as the underlying norm as to why a certain principle should be applied within an organization. In other words, a belief offers normative grounds for the application – or rejection – of a principle. As opposed to the more field-level focus of some institutional work, we focus here on beliefs held by members within the organization, although we acknowledge that field-level norms can strongly influence them. Such beliefs are typically invisible and intangible. For example, many believe that disciplined spending positively affects profitability, so paying less attention to spending will lead to financial weakness. Similarly, members of a certain hospital might believe that patient-friendly behavior positively affects healing, so they would consider behavior that is unfriendly to patients to be unethical. Returning to the earlier example of clinicians making notes in a patient's file, when this is done based upon the principle of patients being well-informed about the care they receive, we may uncover the underlying belief that information is power and can empower patients in making healthier and better-informed health-seeking decisions. Additionally, when the routine of clinicians introducing themselves to patients is driven by the principle that clinician–patient encounters should be made as comfortable for the patient as possible, this may be rooted in the belief that anxiety has a negative influence on patients' health and recovery. Beliefs are seldom explicitly formulated. It is even apparent that people are often not aware of some – if not all – of their beliefs. This is not odd, as it expresses the core of modern society that is characterized by functional rationality (i.e., a focus on the *how* and *what* of actions and thoughts) instead of substantial rationality (i.e., a focus on the *why* of actions and thoughts) (c.f., Mannheim, 1940; Weber, 1978).

As we have indicated, RPBs are interdependent. Routines do not come "out of the blue." Instead, they express a principle. A principle, in turn, is applied for a reason; it is rooted in a belief. Hence, we posit that:

P9. Routines are based on principles, and principles are rooted in beliefs.

RPBs connect the social and technical strings of organizational DNA. In any healthy organization, the interconnected (social and technical) strings should be aligned, which means both strings fit and strengthen each other. For example, to foster patient safety in a hospital, the hospital's structure (technical string) and culture (social string) should be aligned, and thus strengthen each other. A hospital's culture of patient safety would align with and be strengthened by a structure that included specific leadership roles overseeing, enforcing, and advocating for patient safety practices across the organization. In the same way, a hospital's efforts to change its structure by introducing a multidisciplinary task force dedicated to improving patient safety would align with and be strengthened by a culture that prioritizes patient safety. However, if there is misalignment between its structure and culture, the hospital's organizational DNA would be in a state of imbalance, impeding any efforts to realize effective organizational change in improving patient safety. Hence, we propose:

P10. The RPBs of the social and technical strings are interconnected.

Fig. 4.2 shows the interconnectedness described. It demonstrates how the social and technical strings ultimately meet each other in the existence of beliefs and – similar to DNA – "translate" into string-related principles and routines.

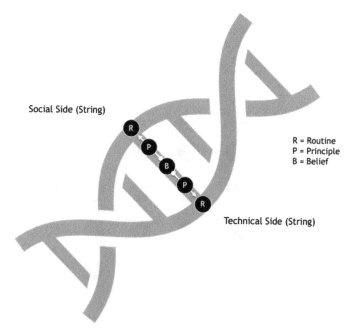

Fig. 4.2.   Interconnected Routines, Principles, and Beliefs (RPBs) as Organizational Deoxyribonucleic Acid (DNA).

RPB ladders bridge the social and technical strings. Each RPB ladder represents a set of standards that are used to identify the building blocks of an organization. Similar to nucleotides in DNA, we suggest that RPB ladders connect the identified organizational social aspects (e.g., culture and people) with the identified organizational technical aspects (e.g., structure and technology). Hence, we posit:

P11. RPB ladders connect the social and technical strings.

P12. A RPB ladder is composed of specific social and technical aspects.

In the socio-technical literature (e.g., Van Amelsvoort, 2000), culture and people are often considered as core social aspects, while structure and technology are viewed as core technical aspects. Although one could distinguish other social and technical aspects, for now we focus upon these core aspects, as represented in the RPB ladders in Fig. 4.3. The previously described example of a clinician writing a note in a patient's medical file illustrates how the routines of People (P) are influenced by their principles and underlying beliefs, reflecting the social string of the organization's DNA. That is, a clinician follows the routine of making a note in the patient's record after a consultation, based on a *principle* of information accessibility, rooted in the *belief* that information can empower patients in making healthier and better-informed health-seeking decisions. At the same time, within the technical string of the organization's DNA, this same *belief* gives rise to the *principle* that appropriate technological solutions can facilitate access to information. In turn, this *principle* generates a routine prompt from the organization's electronic patient record after the scheduled consultation, creating a *routine* enabled by technology (T) to remind clinicians to update the patient's record.

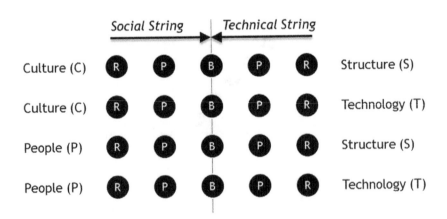

Fig. 4.3.   Routines, Principles, and Beliefs (RPB) Ladders.

CHANGE CONSIDERED FROM THE PERSPECTIVE OF RPBS

In organizations, change is ultimately aimed at establishing lasting effects, as shown in changed routine behaviors. Hence, we posit:

> *P13.* Lasting change in organizations is visible in the change of used social or technical routines.

The levels of desired organizational change differ. The extant literature indicates this through numbered levels, such as first-, second-, and third-order changes (e.g., Argyris & Schon, 1978; Bartunek & Moch, 1987; Dooley, 1997). Each level refers to the depth of change, which suggests that different "things" have to be affected to get the desired change effect. Based on *P9*, we consider these "things" to be: (a) routines based on the currently used principles and beliefs (representing a first-order change – *Improvement* – that targets routines); (b) routines that require new underlying principles based on the currently rooted beliefs (representing a second-order change – *Renewal* – that targets principles); or (c) routines that require new underlying principles and rooted beliefs (representing a third-order change – *Transformation* – that targets beliefs). In other words, the depth of change depends on the levels of required change. Thus, we come to the following proposition:

> *P14.* Organizational change has three levels of depth: RPBs. A Transformation requires change on the level of beliefs and principles to get a desired change in routines, whereas a Renewal requires change on the level of principles and routines without having to change underlying beliefs, and an Improvement requires change only on the level of routines.

In Fig. 4.4, *P14* is depicted as a Transformation with three levels of change: beliefs, principles, and routines. The arrows in the figure represent this progression. Renewal, on the other hand, requires change at two levels: principles and routines. In contrast, routines are the sole focus of Improvement, representing continuous change as shown by the curled arrow in the figure.

From *P10*, we derive that a Transformation is a type of change which necessitates change to the other string's RPBs. If a desired change in the social string requires a change of its belief, the change has to be mirrored in the interconnected technical string, or vice versa, aligning the functional and substantial rationality of the desired change. If this is not the case, the organizational DNA is broken, and the desired change in organizational functioning will not be successfully implemented, consistent with *P1*, *P2*, and *P3*. Thus, the desired change will not last.

Whereas, by definition, a Transformation must be mirrored in the other string in terms of RPBs, a Renewal must also be mirrored in the other string, but

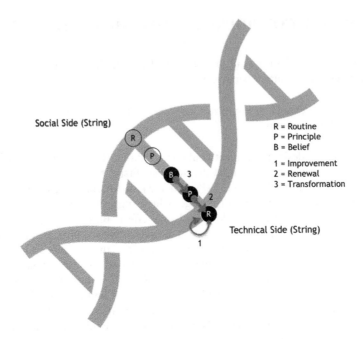

Fig. 4.4.   Change as Improvement, Renewal, and Transformation.

without the need to change the underlying belief. After all, the same belief can be translated into different social and technical principles (see Fig. 4.5). This is true for improvements as well. That is, a change in routines within one string ought to be mirrored in the routines of the other string. However, the underlying belief and principles (social and technical) can remain unchanged. Drawing upon the core of our theory of organizational DNA – namely, *P4* and *P5* – and progressing from *P14*, we apply this theory toward implementing and sustaining change with the following proposition (see also Fig. 4.5):

> *P15.* A Transformation is the deepest type of change which requires changes of RPBs in both the social and technical strings. A Renewal is a deep type of change which requires changes of routines and principles, but not in the underlying beliefs, in both the social and technical strings.

In an organization, changes are triggered in either the social or technical string of its organizational DNA. Recognizing that RPB ladders connect these social and technical strings and are composed of specific social and technical aspects (*P11* and *P12*), we propose the following change pathways to reconnect both strings (see also Fig. 4.6):

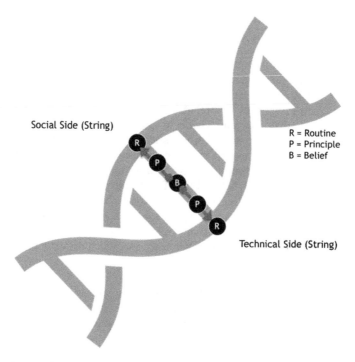

Fig. 4.5.   Changes Transmitted Across Both the Social and Technical Sides of the Organizational Deoxyribonucleic Acid (DNA).

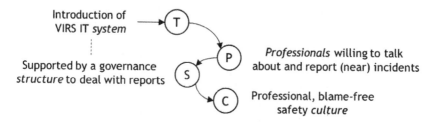

S = Structure, T = Technology, C = Culture, P = People

Fig. 4.6.   Change Pathways for Implementing Voluntary Incident Reporting System (VIRS).

P16. Transformations and Renewals are achievable through two pathways: either initiated in the social string and followed by the technical string or initiated in the technical string and followed by the social string.

P15 and *P16* explain why organizational changes, especially Transformations and Renewals, are difficult to implement. Transformation – the deepest type of change – requires a modification at the core level of beliefs, and thus also requires modifications in principles and routines that are mirrored on both the social and technical sides of the interconnected strings. Similarly, Renewal – a deep change – requires modifications in both principles and routines that are mirrored on both the social and technical sides of the interconnected strings. Thus, both Transformations and Renewals can be construed as a systematic "genetic" manipulation of the existing organizational DNA into a new, desired organizational DNA. *P14* also shows that we must learn to distinguish between Improvement, Renewal, and Transformation before selecting a change strategy. Transformations and Renewals require strategies focusing on approaches and actions in both the social and technical strings. Because these strategies focus on both strings, the organizational DNA will therefore be altered, regardless of the origin of the change (i.e., originating in the social or technical string). By contrast, Improvements – shallow changes – require strategies focusing on either social or technical approaches and actions that do not need to be mirrored on the other side of the interconnected string. Therefore, we conclude with the following proposition:

> *P17.* Both Transformations and Renewals alter organizational DNA, requiring an integral and holistic process that architecturally restructures the interconnection of the social and technical strings.

CASE STUDY: APPLYING RPBS IN PRACTICE IN A HEALTHCARE SETTING

As the strength of a theory is in its feasibility in practice, we focus on a case about a failing change process that is exemplary for many organizations in order to show RPB's explanatory power. The executive board of an academic hospital in the Netherlands concluded that its professional culture and the mindset of its professionals led individuals to avoid speaking about incidents or near-miss incidents, yet the board believed a hospital can only improve its safety record by learning from its mistakes. Therefore, the board decided to introduce a new principle by implementing a voluntary incident reporting system (VIRS), which was an information technology (IT) system for reporting incidents supported by a governance structure to handle the incidents. The purpose of this change was to enact a shift in professional routines from nonreporting to reporting incidents.

A year after the implementation, the executive board wondered why VIRS was hardly used by its medical and nursing professionals and why the nonreporting routines were not changed. The VIRS implementation turned out to be a failure. What went wrong? The hospital's problem was clearly social: the existence of a professional culture of nonreporting, creating an organizational environment that was blame-free, nontransparent, and not structurally organized to facilitate learning from mistakes. The board's solution, on the other hand, was technical: they introduced a new principle (i.e., a protocol with an IT system) aimed at shifting from a nonreporting to a reporting routine among professionals. Applying our theory of organizational DNA, we therefore question: Why did VIRS fail?

In the case of VIRS, the theory of organizational DNA recommends an examination of the beliefs underlying the technical solution and the social situation in order to determine the nature of the change, as described by *P14*. Further, *P16* helps us understand the actual pathway in which the hospital intended to introduce the VIRS IT system. In this instance, change was initiated in the technical string with the introduction of a technical solution – the VIRS IT system. This was supported with a governance structure to encourage professionals to talk about and report incidents (including near-miss incidents) and to establish a professional blame-free safety culture, ultimately connecting to the social string. We analyzed this technical-triggered change pathway with the socio-technical core aspects: technology (T) and structure (S) and people (P) and culture (C). That is, in the organization's core technical aspects, the change was initiated with the introduction of technology (T) and accompanied by a governance structure (S) to support the technology's adoption. In the organization's core social aspects, the change involved people (P) – healthcare professionals – who would use the technology to address incidents and, ultimately, influence the organization's safety culture (C). Fig. 4.6 visualizes this.

Exploring the associated RPBs within this case, the hospital sought to change the *routine* of nonreporting, informed by a changed *principle* with the introduction of the VIRS technology and supporting structure. The *technical belief* set underlying this changed principle was that learning is key for safety improvement and that administrative tasks and procedures (e.g., reporting to management) are a key part of a professional's duty. In contrast, the *social belief* set underlying the organization's culture and professional routine of nonreporting at the time of the change was twofold, rooted in professionalism (Friedson, 1999) and normative isomorphism (DiMaggio & Powell, 1983).

The first belief that professionals held concerned their own role in healthcare. They believed their job comprised only those actions directly related to delivering care to patients; all other tasks, like reporting, did not align with their professional purpose of delivering care, and thus, were not their main professional responsibility. Their second belief was that, as medical professionals, their work could only be assessed and monitored by fellow medical professionals. Therefore, nonmedical professionals, like administrators and managers, could and should not interfere with their day-to-day professional work. These two *beliefs* translated into the *principle* that only medical professionals could monitor, assess, and correct the behaviors of medical professionals (i.e., collegial learning and correcting (Friedson, 1999)), which led to a closed system and culture that was inaccessible for nonprofessionals. Fig. 4.7 visualizes the clash of beliefs between the technical solution and the social situation.

As long as such a clash between beliefs existed, the initiated change could not restructure organizational DNA, and consequently, the success of the VIRS

Clash between Belief Sets

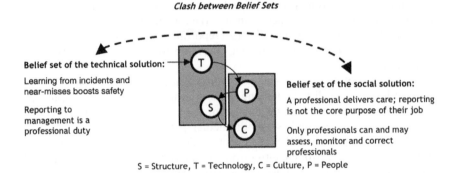

Fig. 4.7.   Clash Between Technical Solution and Social Situation Belief Sets.

introduction remained unfeasible. If instead the executive board had considered the organization's underlying RPBs, the gap between both the technical and social beliefs would have been clear, and with it, a feasible change strategy could have been designed. Fig. 4.8 applies the theory of organizational DNA to explain the failure of the VIRS change as a result of associated RPBs.

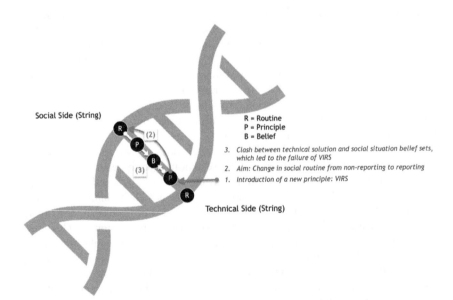

Fig. 4.8.   Theory of Organizational Deoxyribonucleic Acid (DNA) Applied to the Voluntary Incident Reporting System (VIRS) Example to Explain Change Failure.

APPLYING RPBS IN CHANGE PRACTICE

How can RPB-thinking support managers and leaders to get sustainable change results? The theory of organizational DNA and its consideration of associated RPBs helps them in a three-step sequence. First, it is important to identify the nature of the change, described by *P14* as one of RPB. Second, it is important to note the depth of change and how it will affect other levels of the interconnected social and technical strings, as described by *P15*. For instance, a Transformation requires modification of beliefs and principles to influence routines successfully; a Renewal requires modification of principles to influence routines successfully; and, an Improvement requires modification only at the level of the routine (e.g., De Caluwe & Vermaak, 2003; Daft & Noe, 2001). Third, in case of a Transformation and a Renewal, both social and technical strings are subject to change, as addressed in *P9*, *P10*, *P12*, *P16*, and *P17*. Only by addressing associated RPBs can a desired change – initiated in the social or technical strings – be effective, triggered by genetic and sustainable alterations of organizational DNA.

CONCLUSION

The theory of organizational DNA and its consideration of the role of RPBs enables managers and leaders to understand change processes more profoundly and to act as change agents more effectively. The strength of this theory depends upon its usability, including its utility in identifying change pathways, designing optimal change strategies, and implementing changes successfully. To bear the title of a "practical theory," the theory of organizational DNA needs further testing in various organizational contexts and change situations. Therefore, we invite practitioners and scholars to expand the present work by testing and translating the theory of organizational DNA into useful and effective change strategies and approaches. Strategies and approaches that provide organizations with systematic and sustainable change results are critically needed in the ever-growing dynamic organizational context. We believe the theory of organizational DNA builds that foundation.

REFERENCES

Achterbergh, J., & Vriens, D. (2010). *Organizations: Social systems conducting experiments.* Springer.
Alexander, J. A., & D'Aunno, T. A. (1990). Transformation of institutional environments: Perspectives on the corporatization of US health care. In S. S. Mick & associates (Eds.), *Innovations in health care delivery: Insights for organization theory* (pp. 53–85). Jossey-Bass.
Amelsvoort, P. J. L. M. (2000). *The design of work and organisation: The modern sociotechnical systems approach: An overview of the Dutch sociotechnical systems theory.* ST-GROEP.
Argyris, C., & Schon, D. (1978). *Organizational learning: A theory of action perspective.* Addison-Wesley.
Barnett, W. P. (1990). The organizational ecology of the chronological system. *Administrative Science Quarterly, 35*(1), 31–60.
Bartunek, J. M., & Moch, M. K. (1987). First-order, second-order, and third-order change and organization development interventions: A cognitive approach. *The Journal of Applied Behavioral Science, 23*(4), 483–500.

Beer, S. (1985). *Diagnosing the system for organizations.* Wiley.

Cabana, M. D., Rand, C. S., Powe, N. R., Wu, A. W., Wilson, M. H., Abboud, P. A. C., & Rubin, H. R. (1999). Why don't physicians follow clinical practice guidelines?: A framework for improvement. *JAMA, 282*(15), 1458–1465.

Cherns, A. (1987). Principles of sociotechnical design revisited. *Human Relations, 40*(3), 153–161.

Daft, R. L., & Noe, R. A. (2001). *Organizational behavior.* Harcourt College Publishers.

Davis, L. E. (1975). Developments in job design. In P. Warr (Ed.), *Personnel goals and job design* (pp. 1–38). Wiley.

De Caluwe, L., & Vermaak, H. (2003). *Learning to change: A guide for organization change agents.* Sage.

De Sitter, L. U., den Hertog, F., & Dankbaar, B. (1997). From complex organizations with simple jobs to simple organizations with complex jobs. *Human Relations, 50*(5), 497–534.

DiMaggio, P. J., & Powell, W. W. (1983). The iron cage revisited: Institutional isomorphism and collective rationality in organizational fields. *American Sociological Review, 48*, 147–160.

Dooley, K. J. (1997). A complex adaptive systems model of organization change. *Nonlinear Dynamics, Psychology, and Life Sciences, 1*(1), 69–97.

Emery, F. E. (1959). *Characteristics of socio-technical systems.* Tavistock Institute Document 527. Revised in Design of Jobs, L. E. Davis & J. C. Taylor (Eds.), (Vol. 11, pp. 157–186). Penguin Books, 1972.

Feldman, M. S., & Pentland, B. T. (2003). Reconceptualizing organizational routines as a source of flexibility and change. *Administrative Science Quarterly, 48*(1), 94–118.

Fleuren, B. P. I., Stephenson, A. L., Sullivan, E. E., Raj, M., Tietschert, M. V., Sriharan, A., Lai, A. Y., DePuccio, M. J., Thomas, S. C., & McAlearney, A. S. (2021). Even superheroes need rest: A guide to facilitating recovery from work for health-care workers during COVID-19 and beyond. In J. L. Hefner & I. M. Nembhard (Eds.), *The contributions of health care management to grand health care challenges.* Advances in health care management (Vol. 20, pp. 273–282). Emerald Publishing Limited.

Friedson, E. (1999). Theory of professionalism: Method and substance. *International Review of Sociology, 9*(1), 117–129.

Galbraith, J. R. (1973). *Designing complex organizations.* Addison-Wesley.

Gaynor, M., Ho, K., & Town, R. J. (2015). The industrial organization of health-care markets. *Journal of Economic Literature, 53*(2), 235–284.

George, J. M. (2014). Compassion and capitalism: Implications for organizational studies. *Journal of Management, 40*(1), 5–15.

Goldratt, E. M. (1985). *Haystack syndrome: Shifting information out of the data ocean.* North River Press.

Govers, M. J. G., & van Amelsvoort, P. J. L. M. (2023). A theoretical essay on socio-technical systems design thinking in the era of digital transformation. *Gruppe. Interaktion. Organisation. Zeitschrift für Angewandte Organisationspsychologie (GIO), 54*, 27–40.

Greenhalgh, T., Wherton, J., Papoutsi, C., Lynch, J., Hughes, G., A'Court, C., Hinder, S., Fahy, N., Procter, R., & Shaw, S. (2017). Beyond adoption: A new framework for theorizing and evaluating nonadoption, abandonment, and challenges to the scale-up, spread, and sustainability of health and care technologies. *Journal of Medical Internet Research, 19*(11), e367. https://doi.org/10.2196/jmir.8775

Hannan, M. T., & Freeman, J. (1989). *Organization and social structure.* Harvard University Press.

Hannan, M. T., Polos, L., & Carroll, G. R. (2007). *Logics of organization theory: Audiences, code and ecologies.* Princeton University Press.

Hefner, J. L., & Nembhard, I. M. (Eds.). (2021). *The contributions of health care management to grand health care challenges.* Advanced in health care management (Vol. 20). Emerald Publishing Limited.

Howard-Grenville, J. A. (2005). The persistence of flexible organizational routines: The role of agency and organizational context. *Organization Science, 16*(6), 618–636.

Kuipers, H., van Amelsvoort, P., & Kramer, E. (2020). *New ways of organizing. Alternatives to bureaucracy.* ACCO.

Litwin, A. S. (2021). Technological change and frontline care delivery work: Toward the quadruple aim. In J. L. Hefner & I. M. Nembhard (Eds.), *The contributions of health care management to grand health care challenges*. Advances in health care management (Vol. 20, pp. 99–142). Emerald Publishing Limited.

Luhmann, N. (1995). *Social systems*. Stanford University Press.

Mannheim, K. (1940). *Man and society in an age of reconstruction: Studies in modern social structure*. Harcourt, Brace.

Mayo, A. T., Myers, C. G., & Sutcliffe, K. M. (2021). Organizational science and health care. *The Academy of Management Annals, 15*(2), 537–576.

Meyer, J. W., & Rowan, B. (1977). Institutionalized organizations: Formal structure as myth and ceremony. *American Journal of Sociology, 83*(2), 340–363.

Mohr, D., & van Amelsvoort, P. (Eds.). (2015). *Co-creating humane and innovative organizations: Evolutions in the practice of socio-technical system design*. Global STS-D Network.

Moore, H., Dishman, L., & Fick, J. (2021). The challenge of employee retention in medical practices across the United States: An exploratory investigation into the relationship between operational succession planning and employee turnover. In J. L. Hefner & I. M. Nembhard (Eds.), *The contributions of health care management to grand health care challenges* (Vol. 20, pp. 45–75). Emerald Publishing Limited.

Morgan, G. (2006). *Images of organization* (updated ed.). Sage.

Nembhard, I. M., Alexander, J. A., Hoff, T. J., & Ramanujam, R. (2009). Why does the quality of health care continue to lag? Insights from management research. *Academy of Management Perspectives, 23*(1), 24–42.

OECD/EU. (2018). *Health at a glance: Europe 2018: State of health in the EU cycle*. OECD Publishing. https://doi.org/10.1787/health_glance_eur-2018-en

Pava, C. (1983). *Managing new office technology: An organizational strategy*. Simon & Schuster.

Reay, T., Goodrick, E., & D'Aunno, T. (2021). *Health care research and organization theory*. Cambridge University Press.

Rittel, H. W. J., & Webber, M. M. (1973). Dilemmas in a general theory of planning. *Policy Sciences, 4*(2), 155–169.

Scott, W. R. (1987). The adolescence of institutional theory. *Administrative Science Quarterly, 32*(4), 493–511.

Scott, W. R., & Meyer, J. W. (1994). *Institutional environments and organizations: Structural complexity and individualism*. Sage.

Standing, C., Standing, S., McDermott, M., Gururajan, R., & Kiani Mavi, R. (2016). The paradoxes of telehealth: A review of the literature 2000–2015. *Systemic Research, 33*(1), 113–125.

Trist, E. L., & Bamforth, K. W. (1951). Some social and psychological consequences of the longwall-method of coal getting. *Human Relations, 4*(1), 6–24, 37–38.

Trist, E. L., Higging, G. W., Murray, H., & Pollock, A. B. (1963). *Organizational choice*. Tavistock.

Vriens, D., & Achterbergh, J. (2011). Cybernetically sound organizational structures I: De Sitter's design theory. *Kybernetes, 40*(3), 405–424.

Watson, J. D., & Crick, F. H. (1953). Molecular structure of nucleic acids: A structure for deoxyribose nucleic acid. *Nature, 171*(4356), 737–738.

Weber, M. (1978). *Economy and society: An outline of interpretive sociology*. University of California Press.

Will, K. K., Johnson, M. L., & Lamb, G. (2019). Team-based care and patient satisfaction in the hospital setting: A systematic review. *Journal of Patient-Centered Research and Reviews, 6*(2), 158.

Zucker, L. G. (1987). Institutional theories of organization. *Annual Review of Sociology, 13*, 443–464.

CHAPTER 5

INNOVATION DIFFUSION ACROSS 13 SPECIALTIES AND ASSOCIATED CLINICIAN CHARACTERISTICS

Zhanna Novikov[a], Sara J. Singer[b] and Arnold Milstein[c]

[a]UTHealth Houston, USA
[b]Stanford University, USA
[c]Stanford University School of Medicine, USA

ABSTRACT

Diffusion of innovations, defined as the adoption and implementation of new ideas, processes, products, or services in health care, is both particularly important and especially challenging. One known problem with adoption and implementation of new technologies is that, while organizations often make innovations immediately available, organizational actors are more wary about adopting new technologies because these may impact not only patients and practices but also reimbursement. As a result, innovations may remain underutilized, and organizations may miss opportunities to improve and advance. As innovation adoption is vital to achieving success and remaining competitive, it is important to measure and understand factors that impact innovation diffusion. Building on a survey of a national sample of 654 clinicians, our study measures the extent of diffusion of value-enhancing care delivery innovations (i.e., technologies that not only improve quality of care but has potential to reduce care cost by diminishing waste, Faems et al., 2010) for 13 clinical specialties and identifies healthcare-specific individual characteristics such as: professional purview, supervisory responsibility, financial incentive, and clinical tenure associated with innovation diffusion. We also examine the association of innovation diffusion with perceived value of one

Research and Theory to Foster Change in the Face of Grand Health Care Challenges
Advances in Health Care Management, Volume 22, 97–115

ISSN: 1474-8231/doi:10.1108/S1474-823120240000022005

type of care delivery innovation – artificial intelligence (AI) – for assisting clinicians in their clinical work. Responses indicate that less than two-thirds of clinicians were knowledgeable about and aware of relevant value-enhancing care delivery innovations. Clinicians with broader professional purview, more supervisory responsibility, and stronger financial incentives had higher innovation diffusion scores, indicating greater knowledge and awareness of value-enhancing, care delivery innovations. Higher levels of knowledge of the innovations and awareness of their implementation were associated with higher perceptions of the value of AI-based technology. Our study contributes to our knowledge of diffusion of innovation in healthcare delivery and highlights potential mechanisms for speeding innovation diffusion.

Keywords: Diffusion of innovation; value-based care innovations; AI-based technology; healthcare organizations management; survey

INTRODUCTION

Over 50 years ago, Everett Rogers published his theory of the diffusion of innovation, which he defined as the "adoption and implementation of new ideas, processes, products or services" (Rogers, 1962) to explain how and when new ideas spread in organizations. Today, innovation diffusion is still a critical challenge, as now more than ever organizations must find ways to incorporate new ideas, processes, and technologies to effectively compete. In health care, for example, a variety of innovations, including those that rely on changes in personnel, process, culture, and technology, offer promise of substantial improvement in the value of healthcare delivery. Yet, innovation adopters still face barriers (Stornelli et al., 2021). One known problem with adoption and implementation of value-enhancing, care delivery innovations is that while organizations often make innovations immediately available, organizational actors are more wary about adopting new approaches. As a result, innovations remain underutilized, and organizations miss opportunities to improve and advance (Adams et al., 2006). As innovation adoption is vital for organizations to achieve success and remain competitive, it is important to measure and understand the factors that impact innovation diffusion (O'Reilly & Tushman, 2004).

Diffusion of value-enhancing, care delivery innovations in health care is both particularly important and especially challenging. On one hand, stakeholders encourage healthcare organizations to adopt and implement novel practices, procedures, and treatments in order to promote advanced care at the lowest possible cost (Bloem et al., 2017). On the other, healthcare professionals may be wary about adopting new technologies and methods of treatment because they may impact not only patients and practice but also reimbursement. Employees are naturally resistant to changes as changes might lead to loss of status, pay, or comfort (Dent & Goldberg, 1999). Clinicians, therefore, may not rush to diffuse innovations because when adopted and implemented inappropriately, change in care delivery could cause clinical harm and financial and reputational damage (Balas & Chapman, 2018). Ultimately, although value-enhancing care delivery innovations may be embraced at healthcare system and organizational levels, innovations diffuse in practice when healthcare professionals and teams adopt and implement them. Therefore, healthcare professionals play a key role in innovation diffusion by transmitting information regarding availability and performance of care delivery innovations to colleagues (Balas & Chapman, 2018). This inter-colleague diffusion of information occurs through knowledge sharing mechanisms such as professional and social interactions, formal and informal communication, and meetings of professional associations (Fitzgerald et al., 2002). Having knowledge of the existence of innovative ideas and being cognizant of their successful implementation is critical for facilitating their diffusion within organizations (Dearing & Cox, 2018).

Research has shown that individual differences can play a significant role in shaping the success of innovation diffusion efforts, and that these factors interact with organizational context. Factors such as gender, age, and educational background can impact the adoption and implementation of innovative practices (Zhang et al., 2015). Furthermore, different types of innovations, such as technological versus process innovations, may require different skill sets and knowledge to be successfully implemented (Damanpour & Schneider, 2006). Given that individuals vary in their diffusion of care delivery innovations, identifying characteristics of individuals that support value-enhancing care delivery innovations diffusion in health care could increase the ability of those seeking to encourage it to improve the quality of care.

Building on a national sample of 654 clinicians, our study measures the extent of diffusion of value-enhancing care delivery innovations for 13 clinical specialties and identifies individual healthcare-related characteristics associated with diffusion of innovation: professional purview, financial incentive, supervisory responsibility, and clinical tenure. We also evaluate the relationship between knowledge and awareness of current and future care delivery innovations and clinicians' perceived value of one type of care delivery innovation – artificial intelligence (AI) – for assisting them in their clinical work. In doing so, our study contributes to our knowledge of diffusion of innovation in healthcare delivery and highlights potential mechanisms for speeding innovation diffusion.

BACKGROUND

Diffusion of Innovation

Diffusion of innovation in health care is considered a social process that occurs among people in response to learning about an innovation, such as a new evidence-based approach for extending or improving health care (Dearing & Cox, 2018). Focusing on how individuals spread innovations within and across organizations, diffusion of innovation theory suggests the innovation itself, communication channels through which information about novel sources of innovation transmits, social systems consisting of interrelated units engaged in achieving a common goal, and time, i.e., the timeline between becoming aware of an innovation and its implementation, are key elements of innovation diffusion

(Rogers, 1962, 1995). According to innovation diffusion theory, two important factors impact the timeline to innovation implementation – individual knowledge of the innovations and awareness of their implementation – and these factors are often impacted by adopter characteristics (Zhang et al., 2015).

Knowledge of the Innovation and Awareness of Its Implementation

Knowledge is the first requirement for deciding to adopt and diffuse an innovation. Becoming knowledgeable of an innovation means becoming aware of the existence of the innovation and learning about its potential for assisting with clinical care (Rogers, 1962). In becoming knowledgeable, individuals explore and investigate pros and cons of the innovation to determine whether they and their organization should adopt and implement it. When individuals acquire knowledge of an innovation, they may transmit their impressions of the innovation to other organizational actors (Balas & Chapman, 2018). Awareness of an innovation's implementation is also important. When clinicians become aware of organizations that are currently implementing innovations or are planning to implement them, their trust in possible positive outcomes increases relative to their hesitation to change, and their desire to adopt innovations goes up. Taken together, knowledge of the innovation and awareness of its implementation determines how and when innovations will be diffused within and across healthcare organizations (Fitzgerald et al., 2002).

Characteristics of New Adopters

Rogers (1995) characterized innovation adopters according to their willingness to adopt, as innovators (representing about 2.5% of the market), early adopters (13.5%), early majority (34%), late majority (34%), and laggards (16%). In research exploring diffusion of innovation in various settings, studies suggest that individual characteristics and behaviors are positively associated with adopter segments (Zhang et al., 2015). For example, studies found that the two earliest groups of adopters (innovators and early adopters) were characterized by high income, innovativeness (i.e., individual's willingness to change his or her familiar practices), inward focus (i.e., self-efficacy and market "mavenism," being knowledgeable about the market), and previous technology usage and digital skills associated with innovation adoption and diffusion (Dedehayir et al., 2017; Van Braak, 2001). The early majority, those willing to adopt innovations just before the average person, were usually educated individuals, also with high levels of income. The late majority were characterized by skepticism, often adopting innovations only as a result of peer pressure (Haider & Kreps, 2004). Laggards have been characterized by lower incomes and education and show brand loyalty (Uhl et al., 1970).

Understanding which healthcare-related characteristics associate with adopter segments would enable healthcare leaders to speed up dissemination of innovations at the early stages and ensure adoption and implementation across the full spectrum of innovation diffusion. However, most research exploring adopter characteristics has focused on organizational settings outside of health care. Research has yet to explore individual characteristics associated with their innovation adoption, despite evidence suggesting that innovators' characteristics vary by type of innovation (Dedehayir et al., 2017). In this study, we aim to measure care delivery innovations for 13 clinical specialties and to identify adopter characteristics that are relevant to diffusion of innovation in healthcare settings. Specifically, we examine the role of professional purview, supervisory responsibility, financial incentives, and clinical tenure in clinicians' knowledge and awareness of current and future implementation of value-enhanced care delivery innovations, and the relationship between knowledge and awareness of current and future innovation implementation and clinicians' perceived value of AI.

METHODS

Survey Development

The Clinical Excellence Research Center at Stanford University School of Medicine developed the "High-Value Care Method Adoption Survey" to gain knowledge and awareness of the implementation of 62 value-enhancing, innovative approaches recently documented in the clinical literature. For example, primary care providers received questions pertaining to selected aspects of primary care, clinically fragile patients with chronic disease, technology-enabled ambulatory care, high-need high-cost care, dementia care, prescription medication care, spine pain care, ambulatory surgical care, stroke prevention, and acute care (see appendix Table A1 for detail on care delivery domains relevant for each medical specialty).

Following Rogers's (1962, 1995) conceptualization of innovation diffusion, the survey was designed so that individual respondents would answer three questions for each care delivery innovation that applied to their specialty: one focused on *knowledge of the innovations*: "Have you heard of a care method similar to this?"; a second focused on *awareness of current implementation*: "Are you aware of a care organization in your region or state currently using a similar care method?"; and a third focused on *awareness of future implementation*: "Are you aware of a care organization in your region or state planning to use a similar care method?" Yes/no response options were offered for each question. To remove order bias, the survey randomized the order of care delivery innovations and concepts within care delivery innovations displayed to respondents, unless the order was inherent to the care delivery innovation.

The survey also asked participants three questions about their perceptions of the value of AI for assisting them in their clinical work in (1) *clinical decision support*: "assistance for clinicians in identifying clinically important health risk factors, diagnoses, and treatment plan elements," (2) *physical action support*: "assistance for clinicians in detecting and correcting deviations from the physical actions required by the treatment plan, e.g., hand hygiene before patient contact," (3) *automating documentation*: "automating documentation in the electronic health record of verbal interactions and physical examination activity occurring during in-person or virtual patient–clinician interaction." Each of these items measuring *perceived value of AI assistance* used a 10-point rating scale, with 10 indicating the highest value.

In addition to professional specialty, the survey asked four questions about participants. One item measured *professional purview*: "Generally, how broad is your understanding of the nature of care delivery in your clinical specialty." A second item measured *financial incentive*: "What percentage (%) of your total annual professional services income is determined by your performance on measures of cost of care and/or quality." A third item measured *supervisory responsibility*: "What is your level of supervisory responsibility?" Lastly, one item measured *clinical tenure*: "How long have you been practicing clinically, excluding years spent in training programs?"

Survey length differed for different specialties, depending on the number of care delivery innovations relevant for that specialty. Survey length ranged from 5 minutes to 15 minutes.

Sample

The final sample for this survey included a total of 654 frontline clinicians, consisting of random samples of 50 healthcare professionals from 13 medical specialties drawn from Medscape's proprietary market research panel of practicing health professionals who joined Medscape to access its clinical content. Healthcare professionals who do not opt out of market research participation can be sampled for a research study.

To achieve the desired sample, 1,255 respondents accessed Medscape's survey link. Of these, 290 did not qualify because they did not select a valid role (220) or valid speciality (39) or because they were hospital-based pharmacists (31). An additional 311 qualified for specialities that already had 50 respondents by the time they accessed the survey link.

Survey Administration

Medscape administered the survey from November to December 2020. Sample members received invitation and reminder emails if they did not respond.

Measures

Independent Variables. We treated the four demographic items as independent variables: professional purview, financial incentive, supervisory responsibility, and clinical tenure. For each, we created categorical variables, with categories representing four levels of purview (from *limited to the clinical unit where I work* to *extends across multiple states*), four levels of financial incentive (based on quartiles of percentage income at risk for quality), three levels of supervisory responsibility (from *none* to *supervisory responsibility across multiple care delivery units*), and four levels of clinical tenure (from *less than 5 years* to *more than 25 years*), respectively.

Dependent Variables. We created variables measuring the three dimensions of innovation diffusion for the specialty-specific, care delivery innovations for each of the 20 domains of care delivery captured in the survey: *knowledge of the innovations, awareness of current implementation,* and *awareness of future implementation.* For each diffusion innovation dimension within each clinical specialty, we counted the number of 'yes' responses for each value-enhancing innovation, indicating that respondents knew about or were aware of its current or future implementation, respectively. We also created variables measuring the three dimensions of perceived value of AI assistance, focused on *identifying health risk factors, diagnoses, and treatment elements; detecting/correcting deviations from treatment plan;* and *automating documentation.*

Analysis

We used descriptive statistics to report overall diffusion of innovation in terms of clinicians' knowledge of care delivery innovations, awareness of current and future implementation of care delivery innovations, and perceived value of AI technology. We first calculated the average percentage of respondents in each professional discipline reporting knowledge of the care delivery innovations and awareness of current and future implementation (Fig. 5.1). Next, we calculated innovation diffusion scores for knowledge of the innovations, awareness of current implementation, and awareness of future implementation for each respondent in the sample, as well as a summative score measuring total innovation knowledge and awareness. For this purpose, we first calculated the sum of the number of innovations a respondent reported as known, currently implemented, or planned to be implemented. We converted these to proportions by dividing this sum of known, currently implemented, and planned to be implemented innovations by the total number of innovations offered to a respondent. We created a total innovation knowledge and awareness score by summing scores for knowledge, current, and future implementation. We performed bivariate analyses to assess differences in knowledge of the innovations, awareness of current and future implementation, and total innovation knowledge and awareness. Because subgroups for health-related individual characteristics had unequal sample sizes and were not normally distributed, we performed a Kruskal–Wallis H test, a nonparametric alternative to ANOVA that requires neither of these assumptions (Hettmansperger & McKean, 1998), followed by a Mann-Whitney *U*-test (Corder & Foreman, 2014) to determine the effect size for professional purview, financial performance incentives, supervisory responsibility, and clinical tenure on innovation awareness scores. We converted clinical tenure into two categories: less than 16 years and 16 years and more to increase robustness of our results. We adjusted for pairwise comparisons within each row (measuring the differences in knowledge of the innovations, awareness of current and future implementation, and total innovation knowledge and awareness scores among each characteristic) using Bonferroni correction. We performed linear regression analysis to test the

relationship between knowledge of the innovations, awareness of current implementation, awareness of future implementation, and total innovation knowledge
and awareness scores as independent variables and the value of AI technology as
dependent variables.

RESULTS

Respondent Characteristics

Table 5.1 summarizes characteristics of our survey sample. Most respondents
(75.3%) claimed that their professional purview extended at least to the city,
region, or state where they provided care, if not across multiple states. Most also
reported supervisory responsibility across or within a care delivery unit (55.4%);
limited, i.e., 0%–25%, income at risk (68.5%); and clinical tenure between 6 and
25 years (63.6%).

Table 5.1. Sample Characteristics.

Characteristics	Percentage of Respondents
Professional purview	
Limited to the clinical unit where I work	5.5
Limited to the healthcare organization where I work	19.1
Limited to the city, region, or state where I provide care	36.5
Extends across multiple states	38.8
Supervisory responsibility	
No supervisory responsibility	29.7
Supervisory responsibility across or within a care delivery unit	55.4
Supervisory responsibility across multiple care delivery units	15.0
Financial incentive (% income at risk)	
0%–25%	68.5
26%–50%	16.4
51%–75%	10.6
76%–100%	4.6
Clinical tenure	
Less than 5 years	15.1
Between 6 and 15 years	38.1
Between 16 and 25 years	25.5
More than 25 years	21.3
Less than 5 years	15.1

Note: N = 654.

Knowledge and Awareness of Current and Future Implementations Overall and by Clinical Specialty

Overall among respondents, 61.5% reported knowledge of value-enhancing, care delivery innovations relevant for their clinical specialty, 63.2% were aware of current implementation of the innovations by a care organization in their region or state, and 50.4% were aware of planned future implementation of the innovations by a care organization in the region or state (Table 5.2). Across medical specialties, more respondents reported knowledge of care delivery innovations than awareness of current implementation of care delivery innovations, and of planned future implementation, respectively. However, most respondents who reported knowledge of care delivery innovations also reported awareness of organizations currently implementing or planning to implement these innovations. About 75% of the clinicians were aware of at least one of the care delivery innovations relevant for their specialty.

Fig. 5.1 reports descriptive results by specialty. Knowledge of care delivery innovations ranged from 73.3% among obstetricians to 24.2% among emergency department doctors. Awareness of current implementation of care delivery innovations ranged from 70.7% among hospital nurses to 18% among emergency department doctors. Awareness of future implementation of care delivery innovations ranged from 61.4% among pharmacists to 12.6% among emergency department doctors. In general, emergency department doctors, neurologists, and paramedics consistently demonstrated lower levels of innovation diffusion across all three measures, while specialties with higher levels of innovation diffusion were more mixed. Innovation diffusion reported by pharmacists put their specialty among the top three for each of the three measures and oncologists in the top three twice.

Relationship of Clinician Characteristics with Innovation Diffusion

Tables 5.2a and 5.2b report results of bivariate analysis comparing innovation diffusion scores based on other clinician characteristics: their professional purview, supervisory responsibility, performance incentive, and clinical tenure. Respondents whose professional purview extended across multiple states had higher innovation diffusion scores (mean = 0.55, $p < 0.05$ for knowledge of the innovations, mean = 0.39, $p < 0.01$ for awareness of current implementation, mean = 0.33, $p < 0.05$ for awareness of future implementation, mean = 1.28, and $p < 0.01$ for total innovation knowledge and awareness) compared to respondents whose professional purview was more limited (mean ranging from 0.48 to 0.49 for knowledge of the innovations, mean 0.33 for awareness of current implementation, mean ranging from 0.23 to 0.28 for awareness of future implementation, and mean ranging from 1.06 to 1.09 for total innovation knowledge and awareness).

Respondents with higher responsibility, i.e., across multiple care delivery units had higher innovation diffusion scores (mean = 0.53, $p < 0.05$ for knowledge of the innovations, mean = 0.40, $p < 0.05$ for awareness of current implementation, mean = 0.34, $p < 0.01$ for awareness of future implementation, and mean = 1.27,

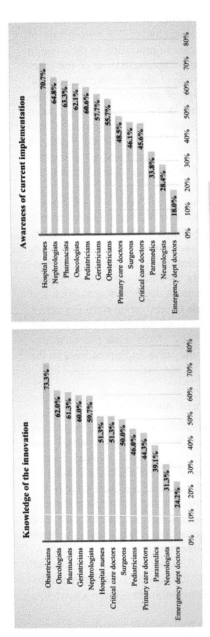

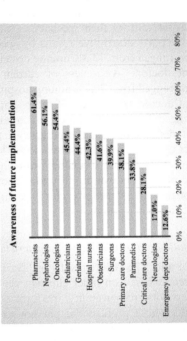

Fig. 5.1. Percent of Respondents Reporting Knowledge of the Innovations and Awareness of Its Current and Future Implementation by Professional Discipline.

Table 5.2a. Knowledge of the Innovations, Awareness of Current Implementation, and Awareness of Future Implementation, and Total Innovation Knowledge and Awareness by Individual Characteristics.

	All Respondents	Professional Purview					Supervisory Responsibility			
		Limited to My Unit (A)	Limited to My organization (B)	Limited to My Region (C)	Extends Across Multiple States (D)	Kruskal–Wallis Test Results	No Responsibility (A)	Across or Within a Care Delivery Unit (B)	Across Multiple Care Delivery Units (C)	Kruskal–Wallis Test Results
Percent of respondents reported knowledge about, and awareness of current and future implementation of care delivery innovations										
Knowledge of the innovations	61.5%	53.1%	56.7%	59.3%	65.9%		55.1%	63.3%	67.1%	
Awareness of current implementation	63.2%	48.3%	52.7%	58.6%	70.4%		53.9%	63.9%	71.9%	
Awareness of future implementation	50.4%	19.7%	34.6%	50.0%	59.5%		30.5%	53.7%	64.6%	
Innovation diffusion score[a]										
Knowledge of the innovations	0.51 (0.26)	0.49 (0.28)	0.49 (.27)	0.48 (0.25)	0.55 (.27) C B	H (3) = 8.58; $p < 0.05$	0.49 (0.25)	0.52 (0.27)	0.53 (0.27)	H (2) = 1.31; $p > 0.05$
Awareness of current implementation	0.35 (0.25)	0.33 (0.26)	0.33 (0.25)	0.33 (0.22)	0.39 (0.26) C B	H (3) = 12.88; $p < 0.01$	0.32 (0.24)	0.36 (.24)	0.40 (0.26) A	H (2) = 10.47; $p < 0.05$
Awareness of future implementation	0.29 (0.27)	0.23 (0.26)	0.24 (0.28)	0.28 (0.26)	0.33 (0.26) B C	H (3) = 17.39; $p < 0.05$	0.22 (0.24)	0.31 (0.26) A	.34 (.29) A	H (2) = 19.27; $p < 0.01$
Total innovation knowledge and awareness	1.16 (0.67)	1.06 (0.61)	1.06 (0.69)	1.09 (0.64)	1.28 (0.67) BC	H (3) = 17.08; $p < 0.01$	1.03 (0.62)	1.19 (0.67) A	1.27 (0.75) A	H (2) = 10.21; $p < 0.05$

[a]The results of innovation diffusion scores are based on Kruskal–Wallis no-parametric test analysis. Two-sided U tests applied for conducting post hoc tests with Bonferroni correction for multiple comparisons. Where letters accompany results, these represent significant differences in innovation scores between segments. For each significant ($p < 0.05$) pair, the letter of the compared smaller category appears in the category with the larger mean. For example, knowledge about care delivery innovations among clinicians whose professional purview extends across multiple states (mean = 0.55, SD = 0.27) is significantly higher (as indicated by the letter B) than that of clinicians whose professional purview is limited to their region (mean = 0.48, SD = 0.25).

Table 5.2b. Knowledge of the Innovations, Awareness of Current Implementation, and Awareness of Future Implementation, and Total Innovation Knowledge and Awareness by Individual Characteristics.

	All Respondents	Financial Incentive					Clinical Tenure		
		0%–25% (A)	26%–50% (B)	51%–75% (C)	76%–100% (D)	Kruskal–Wallis Test Results	Less than sixteen years (A)	Sixteen years and more (B)	Kruskal–Wallis Test Results
Knowledge of the innovations	61.5%	59.5%	62.8%	65.6%	58.8%		68.0%	50.9%	$H(3) = 14.28$; $p > 0.05$
Awareness of current implementation	63.2%	59.4%	64.7%	69.2%	61.2%		65.3%	46.9%	$H(3) = 22.18$; $p < 0.05$
Awareness of future implementation	50.4%	43.3%	55.3%	64.7%	58.9%		38.5%	28.6%	$H(3) = 25.22$; $p < 0.01$
Knowledge of the innovations	0.51 (0.26)	0.49 (0.26)	0.52 (0.24)	0.58 (0.28) A	0.62 (0.30) A	$H(3) = 14.28$; $p < 0.01$	0.50 (0.23)	0.52 (0.30)	$H(3) = 14.28$; $p > 0.05$
Awareness of current implementation	0.35 (0.25)	0.33 (0.23)	0.36 (0.22)	0.45 (0.28) A	0.51 (0.32) A	$H(3) = 22.18$; $p < 0.01$	0.36 (0.21) B	0.33 (0.27)	$H(3) = 22.18$; $p < 0.05$
Awareness of future implementation	0.29 (0.27)	0.26 (0.25)	0.32 (0.26)	0.39 (0.30) A	0.48 (0.34) A	$H(3) = 25.22$; $p < 0.01$	0.27 (0.22) B	0.24 (0.26)	$H(3) = 25.22$; $p < 0.01$
Total innovation knowledge and awareness	1.16 (0.67)	1.07 (0.63)	1.19 (0.64)	1.42 (0.77) A	1.61 (0.88) A	$H(3) = 25.74$; $p < 0.01$	1.14 (0.55) B	1.08 (0.70)	$H(3) = 25.74$; $p < 0.05$

$p < 0.05$ for total innovation knowledge and awareness) compared to respondents with less supervisory responsibility (mean ranging from 0.49 to 0.52 for knowledge of the innovations, mean ranging from 0.32 to 0.36 for awareness of current implementation, mean ranging from 0.22 to 0.31 for awareness of future implementation, and mean ranging from 1.03 to 1.19 for total innovation knowledge and awareness).

Respondents with stronger financial incentives (76–100% of total annual income determined by their performance on measures of the cost of care or quality) had higher innovation diffusion scores (mean = 0.62, $p < 0.01$ for knowledge of the innovation, mean =0.51, $p < 0.01$ for awareness of current implementation, mean = 0.48, $p < 0.01$ for awareness of future implementation, and mean = 1.61, $p < 0.01$ for total innovation knowledge and awareness) compared to respondents with weaker financial incentives (mean ranging from 0.49 to 0.58 for knowledge of the innovation, mean ranging from 0.33 to 0.45 for awareness of current implementation, mean ranging from 0.26 to 0.39 for awareness of future implementation, and mean ranging from 1.07 to 1.42 for total innovation knowledge and awareness).

Respondents with less clinical tenure (less than 16 years) compared to those with more clinical tenure (16 years or more) had higher awareness of current implementation (mean = 0.36 vs. 0.33), awareness of future implementation (mean = 0.27 vs. 0.24), and total innovation knowledge and awareness (mean = 1.14 vs. 1.08).

Relationship Between Innovation Diffusion Scores and Perceived Value of AI Assistance

Table 5.3 reports results of regression analysis relating respondents' innovation diffusion scores to their perceived value of AI assistance for clinical decision support, physical action support, and automating clinical documentation. Awareness of

Table 5.3. Regression Analysis: Relationship Between Knowledge of the Innovations, Awareness of Its Current and Future Implementation, and Perceived Value of AI Assistance.

Innovation Diffusion Score	Form of AI Assistance		
	Clinical Decision Support Est. (SE)	Physical Action Support Est. (SE)	Automating Clinical Documentation Est. (SE)
Knowledge of the innovations	0.45 (0.25)	1.15** (0.31)	0.28 (0.29)
Awareness of current implementation	0.71* (0.30)	1.43** (0.33)	0.12 (0.31)
Awareness of future implementation	0.45 (0.28)	1.12** (0.31)	0.17 (0.29)
Total innovation knowledge and awareness	0.23* (0.11)	0.54** (0.12)	0.08 (0.11)

$*p < 0.05; **p < 0.01$

current implementation and total innovation knowledge and awareness related positively to clinical decision support ($b = 0.71$, SE $= 0.30$, $p < 0.05$ and $b = 0.23$, SE $= 0.11$, $p < 0.05$, respectively). All innovation diffusion scores related positively to physical action support (knowledge of the innovations $b = 1.15$, SE $= 0.31$, $p < 0.01$; awareness of current implementation $b = 1.43$, SE $= 0.33$, $p < 0.01$; awareness of future implementation $b = 1.12$, SE $= 0.31$, $p < 0.01$; and total innovation knowledge and awareness $b = 0.54$, SE $= 0.12$, $p < 0.01$). Innovation diffusion scores did not relate to automating clinical documentation.

DISCUSSION

Innovation diffusion is critical for improving the value of care delivery, and through their knowledge of the innovations and awareness of their implementation, clinicians contribute to innovation diffusion. Our study found that not all clinicians were equally knowledgeable of value-enhancing, care delivery innovations relevant to their clinical specialties and aware of their current and future implementations. Overall, less than two-thirds of clinicians had knowledge and awareness of relevant value-enhancing care delivery innovations, though three-quarters of clinicians were aware of at least one care delivery innovation in their domain. The percentage of knowledge of the innovation and awareness of current and future implementation varied by clinicians' specialty, and individual characteristics of clinicians related to innovation diffusion scores. Clinicians with broader professional purview, higher supervisory responsibility, and stronger financial incentives had higher innovation diffusion scores, indicating greater knowledge and awareness of value-enhancing, care delivery innovations.

Study findings suggest moderate diffusion of value-enhancing, care delivery innovations. If the two-thirds or so of clinicians who reported knowledge about or awareness of implementation of care delivery innovations in their region had adopted the innovations themselves, the market share for value-enhancing innovation would penetrate well into the late majority adopters segment. However, we cannot assume awareness is equivalent to adoption. Achieving significant advances in value-based care sufficient for bending the proverbial cost curve will likely require moving further along Roger's adopter curve. Nevertheless, given clinicians key role in innovation diffusion (Balas & Chapman, 2018), their knowledge and awareness of innovations is a key first step.

Wide variation in knowledge and awareness among clinicians of different specialties suggest extra effort may be required among selected specialties. Pharmacists and oncologists reported the most knowledge of the innovations and awareness of their current and future implementation, while emergency department doctors, neurologists, and paramedics consistently demonstrated least innovation diffusion. Whether this is attributable to characteristics of these specialties or to qualities of the innovations available to these specialties is difficult to discern. One possibility is that emergency department doctors, neurologists, and paramedics face less pressure or have fewer incentives to improve value or remove waste relative to pharmacists, oncologists, and other clinicians. This would explain why they may be less familiar with innovations that improve value as opposed to quality only. Further research should examine this hypothesis and, if confirmed, policy actions may be required to motivate a quest for value in some specialties. Another possibility is that, given the nature of their work, emergency department doctors, neurologists, and paramedics may enjoy fewer opportunities for observing innovation implementations or sharing information with colleagues about them. Emergency doctors and paramedic clinicians typically do shift work, often at night, which may reduce their availability for participating in their organization's innovation efforts. Neurologists tend to work alone, in labs, consulting on cases or in clinic, which may limit their exposure to value-enhancing innovations.

Study findings also suggest that in the case of value-enhancing, care delivery innovations, supervisory responsibility, broad purview, strong financial incentives for quality performance, and less tenure are associated with earlier adoption of innovations. These findings add to the set of individual characteristics associated with adoption identified in previous literature (Dedehayir et al., 2017; Haider & Kreps, 2004; Uhl et al., 1970; Van Braak, 2001). Clinicians with less clinical tenure, often younger, may be less set in their ways and more open and curious about value-enhancing innovation (Woods et al., 2018). Clinicians who occupy higher levels in the organizational hierarchy (e.g., supervisors and clinicians with longer clinical tenure) and those with broader professional purview have greater opportunities for exposure to innovations. This highlights the important role that individuals with more power in organizations must play in leading innovation diffusion in their organizations. It also suggests that it could be helpful to intentionally expose clinicians with less supervisory responsibility and narrower professional purview to care delivery innovations in order to facilitate their adoption and implementation. Such efforts are important because lower level clinicians represent the majority of frontline personnel in health care, and they are vital to reach if innovations are to diffuse sufficiently in organizations. Engaging frontline clinicians in the innovation diffusion process is also critical as they can provide insights and feedback regarding care delivery innovation effectiveness (Tucker et al., 2008). Their engagement in decision-making about innovation also protects against resistance to change. Our findings related to financial incentives indicate that the greater the financial risk for quality performance the more clinicians may be motivated to learn about care delivery innovations. This finding implies a specific mechanism through which financial risk could enhance value-based care.

We also found that innovation diffusion scores indicating greater knowledge and awareness of value-enhancing, care delivery innovations related positively with perceptions of the perceived value of AI-based technology. This relationship was present specifically for perceptions of value of AI in assisting clinicians with clinical decision support and physical action support (deviations from physical actions required by the treatment plan), albeit not for automating clinical documentation, for which recognition of value was consistently high. This suggests that earlier adopters may have greater appreciation for the benefits or fewer concerns about the risks of innovation, at least in the case of AI-based technologies.

This study is not without limitations. First, the survey did not ask respondents directly whether they or their own organization has adopted the care delivery innovations in question, so we are unable to assess this measure of innovation diffusion. Nor did it ask about reasons why clinicians may have regarded a specific innovation as value-enhancing or not given their local needs and culture. Additional research should explore these questions. Second, the survey was administered once, so represents a snapshot in time of innovation diffusion. A subsequent survey is planned and will enable tracking of innovation diffusion over time. Third, we acknowledge that care delivery innovations in larger organizations are predominantly governed by priorities of senior-level managers; if, e.g., they prioritize maximizing fee-for-service (FFS) revenue, care delivery innovations that depress FFS revenue are less likely to be known to or adopted by clinicians. Fourth, our survey was conducted during the COVID-19 pandemic, which could have reduced innovation diffusion if attention and resources were diverted to urgent needs.

CONCLUSION

Our study, nevertheless, offers important insights for healthcare leaders and clinicians. To more rapidly and thoroughly diffuse innovations, layers of organizational actors beyond those with high supervisory responsibility and broad purview should be engaged. Financial incentives that put clinician income at higher risk for value may be a lever for motivating curiosity about value-enhancing innovations. Healthcare organization leaders should monitor the diffusion of innovation and encourage it by raising awareness of innovations and their potential to add value. Selected specialties may be more prone to inertia, requiring regulatory or institutional change.

ACKNOWLEDGEMENTS

This study was funded from pooled philanthropic gifts to Stanford University in support of its Clinical Excellence Research Center. The funders played no role in the design, conduct, or reporting of this research. The authors acknowledge Medscape, which administered the survey and provided the panel of clinicians for the study sample. We acknowledge early support of Thomas Huber DrPH for survey planning and execution.

REFERENCES

Adams, R., Bessant, J., & Phelps, R. (2006). Innovation management measurement: A review. *International Journal of Management Reviews, 8*(1), 21–47.
Balas, E. A., & Chapman, W. W. (2018). Road map for diffusion of innovation in health care. *Health Affairs, 37*(2), 198–204.
Bloem, B. R., Rompen, L., Vries, N. M. D., Klink, A., Munneke, M., & Jeurissen, P. (2017). ParkinsonNet: A low-cost health care innovation with a systems approach from The Netherlands. *Health Affairs, 36*(11), 1987–1996.

Corder, G. W., & Foreman, D. I. (2014). *Nonparametric statistics: A step-by-step approach*. Wiley.

Damanpour, F., & Schneider, M. (2006). Phases of the adoption of innovation in organizations: Effects of environment, organization and top managers. *British Journal of Management, 17*(3), 215–236.

Dearing, J. W., & Cox, J. G. (2018). Diffusion of innovations theory, principles, and practice. *Health Affairs, 37*(2), 183–190.

Dedehayir, O., Ortt, R. J., Riverola, C., & Miralles, F. (2017). Innovators and early adopters in the diffusion of innovations: A literature review. *International Journal of Innovation Management, 21*(08), 1740010.

Dent, E. B., & Goldberg, S. G. (1999). Challenging "resistance to change". *The Journal of Applied Behavioral Science, 35*(1), 25–41.

Faems, D., De Visser, M., Andries, P., & Van Looy, B. (2010). Technology alliance portfolios and financial performance: Value-enhancing and cost-increasing effects of open innovation. *Journal of Product Innovation Management, 27*(6), 785–796.

Fitzgerald, L., Ferlie, E., Wood, M., & Hawkins, C. (2002). Interlocking interactions, the diffusion of innovations in health care. *Human Relations, 55*(12), 1429–1449.

Haider, M., & Kreps, G. L. (2004). Forty years of diffusion of innovations: Utility and value in public health. *Journal of Health Communication, 9*(S1), 3–11.

Hettmansperger, T. P., & McKean, J. W. (1998). Robust nonparametric statistical methods. Kendall's Library of Statistics. Vol. 5 (1st ed., Rather than Taylor and Francis (2010) 2nd ed.). Edward Arnold, John Wiley and Sons, Inc. pp. xiv+467.

O Reilly, C. A., & Tushman, M. L. (2004). The ambidextrous organization. *Harvard Business Review, 82*(4), 74–83.

Rogers, E. M. (1962). *Diffusion of innovations*. The Free Press.

Rogers, E. M. (1995). *Diffusion of innovations* (4th ed.). The Free Press.

Stornelli, A., Ozcan, S., & Simms, C. (2021). Advanced manufacturing technology adoption and innovation: A systematic literature review on barriers, enablers, and innovation types. *Research Policy, 50*(6), 104229.

Tucker, A. L., Singer, S. J., Hayes, J. E., & Falwell, A. (2008). Front-line staff perspectives on opportunities for improving the safety and efficiency of hospital work systems. *Health Services Research, 43*(5p2), 1807–1829.

Uhl, K., Andrus, R., & Poulsen, L. (1970). How are laggards different? An empirical inquiry. *Journal of Marketing Research, 7*(1), 51–54.

Van Braak, J. (2001). Individual characteristics influencing teachers' class use of computers. *Journal of Educational Computing Research, 25*(2), 141–157.

Woods, S. A., Mustafa, M. J., Anderson, N., & Sayer, B. (2018). Innovative work behavior and personality traits: Examining the moderating effects of organizational tenure. *Journal of Managerial Psychology, 33*(1), 29–42.

Zhang, X., Doll, W. J., & Iacocca, K. (2015). Gender, age, and computer self-efficacy in relation to computer anxiety and the use of computers for healthcare information. *Information Technology & People, 28*(1), 78–101.

APPENDIX

Table A1. Care Delivery Domains and Value-Enhancing Innovations Relevant for Each Medical Specialty.

Medical Specialty	Relevant Care Delivery Domains	Examples of Value-Enhancing Care Delivery Innovations
Critical care doctors	Critical care	Economical physiological monitoring technology embedded in Emergency Department and non-ICU hospital beds triggers alerts to a mobile ICU team.
Emergency department doctors	Stroke prevention and acute care	Nurse-led teams use a physician-approved prescribing protocol to approach national benchmarks for hypertension control of >85%.
Geriatrics	Dementia care, late life care	Younger seniors are trained to provide socialization, screening, and referral for unmet medical and social needs of late-life and/or frail seniors.
Hospital nursing	Technology-enabled inpatient care	Predictive analytics software is used to match inpatient nurse staffing for each shift and unit with predictive clinical needs.
Nephrology	Chronic kidney disease (CKD) care, nephrology care	A nurse based in a nephrology practice coordinates care for CKD patients with multiple chronic illnesses during nephrology office visits via tele-connecting with a contracted network of CKD-relevant specialists such as cardiologists, endocrinologists, clinical pharmacologists, dietitians, and occupational therapists in order to reduce travel burden imposed on CKD patients.
Neurology	Stroke prevention and acute care	Following a TIA or mild stroke and a <24 hour evaluation in a hospital emergency department, willing patients who live nearby with a capable adult caregiver are discharged and scheduled for further evaluation via an office visit the next day.
Obstetrics	Maternity care	Hospital-affiliated and immediately adjacent outpatient birth centers with regularly rehearsed rapid hospital transfer protocols are routinely offered to low-risk women desiring less medicalized births by nurse midwives in conjunction with a neonatal specialist.
Oncology	Late-stage cancer care, oncology care regardless of prognosis, oncology care	Oncology teams use nonclinician health coaches to help patients with late-stage cancer in collaboration with their close

Table A1. (*Continued*)

Medical Specialty	Relevant Care Delivery Domains	Examples of Value-Enhancing Care Delivery Innovations
		family periodically select personalized care goals ranging from curative care to comfort care only.
Paramedic	High-need high-cost care, technology-enabled ambulatory inpatient care	Supervised housing is provided for the 10% of the chronic homeless population consuming the greatest share of health, social services, and criminal justice spending.
Pediatrician	Transition of pediatric chronic illness to adult care, early childhood pediatric care	The transitions team establishes tele-mediated connections between patients' prior pediatric specialty providers and new adult care providers to enhance interphysician coordination and supports adult system care-providers until patients are securely integrated.
Hospital pharmacy	Technology-enabled inpatient care	First responders use apps with telehealth consultation connections to nurse practitioners and social workers to reduce preventable ED visits and hospitalizations.
Primary care	Stroke prevention and acute care, ambulatory surgical care, spine pain care, prescription medication care, dementia care, high-need high-cost care, technology-enabled ambulatory care, primary care, clinically fragile patients with chronic disease	Patients at risk for catastrophizing are referred to a behavioral health therapist with rapid access to consultation from a physical medicine specialist.
Surgery	Ambulatory surgical care	Consistent with surgical level of care standards widely employed in the United Kingdom and EU countries, most nonurgent outpatient surgeries for patients without major surgical risk factors are provided in free-standing ambulatory surgical center.

CHAPTER 6

SAFE SURGERY CHECKLIST IMPLEMENTATION: ASSOCIATIONS OF MANAGEMENT PRACTICE AND SAFETY CULTURE CHANGE

Maike Tietschert[a], Sophie Higgins[b], Alex Haynes[c], Raffaella Sadun[b] and Sara J. Singer[d]

[a]Erasmus University Rotterdam, The Netherlands
[b]Harvard University, USA
[c]The University of Texas at Austin, USA
[d]Stanford University, USA

ABSTRACT

Designing and developing safe systems has been a persistent challenge in health care, and in surgical settings in particular. In efforts to promote safety, safety culture, i.e., shared values regarding safety management, is considered a key driver of high-quality, safe healthcare delivery. However, changing organizational culture so that it emphasizes and promotes safety is often an elusive goal. The Safe Surgery Checklist is an innovative tool for improving safety culture and surgical care safety, but evidence about Safe Surgery Checklist effectiveness is mixed. We examined the relationship between changes in management practices and changes in perceived safety culture during implementation of safe surgery checklists. Using a pre-posttest design and survey methods, we evaluated Safe Surgery Checklist implementation in a national sample of 42 general acute care hospitals in a leading hospital network. We measured perceived management practices among managers (n = 99) using the World Management Survey. We measured perceived preoperative safety and safety culture among clinical operating room personnel (N = 2,380 (2016); N = 1,433 (2017)) using the Safe Surgical Practice Survey. We collected data in two consecutive years.

Research and Theory to Foster Change in the Face of Grand Health Care Challenges
Advances in Health Care Management, Volume 22, 117–140
Published under exclusive licence by Emerald Publishing Limited
ISSN: 1474-8231/doi:10.1108/S1474-823120240000022006

Multivariable linear regression analysis demonstrated a significant relationship between changes in management practices and overall safety culture and perceived teamwork following Safe Surgery Checklist implementation.

Keywords: Safety culture; management practice; change; surgical safety; checklists; care transformation

INTRODUCTION

Designing and developing safe healthcare systems has been a persistent challenge in healthcare settings, and in surgery in particular (Arzahan et al., 2022; Institute of Medicine, 2001). Over time, healthcare reforms and improvement efforts have sought to improve safety. Yet, safety remains a concern across the broad spectrum of healthcare delivery with incidence of preventable errors still being a concern (van Dalen et al., 2022). For example, central line-associated bloodstream infection (CLABSI) remains a challenge in intensive care units (Shojania, 2020). Recent developments including the use of telehealth (Guise et al., 2014), electronic health records (Howe et al., 2018), and artificial intelligence (Price II, 2019), designed to improve quality and lower cost in healthcare settings, have nevertheless raised new concerns about safety. Most surgical errors, however, are not caused by technical issues but instead are the result of human factors (van Dalen et al., 2022).

Given the importance to patients and workforce, safety culture, i.e., the values that employees share regarding organizational safety management (Schein, 2010; Singer & Tucker, 2014; Singer & Vogus, 2013a), has received much attention in efforts to improve the quality of health care. An organization is said to have strong safety culture when it encourages employees across hierarchical structures and professional groups to seek solutions to patient safety problems and commits resources to address safety concerns (Agency for Healthcare Research and Quality, 2019). Previous research suggests that safety culture is a critical determinant for achieving better healthcare outcomes. For example, at the level of hospital units, research has shown that cultures promoting safety have led to a reduction of medication errors by 51%, three times fewer nurse back injuries and 27% less urinary tract infections in patients (Hofmann & Mark, 2006). Higher perceptions of safety culture among healthcare providers can also lead to significant reductions in serious complications after surgery of up to 43% (Birkmeyer et al., 2013), and between 7% to 29% reduction in relative risk of surgical mortality (Molina et al., 2016). At the organizational level, research has demonstrated significant improved performance on Patient Safety Indicators (Fan et al., 2016; Singer et al., 2009), such as a relative reduction of 19% in risk of patients obtaining decubitus ulcers, lower incidence of readmissions (Hansen et al., 2011), and reduction in all hospital harm, serious safety events, and mortality (Berry et al., 2020). A recently published systematic review by Arzahan and colleagues (2022) concludes that although the quality of studies examining safety culture requires improvement, almost all studies identified positive associations between safety culture and safety performance.

However, while crucial for healthcare delivery, improving patient safety is organizationally challenging. Improvement requires changing cultural elements, such as vision, values, norms, and artifacts that espouse these values in a given situation, industry, or broader culture (Waddock et al., 2015). Aligning multiple, and sometimes competing, sets of cultural values and norms to affect culture change is complex (A. C. Edmondson, 2016). Improvements to safety culture and performance also require operational changes that facilitate and reinforce these changes (Singer & Vogus, 2013b; Singla et al., 2006). This work includes interventions to improve safety (Morello et al., 2013), such as surgical safety checklists. In general, checklists are "written guides that walk experts through the key steps in a complex procedure" (Guwande, 2010). Checklists in health care seek to improve team-based care, improve handover and compliance with safe practice guidelines to reduce preventable error and unnecessary complications (Sewell et al., 2011). Checklists gained prominence in health care after the World Health Organization (WHO) named Safe Surgery Saves Lives as the second global patient safety challenge in 2008 and introduced the WHO Surgical Safety Checklist in an effort to facilitate uptake by surgical teams worldwide and to reduce surgery-induced harm to patients (Kumar et al., Forthcoming). Since then, checklists have been widely implemented across many health systems. In addition, checklists are increasingly required by health authorities globally, such as the Joint Commission International (JCI) and Accreditation Canada (Kumar et al., Forthcoming; Urbach et al., 2014).

While evidence generally suggests checklists *can* improve safety practices, evidence of effective interventions has been mixed (Molina et al., 2016; Singer & Vogus, 2013b). Research suggests that the use of checklists varies after adoption and often involves inconsistent or incorrect use, resulting in reduced effectiveness in achieving safe practice (Kumar et al., Forthcoming; Molina et al., 2016; Urbach et al., 2014). For tools like checklists to successfully change safety culture, the organizational environment needs to be responsive (Martinez et al., 2015). Critical aspects of the implementation environment include strong leadership commitment and managers who can clearly and persuasively convey the rationale for implementation and effectively demonstrate methods for using it (Singer & Vogus, 2013b). However, empirical evidence of the relationship between management practices, safety culture, and checklist implementation is limited. For this study, we use longitudinal data to assess whether management practice, perceived safety culture, or both change after checklist implementation, and whether more change toward management practices that promote safety relate to perceived improvements in safety culture.

We assess changes in clinical and operational management, including practices that promote safety and perceived safety culture corresponding with a surgical checklist intervention implementation across a large US-based hospital network, as perceived by staff in the operating room (OR). Safety management practices refer to "the policies, strategies, procedures and activities implemented or followed by the management of an organization targeting safety of their employees" and are considered part of the total organizational management (Vinodkumar & Bhasi, 2010). Management practices that promote safety, including operations management for efficiency and standardization, performance monitoring, target setting, and human resource management (Tsai et al., 2015), should be visible to organizational insiders through various actions and programs of the management directed to promote safety (Vinodkumar & Bhasi, 2010). Our results produce insights for health care leaders trying to maximize the impact of organizational changes intended to improve patient safety. Our results are relevant not only for creating safer organizations but also potentially for creating and sustaining change more generally in response to health care's grand challenges, which often require cultural adaptation.

THEORETICAL BACKGROUND

Improving safety in health care requires interrelated changes in human behavior and social structures. This dialectic relationship between structure and practice underpins structuration theory. According to structuration theory, which was first introduced by Antony Giddens in 1984, structure both constrains and enables individual behavior. Structuration theory deviates from previous theories which regarded structure and practice as existing independently of each other. Groves and colleagues (2011) first applied structuration theory to study safety culture. The authors differentiate between actors, i.e., members of groups or society that have agency to do things and to choose whether or not to do them, and structures, i.e., organized sets of rules and resources that reproduce social systems across time and space through structuration. Structures constrain and enable activities of actors (Giddens, 1984; Groves et al., 2011). For safety culture, this theory suggests that changing safety culture requires changing actors' behavior and structures, and that supporting safety culture may require leaders to align safety-oriented structures with other value systems within the organization (Groves et al., 2011). Strong safety culture thus requires leaders who prioritize safety and reliability as a core value of their organization and who provide necessary resources and structures to pursue enhanced reliability (Singer & Vogus, 2013a; Vogus et al., 2010; Zohar & Luria, 2004). Leaders can foster organizational attention toward reliability and safety by creating structures and processes that promote learning from previous activities that threatened, compromised, or strengthened safety (Carroll, 1998; Singer & Tucker, 2014; Singer & Vogus, 2013a; Vogus et al., 2010; Vogus & Singer, 2016).

While leadership can occur at all levels of an organization, managers are uniquely situated to champion safety-oriented leadership that can foster an organization-wide culture promoting safe practice (Singer & Tucker, 2014). Managers in health care are legally and morally obligated to manage their organizations in ways that promote high-quality patient care and seek continuous improvement (Parand et al., 2014). Managers can set targets for performance, motivate certain behaviors that are likely to improve performance toward targets, and monitor progress by comparing behavior to these performance targets (Bloom et al., 2012). Outside the healthcare setting, evidence suggests clearly that management practices impact safety outcomes at the workplace (Parand et al.,

2014; Zohar & Luria, 2004). Within health care, evidence also suggests that management practice is an important contributor to safety outcomes (Parand et al., 2014). Previous research has shown that better management practices are associated with higher quality of care in hospital settings (Tsai et al., 2015). For example, when registered nurses trust their managers, they are more likely to commit to and execute behaviors that promote safety (Blatt et al., 2006; Edmondson, 1999, 2004; Vogus et al., 2010).

Despite its evident relationship to organizational safety, limited empirical evidence exists about changes in management practice and its associations with changes in safety culture during checklist implementation. Previous research often viewed safety culture either as a structural attribute or as the interaction of organizational members rather than as the result of an interplay between macro-level organizational structures and micro-level individual practices (Groves et al., 2011). Also, existing studies of management practice are often not grounded in empirical evidence (e.g., opinion papers or editorials) (Caldwell et al., 2008; Conway, 2008; Gautam, 2005; Goeschel et al., 2010; McGinn & Dave, 2007) or are based on descriptions of managerial behavior to improve safety and quality instead of statistically tested associations (Parand et al., 2014). Yet to be explored empirically is the relationship between a set of specific management practices and safety culture and how management practices and safety culture change after implementation of a patient safety innovation (Singer & Tucker, 2014; Singer & Vogus, 2013b).

The Safe Surgery Checklist is an ideal innovation to study this relationship. Applying structuration theory to checklist implementation, we regard managers as agents that can propagate or alter structures that can hinder or promote safety cultures. As summarized in Fig. 6.1, implementing checklists requires managers

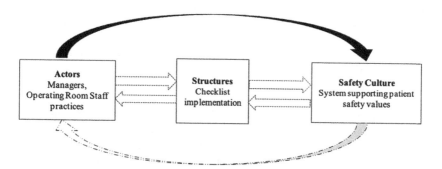

Fig. 6.1. Relationship Between Structures, Actors, and Safety Culture (Figure based on Groves et al., 2011).

to make structural changes that promote and facilitate effective checklist implementation while checklist implementation can in turn provide new structures that impact actors' behavioral practices and can change or promote safety culture.

Based on the above framework, we expect that during checklist implementation, managers need to adapt their practices in ways that promote safety, for example, by creating awareness for checklist implementation and by putting in place relevant procedures and boundary conditions to work. We expect that educating OR staff about the implementation and use of checklists and then implementing checklists will induce structural change to the procedures in the OR. Having conversations about these changes in turn change OR staff's behavior, which translates into changes in perceived safety culture. While the checklist implementation approach that we studied aimed to address all relationships depicted in Fig. 6.1, our data measurement and analysis addressed only the relationship identified by the solid black arrow. We explored the association between change in management practice and safety culture after checklist implementation, using a pre-posttest design across multiple organizations.

METHODS

Setting

We collected data from general acute care hospitals in the United States between 2016 and 2018. All participating hospitals were part of a national hospital network. After a successful pilot study in five of its hospitals as part of the Safe Surgery South Carolina initiative (Molina et al., 2016), the network implemented a system-wide program to encourage use of their version of the WHO Safe Surgery Checklist, which they called a "Safe Procedure Review" (SPR). This name was chosen in order to emphasize that, rather than a checklist only, the new process was intended to be a conversation among members of the surgical team and encompassed three time intervals for safety checks: before the patient is taken into the room; before the incision is made; and before the procedure ends.

For the system-wide Safe Surgery Checklist implementation, the network's senior leaders closely followed the approach of the Safe Surgery South Carolina initiative described by Molina et al. (2016). Implementation was centralized and specifically targeted ORs and their staff as ORs, relative to other procedural areas such as ambulatory surgery centers, showed highest risks of surgical safety incidents. The implementation effort included training activities through a live introductory webinar, which guided hospitals through checklist implementation step-by-step. Additional educational training materials on implementing checklists were also offered, including demonstration videos and spreadsheets to manage the process. Webinars were followed by emails with personalized follow-up, and on-site coaching from regional quality directors.

Sample and Data Collection

Two surveys were administered, one to measure safety culture and one to measure clinical and operational management, including practices that promote safety. The Safe Surgical Practice Survey was administered to understand surgical team members' perspectives on factors affecting patient safety in the OR. With the survey, the network intended to examine the culture of safety in the OR, understand the variances and opportunities for improvement, understand the managerial context of the organization to better support ongoing efforts to improve safety, generate comparative feedback to develop targets for improvement strategies, and learn about best practices.

The Safe Surgical Practice Survey was administered to clinical professionals twice: once in 2016 and once in 2017; a survey about managerial practices was administered to hospital managers once in 2018 and asked respondents retrospectively about management practices in both 2015 and 2017. Safe Surgical Practice Survey respondents were 2,380 clinical professionals at 64 hospitals in 2016 and 1,433 clinical professionals at 55 of the original 64 hospitals in 2017. Respondents included physicians, advanced practitioners (e.g., physician assistants), nurses, perfusionists, and interns/residents/fellows working in surgical services. The Safe Surgical Practice Survey was coupled with the World Management Survey (WMS) in a random sample of 38 hospitals to ask hospital level and middle managers, including clinical and nonclinical OR managers, questions about management practices to understand the extent to which management processes and key performance indicators were adopted within their hospitals. Managerial Practices Survey respondents were 122 management professionals at 76 hospitals. Of these 122, 76 respondents were employed at the hospital in both 2015 and 2017 and were able to provide responses for both years. Management professionals were hospital level senior managers including Chief Executive Officers (CEOs), Chief Nursing Officers (CNOs), and middle managers including clinical and nonclinical OR managers. The surveys were administered by the hospital network. The authors received from the network a deidentified CSV file that included the data for analysis.

Measures

Safety Culture. We measured safety culture using the Safe Surgical Practice Survey. The survey was developed with reference to items from the Agency for Healthcare Research and Quality's (AHRQ) Hospital Survey of Patient Safety Culture, the Patient Safety Climate in Healthcare Organizations Survey, the OR Brief Assessment Tool, and the Safety Climate Sub-Scale from the Safety Attitudes Questionnaire. More information about how the survey was developed and its psychometric characteristics has been described elsewhere (Singer et al., 2015) and is available online (https://www.ariadnelabs.org/2016/04/12/new-safe-surgery-checklist-implementation-guide-offers-a-practical-framework-for-success-with-the-safe-surgery-checklist/). The full survey includes 22 items that ask respondents whether they agree or disagree with statements pertaining to contextual, teamwork, and impact of safety practices of personnel's OR experience. Except for one item, which uses a dichotomous scale to measure whether complications have been averted by use of the checklist, all items were scored on a 7-point Likert response scale. The survey also assessed demographic characteristics of the respondent including their primary professional role, number of years they had worked in that role in any facility, and number of years they had worked in ORs in their current facility. All demographic questions used multiple choice options with the professional role question offering a blank fill-in after the choice of "Other." Respondents were not asked to provide their name or other identifying information.

Management Practices. A modified version of the Management and Organizational Practices Survey (MOPS) (https://www.census.gov/programs-surveys/mops.html) was administered to hospital-level senior managers (e.g., CEOs, Chief Financial Officers [CFOs]) and middle managers including Operations Room Managers at participating hospitals. The MOPS is a modified version of the WMS, which has been utilized extensively across industries, including health care (acute care hospitals), to assess management practices (Tsai et al., 2015; Bloom et al., 2016). More information about the WMS can be found online (https://worldmanagementsurvey.org/). The MOPS – which has been used by the US Census Bureau to track and assess management practices in manufacturing and in service sectors, including health care – translates the WMS methodology based on lengthy telephonic interviews into a simpler questionnaire that respondents can answer anonymously. The survey contained 15 items. Management practices were measured across three key areas. *Monitoring:* how does the organization evaluate performance, including the use of key performance indicators. *Targets:* what is the organization striving for, how does it track outcomes, and what measures are used to make sure targets are achieved. *Incentives:* how are employees motivated to work toward organizational targets and what criteria are used for promotion or lay-off (Bloom et al., 2012). Respondents were told to leave the 2015 boxes empty if they were not working as managers in the hospital at that time. The survey also included a background section asking what year the respondent began working at the hospital and what year the respondent began working as a manager at the hospital. Respondents were required to provide their names, titles, departments, hospitals, and email addresses. The full survey is included in Fig. 3.

Data Analysis

We first examined the data in each survey at the individual respondent level. For both surveys, we excluded respondent-level data if a respondent answered fewer than 50% of survey items. With this much missing data, we had concerns about the reliability of the responses that were provided.

For the culture survey, we reverse scored negatively worded items and examined how data were distributed using histograms. We collapsed respondent-level data, by mean, to the hospital level. As in previous research (Singer et al., 2015), we created an overall "safety culture" measure, which included all Questions (1–21), a team work measure, which included Questions 4–6, Questions 8–9, and Questions 11–15, and a measure assessing the impact of safe practice using a single item ("I would feel safe being treated here as a patient"). We decided to use an overall culture score in addition to the subscores because the subscores omit several key individual items from the survey. A list of all items is provided in Table 6.1. We combined data for 2016 and 2017 at the hospital level. We then examined differences in safety culture at the hospital level. To do so, we plotted differences in the 2016 and 2017 scores of the overall safety culture, teamwork, and impact of safe practice measures.

For the modified MOPS, we also tested for normal distribution of the data and created a management practice score for all respondents, a management practice score for C-suite-level respondents, and a management practice score for middle manager respondents, including clinical and nonclinical OR Managers by calculating unweighted averages across all 15 items. Since the MOPS measures are correlated and intended to serve as a proxy for the firm's true management

Table 6.1. Safety Culture Survey Items.

Item Number	Question[a]	Measure
Q1	Everyone participates in efforts to improve patient safety.	
Q2	Team members are open to changes that improve patient safety even if it means slowing down.	
Q3	Pressure to move quickly from case to case gets in the way of patient safety.	
Q4	Physicians are present and actively participating in patient care prior to skin incision.	Teamwork
Q5	Team discussions (e.g., briefings or debriefings) are common.	Teamwork
Q6	It is difficult to speak up when I perceive problems with patient care.	Teamwork
Q7	The entire team stops at all 3 critical points during the procedure to read the Safe Surgery Checklist (before induction of anesthesia, before skin incision, and before the patient leaves the room).	
Q8	Physicians maintain a positive tone throughout operations.	Teamwork
Q9	All team members work together as a well-coordinated team.	Teamwork
Q10	For complex cases, briefings include planning for potential problems.	
Q11	Team members share key information as it becomes available.	Teamwork
Q12	Physicians are only open to suggestions from other physicians.	Teamwork
Q13	Team members communicate with me in a respectful manner.	Teamwork
Q14	I am treated as a highly valued member of the team.	Teamwork
Q15	It is difficult to discuss medical mistakes.	Teamwork
Q16	The entire team discusses key concerns for patient recovery and management before the patient leaves the room.	
Q17	Using the Safe Surgery Checklist helps my cases run more smoothly.	
Q18	I was given a strong explanation for why it is important to use the Safe Surgery Checklist.	
Q19	The training I received about how to use the Safe Surgery Checklist allowed me to use it effectively during surgical procedures.	
Q20	If I were having an operation, I would want a Safe Surgery Checklist to be used.	
Q21	I would feel safe being treated here as a patient.	
Q22	In the ORs/Procedure Rooms where I work, problems or complications have been averted by the Safe Surgery Checklist	

[a]All questions combined form the overall safety culture measure.

capability, we used these data to create an overall measure for management practice. A list of items is provided in Table 6.2. Respondent-level data were collapsed, by mean, to the hospital level. The safety culture and management practice hospital-level data were merged to create a comprehensive dataset.

Table 6.2. MOPS Survey.

Item Number	Question[a]	Measure
Q1	In 2015 and 2017, what best describes what happened at the hospital in this location when a problem in the care delivery arose? Examples: overcrowding in Emergency Room, cluster of hospital acquired infection. (Mark one box for each year).	Monitoring
Q2	In 2015 and 2017, how many key performance indicators were monitored at this hospital? Examples: metrics on cost, waste, clinical quality, financial performance, absenteeism, patient safety. (Mark one box for each year).	Monitoring
Q3	During 2015 and 2017, how frequently were the key performance indicators reviewed by managers at this hospital? (Mark all that apply). NOTE: A manager is someone who has employees directly reporting to them, with whom they meet on a regular basis, and whose pay and promotion they may be involved with. Examples: Unit Manager, Human Resource Manager, Quality Manager.	Monitoring
Q4	During 2015 and 2017, how frequently were the key performance indicators reviewed by frontline clinical workers at this hospital? (Mark all that apply) NOTE: frontline clinical workers include all clinical staff with nonmanagerial responsibilities, including nurses and physicians.	Monitoring
Q5	During 2015 and 2017, where were the display boards showing clinical quality and other key performance indicators located at this hospital? (Mark one box for each year).	Monitoring
Q6	In 2015 and 2017, what best describes the time frame of clinical or operational (i.e., nonfinancial) targets at this hospital? (Mark one box for each year). Examples of clinical or operational targets: infection rates, readmission rates, wait times, nurse to patient ratios.	Targets
Q7	In 2015 and 2017, how easy or difficult was it for this hospital to achieve its clinical or operational targets? (Mark one box for each year).	Targets
Q8	In 2015 and 2017, who was aware of the clinical or operational targets at this hospital? (Mark one box for each year).	Targets
Q9	In 2015 and 2017, what best describes the time frame of financial targets at this hospital? (Mark one box for each year).	Targets
Q10	In 2015 and 2017, how easy or difficult was it for this hospital to achieve its financial targets? (Mark one box for each year).	Targets
Q11	In 2015 and 2017, who was aware of the financial targets at this hospital? (Mark one box for each year).	Targets
Q12	In 2015 and 2017, what was the primary way frontline clinical workers were promoted at this hospital? (Mark one box for each year).	People
Q13	In 2015 and 2017, what was the primary way managers were promoted at this hospital? (Mark one box for each year).	People
Q14	In 2015 and 2017, when was an underperforming frontline clinical worker reassigned or dismissed at this hospital? (Mark one box for each year).	People
Q15	In 2015 and 2017, when was an underperforming manager reassigned or dismissed at this hospital? (Mark one box for each year).	People
Q16	What year did you start working at this hospital?	
Q17	What year did you start working as a manager at this hospital?	

[a]Survey item 1–15 were combined to measure overall management practice.

To examine relationships between changes in management practices and changes in safety culture, we ran correlations for change in management, C-suite-level managers, middle managers, overall safety culture, teamwork, and impact of safe practice. Because management practices reported by hospital-level senior and middle managers were significantly correlated, we included one measure of management practice per hospital that did not differentiate between senior and middle managerial levels. We also ran correlations of all demographic variables to assess relationships between variables. We then ran three multivariable linear regression analysis models using robust standard errors. In the baseline model, change in safety culture was the dependent variable, and change in management practice was the independent variable. Additionally, we accounted for hospital-level differences by controlling for the number of beds, whether a new CEO, a new CFO, or a new CNO had joined the hospital between 2015 and 2018, whether management respondents had become managers before or after 2016, the number of middle managers, C-suite-level managers, physicians/advanced practitioners (i.e., surgeons, anesthesiologists, CRNAs, and physician assistants), nurses (i.e., surgical technicians and surgical nurses), and other clinical personnel (i.e., perfusionists, interns/residents/fellows, and those responding "other" to the Safe Surgical Practice Survey item asking "What is your primary professional role?") who responded to the survey at each hospital, and the date the hospital were acquired by the national hospital system. We did not correct for the baseline value of safety culture since both our dependent and independent variable consist of change values and both values correlated.

To test the geographic stability of our results, we ran a sensitivity analysis in which we accounted for subregions in which hospitals were located (i.e., Mid Atlantic, East North Central, West North Central, South Atlantic, East South Central, West South Central, and Mountain). We added subregions as control to our models to account for the potential of regional differences in checklist implementation because at the time state hospital associations were pursuing different strategies to encourage surgical checklist uptake throughout the country. An example was the South Carolina initiative for checklist implementation, which was later emulated in other systems. P-values were considered significant if they were less than 0.05. Statistical analyses were conducted using STATA 15.

RESULTS

Sample Characteristics

Sample characteristics are listed in Table 6.1. On average, type of respondents who rated safety culture varied across hospitals. Nurses responded most frequently to our survey, followed by physicians and advanced practitioner respondents. Responses to the manager survey came from middle managers most often. On average, of the 122 managers that responded to our survey, 33 joined the organization after 2016. Of those changes in hospital management, most changes occurred among CNOs (35%), followed by CEOs (33.33%). Changes occurred least frequently among CFOs (19.05%). On average, hospitals had 226.5

beds and had been within the hospital network for 11 years on average. Most hospitals were located in the south of the United States (83.33%).

Descriptive Changes in Safety Culture

Fig. 2 shows changes in safety culture after the intervention at each hospital. On average, perceptions of overall safety culture changed by 0.07 (on a 6-point culture scale). Teamwork culture changed by 0.03. The perceived impact of safe practice changed by 0.025 (see Table 6.3). These relatively low numbers result from the fact that, while most respondents reported a change in their hospital's safety culture, the direction of change differed across hospitals. While some respondents reported a negative change in safety culture, meaning that safety culture was perceived as being higher before the intervention than after the intervention, most respondents reported improvement in safety culture indicated by the positive changes across the three culture measures. The average improvement in perceived safety culture was 0.33, while average reduction in perceived safety culture was −0.20. The average reported improvement in management practice was 0.25, while the average reduction was 0.03. As displayed in Fig. 3, perceived management practice at the hospital level, on average, changed by 0.14 (on a continuous scale from 0 to 1).

Bivariate Relationship Between Change Management Practice and Perceived Safety Culture

Correlations between study variables are presented in Tables 6.4 and 6.5. Change in management practices at the middle manager level was significantly positively

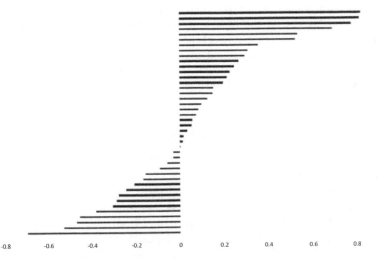

Fig. 2.   Change in Culture per Hospital (6-Point Culture-scale).

Table 6.3. Hospital Demographics.

Characteristic	Obs	Mean	Std. Dev.	Min	Max
Change in Perceptions of Safety Culture					
Overall culture	42	0.07	0.36	−0.70	0.82
Team work	34	0.03	0.42	−0.86	0.91
Impact of safe practice	34	0.03	0.40	−0.82	1.05
Change in Management Practice					
	42	0.14	0.14	−0.12	0.55
Hospital-level characteristics					
Respondents who rated safety culture					
Number of physician/advanced practitioner respondents§					
≤5	24	57.14%			
6–10	13	30.95%			
11–15	3	7.14%			
≥16	2	4.76%			
*Number of nurse respondents***					
≤5	1	2.38%			
6–10	5	11.9%			
11–15	9	21.43%			
≥16	27	64.29%			
Number of other clinical respondents††					
≤5	40	95.24%			
6–10	2	4.76%			
11–15	0	0.0%			
≥16	0	0.0%			
Type of respondents who rated management practice					
Number of C-suite respondents					
0	24	57.14%			
1	17	40.48%			
2	1	2.38%			
3	0	0.0%			
Number of middle management respondents					
0	8	19.05%			
1	27	64.29%			
2	7	16.67%			
3	0	0.0%			
Tenure‡					
Before 2016	9	21.43%			
2016 or after	33	78.57%			
Organizational characteristics					
Change in C-suite					
New CEO*	14	33.33%			

Table 6.3. *(Continued)*

Characteristic	Obs	Mean	Std. Dev.	Min	Max
New CFO*	8	19.05%			
New CNO*	15	35.71%			
Beds	42	226.5	123.455	101	534
Years since acquisition	42	11.02381	4.609048	5	25
		Number of hospitals per region			
Virginia	2	4.76%			
Midwest	4	9.52%			
Northeast	1	2.38%			
South	35	83.33%			
West	2	4.76%			

*Between initial survey and follow-up.
†Date hospital acquired by the national hospital system.
‡Average of all respondents by hospital.
§Physicians/advanced practitioners include anesthesiologists, surgeons, directors of surgical services, certified registered nurse anesthetists (CRNAs), and physician assistants.
**Nurses include surgical nurses and surgical techs.
††Other clinical perspectives include perfusionists, intern/resident/fellow, and respondents selecting "Other" in response to the question asking "What is your primary role?"

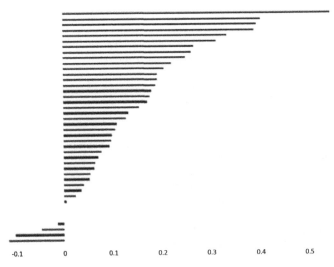

Fig. 3. Change in Management Practice per Hospital (0–1 Scale).

Table 6.4. Correlations of Management and Culture Change Scores.

	1	2	3	4	5
(1) Change in management score	1.00				
(2) Change C-suite management score	−0.14	1.00			
(3) Change middle management score	0.39**	−0.31*	1.00		
(4) Change in teamwork score	0.30**	0.12	0.12	1.00	
(5) Impact of safe practice	0.09	0.04	−0.01	0.67	1.00

**Sig < 0.01 (applies to all correlation tables).
*Sig < 0.05 > 0.01.
†Teamwork measure calculated as the mean of the sum of questions 8–10; questions 12–19 of culture survey.

Table 6.5. Correlations Among Control Variables.

	1	2	3	4	5	6	7	8
(1) Beds								
Initial	1.00							
Follow-up	1.00							
(2) Tenure 2016 and after								
Initial	0.05	1.00						
Follow-up	0.05	1.00						
(3) Acquisition date								
Initial	0.02	−0.20	1.00					
Follow-up	0.02	−0.20	1.00					
(4) Physician/Advanced practitioner perspective								
Initial	0.21	−0.11	0.11	1.00				
Follow-up	0.14	0.19	−0.02	1.00				
(5) Nurse perspective								
Initial	0.33*	−0.08	0.24	0.48**	1.00			
Follow-up	0.18	−0.15	−0.07	−0.09	1.00			
(6) Other healthcare provider perspectives								
Initial	0.24	−0.25	0.25	0.00	0.26	1.00		
Follow-up	−0.06	−0.18	−0.22	−0.10	0.34*	1.00		
(7) C-suite perspective								
Initial	−0.05	−0.14	0.03	−0.13	−0.31*	−0.24	1.00	
Follow-up	0.09	0.21	0.09*	−0.29	−0.07	−0.03	1.00	
(8) Middle management perspective								
Initial	−0.03	0.30	−0.08	0.26	0.11	−0.13	−0.33*	1.00
Follow-up	−0.05	0.45*	−0.08	0.06	−0.01	−0.01	−0.02	1.00

Note: Control variables with a dichotomous scale (New CEO, New CFO, New CNO, Change in C-suite) were excluded from the from the correlation table.

correlated with change in teamwork but not with impact on safe practices. Changes in C-suite-level management were not significantly correlated with changes in any of the safety culture dimensions. However, changes in management practice among middle managers were significantly correlated with changes in management practice at the C-suite level.

Association Between Change Management Practice and Perceived Safety Culture

Table 6.6 presents the results of the multivariable linear regression analyses. We ran separate analytic models to study the relationship between change in management practice and teamwork and the impact of safe practice. Results show a significant positive association between changes in management practice with all three safety culture variables. Associations were strongest between change in management practice and change in teamwork ($\beta = 1.26$, $p < 0.01$), followed by change in the overall culture score ($\beta = 0.83$, $p < 0.01$). Associations were smallest between change in management practice and change in impact of safe practice ($\beta = 0.58$, $p < 0.05$). Results remained relatively stable when accounting for geographical regions.

Table 6.6. Regression Analyses.

	Change in Overall Culture Score		Change in Teamwork Score		Impact of Safe Practice	
	Coef.	(95% CI)	Coef.	(95% CI)	Coef.	(95% CI)
Change in management score	0.83**	0.45–1.21	1.26**	0.70–1.82	0.58*	0.08–1.09
Beds	0.00	0.00–0.00	0.00†	0.00–0.00	0.00	0.00–0.00
New CEO	0.12	−0.04–0.27	0.14	−0.09–0.38	0.04	−0.14–0.22
New CFO	−0.11	−0.29–0.06	−0.06	−0.26–0.14	0.06	−0.13–0.25
New CNO	−0.05	−0.24–0.14	−0.14	−0.35–0.06	−0.16	−0.37–0.04
Change in C-suite	0.17	−0.11–0.44	−0.22†	−0.45–0.01	−0.24	−0.59–0.12
Tenure 2016 and after	0.11†	−0.01–0.23	0.23**	0.11–0.34	0.27**	0.16–0.38
Date of acquisition	0.00	−0.01–0.02	0.00	−0.02–0.02	0.00	−0.02–0.02
Respondents who completed the survey						
Physician/Advanced practitioner	0.02†	0.00–0.04	0.03**	0.01–0.04	0.04**	0.02–0.06
Nurses	−0.01†	−0.01–0.00	−0.01	−0.01–0.00	−0.01**	−0.02–−0.01
Other healthcare provider staff	0.00	−0.03–0.04	0.00	−0.05–0.04	0.02	−0.01–0.05
Middle management	−0.02	−0.12–0.08	0.06	−0.06–0.19	−0.02	−0.15–0.12
C-suite	0.03	−0.10–0.15	−0.02	−0.17–0.14	−0.11	−0.27–0.05
Adjusted R-square	0.20		0.26		0.22	

†$p < 0.1$.
*$p < 0.05$.
**$p < 0.01$.

Among control variables, relationships with change in safety culture varied across models. Only two variables were significantly associated across all three models. Where hospital managers started after 2016, clinical providers in those hospitals reported significantly larger improvements in perceived safety culture. In hospitals where more physicians responded to the Safe Surgical Practice Survey, improvements in safety culture were bigger than in hospitals where fewer physicians responded, although effect sizes are small (0.02–0.04). All other variables were either nonsignificantly related to perceived changes in safety culture or results varied across the three models.

DISCUSSION

This chapter studied the association of change in management practice with change in perceived safety culture during the process of adopting a Safe Surgery Checklist across a national hospital network. We found that, where hospital managers reported greater improvement in management practice after checklist implementation, clinical providers also reported greater increases in perceptions of safety culture overall, teamwork, and the impact of safe practice.

To the best of our knowledge, this is the first study to explore changes in perceived safety culture following checklist implementation using longitudinal data and accounting for changes in management practice. Previous research on checklist implementation has reported inconsistent results with respect to the effectiveness of checklists in improving safety culture and safe practice. While the initial trial of the WHO Safe Surgery Checklist reported significant reductions in mortality from 1.5% to 0.8% (Haynes et al., 2009), subsequent studies have not consistently supported these results. Sewell et al. (2011), for example, did not find significant associations between checklist implementation for emergency and elective orthopedic patients and reduction in early complications and mortality. Urbach et al. (2014) also did not find significant reductions in operative mortality after checklist implementation. Among hospitals in our study, the degree and direction of change in safety culture also varied. While more hospitals showed improvement in safety culture, some also saw declines. These results suggest that changing safety culture through checklist implementation requires consideration of contextual and organizational attributes that might be correlated with both checklist implementation and safety culture (Martinez et al., 2015).

Our study provides empirical evidence for the interplay between human behavior and structuration as conceived in structuration theory. First, we found that, after checklist implementation, management practices and perceived safety culture both change. One explanation of this finding could be that checklist implementation leads to changes in social structures within organizations. Checklists intend to promote use of new protocols and formation of new routines, which employees follow before induction of anesthesia, making a skin incision, and leaving the OR. Gaining commitment to these changes may require managers to interact differently with their teams, leading to changes in management practices. New management practices could also confer changes in the way surgical team members perceive managers' roles and responsibilities, which in turn could impact their perceived safety culture. For example, after the first survey was administered in the hospital network, network-level senior managers presented overall results in webinars and shared hospital-specific reports with hospital-level senior and middle managers. The reports instructed managers to share the survey results with their staff and surgeons, to identify areas of progress and to celebrate these, to develop strategies for continual improvement, to make using the SPR an integral practice, and to emphasize that the SPR process should be led by surgeons. Applying structuration theory to our results sheds light on why management practices and perceived safety culture change after checklist implementation and why we find a significant association between changes in management practice with changes in safety culture.

Previous literature has long emphasized that management practices could be a significant contributor toward effective improvement of safety culture. A systematic literature review conducted by Parand et al. (2014) synthesized literature on managers' role in creating safer healthcare organizations. Our results contribute to this body of work by detailing the importance of not just strong baseline management during implementation of an intervention but also perceived *improvement to management practices* as critical to achieving improvements in safety culture. Our results suggest management practices that promote organizational safety, including monitoring systems to ensure targets are achieved and deploying incentives that allow staff to work toward goals, correlate with higher perceptions of safety culture.

Management practice correlated most strongly with the teamwork component of safety culture. Surgical teams require seamless coordination across different professional specialties (Healey et al., 2006), who carry different values and language based on their professional affiliations (Hall, 2005). Previous studies have reported failure of effective teamwork to be among the strongest contributors toward errors such as wrong site surgeries (Commission, 1998; Makary et al., 2006; Russ et al., 2013). Effective teamwork in surgery requires clear specification of what the team should be doing, when, and how. In practice, however, perceptions of what constitutes safety differ across different professional groups (Singer et al., 2010; Vogus et al., 2010).

Our findings suggest an important interplay between culture and management practice. More specifically, managers may play an important role in framing how regulatory and operational changes impact culture, both overall and indirectly through team functioning. According to Gibson and Kaplan (Gibbons & Kaplan, 2015), managers can intervene in the regulative as well as constitutive aspects of culture based on relational contracts: effort conventions that an organization and individuals within the organization adopt. In terms of our results, regulative aspects of safety culture consider changing the value of action, for example, by encouraging nurses to speak up, and constitutive aspects by helping surgical team members across professional groups to arrive at a common understanding that disagreement can be a positive behavior if it prevents errors from happening. Management practices can thus both provide formal structures that enable a culture of safety as well as informal mechanisms that build agreement about the purpose of a checklist, its rightful use, and the evaluation of checklist compliance (Gibbons & Kaplan, 2015; Hofmann & Morgeson, 1999; Nembhard & Edmondson, 2006).

Our results also suggest that change in safety culture was larger in organizations where new managers joined the organization after 2016. Previous research, which depicts culture as a toolkit that individuals and organizations use for sensemaking (Swidler, 1986, 2013), has reported that organizations can support cultural change by hiring organizational members that infuse new cultural material and contribute to cultural change if those resources are adopted and diffuse throughout the organization (Harrison & Corley, 2011). Managers who were newly hired during the checklist implementation process could have been selected because they have experience in changing culture toward a focus on safety and in that way offer new resources to the organization. Alternatively their new status in the organization could have created opportunity to evoke bigger change. In any case, these results suggest that changes in management team members may contribute to larger changes in culture.

Safety in surgery and health care more broadly has gained attention since being brought to light in the early 2000s and, consequently, more hospitals are measuring safety culture (Sorra & Dyer, 2010). While these trends are encouraging, scholarship has yet to fully discover the antecedents and effects of safety culture. For example, Arzahan and colleagues (2022) call for studies that combine proactive and reactive assessments of safety culture to explore alignments of safety awareness with safety management systems. We believe that our study advances safety research and research on safety culture by examining statistically the dialogic relationship between human behavior and structural changes. In doing so, we followed suggestions by Groves and colleagues (2011) to study safety culture as a system of reciprocal interactions between individual agency and organizational structures to explore a more comprehensive set of malleable elements that can help to develop, sustain, or improve safety cultures.

Our results have implications for practice and research. For practice, our results show the importance of the perception of improved management practice alongside checklist implementation to enhance safety culture. Frontline healthcare professionals want to see action that demonstrates manager support for the change they seek to implement. Managers have many tools at their disposal. Developing performance indicators that are specifically targeted toward safer practice is one way of doing so. Another way is to develop a reward system that emphasizes open communication around issues of safety: celebrating near-misses could be one way. When changing safety culture, managers should hence critically examine existing practices and make adjustments where needed. Our results show that changes toward better teamwork, in particular, requires infrastructure that supports interprofessional collaboration.

When studying culture change toward safety, and potentially culture change more generally, it may be important to consider actors' behavior, and particularly managers' behavior, in combination with structural and organizational factors. Mixed results of checklist effectiveness may stem from the fact that organizational structures and relevant actor practices are not well aligned. Although it was beyond the scope of this study to examine precisely how checklists were implemented, our results show that general management practices, oriented toward the efficient and effective functioning of operational and human resources, can explain some of the variation observed across organizations in the extent to which checklist implementation changes safety culture. Management and culture are both concepts that are hard to measure as they include multiple dimensions and have been variously defined. Yet, although previous research has been largely descriptive, our study shows that management practice, safety culture, and their association can be measured and quantified. The MOPS and the Safe Surgical Practice Survey have proven to be useful instruments to do so. Future research could explore processes through which human behavior, structures, and processes interact to enact, enable, and elaborate safety culture and safe surgery practice and how the implementation of checklists impacts the dialogic relationship between practices and structures (Groves et al., 2011).

A number of limitations should be considered when interpreting our study findings. First, although we have a larger number of individual respondents, our sample at the organizational level (42 hospitals) is small. Nevertheless, we were able to demonstrate significant relationships between changes in management practice and safety culture. Future studies should replicate our approach in larger samples. Second, while we received a sizable number of responses from each hospital, unfortunately, the survey was administered by the health network in a way that did not allow us to know how many individuals received the survey. Thus, it is possible our results are biased due to nonresponse. Third, the hospitals that we studied were all owned by the same hospital network. Common network membership could result in similar policies and procedures across hospitals and in potentially more similar management practices and cultures, reducing variance in our sample. Replicating our study across hospitals with different ownership types could result in even larger effects of checklist implementation and would be an interesting avenue for further exploration. Fourth, the hospitals in our study already had some checklists in use, albeit not with a structured approach for implementation, which could result in underestimation of the effect of checklist use on change in safety culture. Again, this suggests our findings may be conservative. Given that we do find significant associations, we expect this effect to be even larger across hospitals that do not use any type of checklists before intervention. Fifth, although we measured our concepts before and after checklist implementation, we were not able to assess the degree to which individual hospitals or departments translated the system-wide strategy and procedure to checklist implementation at their location. Given the hierarchical structure of the hospital system and its structured process for briefing and implementation, the hospital system attested to little variation across hospitals. Including a variable for regional differences would have accounted for some of this variation if it were present, yet this variable did not alter our results significantly. Sixth, the management survey collected retrospective data. Collecting data retrospectively could potentially induce recall bias. Furthermore, we only collected data on management practices by managers themselves. Frontline healthcare professionals could perceive management practices and change thereof differently. Future research should repeat our study using repeated measures that are not retrospective and measuring management practice across different levels at the organization. Finally, we only studied one organizational attribute, management practice, that could be correlated with safety culture. Future studies should consider additional attributes that could influence organizations' ability to change toward a culture that values safety.

CONCLUSIONS

Our results suggest that the changes in safety culture encouraged by implementation of the Safe Surgery Checklist are significantly related to changes in management practices. Overall safety culture and perceived teamwork were positively associated with improvements in management practice following implementation of the checklist. Our study indicates the importance of the relationship between management practices and safety culture when implementing the Safe Surgery Checklist. Hospitals should approach checklist implementation in a structured and rigorous way in order to achieve the maximum benefit to health and safety outcomes.

REFERENCES

Agency for Healthcare Research and Quality. (2019). *Culture of safety*. https://psnet.ahrq.gov/primers/primer/5/culture-of-safety

Arzahan, I. S. N., Ismail, Z., & Yasin, S. M. (2022). Safety culture, safety climate, and safety performance in healthcare facilities: A systematic review. *Safety Science, 147*, 105624.

Berry, J. C., Davis, J. T., Bartman, T., Hafer, C. C., Lieb, L. M., Khan, N., & Brilli, R. J. (2020). Improved safety culture and teamwork climate are associated with decreases in patient harm and hospital mortality across a hospital system. *Journal of Patient Safety, 16*(2), 130–136.

Birkmeyer, N. J., Finks, J. F., Greenberg, C. K., McVeigh, A., English, W. J., Carlin, A., ... Birkmeyer, J. D. (2013). Safety culture and complications after bariatric surgery. *Annals of Surgery, 257*(2), 260–265.

Blatt, R., Christianson, M. K., Sutcliffe, K. M., & Rosenthal, M. M. (2006). A sensemaking lens on reliability. *Journal of Organizational Behavior: The International Journal of Industrial, Occupational and Organizational Psychology and Behavior, 27*(7), 897–917.

Bloom, N., Genakos, C., Sadun, R., & Van Reenen, J. (2012). Management practices across firms and countries. *Academy of Management Perspectives, 26*(1), 12–33.

Bloom, N., Lemos, R., Sadun, R., Scur, D., & Van Reenen, J. (2016). International data on measuring management practices. *American Economic Review, 106*(5), 152–156.

Caldwell, C., Butler, G., & Grah, J. (2008). Breakthrough quality: What the board must do. *Trustee: The Journal for Hospital Governing Boards, 61*(6), 32–33, 31.

Carroll, J. S. (1998). Organizational learning activities in high-hazard industries: The logics underlying self-analysis. *Journal of Management Studies, 35*(6), 699–717.

Commission, J. (1998). Sentinel events: Evaluating cause and planning improvement. *Oakbrook Terrace (IL): Joint Commission of Health Care Organizations.*

Conway, J. (2008). Getting boards on board: Engaging governing boards in quality and safety. *Joint Commission Journal on Quality and Patient Safety, 34*(4), 214–220.

van Dalen, A. S. H. M., Jung, J. J., van Dijkum, E. J. N., Buskens, C. J., Grantcharov, T. P., Bemelman, W. A., & Schijven, M. P. (2022). Analyzing and discussing human factors affecting surgical patient safety using innovative technology: Creating a safer operating culture. *Journal of Patient Safety, 18*(6), 617–623.

Edmondson, A. (1999). Psychological safety and learning behavior in work teams. *Administrative Science Quarterly, 44*(2), 350–383.

Edmondson, A. C. (2004). Learning from mistakes is easier said than done: Group and organizational influences on the detection and correction of human error. *The Journal of Applied Behavioral Science, 40*(1), 66–90.

Edmondson, A. C. (2016). Wicked problem solvers. *Harvard Business Review, 94*(6), 52–59, 117.

Fan, C. J., Pawlik, T. M., Daniels, T., Vernon, N., Banks, K., Westby, P., ... Makary, M. A. (2016). Association of safety culture with surgical site infection outcomes. *Journal of the American College of Surgeons, 222*(2), 122–128.

Gautam, K. S. (2005). A call for board leadership on quality in hospitals. *Quality Management in Health Care, 14*(1), 18–30.

Gibbons, R., & Kaplan, R. S. (2015). Formal measures in informal management: Can a balanced scorecard change a culture? *The American Economic Review, 105*(5), 447–451.

Giddens, A. (1984). *The construction of society: Outline of the theory of structuration.* University of California Press.

Goeschel, C. A., Wachter, R. M., & Pronovost, P. J. (2010). Responsibility for quality improvement and patient safety: Hospital board and medical staff leadership challenges. *Chest, 138*(1), 171–178.

Groves, P. S., Meisenbach, R. J., & Scott-Cawiezell, J. (2011). Keeping patients safe in healthcare organizations: A structuration theory of safety culture. *Journal of Advanced Nursing, 67*(8), 1846–1855.

Guise, V., Anderson, J., & Wiig, S. (2014). Patient safety risks associated with telecare: A systematic review and narrative synthesis of the literature. *BMC Health Services Research, 14*(1), 1–15.

Guwande, A. (2010). *The checklist manifesto.* Picadur.

Hall, P. (2005). Interprofessional teamwork: Professional cultures as barriers. *Journal of Interprofessional Care, 19*(Suppl. 1), 188–196.

Hansen, L. O., Williams, M. V., & Singer, S. J. (2011). Perceptions of hospital safety climate and incidence of readmission. *Health Services Research, 46*(2), 596–616.

Harrison, S. H., & Corley, K. G. (2011). Clean climbing, carabiners, and cultural cultivation: Developing an open-systems perspective of culture. *Organization Science, 22*(2), 391–412.

Haynes, A. B., Weiser, T. G., Berry, W. R., Lipsitz, S. R., Breizat, A.-H. S., Dellinger, E. P., & Lapitan, M. C. M. (2009). A surgical safety checklist to reduce morbidity and mortality in a global population. *New England Journal of Medicine, 360*(5), 491–499.

Healey, A. N., Undre, S., & Vincent, C. A. (2006). Defining the technical skills of teamwork in surgery. *BMJ Quality and Safety, 15*(4), 231–234.

Hofmann, D. A., & Mark, B. (2006). An investigation of the relationship between safety climate and medication errors as well as other nurse and patient outcomes. *Personnel Psychology, 59*(4), 847–869.

Hofmann, D. A., & Morgeson, F. P. (1999). Safety-related behavior as a social exchange: The role of perceived organizational support and leader–member exchange. *Journal of Applied Psychology, 84*(2), 286.

Howe, J. L., Adams, K. T., Hettinger, A. Z., & Ratwani, R. M. (2018). Electronic health record usability issues and potential contribution to patient harm. *JAMA, 319*(12), 1276–1278.

Institute of Medicine. (2001). *Crossing the quality chasm: A new health care system for the 21st century.* Institute of Medicine.

Kumar, S., Swaminathan, R., Mohamed, R., Dadhich, S., Chilumukuru, N., & Changerath, R. (Forthcoming). A review of evolution, implementation, impact and improvisation of who surgical safety checklist-the panacea for safe surgical practice. *European Journal of Molecular & Clinical Medicine, 10*(2).

Makary, M. A., Sexton, J. B., Freischlag, J. A., Holzmueller, C. G., Millman, E. A., Rowen, L., & Pronovost, P. J. (2006). Operating room teamwork among physicians and nurses: Teamwork in the eye of the beholder. *Journal of the American College of Surgeons, 202*(5), 746–752.

Martinez, E. A., Beaulieu, N., Gibbons, R., Pronovost, P., & Wang, T. (2015). Organizational culture and performance. *The American Economic Review, 105*(5), 331–335.

McGinn, P., & Dave, R. (2007). What is the board's role in quality? *Trustee: The Journal for Hospital Governing Boards, 60*(8), 40–44.

Molina, G., Jiang, W., Edmondson, L., Gibbons, L., Huang, L. C., Kiang, M. V., … Singer, S. J. (2016). Implementation of the surgical safety checklist in South Carolina hospitals is associated with improvement in perceived perioperative safety. *Journal of the American College of Surgeons*, *222*(5), 725–736.

Morello, R. T., Lowthian, J. A., Barker, A. L., McGinnes, R., Dunt, D., & Brand, C. (2013). Strategies for improving patient safety culture in hospitals: A systematic review. *BMJ Quality and Safety*, *22*(1), 11–18.

Nembhard, I. M., & Edmondson, A. C. (2006). Making it safe: The effects of leader inclusiveness and professional status on psychological safety and improvement efforts in health care teams. *Journal of Organizational Behavior: The International Journal of Industrial, Occupational and Organizational Psychology and Behavior*, *27*(7), 941–966.

Parand, A., Dopson, S., Renz, A., & Vincent, C. (2014). The role of hospital managers in quality and patient safety: A systematic review. *BMJ Open*, *4*(9), e005055.

Price, W. N., II (2019). *Risks and remedies for artificial intelligence in health care*. https://www.brookings.edu/research/risks-and-remedies-for-artificial-intelligence-in-health-care/

Russ, S., Rout, S., Sevdalis, N., Moorthy, K., Darzi, A., & Vincent, C. (2013). Do safety checklists improve teamwork and communication in the operating room? A systematic review. *Annals of Surgery*, *258*(6), 856–871.

Schein, E. H. (2010). *Organizational culture and leadership* (Vol. 2). John Wiley & Sons.

Sewell, M., Adebibe, M., Jayakumar, P., Jowett, C., Kong, K., Vemulapalli, K., & Levack, B. (2011). Use of the WHO surgical safety checklist in trauma and orthopaedic patients. *International Orthopaedics*, *35*(6), 897–901.

Shojania, K. G. (2020). *Beyond CLABSI and CAUTI: Broadening our vision of patient safety*. In (Vol. 29, pp. 361–364). BMJ Publishing Group Ltd.

Singer, S., Lin, S., Falwell, A., Gaba, D., & Baker, L. (2009). Relationship of safety climate and safety performance in hospitals. *Health Services Research*, *44*(2p1), 399–421.

Singer, S. J., Jiang, W., Huang, L. C., Gibbson, L., Kian, M., Edmondson, L., Gawande, A. A., & Berry, W. R. (2015). Surgical team member assessment of the safety of surgery practice in 38 South Carolina hospitals. *Medical Care Research and Review*, *72*(3), 298–323. https://doi.org/10.1177/1077558715577479

Singer, S. J., Rosen, A., Zhao, S., Ciavarelli, A. P., & Gaba, D. M. (2010). Comparing safety climate in naval aviation and hospitals: Implications for improving patient safety. *Health Care Management Review*, *35*(2), 134–146.

Singer, S. J., & Tucker, A. L. (2014). *The evolving literature on safety WalkRounds: Emerging themes and practical messages*. BMJ Publishing Group Ltd.

Singer, S. J., & Vogus, T. J. (2013a). Reducing hospital errors: Interventions that build safety culture. *Annual Review of Public Health*, *34*, 373–396.

Singer, S. J., & Vogus, T. J. (2013b). *Safety climate research: Taking stock and looking forward*. BMJ Publishing Group Ltd.

Singla, A. K., Kitch, B. T., Weissman, J. S., & Campbell, E. G. (2006). Assessing patient safety culture: A review and synthesis of the measurement tools. *Journal of Patient Safety*, *2*(3), 105–115.

Sorra, J. S., & Dyer, N. (2010). Multilevel psychometric properties of the AHRQ hospital survey on patient safety culture. *BMC Health Services Research*, *10*(1), 1–13.

Swidler, A. (1986). Culture in action: Symbols and strategies. *American Sociological Review*, 273–286.

Swidler, A. (2013). *Talk of love: How culture matters*. University of Chicago Press.

Tsai, T. C., Jha, A. K., Gawande, A. A., Huckman, R. S., Bloom, N., & Sadun, R. (2015). Hospital board and management practices are strongly related to hospital performance on clinical quality metrics. *Health Affairs*, *34*(8), 1304–1311.

Urbach, D. R., Govindarajan, A., Saskin, R., Wilton, A. S., & Baxter, N. N. (2014). Introduction of surgical safety checklists in Ontario, Canada. *New England Journal of Medicine*, *370*(11), 1029–1038.

Vinodkumar, M., & Bhasi, M. (2010). Safety management practices and safety behaviour: Assessing the mediating role of safety knowledge and motivation. *Accident Analysis & Prevention*, *42*(6), 2082–2093.

Vogus, T. J., & Singer, S. J. (2016). Creating highly reliable accountable care organizations. *Medical Care Research and Review, 73*(6), 660–672.

Vogus, T. J., Sutcliffe, K. M., & Weick, K. E. (2010). Doing no harm: Enabling, enacting, and elaborating a culture of safety in health care. *Academy of Management Perspectives, 24*(4), 60–77.

Waddock, S., Meszoely, G. M., Waddell, S., & Dentoni, D. (2015). The complexity of wicked problems in large scale change. *Journal of Organizational Change Management*.

Zohar, D., & Luria, G. (2004). Climate as a social-cognitive construction of supervisory safety practices: Scripts as proxy of behavior patterns. *Journal of Applied Psychology, 89*(2), 322.

SECTION 3

ORGANIZATIONAL PREPAREDNESS AND RESPONSE IN THE FACE OF ACUTE CRISIS

CHAPTER 7

HOSPITAL FINANCES DURING THE FIRST TWO YEARS OF THE COVID-19 PANDEMIC: EVIDENCE FROM WASHINGTON STATE HOSPITALS

Nathan W. Carroll, Shu-Fang Shih, Saleema A. Karim and Shoou-Yih D. Lee

Virginia Commonwealth University, USA

ABSTRACT

The COVID-19 pandemic created a broad array of challenges for hospitals. These challenges included restrictions on admissions and procedures, patient surges, rising costs of labor and supplies, and a disparate impact on already disadvantaged populations. Many of these intersecting challenges put pressure on hospitals' finances. There was concern that financial pressure would be particularly acute for hospitals serving vulnerable populations, including safety-net (SN) hospitals and critical access hospitals (CAHs). Using data from hospitals in Washington State, we examined changes in operating margins for SN hospitals, CAHs, and other acute care hospitals in 2020 and 2021. We found that the operating margins for all three categories of hospitals fell from 2019 to 2020, with SNs and CAHs sustaining the largest declines. During 2021, operating margins improved for all three hospital categories but SN operating margins still remained negative. Both changes in revenue and changes in expenses contributed to observed changes in operating margins. Our study is one of the first to describe how the financial effects of COVID-19 differed for SNs, CAHs, and other acute care hospitals over the first two years of the pandemic. Our results highlight the continuing financial vulnerability of SNs and demonstrate how the factors that contribute to profitability can shift over time.

Research and Theory to Foster Change in the Face of Grand Health Care Challenges
Advances in Health Care Management, Volume 22, 143–160
Copyright © 2024 Nathan W. Carroll, Shu-Fang Shih, Saleema A. Karim and Shoou-Yih D. Lee
Published under exclusive licence by Emerald Publishing Limited
ISSN: 1474-8231/doi:10.1108/S1474-823120240000022007

Keywords: Hospital financial management; COVID-19; safety-net hospitals; critical access hospitals; financial performance

INTRODUCTION

Volume 20 of *Advances in Healthcare Management* highlighted a number of grand challenges facing the healthcare system, including the imperative to care for vulnerable populations, the need to sustain the organizations providing care, and the challenges associated with navigating the pandemic (Hefner & Nembhard, 2021). In this chapter, we describe how hospitals at the intersection of these three challenges have navigated the pandemic period. In particular, we examine how the financial performance of hospitals caring for vulnerable populations has differed from the financial performance of other hospitals. We focus on urban safety-net (SN) hospitals and rural critical access hospitals (CAHs). Understanding how these particular hospitals performed financially is critical, because these hospitals are often the sole points of access to hospital care for many vulnerable, resource-poor communities (Coughlin et al., 2021). Moreover, these facilities experienced worse prepandemic financial performance, making them some of the least prepared to weather the financial rigors of the pandemic (Gaffney & Michelson, 2023), and raising concerns about hospital closures and, in turn, a loss of access to care for vulnerable populations (Boserup et al., 2021; Orlando & Field, 2021).

SN and CAHs: Key Access Points for Vulnerable Populations

Our research focuses on two types of hospitals that serve vulnerable populations: SN and CAHs. While there is no universally agreed upon definition for which facilities are SN hospitals, a 2000 Institute of Medicine report defined them as providers that deliver a significant level of care to uninsured patients, Medicaid beneficiaries, and other vulnerable patients (Lewin & Altman, 2000). Not surprisingly, these hospitals face distinct challenges attracting financial resources. SN hospitals are also, often, the primary care providers for large populations of racial and ethnic minorities (Hefner et al., 2021) and are most often located in urban areas (Popescu et al., 2019).

The other category of hospitals on which our work focuses are CAHs. Unlike SN status, CAH status is a formal designation made by the Centers of Medicare and Medicaid Services (CMS). In order to be designated a CAH, a hospital must be located over 35 miles from the nearest hospital (15 miles if the terrain poses particular transportation difficulties), or have been deemed a "necessary provider" by the state in which they are located (Casey et al., 2015). As a result, most CAHs are located in rural areas. CMS began the CAH program in the late 1990s to help financially sustain rural hospitals that were struggling under Medicare's prospective payment system. CAHs receive cost-based reimbursement from Medicare and many states' Medicaid programs rather than prospective payments. CAHs generally have worse financial performance than other rural hospitals (Holmes et al., 2013). The patient populations served by CAHs face relatively high rates of poverty, low employment rates, and significant challenges accessing transportation (Lahr et al., 2021).

Financial Performance for all Hospitals During COVID-19

At the onset of the COVID-19 pandemic, prior to the availability of data on its financial impacts, several studies utilized historical financial data from before the pandemic to assess hospitals' financial preparedness (Khullar et al., 2020; Nikpay & Smith, 2020). Furthermore, some studies utilized this method to speculate on the probable financial impacts of the pandemic on hospitals and other healthcare providers (Carroll & Smith, 2020; Cutler et al., 2020). Another set of papers examined effects of the pandemic on hospital volumes and finances in the earliest months of the pandemic (Birkmeyer et al., 2020; Jiang et al., 2020).

More recently, two studies examined the pandemic's effects over a slightly longer period. Rhodes et al. (2023) found that hospital margins declined by an average of 5.3 percentage points in 2020 (relative to 2019) and that these declines in margin were driven primarily by declines in operating revenue, though increased expenses also contributed to poor financial outcomes. Rhodes et al. (2023) also examined the financial effects of the pandemic on SN or rural hospitals as compared to other hospital types, and did not observe differences between hospital types. However, because of differences in hospital fiscal years and the challenge of aligning financial reporting with pandemic periods, the hospitals in this research were only exposed to an average of 6 months of the pandemic. A second paper by Wang et al. (2022) examined 2020 operating margins for hospitals with a fiscal year that aligned with the 2020 calendar year. The study found declines in operating margins and noted that these declines seemed to be similar for rural and nonrural hospitals. These two studies provided evidence on the financial preparedness and resilience of healthcare organizations during the early period of the COVID-19 pandemic. However, neither of them evaluated the prolonged impacts of the pandemic on the financial stability of hospitals. Furthermore, they focused on rural hospitals rather than CAHs (Rhodes et al., 2023; Wang et al., 2022).

The most recent analysis of hospital finances came from the consulting firm Kauffman Hall through their "National Hospital Flash Reports," which offered information on margins, revenue, and expenses from a proprietary sample of 900 US hospitals. Kauffman Hall reported that operating margins declined by 4.9 percentage points during 2020, and that these declines were driven by a combination of declining revenue and rising expenses (Kaufman Hall, 2021). A follow-up report in January of 2022 suggested that during 2022, hospital operating margins rose relative to the first year of the pandemic, but that margins still lagged their prepandemic levels (Kaufman Hall, 2022). The findings suggested that the volume of services hospitals offered during the last half of 2021 increased, but that the financial benefits associated with these revenue increases were limited because hospitals were being forced to cancel profitable elective surgeries to accommodate rising COVID-19-related hospitalizations. Although these reports provided a general understanding of the average performance of hospitals nationally, they did not distinguish between different hospital types, limiting their ability to evaluate if hospitals serving vulnerable populations were disproportionately affected by the COVID-19 pandemic.

The aim of our study is to examine the financial performance of various hospital types over the initial two years of the COVID-19 pandemic and to determine factors that influenced these changes in financial performance. Our research extends prior work in three primary ways. First, our research compares the effects of the pandemic on SNs, CAHs, and other acute care hospitals. Distinguishing between different hospital types is crucial as each type serves a unique patient population, draws employees from different labor markets, and operates within different reimbursement environments. These variations may result in different impacts of the COVID-19 pandemic on each type of hospital. Moreover, understanding the financial performance of these hospital types is important given their role in ensuring access to care for vulnerable communities and their often precarious financial position in the years prior to COVID-19. Second, our dataset includes data on factors that affect hospital operating margins, including not only revenue and expenses but also service volumes, revenue by payer, and categories of expense. These additional data allow us to gain a better understanding of the factors driving observed changes in revenue and expenses that impact hospital margins. Understanding the unique advantages and vulnerabilities of each hospital type will offer payers and policymakers' insight into strategies that can effectively support these facilities in maintaining financial sustainability. Finally, this research extends work from Wang et al. (2022) and Rhodes et al. (2023) by examining hospitals' financial experience throughout the second year of the pandemic as well as the first. This is an important contribution since the factors affecting hospital finances, and the financial impact of the pandemic, may have shifted over time. It is unlikely that the experiences of hospitals during the first six months of the COVID-19 pandemic will be indicative of their experiences in subsequent periods.

STUDY DATA AND METHODS

Study Data

The main source of financial data used in this analysis are financial reports from Washington State hospitals submitted to the Washington State Department of Health. Reports cover each calendar quarter from 2019–2021. Unlike the Medicare Cost Reports, which are widely used in hospital financial research, the quarterly Washington State financial reports that make up our dataset are reported on a consistent time period regardless of hospital fiscal year. Hospitals' organization and market characteristics are used to identify differences in the three groups of hospitals we construct. These data come from the American Hospital Association (AHA) 2019 Annual Survey, the Area Health Resource File (AHRF), and the Medicare Impact File.

The initial sample of Washington hospitals included 91 facilities after excluding specialty hospitals (e.g., long-term acute care hospitals, rehabilitation hospitals) that were likely subject to completely different pressures during the pandemic. We excluded five hospitals that targeted special populations (i.e., cancer patients and children), and four hospitals with margins less than 50% (which we considered to be erroneous values). Finally, we removed 20 hospitals from the sample with one or more missing quarters of data. The final sample is a balanced panel of 62 hospitals and 744 hospital-quarter observations.

Hospital Category Variables

This is an exploratory study seeking to identify differences in financial performance for different categories of hospitals over the first two years of the pandemic, and then to identify factors that caused changes in these hospitals' financial performance. To accomplish this, we first created three categories of hospitals: CAHs, SNs, and other acute care hospitals. CAHs were identified through the AHA annual survey data. Consistent with other studies, SN status was assigned based on a hospital's being in the top quartile of disproportionate share (DSH) patient percentage as reported on the Medicare Impact File (Gilman et al., 2014, 2015; Favini et al., 2017). The remaining hospitals constitute the group which we refer to as other acute care hospitals. These are general, medical surgical facilities, excluding specialty hospitals, ambulatory surgery centers, and hospitals serving select populations (e.g., Veterans Affairs hospitals, children's hospitals). To understand differences in the three hospital categories, we calculated mean values for each category for a set of organizational and market characteristics drawn from the AHA annual survey and the AHRF.

Financial Outcomes

Next, we used operating margins, calculated as operating income divided by operating revenue, as the dependent variable. In the Washington State financial reports, operating revenue includes net patient revenues as well as a category of other operating revenue which consists of a variety of revenue sources including parking, joint venture revenue, cafeteria revenue, and grants. Unfortunately, it is unclear how provider relief funds were accounted for in the Washington data, and there was variation in how relief funds were reported in audited financial statements (AICPA, 2021). We believe that the changes in margins we observe are primarily the result of changes in hospital operations, though it is possible that these may be influenced by the inclusion of some amount of relief funding – see the Discussion section for further consideration of this limitation.

To understand the factors contributing to changes in operating margins, we examined hospitals' revenue by payer (from Medicare, Medicaid, Self-pay, and other payers including commercial payers). We also examined changes in the volume of acute care discharges, ER visits, outpatient visits, and outpatient surgeries, and changes in expenses including supply expenses and expenses for employee salaries and benefits. In addition, we included variables capturing bad debt expense and charity care. In the Washington State data, these line items are reported separately rather than reported as part of the total expenses or a deduction from revenue.

We standardized each of these measures to help facilitate meaningful comparison between each of the three hospital categories. We chose to standardize by bed size rather than a measure of volume (e.g., discharges) because we wanted these measures to reflect overall changes in revenues generated and expenses incurred rather than drastic shifts in volume providers experienced during the pandemic (Birkmeyer et al., 2020).

Analysis

We calculated differences in each financial measure for each category of hospitals over the first two years of the pandemic, from calendar years 2019 to 2020, and then from 2020 to 2021. This analysis allowed us to understand the financial challenges hospitals faced in the first year of the pandemic, when the strictest lockdown measures and limits on nonemergency procedures were in place. Further, the comparisons highlighted the impact of COVID-19-related factors on SN and CAH facilities that provide access to vulnerable populations and how the effects differed from those on other acute care hospitals. We made the same between-group comparisons for the 2020–2021 period so that we could examine how the financial performance of hospital groups changed as the most severe COVID-19 restrictions ended. We used t-tests to assess whether our estimates were statistically significantly different from zero. We report whether changes are statistically significantly different from zero at significance levels of 0.01, 0.05, and 0.1.

We chose not to employ multivariate regression models to analyze the data for two reasons. First, we were interested in understanding the pandemic experience of different types of hospitals. Thus, understanding the impact of the pandemic on hospitals "holding other factors constant" was, in a sense, of somewhat limited utility. This study was focused on describing changes in margins for each hospital category during the pandemic. If, for example, changes in SN operating margins could be explained by, say, change in insurance rates or median incomes in the local market, it did not change the fact that SNs must find ways to support operations with less profit than they earned before the pandemic. Future research can more thoroughly investigate the factors affecting observed changes in financial performance. Our second reason for using simple comparisons of means was that our sample size was relatively small to begin with, and we did not have sufficient observations to segment our sample by hospital type covariates, year covariates, and covariates that describe other hospital and market characteristics.

STUDY RESULTS

Sample Characteristics

Table 7.1 shows the characteristics of the hospitals in the sample. Over 75% of both SN and other acute-care hospitals were system-affiliated, whereas less than a

Table 7.1. 2019 Operating and Market Characteristics.

	Safety-Net (Mean/SD)	CAH (Mean/SD)	Other Acute (Mean/SD)
System-affiliated	0.85	0.30	0.79
	(0.38)	(0.47)	(0.41)
For-profit	0	0.050	0.069
	(0)	(0.22)	(0.26)
Not-for-profit	0.77	0.30	0.69
	(0.44)	(0.47)	(0.47)
Government	0.23	0.65	0.21
	(0.44)	(0.49)	(0.41)
Bed size	316	24.1	208.8
	(202.5)	(11.5)	(134.1)
Rural	0	0.30	0
	(0)	(0.47)	(0)
HHI	0.59	0.93	0.69
	(0.40)	(0.16)	(0.33)
Median Household Income 2019 ($)	79,681	62,984	81,078
	(20,026)	(15,062)	(15,760)
% Below poverty level	11.4	14.5	10.3
	(2.48)	(4.58)	(2.19)
% Without health ins	7.65	9.28	7.58
	(1.99)	(2.10)	(1.40)
Unemployment rate	4.60	5.46	4.25
	(1.61)	(1.40)	(1.20)
Educational attainment	9.08	10.1	8.05
% less than high school	(4.54)	(5.25)	(2.44)
	90.9	89.9	92.0
% greater than h.s.	(4.54)	(5.25)	(2.44)
	35.4	30.4	35.7
% w/4+ years of college	(14.9)	(13.9)	(10.5)
	0.85	0.30	0.79
Observations	13	20	29

quarter of CAHs were part of a system. For-profit ownership was relatively rare across all hospital categories with the majority of CAHs being government owned (usually by local governments) and the majority of SN and other acute care hospitals being owned by not-for-profit organizations. SN facilities were the largest by bed size (mean = 316) with other acute care hospitals having a smaller mean bed size (209) and CAHs having a significantly smaller mean bed size (24). Not surprisingly, given the requirements for CAH designation, 30% of CAHs were in a rural core–based statistical area and CAHs operated in the least competitive markets while the Herfindahl–Hirschman Index (HHI) for SNs and other acute care hospitals were similar. As expected, SNs and CAHs were located in counties with high levels of poverty and lower median household income than other acute care hospitals.

Annual Operating Margins

Fig. 7.1 shows annual operating margins for CAHs, SNs, and other general acute care facilities for the first two years of the pandemic, as compared to 2019. The experience of each of these facilities was markedly different. CAH margins were negative prior to the pandemic (−2.05%), fell further during 2020 (to −3.31%), and then improved markedly in 2021, rising to 2.24%. SN facilities, like CAHs, began in 2019 with negative margins (−0.04%), which also fell during the pandemic (to −2.68%) and then remained negative in 2021 (at −1.75%). Finally, other general acute care hospitals began the period with positive margins averaging 3.64% in 2019. Their margins fell to −1.93% in 2020 but partially recovered and became positive again in 2021, averaging 1.65%.

Factors Affecting Operating Results for CAHs

Table 7.2 shows changes in CAHs financial performance between 2019 and 2021. During 2020, despite concerns about patients' reluctance to seek care and restrictions on elective surgeries potentially affecting hospital revenues, CAHs actually enjoyed a statistically and practically significant increase in operating revenue of $78,159 per bed ($p < 0.01$). This increase in revenue was driven by a combination of smaller increases in revenue across payers, with the exception of

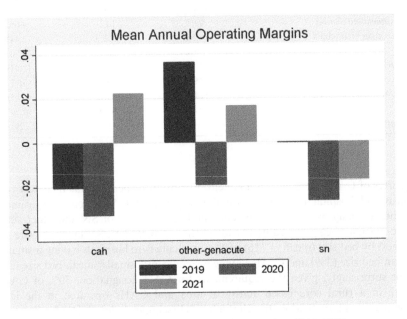

Fig. 7.1.   Mean Hospital Operating Margins: 2019–2021.

Table 7.2. Changes in Financial Measures – Critical Access Hospitals.

	2019 (Mean/SD)	Change From '19 to '20 (Mean/SD)	Change From '20 to '21 (Mean/SD)
Operating margin	−0.021	−0.013	0.056***
	(0.088)	(0.045)	(0.069)
Revenues (per Bed)			
Total operating	1,628,932	78,159***	223,851***
	(815,363)	(71,827)	(255,864)
Medicare	710,021	3,145	123,111***
	(413,659)	(119,125)	(117,288)
Medicaid	231,990	6,453	38,750***
	(146,697)	(34,668)	(49,964)
Self-pay	60,334	1,824	2,648
	(44,599)	(25,841)	(20,721)
Other payers	568,769	−5,533	91,272***
	(343,654)	(43,485)	(110,248)
Volumes (per Bed)			
Acute care discharges	17.8	−2.37***	0.77
	(12.2)	(3.50)	(2.92)
Emergency Room visits	280.1	−49.6***	40.3***
	(161.3)	(35.8)	(38.0)
Outpatient visits	2,614	−22.9	412
	(1,992)	(518)	(1,165)
Outpatient surgeries	22.4	−0.52	10.4**
	(23.7)	(5.75)	(21.5)
Expenses (per Bed)			
Total operating expenses	1,521,455	119,178***	117,491***
	(721,140)	(109,880)	(115,837)
Supplies	179,550	12,368**	25,843***
	(134,177)	(23,325)	(34,410)
Salary and benefits	869,136	76,127***	63,083***
	(428,961)	(79,658)	(71,184)
Uncompensated Care (per Bed)			
Bad debt	52,452	−10,148	5,011
	(43,837)	(27,440)	(49,928)
Charity care	51,007	−6,283	−1,664
	(53,546)	(17,804)	(24,957)
Observations			20

Note: Stars refer to significance levels determined by a *t*-test analyzing whether the change was different than zero. *** denotes $p < 0.01$, **$p < 0.05$, *$p < 0.1$.

other commercial payers. Interestingly, these increases in revenue did not appear to be driven by increases in the volume of services provided since CAHs experienced, on average, declines in the mean number of acute care discharges, ER visits, outpatient visits, and outpatient surgeries delivered. Despite declines in the provision of services, CAHs experienced increases in total operating expenses, with a mean increase of $119,178 per bed ($p < 0.01$). This increase was driven primarily by increases in the costs of supplies (mean of $12,368, $p < 0.01$) and salary and benefits (mean of $76,127, $p < 0.01$).

During 2021, CAH margins improved, above where they had been in 2019 (mean of 5.6% compared to -2.1%). Like in 2020, their revenues increased, but in 2021, the magnitude of these increases was larger, with an average increase in operating revenue of $223,851 compared to 2021 ($p < 0.01$). This increase was driven by increases in revenues per bed coming from all payer types. Unlike in 2020, the 2021 increases in revenue were supported by increases in all the measured types of utilization. These included a statistically significant increase in ER visits (mean $= 40.3$, $p < 0.01$), as well as a substantial increase in outpatient surgeries (mean $= 10.4$, $p < 0.05$), that was much larger in magnitude than the slight decrease in outpatient surgeries during 2020.

Factors Affecting Operating Results for SN Hospitals

Table 7.3 describes changes in financial performance for SN hospitals over the course of the pandemic. SN margins fell drastically in 2020, dropping by 2.6 percentage points, then rose by almost a percentage point in 2021, while still remaining negative. The 2020 decline in margins was caused by a combination of declining revenue and increasing expenses. Revenue declines were seen across all payers, though only the $34,352 mean decline in Medicare payments was statistically significant ($p < 0.05$). Declines in volumes for all service types contributed to declining revenue, although the most significant declines were seen in acute care discharges (mean decline $= 3.66$ discharges per bed, $p < 0.01$) and ER visits (mean decline $= 40.3$, $p < 0.01$). Expenses increased slightly and the increase was not statistically significant.

Improvements in margins in 2021 were driven by a $155,550 mean per bed increase in total revenue ($p < 0.01$), which reflected an increase in revenue from all payers with the exception of self-pay revenue. These increases in revenue were paired with increases in the volume of services provided, coming primarily from a 15.4 mean increase in ER visits per bed ($p < 0.05$) and a mean increase in outpatient visits per bed of 135 ($p < 0.01$). The increase in mean expenses ($130,713 per bed, $p < 0.01$) was only slightly lower than the mean increase in revenue. Increasing operating expenses were driven by increases in both supply expenses and salary/benefit expenses.

Factors Affecting Operating Results for Other Acute Care Hospitals

Table 7.4 shows changes in other acute care hospitals' financial performance from 2019 to 2021. Of all three hospital types, other acute care hospitals had the largest mean decline in margins (5.6 percentage points) in 2020, but this group started 2019 with the strongest margins and, unlike SN facilities, was able to enjoy positive margins in 2021. Other acute care hospitals also experienced a mean decline in operating revenue during 2020 of $22,460 per bed. The revenue changes

Table 7.3. Changes in Financial Measures – Safety-Net Hospitals.

	2019 (Mean/SD)	Change From 2019 to 2020 (Mean/SD)	Change From 2020 to 2021 (Mean/SD)
Operating margin	−0.00037	−0.026*	0.0092
	(0.039)	(0.049)	(0.039)
Revenues (per Bed)			
Total operating	1,744,724	−15,369	155,550***
	(671,245)	(120,757)	(124,658)
Medicare	499,091	−34,352**	60,188***
	(186,772)	(43,789)	(32,231)
Medicaid	274,997	−22,172	36,221**
	(151,125)	(63,845)	(50,689)
Self-pay	80,402	−7,995	−2,959
	(65,844)	(17,870)	(14,489)
Other payers	870,139	−14,292	69,202***
	(343,861)	(79,649)	(49,464)
Volumes (per Bed)			
Acute care discharges	40.5	−3.66***	0.79
	(14.8)	(3.94)	(2.97)
ER visits	197	−40.3***	15.4**
	(110)	(35.7)	(19.4)
Outpatient visits	1,262	−41.3	135***
	(1,017)	(309)	(142)
Outpatient surgeries	24.2	−1.47	1.11
	(15.5)	(4.43)	(5.17)
Expenses (per Bed)			
Total operating expenses	1,604,847	45,868	130,713***
	(617,100)	(182,060)	(114,218)
Supplies	263,349	−6,266	26,177**
	(118,547)	(30,772)	(24,775)
Salary and benefits	768,996	52,170*	65,682***
	(369,031)	(100,562)	(63,279)
Uncompensated Care (per Bed)			
Bad debt	32,165	13,461	−1,813
	(34,074)	(36,000)	(15,512)
Charity care	101,768	−19,177**	1,098
	(59,834)	(31,652)	(22,428)
Observations			13

Note: Stars refer to significance levels determined by a *t*-test analyzing whether the change was different than zero. *** denotes $p < 0.01$, **$p < 0.05$, *$p < 0.1$.

by payer were mixed and included small increases in revenue from Medicaid and self-pay patients. The decline in total revenue was not statistically significant, and among individual payer categories, only the decline in Medicare revenue was statistically significant (mean decline = 36,028, $p < 0.05$). Contributing to the

Table 7.4. Changes in Financial Measures – Other Acute Care Hospitals.

	2019 (Mean/SD)	Change From 2019 to 2020 (Mean/SD)	Change From 2020 to 2021 (Mean/SD)
Operating margin	0.036	−0.056***	0.036**
	(0.074)	(0.064)	(0.070)
Revenues (per Bed)			
Total operating	1,851,959	−22,460	159,596.9***
	(584,016)	(200,860)	(201,543)
Medicare	631,952	−36,028**	99,994***
	(338,775)	(71,002)	(113,630)
Medicaid	223,762	3,998	34,111***
	(99,699)	(110,046)	(31,226)
Self-pay	74,569	3,919	−6,642
	(50,644)	(28,259)	(22,937)
Other payers	934,857	−49,452	68,564***
	(357,495)	(164,520)	(121,921)
Volumes (per Bed)			
Acute care discharges	44.9	−3.53***	−1.61
	(12.0)	(6.13)	(7.75)
ER visits	227	−39.0***	18.1***
	(105)	(27.6)	(18.3)
Outpatient visits	1,606	−66.0	200.4***
	(1,128)	(398)	(277)
Outpatient surgeries	33.1	−3.11***	0.12
	(23.0)	(4.86)	(17.9)
Expenses (per Bed)			
Total operating expenses	1,655,207	69,372*	111,413***
	(573,810)	(185,247)	(143,901)
Supplies	290,227	−2,847	25,312***
	(147,067)	(42,548)	(24,998)
Salary and benefits	780,523	48,669***	70,709***
	(364,083)	(86,804)	(64,042)
Uncompensated Care (per Bed)			
Bad debt	28,737	21,535	−6,530
	(62,134)	(69,792)	(30,851)
Charity care	95,808	−25,762**	−2,490
	(90,479)	(64,306)	(13,910)
Observations			29

Note: Stars refer to significance levels determined by a *t*-test analyzing whether the change was different than zero. *** denotes $p < 0.01$, **$p < 0.05$, *$p < 0.1$.

decline in revenues were declines in acute care discharges (mean of 3.53 per bed, $p < 0.01$), ER visits (decline of 39 visits per bed, $p < 0.01$), and outpatient surgeries (mean decline of 3.11 per bed, $p < 0.01$). Mean operating expenses increased for this group by \$69,372 per bed ($p < 0.1$) between 2019 and 2021, driven largely by an increase in salary and benefits of \$48,669 per bed ($p < 0.01$).

During 2021, other acute-care hospitals experienced increases in both total operating revenue, and revenue from all payers with the exception of self-pay patients. The mean increase in operating revenue per bed was \$159,597 ($p < 0.01$), which was greater than the mean decrease in operating revenue during 2020. Revenue from all payers, with the exception of self-pay, increased. Supporting these increases in revenue were increases in the volume of ER visits (mean = 18.1, $P < 0.01$) and outpatient visits (mean = 200.4, $p < 0.01$). Operating expenses rose in 2021 as well, increasing by a mean of \$111,413 ($p < 0.01$). This increase was driven by increases in both supply expense and salary and benefits expense.

DISCUSSION

Our research highlights several important effects of the COVID-19 pandemic on hospital finances. First, there were substantial decreases in operating margins across all hospital types during 2020, but the extent of recovery from financial stress differed among hospital types. Other acute care hospitals regained positive margins in the year 2021, though these improvements were dulled by rising salary and supply expenses. CAHs were less impacted by increasing labor and supply costs, owing to their cost-based reimbursement from Medicare and Washington State Medicaid. As a result, CAHs witnessed significant advancements in their operating results during the year 2021. On the contrary, SN hospitals faced the most significant challenges during the pandemic and are the only group to incur negative operating margins in both 2020 and 2021.

Practice and Policy Implications

These results have significant implications for both hospital management and health policy. The fluctuations in operating results over time suggests the necessity of continuing to monitor the financial impact of the rapidly changing pandemic on hospitals and the importance of understanding the heterogeneous effects on different types of hospitals. Multiple studies have demonstrated that COVID-19 has exacerbated health and healthcare disparities among specific populations, particularly those who are underserved or have low incomes. The continued poor financial performance of SN hospitals suggests these facilities may need additional funding support as funding from the CARES Act and other relief sources ends.

Our results also suggest important implications for management and research as it relates to periods of rapid change in general. One important implication for policymakers and academic researchers is to take a long-term perspective when evaluating the year-to-year changes in organizations' financial performance. This includes understanding the context of organizations' initial financial health at the outset of a period of significant change, and the cumulative effect that year-to-year changes in profitability can have on an organization's financial well-being. For instance, in our sample of hospitals, CAHs enjoyed the highest 2021 margins, even higher than mean margins for other acute care hospitals, despite past concerns about the financial stability of CAHs. Looking at this figure in isolation would ignore the fact that by 2021, CAHs had already been forced to muster the financial resources required to sustain losses in 2019 and 2020, and that these previous losses likely eroded CAHs cash savings and equity. Similarly, SN facilities sustained significant losses in both 2020 and 2021, and returning to even a prepandemic state of financial health will require several years of margins of much greater magnitude than SNs enjoyed in 2019. In periods of rapid and significant change, monitoring the financial health of organizations should be an ongoing effort that requires understanding a long trajectory of each organization's financial performance and the persistent impact that past losses can have on a hospital's present resources.

These recommendations are consistent with best practices proposed by finance professional groups, including the Government Finance Officers Association (2023). Currently, the Medicare Payment Advisory Commission (MedPAC) is responsible for monitoring the financial health of hospitals receiving Medicare fee-for-service payments (including SN hospitals) and advising Congress on the adequacy of Medicare payments. Similarly, CMS' Flex Monitoring team helps to track the financial status of CAHs, to identify financial challenges, and to make policymakers aware of these challenges. However, both of these organizations rely heavily on the Medicare Cost Report data to carry out their financial monitoring mandates. Unfortunately, Medicare Cost Report data lack important financial information, including cash flow information, that would improve analysts' ability to monitor long-term financial trends that could ultimately affect hospital sustainability and communities' access to care. Requiring hospitals to submit audited financial statements to these federal agencies could improve their ability to monitor hospitals' financial status (Kane & Magnus, 2001).

Theoretical Implications

These results also have implications for theories that describe how organizations can successfully access necessary resources, emphasizing that the characteristics that make hospitals profitable can shift during times of significant change. In 2019, the "other acute care hospital" group had the highest margins in our sample. These hospitals operated in an environment that was primarily fee-for-service. As a result, the resources that supported these facilities' financial success were the ability to provide high volumes of services to a well-resourced patient population. During 2019, these resources were plentiful for the other acute care hospital group, which boasted the highest utilization volumes (discharges and outpatient surgeries) and were located in communities with the highest insurance rates and household incomes. CAHs performed worse financially in 2019. These facilities lacked the resources that facilitated success from fee-for-service payers since CAHs were located in areas with lower incomes and lower insurance rates. CAHs also received cost-based reimbursement from Medicare and Washington

State's Medicaid agency, which limited their financial gains. However, during the pandemic, it seems that the characteristics that had contributed to CAHs relatively poor financial performance were no longer a liability.

In the second year of the pandemic, the cost-based reimbursement that CAHs received compensated these facilities for the rapidly increasing supply and wage expenses that all three categories of hospitals experienced. During 2021, the CAH group experienced the largest improvement in operating margin of all three hospital groups. This improvement was driven by a significant increase in revenue per bed, despite providing lower per-bed numbers of admissions, ER visits, and outpatient surgeries than in 2019 or 2020. The increases in supply and salary expense that eroded profits for other providers helped to increase revenue for the CAHs. Because of wage and supply inflation during the pandemic period, the cost-based reimbursement system that may have contributed to CAHs relatively poor prepandemic financial performance was now an avenue through which hospitals could successfully attract financial resources. The low rates of insurance and income in CAH markets were of less importance in determining hospitals' ability to attract financial resources than they had been previously.

The experience of CAHs during COVID-19 emphasizes the importance of understanding how significant changes in the environment can affect the organizational and environmental characteristics that allow healthcare organizations to compete successfully for resources. This is particularly important for organizational scholars conducting research in healthcare management, since such research often relies on resource-based theories such as the resource-based view of the firm or resource dependency theory. Our results suggest that when scholars employ these theories to understand how organizations are coping with periods of significant change, they should be careful in identifying the characteristics that allow the firm to successfully compete for resources, because these characteristics can shift over time. Shifts in the characteristics that afford healthcare organizations access to resources are likely to be a concern going forward as reimbursement systems evolve. In the future, new "value-based" payment systems may shift resources to providers with characteristics that are not currently rewarded under traditional fee-for-service reimbursement. These characteristics could include the ability to manage population health or the ability to manage patient costs across a continuum of care.

Just as the factors that help organizations successfully compete for resources can change over time, these factors can also differ from one healthcare delivery system to another. As a result, the financial impact of environmental stresses can vary based on how healthcare organizations are funded or reimbursed. For instance, financial losses during COVID-19 have been more drastic among US healthcare organizations than for healthcare organizations in England, Germany, and Israel. These differences arise as a result of the US's dependence on reimbursement methods tied to the volume of medical services provided (Waitzberg et al., 2021). Even within the United States, healthcare organizations' financial performance during COVID-19 has prompted calls to consider other funding structures, including global budget strategies similar to those used by other countries to finance health services (Fried et al., 2020). Further research is needed to understand how COVID-19 has affected the financial sustainability of healthcare organizations, such as those in the Veterans Health Administration, that operate under different funding mechanisms and treat particular patient populations. Such research will improve our understanding of different funding arrangements' ability to endure external shocks and maintain financial sustainability.

Limitations

This study's primary limitation is that it only included observations from a single state. Focusing only on hospitals in Washington State afforded us access to an unusually rich dataset that was more recent than other available data. However, the trends and effects that we observed may not be representative of the experience of hospitals nationally. In this chapter, we sought to understand how the pandemic affected hospitals' core operations, and we focused on analyzing changes in operating margins and some of the determinants of these margins. However, we should also acknowledge that many hospitals may have access to significant nonoperating sources of funds including returns from financial investments. We excluded these nonoperating funds from our analyses to focus on understanding how the pandemic affected hospital operations, without considering the effects of swings in the financial markets. As a result of this choice, our profitability estimates did not reflect all the sources of funds available to hospitals and nonoperating funds did provide a significant increase to many hospitals' margins (Kaufmann Hall, 2022; Wang et al., 2022). Another reason that we focused on operating results was to examine financial effects in the absence of CARES Act funding available to hospitals. Unfortunately, we cannot be confident that our data did not include any funding from the CARES Act, since it is unclear how provider relief funds were accounted for in Washington State. According to the Association of International Certified Professional Accountants (2021), there were varying practices even in audited financial statements. This presents a limitation in our analysis, as we are unable to accurately determine the exact extent to which relief funding may have influenced the changes in hospital margins we observe. This limitation aside, we believe that the changes in margins primarily stem from changes in hospital operations, but cannot completely rule out the potential impact of relief funding. While our analyses were focused on changes in hospital profitability, we must acknowledge that there are other factors that determine an organization's financial health, including the adequacy of the organization's cash holdings and its degree of leverage. Better understanding COVID-19's impact on those financial characteristics is an excellent opportunity for future research. Despite these limitations, this study offers valuable insight into how financial results differed for CAHs, SNs, and other acute care hospitals over the first two years of the pandemic.

CONCLUSION

Despite consistent declines in margins for all hospital types in 2020, the three types of hospitals we examined (CAHs, SNs, and other acute care hospitals) differed markedly in their 2021 financial results as well as their financial results in the year prior to the pandemic. From a policy perspective, the successful rebound for CAHs in 2021 underlies the fact that providers operating under alternative reimbursement systems can have different financial responses to significant market changes. This seemingly obvious fact will be important to keep in mind in the future as the variation in reimbursement models to which hospitals are exposed increases. More immediately, policymakers need to be concerned about the slow recovery of SNs. From a theory perspective, our results highlight the importance of understanding the ways in which organizations compete for resources, and the fact that periods of great change can alter the characteristics and strategies that affect hospital financial performance.

REFERENCES

AICPA. (2021). Q&A section 6400: Health care entities: 0.63 background to sections 6400.64-.70– CARES Act provisions specific to health care entities. AICPA.

Birkmeyer, J. D., Barnato, A., Birkmeyer, N., Bessler, R., & Skinner, J. (2020). The impact of the COVID-19 pandemic on hospital admissions in the United States. *Health Affairs, 39*(11), 2010–2017.

Boserup, B., McKenney, M., & Elkbuli, A. (2021). The financial strain placed on America's hospitals in the wake of the COVID-19 pandemic. *The American Journal of Emergency Medicine, 45*, 530.

Carroll, N. W., & Smith, D. G. (2020). Financial implications of the COVID-19 epidemic for hospitals: A case study. *Journal of Health Care Finance, 46*(4), 11–22.

Casey, M. M., Moscovice, I., Holmes, G. M., Pink, G. H., & Hung, P. (2015). Minimum-distance requirements could harm high-performing critical-access hospitals and rural communities. *Health Affairs, 34*(4), 627–635. https://doi-org.proxy.library.vcu.edu/10.1377/hlthaff.2014.0788

Coughlin, T. A., Ramos, C., & Samuel-Jakubos, H. (2021). *Safety net hospitals in the COVID-19 crisis: How five hospitals have fared financially.* Urban Institute.

Cutler, D. M., Nikpay, S., & Huckman, R. S. (2020). The business of medicine in the era of COVID-19. *JAMA, 323*(20), 2003–2004.

Favini, N., Hockenberry, J. M., Gilman, M., Jain, S., Ong, M. K., Adams, E. K., & Becker, E. R. (2017). Comparative trends in payment adjustments between safety-net and other hospitals since the introduction of the hospital readmission reduction program and value-based purchasing. *JAMA, 317*(15), 1578–1580.

Fried, J. E., Liebers, D. T., & Roberts, E. T. (2020). Sustaining rural hospitals after COVID-19: The case for global budgets. *JAMA, 324*(2), 137–138.

Gaffney, L. K., & Michelson, K. A. (2023). Analysis of hospital operating margins and provision of safety net services. *JAMA Network Open, 6*(4), e238785.

Gilman, M., Adams, E. K., Hockenberry, J. M., Wilson, I. B., Milstein, A. S., & Becker, E. R. (2014). California safety-net hospitals likely to be penalized by ACA value, readmission, and meaningful-use programs. *Health Affairs, 33*(8), 1314–1322.

Gilman, M., Hockenberry, J. M., Adams, E., Milstein, A. S., Wilson, I. B., & Becker, E. R. (2015). The financial effect of value-based purchasing and the hospital readmissions reduction program on safety-net hospitals in 2014: A cohort study. *Annals of Internal Medicine, 163*(6), 427–436.

Government Finance Officers Association. (2023). Best practices – The use of trend data and comparative data for financial analysis. https://www.gfoa.org/materials/the-use-of-trend-data-and-comparative-data-for-financial/. Accessed on May 10, 2023.

Hefner, J. L., Hogan, T. H., Opoku-Agyeman, W., & Menachemi, N. (2021). Defining safety net hospitals in the health services research literature: A systematic review and critical appraisal. *BMC Health Services Research, 21*(1), 278. https://doi-org.proxy.library.vcu.edu/10.1186/s12913-021-06292-9

Hefner, J. L., & Nembhard, I. M. (Eds.). (2021). *The contributions of health care management to grand health care challenges. Advances in healthcare management* (Vol. 20). Emerald Publishing Limited.

Holmes, G. M., Pink, G. H., & Friedman, S. A. (2013). The financial performance of rural hospitals and implications for elimination of the critical access hospital program. *The Journal of Rural Health : Official Journal of the American Rural Health Association and the National Rural Health Care Association, 29*(2), 140–149. https://doi-org.proxy.library.vcu.edu/10.1111/j.1748-0361.2012.00425.x

Jiang, J. X., Bai, G., Gustafsson, L., & Anderson, G. F. (2020). *Canary in a coal mine? A look at initial data on COVID-19's impact on U.S. hospitals.* Commonwealth Fund.

Kane, N. M., & Magnus, S. A. (2001). The Medicare cost report and the limits of hospital accountability: Improving financial accounting data. *Journal of Health Politics, Policy and Law, 26*(1), 81–106.

Kaufman Hall. (2021). *National hospital flash report.*

Kaufman Hall. (2022). *National hospital flash report: January 2022.* Kaufman Hall.

Khullar, D., Bond, A. M., & Schpero, W. L. (2020). COVID-19 and the financial health of US hospitals. *JAMA, 323*(21), 2127–2128.

Lahr, M., Chantarat, T., Quick, M., Pick, M., & Moscovice, I. (2021). How critical access hospitals are addressing the social needs of rural populations. https://www.flexmonitoring.org/sites/flexmonitoring.umn.edu/files/media/FMT_PB61_2021.pdf. Accessed on December 9, 2022.

Lewin, M. E., & Altman, S. (2000). Institute of medicine. In *America's health care safety net: Intact but endangered.*

Nikpay, S., & Smith, D. G. (2020). Hospital financial preparedness and COVID-19. *Journal of Health Care Finance, 46*(4).

Orlando, A. W., & Field, R. I. (2021). Measuring the COVID-19 financial threat to hospital markets. *INQUIRY: The Journal of Health Care Organization, Provision, and Financing, 58.* https://doi.org/10.1177/00469580211059985

Popescu, I., Fingar, K. R., Cutler, E., Guo, J., & Jiang, H. J. (2019). Comparison of 3 safety-net hospital definitions and association with hospital characteristics. *JAMA Network Open, 2*(8), e198577. https://doi-org.proxy.library.vcu.edu/10.1001/jamanetworkopen.2019.8577

Rhodes, J. H., Santos, T., & Young, G. (2023). The early impact of the COVID-19 pandemic on hospital finances. *Journal of Healthcare Management, 68*(1), 38–55.

Waitzberg, R., Quentin, W., Webb, E., & Glied, S. (2021). The structure and financing of health care systems affected how providers coped with COVID-19. *The Milbank Quarterly, 99*(2), 542–564.

Wang, Y., Bai, G., & Anderson, G. (2022). COVID-19 and hospital financial viability in the US. *JAMA Health Forum, 3*(5), e221018.

CHAPTER 8

SUSTAINING PREPAREDNESS IN HOSPITALS

Elveta D. Smith

University of North Carolina at Wilmington, USA

ABSTRACT

Purpose: *The years following the 9/11/2001 terrorists attacks saw a marked increase in community and hospital emergency preparedness, from communications across community networks, development of policies and procedures, to attainment and training in the use of biological warfare resources. Regular drills ensured emergency and health care personnel were trained and prepared to address the next large-scale crisis, especially from terrorist and bioterrorist attacks. This chapter looks at some of the more familiar global health issues over the past two decades and the lessons learned from hospital responses to inform hospital management in preparation for future incidents.*

Search Methods: *This study is a narrative review of the literature related to lessons learned from four major events in the time period from 2002 to 2023 – SARS, MERS, Ebola, and COVID-19.*

Search Results: *The initial search yielded 25,913 articles; 57 articles were selected for inclusion in the study.*

Discussion and Conclusions: *Comparison of key issues and lessons learned among the four major events described in this article – SARS, MERS, Ebola, and COVID-19 – highlight that several lessons are "relearned" with each event. Other key issues, such as supply shortages, staffing availability, and hospital capacity to simultaneously provide care to noninfectious patients came to the forefront during the COVID-19 pandemic. A primary, ongoing concern for hospitals is how to maintain their preparedness given competing priorities, resources, and staff time. This concern remains post-COVID-19.*

Research and Theory to Foster Change in the Face of Grand Health Care Challenges
Advances in Health Care Management, Volume 22, 161–178
Copyright © 2024 Elveta D. Smith
Published under exclusive licence by Emerald Publishing Limited
ISSN: 1474-8231/doi:10.1108/S1474-823120240000022008

Keywords: SARS; MERS; Ebola; COVID-19; bioterrorism; lessons learned

INTRODUCTION

Many of us remember where we were and what we were doing on the morning of September 11, 2001. As the unfolding horror of terrorist attacks on American soil struck fear and incredulity in the hearts of Americans, first responders and health care personnel were immersed in a new kind of emergency. Sure, many communities had drills of what to do in an emergency, but when reality struck, it was as if much of that had been a television show or local play. In the days immediately following September 11, as the news was released of anthrax being mailed, everyone became wary of receiving mail and packages, and communities within fallout distance of any military base were on heightened alert.

The next few years saw a marked increase in emergency preparedness, from communications across community networks, development of policies and procedures, to attainment and training in the use of biological warfare resources. Regular drills ensured emergency and health care personnel were trained and prepared to address the next large-scale crisis, especially from terrorist and bioterrorist attacks. There were viral epidemics overseas, like SARS, MERS, and Ebola, but limited exposure in the United States. When bird flu (H1N1 in 2007) and swine flu (H5N1 in 2009) were predicted to wreak havoc on American communities, these policies and procedures may have still been fresh enough in our minds.

However, when the COVID-19 global pandemic began in March 2020, health care providers seemed to be overwhelmed from the beginning. Isolation procedures, including policies on personal protective equipment use and reuse, in emergency rooms were either forgotten or overwhelmed by the sheer volume of patients presenting with COVID-19 symptoms (Cohen & van der Meulen Rodgers, 2020; Mehrotra et al., 2020). Considering those symptoms included respiratory distress, one would assume these patients were immediately triaged into isolation areas, and health care providers took additional precautions in testing, diagnosis, and treatment. With the high volume of health care providers who contracted COVID-19, these precautions were either inadequate or implemented too late (Godshall & Banach, 2021). This could not be the result of ignorance of the growing potential for impact or of the presenting signs and symptoms and was also not an unprecedented situation, although not to this level.

This situation was not confined to hospitals, urgent care centers, or physician practices. In general, the official warnings and notices about the contagion and needed precautions lagged behind the news and social media. Even so, it would appear that public belief in the credibility of those two communication outlets was low because, although stress was created, no actionable instructions were provided, and seemingly few administrators implemented emergency precautions immediately. Some did not do so before the government declared a public emergency, and states began restricting congregating and closed businesses to try and halt the rapid spread of COVID-19. These measures appeared to be a case of "closing the barn door after the horses have escaped." When did health care providers and state and local emergency management organizations begin relying on the government and political establishment to determine there is a health care crisis? These recent situations have led to research into the levels and types of emergency preparedness communities across the United States. D'Emidio et al. (2022) report that between 2002 and 2021, the Federal Emergency Management Agency (FEMA) has provided more than $52 billion in grants supporting state and local emergency preparedness. While the investments in those earlier years were driven by terrorist events of September 11, 2001, D'Emidio et al. (2022) point out that incidents have seen increasing frequency and severity, as well as a variety of national disasters.

COVID-19 certainly is not the first instance of threatened or actual public health emergencies. While we will not go back to the outbreak of the so-called Spanish flu near the end of World War I, this narrative review will look back to 2001 when the terrorist attacks on September 11, 2001, threw the United States into a tailspin. In this time of both civil and global unrest, the reality of continued threats and incidences of viral and biological, not to mention nuclear, contamination is a possibility. Ongoing preparation and practice of emergency communications and procedures are imperative. The world cannot afford to be caught unprepared to deal with the next such emergency. This chapter looks at some of the more familiar global health issues over the past two decades and the lessons that can be learned from hospital response to inform hospital management in preparation for future incidents. The situations included in this review include the September 11, 2001, terrorist attacks on American soil that highlighted the lack of preparedness for major emergencies, Severe Acute Respiratory Syndrome (SARS-CoV-1) in 2003, Middle East Respiratory Syndrome Coronavirus (MERS-CoV), Ebola Virus Disease (EVD), and, finally, the novel 2019 Coronavirus Disease (SARS-CoV-2 referred to as COVID-19).

METHODS

This study is a narrative review of the literature related to lessons learned from five major events in the time period from 2002 to 2023. Databases used were PUBMED, CINAHL Plus, CDC.gov, WHO.int. Article inclusion criteria were bioterrorism, SARS, MERS, Ebola, COVID-19, and "lessons learned." The article also had to be based in North America. Articles with specific disease or treatment foci were excluded. The initial search yielded 25,913 articles; 1,142 of these were selected based on the inclusion and exclusion criteria. From these, 130 articles were selected based on title review; from that list, 57 articles were selected based on abstract review pending full article review with 57 selected for inclusion in the study.

The following section presents a summary of the research on the lessons learned from these four large-scale viral epidemics, and then Table 8.1 identifies lessons common to these four case studies and therefore important for hospital administration to remember in preparation for future incidents.

Table 8.1. Comparison of Key Lessons Identified.

Key Issues	SARS	MERS	Ebola	Covid-19
Communication – conflicts	X	X	X	X
Incident Command Centers – development and training	X		X	X
Ability to rapidly increase availability of specialty beds/surge of patients	X		X	X
Preparation of first responders	X		X	
Intake documentation/screening tool identifying travel/EHR		X	X	X
Ability to quickly recognize signs and symptoms to take preventative measures		X	X	
Vigilant infection control processes		X	X	X
Use common sense in treating new (undiagnosed) diseases		X		
PPE issues – availability, standardization, cost			X	X
Point-of-care labs and diagnostic testing			X	X
Increase number of negative pressure/isolation rooms			X	X
Regular drills and training at all levels, especially locally			X	X
Transportation safety of infectious patients – in house and between locations/facilities			X	
Supply shortages – restocking availability, Federal and State stockpile				X
Staffing – availability, being infected, fears for self and family, well-being				X
Capacity to continue care for noninfectious patients safely				X

RESULTS

Bioterrorism Sparks Emergency Readiness Responses

In the days following the airplane hijackings and crashes on September 11, 2001, a number of additional incidences occurred with chemicals being mailed or shipped to various political and public personalities. These events were very real to anyone with media access, and the horror of the events and their aftermath led to a sense of outrage, nationalism, and camaraderie. The media coverage brought instant awareness to the public attention, creating continued stress and concern about possible anthrax or other chemicals contaminating the postal distribution centers. Attention and preparations were narrowly focused on the current events – being prepared for plane crashes/mass casualties or bioterrorist attacks. Niska and Burt (2005) report that even the federal government had a narrow focus, funding hospital preparedness for bioterrorism attacks through the Bioterrorism Hospital Preparedness Program of the Health Resources and Services Administration (HRSA) in 2002. A survey of state and territorial health departments in late 2001 revealed that nearly half of the public health epidemiologists had no formal epidemiologic training (CDC MMWR, 2003). D'Emidio et al. (2022) report that between 2002 and 2021, the FEMA has provided more than $52 billion in grants supporting state and local emergency preparedness. As Gensheimer (2004) pointed out, there is overlap in preparedness preparation for bioterrorism and infectious disease so the opportunity was right to use funds to prepare the infrastructure and readiness at all levels for such emergencies.

The financial assistance for preparedness began in 2002, but even then it took time for assistance to be distributed down through the levels of government to reach the state, county, city, and facility level. Early preparations included expanding communication abilities between various federal agencies, like the Centers for Disease Control and Prevention (CDC), Health and Human Services (HHS), FEMA, and Homeland Security, and within state and local emergency response agencies and hospitals; training in bioterrorism and hospital acquisition and training in the use of decontamination shelters and hazmat protections all the way to the local hospital level; updating policies and procedures to include the expanded collaborations; training and drills in use of the communications and equipment; and use of after-action reports to improve in areas found lacking, then repeating the drills until most community participants felt confident in their ability to respond and perform as needed to an emergency. While the investments in those earlier years were driven by terrorist events of September 11, 2001, D'Emidio et al. (2022) point out that emergency incidents have seen increasing frequency and severity, as well as a variety of national disasters. Even during the emergency preparedness activities between 2002 and 2006, there continued to be international threats with potential to invade the United States. One of these was a new coronavirus, SARS.

SARS

Since 2002, the previously unknown coronavirus, SARS, has been of medical and scientific interest because of its "lethal nature and epidemic potential" (Hui & Zumla, 2019). The first case of SARS, called "atypical pneumonia," was identified in Foshan, China, in November 2002. Many health care workers were exposed, and one such physician subsequently visited Hong Kong, "where an outbreak of this severe pneumonia then occurred" (Hui & Zumla, 2019). It took several months, and hundreds of cases before the World Health Organization (WHO) then labeled it "severe acute respiratory syndrome" on March 15, 2003; then eight days later, a novel β coronavirus (SARS-CoV) was confirmed as the cause of the atypical pneumonia cases.

The first SARS case in North America occurred in Canada in March 2003, with outbreaks in Toronto hospitals. Many of these cases were traced to failures in infection control procedures. As noted by Booth and Stewart (2005) and others, there are transmission opportunities in health care that even proper infection control procedures may not prevent, such as medical procedures of intubation, bronchoscopy, and cardiopulmonary resuscitation (Zawilińska & Kosz-Vnenchak, 2014).

According to the CDC (n.d.), there were 29 probable cases, eight confirmed, and 137 suspect cases of SARS reported, all having traveled to other countries where SARS was spreading. The CDC worked closely with the WHO, as well as state and local health departments, bringing their global experiences and expertise to bear in providing local investigations and assistance (CDC, n.d.).

Then, in July 2003, the WHO declared the SARS epidemic over. During that nine month period, there were 8,096 cases with 774 deaths in 29 countries and regions. "It was evident that the global public health, medical, and scientific communities were not adequately prepared for the emergence of SARS. There were major disruptions to international air travel and major impacts on the health services and business in the affected countries. Since July 2003, there were at least four reappearances of SARS" as of the publication of the referenced article (Hui & Zumla, 2019). The later appearance of a SARS covariant in China occurred in late 2019, and is addressed later in this article under COVID-19 (SARS-CoV).

Although SARS was active in 2003 and 2004, while the United States was actively developing and improving its ability to respond to such incidents, the SARS responses shed light on the aspects of preparedness that needed attention. These needs included:

- Improved *communication* at all levels to reduce conflicting guidelines (Booth & Stewart, 2005; Moore et al., 2005);
- Training and drills in the importance and *use of Incident Command Centers to coordinate communication* (Rebmann et al., 2007);
- Ability to *rapidly increase the number of specialty beds (ICU)* (Booth & Stewart, 2005);
- Ability to *continue some aspect of patient care for nonepidemic chronic patients* (Booth & Stewart, 2005);
- Training and *preparation of emergency medical responders* who may interact with infectious patients before they are transported and diagnosed at the hospital (Verbeek et al., 2004).

Khabbaz (2013) also stressed the importance of improving and growing public health capacities before the next major crisis occurred. As D'Emidio et al. (2022) point out, emergency incidents are seeing increasing frequency and severity on a global scale. As Hui and Zumla (2019) pointed out, numerous cases of SARS were spread across the world, from airflow in hotels and airplanes, surfaces, close contact with infected individuals, and especially from hospital transmissions (21% of cases globally were health care workers), all in a matter of four months, even in 2003. Were these "lessons learned" or "lessons observed but not learned" (Parker, 2020)?

MERS

The MERS-CoV is another zoonotic disease that initially spread from animals to humans, in this case, camels. MERS, first identified in Jordan in 2012 (Al-Abdallat et al., 2014), has a 35% mortality rate, and the greatest number of cases are human to human within health care systems. A majority of reported MERS-CoV cases have been from Saudi Arabia which noted a marked increase in reported cases in early 2014 (Oboho et al., 2015). Research into the causes of the increase related to contact with health care facilities and employees, other patients, or both (Oboho et al., 2015). Because of such high person-to-person transmission of MERS in health care settings, Assiri et al. (2013) emphasize the importance of surveillance and infection control measures.

Although the majority of cases have been in Saudi Arabia, travel to the Middle East resulted in cases confirmed in at least 27 other countries, including the United States (Azhar et al., 2019). As a result of one Korean traveler to the Arabian peninsula returning home sick, then visiting several hospitals before being diagnosed, 186 cases were reported in South Korea, with 181 of those cases being associated with hospital transmission, including 25 health care workers (Azhar et al., 2019).

Given the respiratory nature of the disease, and because nosocomial infection is a potential, the Korean doctors also warned that "early active quarantine might help reduce the size of the outbreak," (Kang et al., 2017). Al-Abdallat et al. (2014) report that quick isolation and "rigorous infection control practices" may have been instrumental in preventing transmissions at the hospitals in Jordan. The typical presenting symptoms of patients with MERS-CoV are fever, cough, and shortness of breath, with predominate spread by large respiratory droplets during coughing and sneezing (Zumla & Hui, 2014).

Although SARS-CoV and MERS-CoV have many similar symptoms, a few key differences should be noted. One important point is that "nosocomial infections of MERS typically occur early within the first week of illness, whereas those of SARS occur mainly in the second week of illness when the patient's upper airway viral load peaks on day 10 of illness" (Hui et al., 2014). Other differences are that MERS-CoV progresses to respiratory failure much quicker than SARS, MERS has a higher fatality rate, and occurs more frequently in males averaging 45 years of age, who have more comorbid conditions (Hui et al., 2014). Realizing that these presenting symptoms are also common with other illnesses and diseases, perhaps regular precautions should be maintained and enforced. All hospitals should have established policies and procedures for the quick identification of suspected or known MERS-CoV cases and should implement appropriate infection prevention measures. As noted above, one traveler came in contact with the virus then traveled home, thereby spreading the infection to 186 others (181 in hospitals) with 36 deaths.

Several recommendations have been made to address such infectious diseases. Omrani and Shalloub (2015) identified six key actions based on the MERS epidemic:

(1) The ease and frequency of travel that resulted in MERS, ultimately affecting 27 countries globally, supports the importance of the intake questionnaire to health care facilities. *Identifying recent travel or contact with anyone having traveled to the Middle East* can enable early precautions to prevent spread.
(2) *Fast and early recognition of disease* is critical to diagnosing and treating emerging infectious disease (EID).
(3) Common elements of the quick spread of virus, especially in hospitals, are overcrowded emergency departments (EDs) and the lack of sufficient

infection control procedures. *Remaining vigilant can prevent the unintentional spread when undiagnosed patients are present.*

(4) Especially with new diseases, presenting symptoms may not be consistent. Early precautions should not be considered as the whole story with such strict adherence that the natural progression of both the disease and different manifestations are not addressed. *Common sense in treating new diseases* must be coupled with the emerging scientific evidence.

(5) MERS is another zoonotic disease. In recent years, numerous contagions have been traced to monkeys, camels, chickens, bats, pigs, and others. Community *awareness that handling animals* should be accompanied with strict handwashing and precautions is important.

(6) *Social media is both an opportunity to communicate* accurate real-time data, but can also have great negative effects if used carelessly or inappropriately.

Ebola

Ebola viruses were initially identified in 1976 in the central African country of Zaire, now part of the Democratic Republic of the Congo. Over the next 37 years, sporadic outbreaks were noted in four other central African countries (Coltart et al., 2017). Then in 2013, a young child in Guinea contracted the virus and died within five days, marked the beginning of the largest, deadliest Ebola outbreak in history, with 28,646 cases and 11,323 deaths reported (WHO.int/ health-topics/ebola). Early symptoms of Ebola include "malaise, fatigue, muscle weakness, and/or myalgia, preceding or concurrent with fever $>100.4^0$F or $>38^0$C" (Baseler et al., 2017). As a result, the illness was initially thought to be cholera as it spread to Sierra Leone and Liberia. These symptoms are quickly followed in the first week by severe nausea, vomiting, and profuse watery diarrhea for five to seven more days, which quickly contribute to severe dehydration leading to multiple organ failures and death. Since the symptoms typically present before the virus is detectable in blood tests, there were initial delays in diagnosis, allowing for quick spread of the virus to caregivers and health care staff (Baseler et al., 2017). Over time, the virus has presented in different African countries with slight variations, so there are now six known types of Ebola.

Additional impacts noted were from diversion of resources from other urgent or life-threatening illnesses (Malvy et al., 2019). Diseases such as malaria, HIV, and tuberculosis require regular treatment, and resource availability, including health care personnel and physically safe locations for treatment, were limited. The immunocompromised condition of these patients put them at increased risk when exposed to Ebola. Being prepared for viral outbreaks, epidemics and pandemics could also reduce the impact of resource diversion from other illnesses, allowing overall health care services to safely continue, even if on a modified basis.

Some key actions to control the outbreaks of Ebola included early case identification and rapid isolation (Ohimain & Silas-Olu, 2021). Because the presenting symptoms of Ebola are similar to other diseases, such as malaria, identification may be delayed unless there is already a known presence of Ebola in the vicinity. While photographs of patients with Ebola depict the hemorrhagic presentation, this is not the most obvious or first symptoms of Ebola. Hemorrhage is often internal as part of the multisystem breakdown within the body as the disease rapidly progresses. This is one reason the virus name was changed from Ebola Hemorrhagic Fever to EVD (Kuhn et al., 2019).

With the arrival of Ebola in the United States in 2014, the disease suddenly became a real and present danger, no longer a faraway problem for others. When the Ebola virus first presented in the United States, a traveler presented in Texas that was not expected and had not been diagnosed. Two health care workers at that hospital were infected and the patient ultimately died (Chevalier et al., 2014). This brought the reality of these foreign-born infectious diseases and their ability to come into the United States and bring death to a mostly unsuspecting and unprepared population, to the forefront. "The development of a readily available screening tool for highly hazardous communicable diseases with up-to date guidance is, therefore, imperative for successful identification, isolation, and care" (Schwedhelm et al., 2020). After that, four cases were expected because they were health care workers who had contracted the disease in Africa and were returned home for treatment and care at specifically identified medical centers that were prepared for Ebola patient care. In total, 11 patients were treated in the United States, but they made a tremendous impact on hospital preparedness.

With the creation of a tiered system and certain regional facilities being quickly prepared with isolation units and some trained staff, they also prepared another tier of hospitals that were better prepared at identifying and isolating and then transporting potential Ebola patients to those regional facilities for care. The frontline hospitals typically had less isolation potential or opportunity or ability and fewer trained, sometimes no trained, staff to deal with such an infectious disease, whether diagnosed or undiagnosed. This level of hospital is the category where the Texas hospital fell and where most of the rest of the hospitals in the country knew they were and they panicked. Health care Emergency Medical Services (EMS) did not know how to treat or prepare to transport patients. Patients showed up at the ED with the fear that they may have Ebola because they had a fever or because they were nauseous, and quickly the EDs of hospitals were swamped with fearful people to see if they had contracted the disease, although they had neither traveled out of the United States nor been exposed to anyone who had traveled out of the United States. Due to this surge of patients into hospitals requiring testing and then having to wait for the results, having isolated places for these patients to receive care while they awaited the results, immediately caused a backlog in hospitals and the EDs. This often resulted in potentially infectious patients being transferred to the intensive care unit in order to have a form of isolation and to have the additional equipment they may need. This displaced other critical care patients that were not related to any expected infectious disease.

This displacement of chronic and critically ill noninfectious patients caused even more difficulty and stress for staff, administrators, and the community. While administrators report that they managed because the majority of patients who presented to the ED in fear were not contagious, therefore, they were quicker resolutions, and the emergency lasted only a matter of weeks or months, the use of personal protective equipment drastically increased, and the toll on frontline staff was severe. Administrators (CDC, oei-06-15-00230, 2018) reported that while they succeeded in enduring or surviving this all too real drill they doubted their facility's ability to sustain that level of treatment preparation and care should it have lasted much longer, or been more intense or had more victims. This preparation for such a surge of infectious patients, for the illness to be manifested as true infections, rather than fearful community residents, could easily over-whelm both facilities' staff and the entire health care system at the local level. There were recommendations after the fact that helped facilities continue to prepare for just such an eventuality, with Ebola preparation becoming the model used by many hospitals and health systems to prepare for the next infectious disease outbreak. Following are some of these recommendations that may be compared with the previous recommendations from both the SARS and MERS contagions. Note the recommendations from those epidemics when they had very little physical impact on the United States show we are not continuously prepared for a real threat to the United States.

Ongoing concerns identified from the EVD experience include the following:

- *Communication* – coordination and centralized: information sharing through various levels of government emergency management still conflicts between different sources; information often occurs through media and social networks before official channels, spreading false information and creating unhelpful anxiety and fearful responses; having a central source of accurate communication separate from the political establishment so it is more scientifically accurate and consistent; coordinated incident command centers at each level of the US health care emer-gency system, from federal to the local entities; include bidirectional feedback to improve speed, clarity, and background of guidance; regularly update top state officials on the sate of the *incident command system* policies and procedures using real examples (Chevalier et al., 2014; Dwyer et al., 2017; Garibaldi et al., 2016; Hewlett et al., 2015; Johnson et al., 2015; Meyer et al., 2018; Morgan et al., 2015; Parker, 2020; Patel et al., 2017; Rosenfeld et al., 2009; Silva et al., 2022; Toppenberg-Pejcic et al., 2019).
- *PPE supply challenges: lack of standardization* across manufacturers make training and fitting difficult; production outside the United States may hamper quick *availability during surges* in need, need to improve the national stockpile amount and process (DuBose et al., 2018; Hewlett et al., 2015; Leonhardt et al., 2016; Meyer et al., 2018; Morgan et al., 2015; Patel et al., 2017; Varkey & Ribner, 2016; Yarbrough et al., 2016).
- *Isolation, negative pressure, and decontamination space*, pre- and postadmission: ability to *provide point-of-care ability for labs* and other testing; include public health in all planning and assessment; need to *strengthen isolation and quar-antine* and collaborate with others about promising improvements; physical layout of facility minimize exposure and contamination, including unidirec-tional flow of providers and materials in and out of isolation areas; separate

entrances for potentially contagious patients; *use of Isolation Communication Management System (iSOCOMS) to communicate in and with isolation units* (DuBose et al., 2018; Dwyer et al., 2017; Fairley et al., 2016; Garibaldi et al., 2016; Gossen et al., 2020; Herstein et al., 2021; Hewlett et al., 2015; Le et al., 2017; Meyer et al., 2018; Schwedhelm et al., 2020; Varkey & Ribner, 2016).

- Practice *infection control* before the patient presents to the ED: emphasize a *culture of safety*; conduct regular training; conduct *regular full-scale drills to practice and improve processes and procedures, including all aspects of local emergency management*; ensure local EMS is part of the incident command structure; *improve EMS training; include EMS and 911 dispatch staff in preparedness and planning; training and practicing donning and doffing PPE correctly; stress importance of documented after-action reports to improvement*; (DuBose et al., 2018; Dwyer et al., 2017; Fairley et al., 2016; Hewlett et al., 2015; Jacobsen et al., 2016; Light, 2009; Meyer et al., 2018; Morgan et al., 2015; Parker, 2020; Toppenberg-Pejcic et al., 2019; Varkey & Ribner, 2016).
- *Onsite laboratory with isolation and diagnostic capabilities*: limit lab specimens and procedures to point-of-care in patient's room or in a biological safety cabinet in the isolation area; *include laboratory personnel in preparedness and planning meetings* (DuBose et al., 2018; Dwyer et al., 2017; Garibaldi et al., 2016; Hewlett et al., 2015; Johnson et al., 2015; Varkey & Ribner, 2016).
- *Transportation concerns* in and out of facility: *use ICS to coordinate*; repeated drills to be ready; sufficient PPE for patient in transport; *first responders may be first contact with infectious patients so constant preparedness is essential* (Hewlett et al., 2015; McCoy et al., 2014).
- *Ability to anticipate highly infectious diseases (HIDs) and quickly identify and isolate persons under investigation*: need to develop a "readily available **screening tool for HIDs** with current guidance" (Schwedhelm et al., 2020); use mHealth applications to *track outbreaks*; (Jacobsen et al., 2016).

SARS-COVID-19

The CDC issued a travel advisory about the novel coronavirus in China in January 2020. On January 7, 2020, the CDC activated its emergency response system (ERS) to provide better support for the COVID-19 response. On January 17, the CDC began screening of passengers entering the United States from direct or connecting flights from Wuhan, China (WHO), and on the same day, the CDC updated their Health Alert Network (HAN) advisory informing state and local health departments and health care providers about the outbreak. A Geosentinal Alert (2020) was posted on January 21, 2020, notifying users of the presence of the novel coronavirus in China and to take precautions and notify public health officials of any suspected cases. On January 23, 2020, the first case in the United States was reported to the WHO, from the state of Washington (CDC, 2020).

The CDC has a process to continually monitor, evaluate, and respond to infectious disease outbreaks, natural or human-made disasters, and security events. Between 2013 and 2018, the most common threats the CDC responded to were infectious diseases. When the CDC's Incident Management System (IMS) is activated, the Emergency Management Program (EMP) utilization distributes a HAN notice, which is a vital public health incident message (Rico et al., 2021). During a public health crisis, communication, both internal and external, is essential (Godshall & Banach, 2021). Evidence shows that communication and education were lacking from the beginning of the COVID-19 outbreak in the United States, with HHS personnel screening evacuees arriving at federal quarantine sites, while not being properly protected (OIG, 2022). While the CDC said it used evolving COVID-19 data as well as documents from previous epidemics and planning documents, the OIG's internal review reported that "CDC's approach did not align with assumptions outlined in these documents and ... CDC did not have a comprehensive plan for recommending travel-related containment measures that weighed the risks" (OIG, 2022).

The Department of Health and Human Services conducted a "pulse survey" early in the COVID-19 pandemic (March 23–27, 2020) to identify the major issues hospitals were facing. Twelve key concerns were already evident at the very beginning of the COVID-19 pandemic. In their report OEI-06-20-00300, the OIG found the following concerns:

(1) Severe shortage of testing supplies;
(2) Extended wait times for test results;
(3) Extended patient hospital stays awaiting test results, straining ED and ICU bed availability;
(4) Widespread shortages of PPE;
(5) Lack of robust supply chain delays or prevents PPE restocking;
(6) Uncertainty of PPE availability from Federal/State stockpiles;
(7) Sharp increases in PPE prices;
(8) Shortage of specialized providers to meet patient surge;
(9) Concerns over virus exposure exacerbating staffing shortages or causing overwork;
(10) Capacity concerns for infectious and all other patients, advance preparation of alternate care sites;
(11) Shortage of critical supplies, materials, and support for surge of patients;
(12) Changing and sometimes inconsistent guidance from Federal, State, and local authorities pose challenges and confusion for hospitals and the public.

Gudi and Tiwari (2020) noted that aggressive social distancing practices may drastically reduce the actual number of COVID-19 cases from the potential peak of nine million. The rapid spread, highly contagious nature, and high mortality of COVID-19 should help governments and local health care leaders understand their strengths and weaknesses and better prepare for the, inevitable, next EID (Gudi & Tiwari, 2020). Herstein et al. (2021) reviewed the four phases of emergency management from the National Incident Management System (NIMS) and what the COVID-19 pandemic taught us about being prepared. Enhancing facility infrastructures to provide additional negative pressure rooms for isolation, planning, training, and drills to be prepared for the next emergency, create and rotate supply caches, clearly defined surge plans, were identified again. Enabling a comprehensive telemedicine platform, anticipated prolonged increased volumes of patients, the potential for utilizing alternate sites of care, and creating a technology infrastructure to enable remote work capabilities were newly identified (Herstein et al., 2021).

A key aspect of care that was identified by Maldonado et al. (2020) is ethical decision-making in the face of limited resources, as well as the infectious potential to health care workers. When there are limited resources and more patients need the resources, decisions must be made about the allocation of those resources, usually on a case-by-case basis. During COVID-19, the availability of ventilators and the inability to acquire more became a very real issue. Decisions about additional treatments for COVID-19 patients, such as intubation, CPR, and surgery, all became ethical decisions that had to be made at bedside.

Because of the zoonotic origins of the coronavirus infections, Mujica et al. (2020) note that there may even be dangers from some pets, such as cats, ferrets, or macaque monkeys. As we have seen from the three previous epidemics, the commonality of their sources relates back to animal contact. Perhaps the hospital intake questionnaire should ask, if there is no foreign travel noted, is there a presence of animals/pets? After the worst part of the COVID-19 pandemic was past, the ongoing concerns that have been identified include the following:

• Communication at all levels still needs improvement;
• Supply manufacture and accessibility is still an issue;
• Staffing shortages and staff well-being are a key concern;
• Capacity (beds, staff, materials) for mass infections is still an issue;
• Caring for noninfectious patients with chronic or critical illness or health needs should not be delayed or overlooked;
• The EHR screening questionnaire should continue to be used to keep awareness high;
• Improve infrastructure to add more negative pressure rooms;
• Review after-action reports and act on lessons identified;
• Identify and arrange for alternate care sites in advance of need;
• Create and rotate supply caches;
• Use training and drills regularly to fight complacency and the lack of urgency in infection control;
• Computer modeling should be developed to both track EID and potential trends for transmission.

(OIG, 2020; Herstein et al., 2021; Hoelscher & McBride, 2020).

Key Lessons Learned for Hospital Administration Preparedness

Table 8.1 compares the key lessons identified from each of the four infectious diseases, SARS, MERS, EVD, and COVID-19. While improvements are evident from these experiences, it is imperative that during the recovery time post-COVID, the concept of "returning to life as it once was" is no longer an option. The next unidentified HID is coming. It is not time to panic but to take action. Health care administrators should review after-action reports. Make corrections and updates to policies and procedures. Conduct drills and exercises involving all local agencies that have been so important throughout the COVID-19 pandemic. Strengthen collaborations and build additional support networks. Stock PPE and supplies that were so difficult to obtain during the surge of patients in 2020–2021. And train new employees maintaining a high level of vigilance in infection control. As Johnathan Quick (2018) reminds us, "It's not a matter of IF, but WHEN."

CONCLUSION

Varkey and Ribner (2016) remind us that "infectious diseases have no borders." They continue that being unprepared for Ebola was "particularly jarring given that outbreaks of SARS (severe acute respiratory syndrome), H1N1 influenza, and MERS (Middle East respiratory syndrome) have marked the last decade." As Parker (2020) states, "The SARS-CoV-2 virus and ongoing pandemic caught the world by surprise and is a stark demonstration of risks coming from microbial threats. This provocative 'lesson observed' assessment is a wakeup call for action at higher levels to confront another challenge – complacency and lack of urgency." Herstein et al. (2021) notes, "Too often in emergency management, plans are developed, agreed upon, written into policy, and then stored on shelves until a regulatory requirement or emergency motivate their use." Meyer reminds us that "that budget shortfalls and waning staff interest post-event" are real challenges hospitals face in their daily routines. Studies conducted by the US Department of Health and Human Services (DHHS) (2018) confirm that an ongoing concern for preparedness is the "challenges to maintaining their preparedness given competing priorities, hospital resources and staff time." This concern remains post-COVID-19.

ACKNOWLEDGMENTS

I would like to acknowledge and thank, Stephanie Duea, PhD, for her assistance and encouragement.

REFERENCES

Al-Abdallat, M. M., Payne, D. C., Alqasrawi, S., Rha, B., Tohme, R. A., Abedi, G. R., Al Nsour, M., Iblan, I., Jarour, N., Farag, N. H., Haddadin, A., Al-Sanouri, T., Tamin, A., Harcourt, J. L., Kuhar, D. T., Swerdlow, D. L., Erdman, D. D., Pallansch, M. A., Haynes, L. M., … Jordan MERS-CoV Investigation Team. (2014). Hospital-associated outbreak of Middle East respiratory syndrome coronavirus: A serologic, epidemiologic, and clinical description. *Clinical Infectious Diseases: An Official Publication of the Infectious Diseases Society of America*, 59(9), 1225–1233. https://doi.org/10.1093/cid/ciu359
Assiri, A., McGeer, A., Perl, T. M., Price, C. S., Al Rabeeah, A. A., Cummings, D. A., Alabdullatif, Z. N., Assad, M., Almulhim, A., Makhdoom, H., Madani, H., Alhakeem, R., Al-Tawfiq, J. A.,

Cotten, M., Watson, S. J., Kellam, P., Zumla, A. I., & Memish, Z. A., & KSA MERS-CoV Investigation Team. (2013). Hospital outbreak of Middle East respiratory syndrome coronavirus. *New England Journal of Medicine, 369*(5), 407–416. https://doi.org/10.1056/NEJMoa1306742

Azhar, E. I., Hui, D. S. C., Memish, Z. A., Drosten, C., & Zumla, A. (2019). The Middle East respiratory syndrome (MERS). In *Infectious disease clinics of North America* (Vol. 33, pp. 891–905). Elsevier.

Baseler, L., Chertow, D. S., Johnson, K. M., Feldmann, H., & Morens, D. M. (2017). The pathogenesis of Ebola virus disease. *Annual Review of Pathology, 12*, 387–418. https://doi.org/10.1146/annurev-pathol-052016-100506

Booth, C. M., & Stewart, T. E. (2005, January). Severe acute respiratory syndrome and critical care medicine: The Toronto experience. *Critical Care Medicine, 33*(1 Suppl. 1), S53–S60. PMID: 15640680. https://doi.org/10.1097.01.ccm.0000150954.88817.6

CDC, oei-06-15-00230. (2018). Hospitals reported improved preparedness for emerging infectious diseases after the Ebola outbreak. Office of Inspector General. USDHHS. https://oig.hhs.gov/oei/reports/oei-06-15-00230.pdf

CDC. (n.d.). SARS basic fact sheet. https://www.cdc.gov/sars/about/fs-sars.html

CDC. (2003). Assessment of epidemiologic capacity in state and territorial health departments – United States, 2001. *Morbidity and Mortality Weekly Report, 52*(43), 1049–1064.

CDC. (2020). CDC in action: Working 24/7 to stop the threat of COVID-19. https://www.cdc.gov/budget/documents/COVID-19/CDC-247-Response-to-COVID-19-fact-sheet.pdf

Chevalier, M. S., Chung, W., Smith, J., Weil, L. M., Hughes, S. M., Joyner, S. N., Hall, E., Srinath, D., Ritch, J., Thathiah, P., Threadgill, H., Cervantes, D., & Lakey, D. L. (2014, November 21). Centers for disease control and prevention (CDC). Ebola virus disease cluster in the United States–Dallas County, Texas, 2014. *Morbidity and Mortality Weekly Report, 63*(46), 1087–1088. Erratum in: *Morbidity and Mortality Weekly Report*. 2014 Dec 5; *63*(48), 1139. PMID: 25412069; PMCID: PMC5779510.

Cohen, J., & van der Meulen Rodgers, Y. (2020). Contributing factors to personal protective equipment shortages during the COVID-19 pandemic. *Preventive Medicine, 141*, 106263, ISSN 0091-7435. https://doi.org/10.1016/j.ypmed.2020.106263. https://www.sciencedirect.com/science/article/pii/S0091743520302875

Coltart, C. E., Lindsey, B., Ghinai, I., Johnson, A. M., & Heymann, D. L. (2017). The Ebola outbreak, 2013–2016: Old lessons for new epidemics. *Philosophical Transactions of the Royal Society of London - Series B: Biological Sciences, 372*(1721), 20160297. https://doi.org/10.1098/rstb.2016.0297

D'Emidio, T., Fox, J., Spaner, J., & Usher, O. (2022, August). *Building resilience: The history and future of US crisis management.* McKinsey & Company. https://www.mckinsey.com/capabilities/risk-and-resilience/our-insights/building-resilience-the-history-and-future-of-us-crisis-management?cid=other-eml-alt-mip-mck&hdpid=4677c294-dbc4-4333-990c-62aedccdb952&hctky=12988591&hlkid=d33d1a1888ab4faf89395d4a2b0f82f0

DuBose, J. R., Matić, Z., Sala, M. F. W., Mumma, J. M., Kraft, C. S., Casanova, L. M., Erukunuakpor, K., Durso, F. T., Walsh, V. L., Shah, P., Zimring, C. M., & Jacob, J. T., & CDC Prevention Epicenters Program. (2018, August). Design strategies to improve healthcare worker safety in biocontainment units: Learning from Ebola preparedness. *Infection Control & Hospital Epidemiology, 39*(8), 961–967. Epub 2018 Jun 18. PMID: 29909821. https://doi.org/10.1017/ice.2018.125

Dwyer, K. S., Misner, H., Chang, S., & Fajardo, N. (2017, September/October). An interim examination of the US public health response to Ebola. *Health Secur, 15*(5), 527–538. Epub 2017 Oct 10. PMID: 28994617. https://doi.org/10.1089/hs.2016.0128

Fairley, J. K., Kozarsky, P. E., Kraft, C. S., Guarner, J., Steinberg, J. P., Anderson, E., Jacob, J. T., Meloy, P., Gillespie, D., Espinoza, T. R., Isakov, A., Vanairsdale, S., Baker, E., & Wu, H. M. (2016, January 18). Ebola or not? Evaluating the ill traveler from Ebola-affected countries in West Africa. *Open Forum Infectious Diseases, 3*(1), ofw005. PMID: 26925428; PMCID: PMC4766384. https://doi.org/10.1093/ofid/ofw005

Garibaldi, B. T., Kelen, G. D., Brower, R. G., Bova, G., Ernst, N., Reimers, M., Langlotz, R., Gimburg, A., Iati, M., Smith, C., MacConnell, S., James, H., Lewin, J. J., Trexler, P., Black, M. A., Lynch, C., Clarke, W., Marzinke, M. A., Sokoll, L. J, . . . Maragakis, L. L. (2016, May). The creation of a biocontainment unit at a tertiary care hospital. The Johns Hopkins medicine experience. *Annals of the American Thoracic Society, 13*(5), 600–608. PMID: 27057583. https://doi.org/10.1513/AnnalsATS.201509-587PS

Gensheimer, K. F. (2004, June). Challenges and opportunities in pandemic influenza planning: Lessons learned from recent infectious disease preparedness and response efforts. *International Congress Series, 1263*, 809–812. Epub 2004 Jun 30. PMID: 32288145; PMCID: PMC7134731. https://doi.org/10.1016/j.ics.2004.01.021

Godshall, C. E., & Banach, D. B. (2021). Pandemic preparedness. In *Infectious disease clinics of North America* (Vol. 35, pp. 1077–1089). Elsevier.

Gossen, A., Mehring, B., Gunnell, B. S., Rheuban, K. S., Cattell-Gordon, D. C.., Enfield, K. B., & Sifri, C. D. (2020, June). The isolation communication management system. A telemedicine platform to care for patients in a biocontainment unit. *Annals of the American Thoracic Society, 17*(6), 673–678. PMID: 32357069; PMCID: PMC7258411. https://doi.org/10.1513/AnnalsATS.202003-261IP

Gudi, S. K., & Tiwari, K. K. (2020, April). Preparedness and lessons learned from the novel coronavirus disease. *The International Journal of Occupational and Environmental Medicine, 11*(2), 108–112. PMID: 32218558. PMCID: PMC7205510. https://doi.org/10.34172/ijoem.2020.1977

Herstein, J. J., Schwedhelm, M. M., Vasa, A., Biddinger, P. D., & Hewlett, A. L. (2021, October 13). Emergency preparedness: What is the future? *Antimicrobial Stewardship & Healthcare Epidemiology, 1*(1), e29. PMID: 36168490; PMCID: PMC9495548. https://doi.org/10.1017/ash.2021.190

Hewlett, A. L., Varkey, J. B., Smith, P. W., & Ribner, B. S. (2015, August). Ebola virus disease: Preparedness and infection control lessons learned from two biocontainment units. *Current Opinion in Infectious Diseases, 28*(4), 343–348. PMID: 26098504; PMCID: PMC4743738. https://doi.org/10.1097/QCO.0000000000000176

Hoelscher, D., & McBride, S. (2020, October). Usability and the rapid deployable infectious disease decision support system. *CIN: Computers, Informatics, Nursing [Internet], 38*(10), 490–499. [cited 2023 May 15].

Hui, D. S., Memish, Z. A., & Zumla, A. (2014, May). Severe acute respiratory syndrome vs. the Middle East respiratory syndrome. *Current Opinion in Pulmonary Medicine, 20*(3), 233–241. https://doi.org/10.1097/MCP.0000000000000046

Hui, D. S., & Zumla, A. (2019). Severe acute respiratory syndrome: Historical, epidemiologic, and clinical features. In *Infectious disease clinics of North America* (Vol. 33, pp. 869–889). Elsevier.

Jacobsen, K. H., Aguirre, A. A., Bailey, C. L., Baranova, A. V., Crooks, A. T., Croitoru, A., Delamater, P. L., Gupta, J., Kehn-Hall, K., Narayanan, A., Pierobon, M., Rowan, K. E., Schwebach, J. R., Seshaiyer, P., Sklarew, D. M., Stefanidis, A., & Agouris, P. (2016, March). Lessons from the Ebola outbreak: Action items for emerging infectious disease preparedness and response. *EcoHealth, 13*(1), 200–212. Epub 2016 Feb 25. PMID: 26915507; PMCID: PMC7087787. https://doi.org/10.1007/s10393-016-1100-5

Johnson, D. W., Sullivan, J. N., Piquette, C. A., Hewlett, A. L., Bailey, K. L., Smith, P. W., Kalil, A. C., & Lisco, S. J. (2015, June). Lessons learned: Critical care management of patients with Ebola in the United States. *Critical Care Medicine, 43*(6), 1157–1164. PMID: 25756410. https://doi.org/10.1097/CCM.0000000000000935

Kang, C. K., Song, K. H., Choe, P. G., Park, W. B., Bang, J. H., Kim, E. S., Park, S. W., Kim, H. B., Kim, N. J., Cho, S. I., Lee, J. K., & Oh, M. D. (2017). Clinical and epidemiologic characteristics of spreaders of Middle East respiratory syndrome coronavirus during the 2015 outbreak in Korea. *Journal of Korean Medical Science, 32*(5), 744–749. https://doi.org/10.3346/jkms.2017.32.5.744

Khabbaz, R. F. (2013, December 3). Still learning from SARS. *Annals of Internal Medicine, 159*(11), 780–781. [Internet]. [cited 2023 May 15].

Kuhn, J. H., Adachi, T., Adhikari, N. K. J., Arribas, J. R., Bah, I. E., Bausch, D. G., Bhadelia, N., Borchert, M., Brantsæter, A. B., Brett-Major, D. M., Burgess, T. H., Chertow, D. S., Chute, C.

G., Cieslak, T. J., Colebunders, R., Crozier, I., Davey, R. T., de Clerck, H., Delgado, R.,
    Evans, L., & Yoti, Z. (2019). New filovirus disease classification and nomenclature. *Nature
    Reviews Microbiology, 17*(5), 261–263. https://doi.org/10.1038/s41579-019-0187-4

Le, A. B., Biddinger, P. D., Smith, P. W., Herstein, J. J., Levy, D. A., Gibbs, S. G., & Lowe, J. J. (2017
    May/June). A highly infectious disease care network in the US healthcare system. *Health Secur,
    15*(3), 282–287. PMID: 28636444. https://doi.org/10.1089/hs.2016.0073

Leonhardt, K. K., Keuler, M., Safdar, N., & Hunter, P. (2016, August). Ebola preparedness planning
    and collaboration by two health systems in Wisconsin, September to December 2014. *Disaster
    Medicine and Public Health Preparedness, 10*(4), 691–697. Epub 2015 Sep 15. PMID: 26370206.
    https://doi.org/10.1017/dmp.2015.103

Light, R. B. (2009). Plagues in the ICU: A brief history of community-acquired epidemic and endemic
    transmissible infections leading to intensive care admission. *Critical Care Clinics, 25*(1), 67–81.
    PMID: 19268795; PMCID: PMC7135779. https://doi.org/10.1016/j.ccc.2008.11.002

Maldonado, F., Rafael, F. J., Shinall, M. C., Ely, E. W., & Shinall, M. C., Jr. (2020, October).
    Coronavirus disease 2019: Withdrawing mechanical ventilation to reallocate life support under
    crisis standards of care-nonequivalence of the equivalence thesis. *Critical Care Medicine,
    48*(10), e994–e996. [Internet]. [cited 2023 May 15].

Malvy, D., McElroy, A. K., de Clerck, H., Günther, S., & van Griensven, J. (2019). Ebola virus
    disease. *The Lancet, 393*, 936–948. http://doi.org/10.1016/S0140-6736(18)33132-5

McCoy, C. E., Lotfipour, S., Chakravarthy, B., Schultz, C., & Barton, E. (2014, November).
    Emergency medical services public health implications and interim guidance for the Ebola virus
    in the United States. *Western Journal of Emergency Medicine, 15*(7), 723–727. Epub 2014 Oct
    10. PMID: 25493108; PMCID: PMC4251209. https://doi.org/10.5811/westjem.2014.10.24155

Mehrotra, P., Malani, P., & Yadav, P. (2020, May). Personal protective equipment shortages during
    COVID-19—Supply chain–Related causes and mitigation strategies. *JAMA Health Forum.*
    https://doi.org/10.1001/jamahealthforum.2020.0553

Meyer, D., Kirk, S. T., Schoch-Spana, M., Shearer, M. P., Chandler, H., Thomas, E., Rose, D. A.,
    Carbone, E. G., & Toner, E. (2018, May). Lessons from the domestic Ebola response:
    Improving health care system resilience to high consequence infectious diseases. *American
    Journal of Infection Control, 46*(5), 533–537. Epub 2017 Dec 15. PMID: 29249609; PMCID:
    PMC8666128. https://doi.org/10.1016/j.ajic.2017.11.001

Moore, D. M., Gilbert, M., Saunders, S., Bryce, E., & Yassi, A. (2005, June). Occupational health and
    infection control practices related to severe acute respiratory syndrome: Health care worker
    perceptions. *AAOHN Journal, 53*(6), 257–266. [Internet]. [cited 2023 May 15].

Morgan, D. J., Braun, B., Milstone, A. M., Anderson, D., Lautenbach, E., Safdar, N., Drees, M.,
    Meddings, J., Linkin, D. R., Croft, L. D., Pineles, L., Diekema, D. J., & Harris, A. D. (2015,
    June). Lessons learned from hospital Ebola preparation. *Infection Control & Hospital Epide-
    miology, 36*(6), 627–631. PMID: 25994323. https://doi.org/10.1017/ice.2015.61

Mujica, G., Sternberg, Z., Solis, J., Wand, T., Carrasco, P., Henao-Martínez, A. F., & Franco-Paredes, C.
    (2020, November 30). Defusing COVID-19: Lessons learned from a century of pandemics. *Tropical
    Medicine and Infectious Disease, 5*(4), 182. PMID: 33266051; PMCID: PMC7709642. https://doi.
    org/10.3390/tropicalmed5040182

Niska, R. W., & Burt, C. W. (2005). *Bioterrorism and mass casualty preparedness in hospitals: United
    States, 2003.* CDC Advance Data 364.

Oboho, I. K., Tomczyk, S. M., Al-Asmari, A. M., Banjar, A. A., Al-Mugti, H., Aloraini, M. S.,
    Alkhaldi, K. Z., Almohammadi, E. L., Alraddadi, B. M., Gerber, S. I., Swerdlow, D. L.,
    Watson, J. T., & Madani, T. A. (2015). 2014 MERS-CoV outbreak in Jeddah–A link to health
    care facilities. *New England Journal of Medicine, 372*(9), 846–854. https://doi.org/10.1056/
    NEJMoa1408636

Oei-06-15-00230. (2018). Hospitals reported improved preparedness for emerging infectious diseases
    after the Ebola outbreak. Office of Inspector General. USDHHS. https://oig.hhs.gov/oei/
    reports/oei-06-15-00230.pdf

Oei-06-20-00300. (2020). Hospital experiences responding to the Covid-19 pandemic: Results of a
    national pulse survey March 23–27, 2020. Office of Inspector General. USDHHS. https://oig.
    hhs.gov/oei/reports/oei-06-20-00300.pdf

Ohimain, E. I., & Silas-Olu, D. (2021). The 2013–2016 Ebola virus disease outbreak in West Africa. *Current Opinion in Pharmacology, 60*, 360–365. https://doi.org/10.1016/j.coph.2021.08.002Ohimain

OIG. (2022, November 3). During the initial COVID-19 response, HHS personnel who interacted with potentially infected passengers had limited protections. Office of the Inspector General, USDHHS. https://oig.hhs.gov/oei/reports/OEI-04-20-00360.pdf

Omrani, A. S., & Shalhoub, S. (2015, November). Middle East Respiratory Syndrome Coronavirus (MERS-CoV): What lessons can we learn? *Journal of Hospital Infection, 91*(3), 188–196. Epub 2015 Aug 22. PMID: 26452615; PMCID: PMC7114843. https://doi.org/10.1016/j.jhin.2015.08.002

Parker, G. W. (2020, August). Best practices for after-action review: Turning lessons observed into lessons learned for preparedness policy. *Rev Sci Tech, 39*(2), 579–590. PMID: 33046918. https://doi.org/10.20506/rst.39.2.3108

Patel, A., D'Alessandro, M. M., Ireland, K. J., Burel, W. G., Wencil, E. B., Rasmussen, S. A. (2017, June). Personal protective equipment supply chain: Lessons learned from recent public health emergency responses. *Health Security, 15*(3), 244–252.

Quick, J. D. (2018). *The end of epidemics* (p. 68). Martin's Press. ISBN: 9781250117779.

Rebmann, T., English, J. F., & Carrico, R. (2007, August). Disaster preparedness lessons learned and future directions for education: Results from focus groups conducted at the 2006 APIC conference. *American Journal of Infection Control, 35*(6), 374–381. PMID: 17660007; PMCID: PMC7132723. https://doi.org/10.1016/j.ajic.2006.09.002

Rico, A., Sanders, C. A., Broughton, A. S., Andrews, A., Bader, F. A., & Maples, D. L. (2021). CDC's emergency management program activities – Worldwide, 2013–2018. Atlanta, GA. *Morbidity and Mortality Weekly Report, 70*(2), 36–39.

Rosenfeld, L. A., Fox, C. E., Kerr, D., Marziale, E., Cullum, A., Lota, K., Stewart, J., & Thompson, M. Z. (2009, March–April). Use of computer modeling for emergency preparedness functions by local and state health officials: A needs assessment. *Journal of Public Health Management and Practice, 15*(2), 96–104. PMID: 19202407. https://doi.org/10.1097/01.PHH.0000346004.21157.ef

Schwedhelm, M. M., Herstein, J. J., Watson, S. M., Mead, A. L., Maddalena, L., Liston, D. D., & Hewlett, A. L. (2020, November). Can you catch it? Lessons learned and modification of ED triage symptom- and travel-screening strategy. *Journal of Emergency Nursing, 46*(6), 932–940. Epub 2020 Apr 16. PMID: 32340737; PMCID: PMC7160057. https://doi.org/10.1016/j.jen.2020.03.006

Silva, M., Tallman, P., Stolow, J., Yavinsky, R., Fleckman, J., & Hoffmann, K. (2022, August 30). Learning from the past: The role of social and behavior change programming in public health emergencies. *Global Health Science and Practice, 10*(4), e2200026. PMID: 36041834; PMCID: PMC9426983. https://doi.org/10.9745/GHSP-D-22-00026

Toppenberg-Pejcic, D., Noyes, J., Allen, T., Alexander, N., Vanderford, M., & Gamhewage, G. (2019, April). Emergency risk communication: Lessons learned from a rapid review of recent gray literature on Ebola, Zika, and yellow fever. *Health Communication, 34*(4), 437–455. [Internet]. [cited 2023 May 15].

Varkey, J. B., & Ribner, B. S. (2016, June). Preparing for serious communicable diseases in the United States: What the Ebola virus epidemic has taught us. *Microbiology Spectrum, 4*(3). PMID: 27337477; PMCID: PMC4922497. https://doi.org/10.1128/microbiolspec.EI10-0011-2016

Verbeek, P. R., McClelland, I. W., Silverman, A. C., & Burgess, R. J. (2004, September). Loss of paramedic availability in an urban emergency medical services system during a severe acute respiratory syndrome outbreak. *Academic Emergency Medicine, 11*(9), 973–978. [Internet]. [cited 2023 May 15].

Yarbrough, M. I., Ficken, M. E., Lehmann, C. U., Talbot, T. R., Swift, M. D., McGown, P. W., Wheaton, R. F., Bruer, M., Little, S. W., & Oke, C. A. (2016). Respirator use in a hospital setting: Establishing surveillance metrics. *Journal of the International Society for Respiratory Protection, 33*(1), 1–11. https://stacks.cdc.gov/view/cdc/41190

Zawilińska, B., & Kosz-Vnenchak, M. (2014). General introduction into the Ebola virus biology and disease. *Folia Medica Cracoviensia, 54*(3), 57–65.

Zumla, A., & Hui, D. S. (2014). Infection control and MERS-CoV in health-care workers. *Lancet, 383*(9932), 1869–1871. https://doi.org/10.1016/S0140-6736(14)60852-7. London, England.

SECTION 4

SOCIOPOLITICAL AND DEMOGRAPHIC SHIFTS REQUIRE PREPAREDNESS OUTSIDE OF ACUTE CRISIS

CHAPTER 9

THE COPRODUCTION OF HEALTH FRAMEWORK: SEEKING INSTRUCTIVE MANAGEMENT MODELS AND THEORIES

Anne M. Hewitt

Seton Hall University, USA

ABSTRACT

At the beginning of the 21st century, multiple and diverse social entities, including the public (consumers), private and nonprofit healthcare institutions, government (public health) and other industry sectors, began to recognize the limitations of the current fragmented healthcare system paradigm. Primary stakeholders, including employers, insurance companies, and healthcare professional organizations, also voiced dissatisfaction with unacceptable health outcomes and rising costs. Grand challenges and wicked problems threatened the viability of the health sector. American health systems responded with innovations and advances in healthcare delivery frameworks that encouraged shifts from intra- and inter-sector arrangements to multi-sector, lasting relationships that emphasized patient centrality along with long-term commitments to sustainability and account-ability. This pathway, leading to a population health approach, also generated the need for transformative business models. The coproduction of health framework, with its emphasis on cross-sector alignments, nontraditional partner relationships, sustainable missions, and accountability capable of yielding return on investments, has emerged as a unique strategy for facing disruptive threats and challenges from nonhealth sector corporations. This chapter presents a coproduction of health framework, goals and criteria, examples of boundary spanning network alliance models, and operational (integrator, convener, aggregator) strategies. A comparison of important organizational science theories, including institutional theory, network/network analysis theory, and resource dependency theory, provides

Research and Theory to Foster Change in the Face of Grand Health Care Challenges
Advances in Health Care Management, Volume 22, 181–210
Copyright © 2024 Anne M. Hewitt
Published under exclusive licence by Emerald Publishing Limited
ISSN: 1474-8231/doi:10.1108/S1474-823120240000022009

suggestions for future research directions necessary to validate the utility of the coproduction of health framework as a precursor for paradigm change.

Keywords: Coproduction of health framework; multi-sector health relationships; grand challenges in health care; organizational science theory and health care; population health; boundary spanning

INTRODUCTION

If the American health sector could reach consensus on a single point, the outcome would be universal recognition of the need for immediate and transformative change. In this case, the desired change may not be a classic scientific revolution, as described in the original treatise on paradigms, but a similar mandate to implement "universally recognized scientific achievements that for a time provide model problems and solutions to a community of practitioners" (Kuhn, 1962, p. viii). Paradigms present a particular worldview or perspective based on a set of theories or shared beliefs that include action strategies and frameworks designed to solve a problem (Kivunjal & Kuyini, 2017).

Why the discussion of a paradigm change? Today's contemporary circumstances place the US health sector at the intersection of grand health challenges and wicked problems. Grand health challenges refer to unresolved problems that present as extremely complex with nonlinear interactions and radical uncertainty (Colquitt & George, 2011; Ferraro et al., 2015; George, 2014; Hefner & Nembhard, 2022). The magnitude and velocity of these challenges creates critical barriers "that, if removed, would help solve an important societal problem with a high likelihood of global impact through widespread implementation" (George et al., 2016). Challenges with no easy solutions are also known as wicked problems, "because they involve many interdependent, changing, and difficult to define factors" (Nembhard et al., 2020), and because the underlying problem is often a symptom of other problems (Head & Alford, 2015; Rattel & Webber, 1973). Grand health challenges will not respond to a single health organization's effort. Today's healthcare systems face multiple and, in some cases unprecedented obstacles including unsustainable financial losses, severe staffing shortages and burnout, high drug prices, disappointing health outcomes, and unparalleled inflationary pressures (Hughes, 2022).

Why introduce the coproduction of health framework as capable of facilitating a healthcare delivery paradigm change? Evidence suggests that previous "provider-centric" health models used to solve current health challenges and problems were lacking in positive outcomes (Bovaird, 2007), and resulted in a nationally recognized need for alternative models of social delivery (Realpe & Wallace, 2010). Health policymakers also sought to promote social capital already available within communities (Needham & Carr, 2009), while other health stakeholders stressed a strong desire to shift from individual patient engagement and participation to a stronger accountability for all parties (payer, provider, and patient) (Felipe et al., 2010). The coproduction of health approach, described as "community organizations, clinicians, social services, government agencies, and the service recipients (patients) engaged in and focused on the well-being of a population" (Wagner & Hewitt, 2022), integrates key elements previously identified by health scholars (Batalden et al., 2016; Beresford et al., 2021; Bodenheimer & Sinsky, 2014; Brandsen & Honingh, 2018; Ostrom, 1996).

This chapter seeks to:

- briefly summarize and interpret the contemporary health drivers of change leading to this transformative inflection point;
- review the contributions of important healthcare delivery transformations and innovations;
- examine supporting organization science theories;
- clarify the potential utility of the coproduction of health framework.

By examining the coproduction of health's development pathway and underlying theoretical constructs, health management professionals may gain important insights that enable advances toward a necessary paradigm shift that will meet our contemporary healthcare delivery system's sustainability challenge.

IDENTIFICATION AND DISSOLUTION OF THE CURRENT HEALTH PARADIGM

Accumulating evidence seems almost irrefutable that the US system of healthcare is struggling with unimpressive impacts on quality, cost, and overall health outcomes (Hilts et al., 2021; Tikkanen & Abrams, 2020). Important concerns and critiques became evident early in the 21st century including major impact reports from health policy experts, professional organizations, government agencies, and nonprofit organizations (Cordani, 2020; Hostetter & Klein, 2022; NAM, 2000, 2001; NPP, 2008). Criticisms targeted both the safety and quality of healthcare delivery and the discrepancy between unacceptable health outcomes, such as a lower life expectancy and higher infant mortality rates, and the increasing outlay of healthcare expenditures (Martin et al., 2022; United Health Foundation, 2022; Wernau & Kamp, 2022). Current reports suggest that the lifetime cost of health care averages $700,000 while the number of uninsured individuals continues to rise (Grieve, 2022; Tolbert et al., 2020).

The unexpected and unprecedented pandemic challenge to the entire health sector, including primary, post, and acute care, the biotech and pharmaceutical industry, and the public health system, resulted in over one million US COVID-19 deaths (New York Times, 2023). The pandemic generated negative and residual impacts on health systems' financial margins and sustainability (Qualifacts & NCBH, 2020), workforce burnout, shortages of front-line workers, and retention/recruitment difficulties which have added cost difficulties due to a reliance on per diem health practitioners (Absher, 2022; ASPE, 2022a).

The heroic first responders to this major 21st century plague showed resilience, innovation, and laudatory responses, yet the health outcomes uncovered system gaps in care coordination, weaknesses in organizational planning both within and across the health and other industry sectors and exposed the unacceptable level of health disparities in marginalized and at-risk populations (Vasquez Reyes, 2020). Despite years of concerted efforts and massive national campaigns, such as the Healthy People initiatives, the COVID-19 pandemic response resulted in health disparities across testing, access to vaccinations, treatment, and increased mortalities among vulnerable groups (Abbott, 2022; Bakshi, 2021). Epidemiological reports pinpointed the role of social determinants of health on population health outcomes as the prime factor leading to disparities (Thornton & Yang, 2023).

This brief review describes a national health sector in crisis with the convergence of unsustainable costs, system inequities, and significant operational and delivery model challenges leading to undesirable health outcomes. See Table 9.1.

This turbulent environment suggests health systems in organizational distress and struggling to resolve challenges and problems that the past healthcare paradigm cannot solve.

Table 9.1. Health Sector Contemporary Grand Challenges and Wicked Problems.

Quality and Safety of Care Issues	Health Inequities/and Disparities Social determinants of health (SDOH)	System Delivery Gaps/Care Coordination	Unsustainable Costs/ Burden to Consumer

ADVANCING PROGRESS: EXAMPLES OF HEALTH SYSTEMS' TRANSITIONS AND TRANSFORMATIONS

The perplexing sector problems of the last two decades were not ignored by health systems, as important and diverse advances steadily emerged. Existing evidence shows significant progress in developing health policies, technological (digital) and clinical achievements, cultural shifts, organizational restructuring, and healthcare delivery frameworks and models (Brandsen et al., 2018; Hostetter & Klein, 2022; Murphy et al., 2019). Whether revisions of current models or unique health delivery innovations, these initiatives and strategies helped directly and indirectly move the health system along the pathway toward a coproduction of health framework.

Health Policy Transformations

- The most significant health policy development during this transition era, The Patient Protection and Affordability Care Act (ACA) of 2010 has been compared to the major health industry legislation of the 1960s that introduced Medicare and Medicaid mandates (Goldstein et al., 2016; PPACA, 2010). This statute impacted individual consumers' insurance options, the availability and delivery of care, and the cost of care for many Americans. But the ACA's primary contribution to the improvement of American health may be the transition of the healthcare exchange system to a value over volume agenda where health providers are rewarded and incentivized to ensure their patients remain healthy (Buehler et al., 2018). Although experts continue to debate the utility of the ACA, positive impacts are reported in areas such as health and marketplace coverage and uninsured rates, Medicaid expansion, and expanded preventive care (ASPE, 2022b). The impact of this legislation provided a strong impetus for new alignments and accountability among provider, payer, and patients and helped to strengthen the coproduction of health premise.

Technological Achievements: Digital and Clinical

- During this general timeframe, significant legislative mandates supported concurrent health information technology (HIT) achievements that encompassed the complex functions of processing, storing, and exchanging health information in the digital environment (Johri, 2022). The passage of the Health Information Technology for Economic and Clinical Health (HITECH) Act of 2009 (CMS.gov, 2010) increased adoption rates of HIT and advanced reporting metrics derived from electronic health records (EHRs). Other benefits included direct financial incentives to providers (Brown et al., 2019; CMS.gov, 2010; HIPAA Journal, 2020). Together, the HITECH Act combined with the requirements of The Health Insurance and Portability and Accountability Act (HIPAA), defined standards to protect personal health data and the security of health information and boosted digital options for health systems operation and care delivery (HIPAA, 1996; US DHHS, 2017). The passage of the Medicare Access and Chip Reauthorization Act (MACRA) in 2015, introduced both risk and bonus sharing options (Findlay, 2017), by supporting technology platform developments capable of aligning communication among providers, healthcare organizations, and payers (Dunn, 2021a).
- Healthcare systems have benefited from the integration of EHRs serving as universal repositories of patient's health information. EHRs enhanced the interoperability of HIT systems and the capacity to provide real-time information instantly and securely to authorized users (ONC, 2023). Experts view EHRs as key to the adoption of artificial intelligence in health care along with enterprise technology advances including data analytics and predictive modeling (Johri, 2022). Access to real-time patient data through the rapid adoption of digital wearables and home monitoring (Samuel, 2022) along with the emergence of telehealth/telemedicine and innovative hospital at home options (Bestsennyy et al., 2022; Byrne, 2020), illustrate the impact of technology advancements leading to opportunities for cross-sector collaborations between providers and patients.
- The integration of artificial intelligence also benefitted clinical outcomes based on advanced communications and improved interactions among systems,

patients, and providers (Dunn, 2021a). Other medical improvements and
enhancements included genomics (genetic mapping) (Collins & Varmus, 2015),
tissue engineering (Khademhosseini & Langer, 2019), imaging technology
(Kabasawa, 2022), and improved robotics (Millar, 2022). These clinical
achievements supported a trajectory toward the goal of precision medicine and
the ability to tailor healthcare for the individual that aligned with a person's
genes, environment, and lifestyle (Holst, 2015; Medline, 2022). Although precision medicine and population health may seem like contradictory concepts,
these two health strategies serve as key components for value-based care (AHA,
2021) a significant component of the coproduction of health approach.

Enhanced Health Organizational Structures

- Health sector organizations, whether major health systems or independent
  hospitals, strive to complete strategic business activities that maintain sustainability, competitive advantage, and explore future opportunities (Fiorio
  et al., 2018). The Accountable Care Organization, a Patient Protection and
  Affordable Care Act (PPACA) introduced organizational option, offered an
  opportunity to provide care benefits such as the integration of an expanded care
  continuum and the adoption of value-based payment models (Schwartz et al.,
  2020). As of 2022, Centers for Medicare & Medicaid Services (CMS) reported
  more than 483 Accountable Care Organizations (ACOs) enrolled in the Shared
  Saving Program (CMS, 2022), showing a steady progression toward the value
  alignment between payers and providers necessary for the coproduction of
  health.
- Technology-enhanced workflow and workforce operations improvements
  resulted in increased process speed, scope, and interoperability between payers,
  providers, and patients (Sweeney, 2022). This new capability to effectively
  manage large scale health organizations enabled further strategic restructuring
  and reengineering as evidenced by an increase mergers and acquisition activity
  (Dunn, 2021b) and the creation of dominant regional or national systems
  (NIHCM, 2020). From 1998 to 2017, 1,600 hospital mergers occurred
  (Gaynor, 2020) with 1,400 health services deals finalized in 2021 valued at 217
  billion dollars (PWC, 2023). Recent indications suggest hospital merger activity
  dropped significantly in 2022, which may or may not be attributed to the recent
  pandemic (Kacik, 2023). The synergies produced from the rise of ACOs, and
  the increased numbers of mergers and acquisitions resulted in opportunities for
  further health sector integration (coproduction of health) (van Oorschot et al.,
  2022), and opportunities to transform care for vulnerable populations (AHA
  Fact Sheet, 2023).

Health Management Adapting to Cultural Shifts

- The rapid ascent of technology and digital communication within the last two decades appear to be directly linked to the democratization of information, accessibility of health knowledge via internet sources, and individuals taking more responsibility for health services received (Brandsen et al., 2018). The upswing of health consumerism, whether wholly attributed to the pressures and impact of COVID-19 or a continuation of an evolving process, became evident in 2021 when a Press Ganey survey reported more than 50% of consumers used the internet to find and select a new primary care provider, and respondents were more than twice as likely to use digital sources than a doctor's referral to choose a primary care doctor (Gordon, 2021). This cultural shift resulted in the patient/consumer moving to the center of any healthcare delivery model (Batalden et al., 2016), and a stronger commitment to involvement with the coproduction of health process (Filipe et al., 2017; Kaplan, 2016).
- An equally important national awakening and cultural shift occurred in response to the unacceptable situation of significant and multiple gaps in care and health disparities amplified by COVID-19 (Abbott, 2022). To counteract the negative impact of detrimental social drivers of health, health systems recognized the need for investment in and with community organizations to produce quality healthcare for all (Castrucci & Auerbach, 2019; Murphy, 2017; Shashank, 2017) and a stronger commitment to anti-racism and social justice (Balser et al., 2021). Together, these significant cultural changes helped set the precedent for contemporary health systems to migrate beyond the brick-and-mortar physical locations as a stronger partner to improve the quality of care via community alignment.

This brief retrospective review describes important national health system responses to both the mounting criticism of health outcomes and the profound 21st century challenges and problems. Table 9.2 summarizes these major transitions and transformations ranging from health policy mandates to substantial cultural changes and consumer expectations.

The healthcare delivery system transformations, enabled by technological advances, produced improved patient experience and outcomes, empowered a pivot to precision medicine models, and facilitated unprecedented organizational restructuring. These advances addressed the most pressing operational challenges but lacked a coherent integrative framework for the future.

Table 9.2. Health Sector Shifts Toward a Coproduction of Health Model.

National Health Policy Standards/ Incentives	Technological Achievements – Digital/Clinical	Health Organizational Transformations/ Innovative ACO Model	Shifts in Cultural Expectations – Consumerism/Multi-Sector Collaboration

THE POPULATION HEALTH FRAMEWORK AS A PARADIGM CHANGE PRECURSOR/ENABLER

The 21st century produced several valuable healthcare delivery frameworks that offered guidance for addressing imminent and challenging problems including the population health framework, the Triple Aim, the Cultural of Health, and other prominent industry models. In 2003, Kindig and Stoddart (2003) defined population health as requiring a primary focus on groups (populations) combined with an emphasis on health outcomes. This definition provided a crucial distinction from public, community, and global health which function within geographic bounded areas and lack outcome to cost alignment (Hewitt, 2022). Population health shares commonalities with other approaches via the integration of the public health's focus on social, economic, and cultural factors (IOM, 2002), and the adoption of community and global health strategies for integrating local health organizations, providers, and stakeholders initiatives that target health equity and socioeconomic disparities (Bresnick, 2017; Coburn et al., 2003).

In 2008, The Triple Aim model emerged to become one of healthcare's primary recognized frameworks and a goal accepted industry-wide (Berwick et al., 2008; IHI, 2022). By aligning access, cost, and quality, the Triple Aim provided a unifying direction that garnered national support and advocacy (Whittington et al., 2015). The iron triangle's premise offered a unique rationale for transitioning away from the standard fee-for-service approach (Delaronde, 2019). Although, now known as the Quadruple Aim, with the addition of productivity, well-being, or health equity as the fourth aim (Feeley, 2017), the framework underpins the primary principles of population health management – quality care and reducing per capital costs of care (Miller, 2022).

Two other national frameworks, the *Health in All Policies* (HiAP) and the *Culture of Health* (Chandra et al., 2017; Culture of Health Framework, n.d.; OADPS, 2016) also captured the interest of health systems and public health advocates. The HiAP is a collaborative multi-sector approach for improving population health by stressing health considerations in all decision-making practices. The framework emphasizes health equity, clinical and community prevention services, empowering people, and establishing healthy and safe community environments (OADPS, 2016). Like the HiAP, the Culture of Health supports strong cross-sector collaboration across communities but also integrates population health strategies that encourage the "appropriate use of healthcare services" and "risk reduction monitoring" (Chandra et al., 2017; Riley, 2010). The Culture of Health framework continues to be one of the most recognized widely adopted frameworks in the United States. Both approaches recommend the participation of nonhealth sector stakeholders integrate a community/municipality focus on eliminating health disparities, and a prevention and wellness perspective.

The impact of these initial frameworks and models led to a steady progression away from the traditional medical model with its emphasis on the individual and acute, reactive, and episodic model of care (George et al., 2022; Kumar & Chattu, 2018; The Medical Model, 2012) and aided the transition to a population health approach (Shahzad et al., 2019). Population health models illustrate the need for intersectoral collaboration (Friedman & Starfield, 2003) and suggest that establishing partnerships both intersector (physician-owned primary care) and with the public sector (public health), healthcare organizations can improve health outcomes (Shahzad et al., 2019) and increase value cocreation, (Gronroos, 2011). Together, Triple Aim, HiAP, and Culture of Health supplied workable and sustainable healthcare delivery examples for population health.

The American Hospital Association (AHA) in collaboration with other major national health stakeholders, and the Population Health Alliance (PHA), a major multi-stakeholder industry organization, also recognized the need for population health management models to help guide industry transitions (AHA, 2023; PHA, n.d.) The PHA-Population Health Management framework follows a process workflow of population assessment, stratification, person-centric interventions, and impact evaluation (PHA, 2018). The AHA's Population Health Framework identifies two strategic goals – community well-being and population health management with a concurrent emphasis on three implementation strategies – integrated care models, chronic complex care, and community partnerships (AHA, 2023). Inherent within both models is the theme of social accountability not only to the population but also the community. Table 9.3 summarizes the relationships between previous health models and guidelines and the two most recent industry frameworks that include process and implementation strategies.

Today, the health sector views population health management strategies as an effective framework for managing the cause of disease as well as the delivery of healthcare in a more efficient and effective way (Kohli & De Biasi, 2017). Despite the recent health system delivery transformations and achievements and the development of guiding models and frameworks, added challenges, in the form of major disruptions, have appeared to encompass the entire health sector.

Table 9.3. Important Health Management Frameworks and Models of the 21st Century.

Population Health	Triple Aim	Health in All Policies	Culture of Health
The American Hospital Association's (AHA's) Population Health Framework		The Population Health Alliance's (PHA's) Population Health Management	

THE CRISIS OF DISRUPTION LEADING TO A COPRODUCTION OF HEALTH SOLUTION

Disruption refers to an event that interferes with the normal, whether that be a process or activity or a way of doing business (Dunn, 2021c). Disruptive innovation often occurs when businesses build delivery models very different from traditional services, such as when convenient care clinics emerged and followed a standard protocol to diagnose and treat consumers versus the primary care model which relied on physician's expertise for patient care (Christensen et al., 2015).

Within the traditional healthscape, the management of institutions, medical practices, state, and federal agencies; and public health organizations were separate activities and seen as distinct in many ways with separate missions (Bialek et al., 2020). Although, health systems and local community hospitals continually coordinated efforts with public health agencies and other local nonprofit agencies to improve community health over the years, the results yielded limited efforts capable of sustaining major health initiatives (Hewitt & Dykstra, 2022). The PPACA, to ensure fair health coverage along with afford-ability (US CMMS, n.d.) mandated community health needs assessments (CHNAs). CHNAs required health systems and local public health agencies to collaborate closely and develop strategic community health improvement plans (CHIPs) (IRS, 2020). This health policy supported blending the overlapping system functions of public health and healthcare to improve population health outcomes (Hardcastle et al., 2011; Jacobson & Parmet, 2018). The CHNA mandates produced an initial disruption to the status quo relationships between the typical hospital/public health and community agency alignments. As man-agement continues to support hospital-community partnerships, opportunities emerge for breaking down silos and fragmented care, improving cross-sector communication, and aligning appropriate interventions with specific at-risk populations (Hilts et al., 2021).

A second type of health sector disruption occurred in 2018, when three non-health sector organizations with finance, retail, and insurance industry strengths, announced the formation of a new healthcare company (Haven), with the coproduction of health as the primary goal (Gawande, 2019; Tozzi, 2019). Although this innovative alliance dissolved after only three years (LaMonica, 2021), the Haven example provided a prototype for other industry sectors to enter the healthscape (Hewitt, In press). Within two years, the AHA identified six major corporations as potential disruptors with aspirations to enter the health-care delivery system and interrupt the normal process of doing business (AHA, 2020). The impact of disruptive innovation underscored the threat of nonsector companies as direct participants and competitors with their competing capabil-ities to provide quality healthcare at a lower cost by leveraging in-house strengths in sophisticated technologies, size, scope, and consumer expertise (Bruce & Twenter, 2022; Hewitt, In press).

The rapid entry of private equity into the health sector arena illustrates a third example of disruption as venture capital funding invested $206 billion into more than 1,400 healthcare acquisitions in 2021 (Schulte, 2022). Although, venture capitalists have always had a role and influence on funding diverse health tech-nologies initiatives (Lehoux et al., 2016), private equity firms began to purchase almost every type of health sector component: hospitals, health systems, ambu-latory surgical centers, imaging, medical practices and special groups, medical devices, pharmaceutical, biotechnology, healthcare technology systems, consul-ting, and value-based care companies (Birk, 2023; Bruch et al., 2022; Singh et al., 2022; Zhu et al., 2020). Corporate investment now appears to be acquiring primary care organizations and introducing an innovation model based on total-cost, value-based care where providers receive payment to manage the total cost of care for their patients, with payment flexibility-based on the magnitude of the patients' health risks and the provider's performance on quality metrics (Shah et al., 2023). Table 9.4 identifies these major disruption examples.

Table 9.4. Recent Health Sector Disruption Examples.

Health Policy community health needs assessments (CHNA) Mandate	Merger/Acquisition Rapid Increases	Nonsector Entrants	Venture Capital Targeted Funding

The rapid rise of mergers and acquisitions, along with nonhealth sector entrants and third-party funding disrupted the healthcare business model and accelerated the need for innovative business responses. Redesigning healthcare organizations and strategies will likely not only necessitate multi-sector collaboration but also align both clinical and nonclinical services with community social and provider networks (Farmanova et al., 2019). Engaging in multi-sector alignments may require collaboration with local or regional competitors. Co-coopetition occurs in a situation when competing organizations cooperate at times for other purposes (Chalhoub, 2007; LeTourneau, 2004). Radical collaboration, describes collaborations with nontraditional or unexpected organizations to obtain important health goals that require integration of shared decision-making and accountability (Wagner & Hewitt, 2022). Both strategies provide options necessary for the coproduction of health process. The AHA recently stated "the management of a population's health is promoted via a co-production of health model that emphasizes care coordination and patient engagement and is supported by appropriate fiscal models and evidence-based practice" (AHA, 2023).

THE EMERGING COPRODUCTION OF HEALTH FRAMEWORK

The recent disruptions to the American health delivery system may have resulted in unintended consequences with the health sector opting for the coproduction of health approach as an opportune business strategy. Fig. 9.1 summarizes the previously reviewed health sector pathway from the drivers of change to the transformational health system responses that enabled the coproduction of health to emerge as a valid organizational strategy.

This development process also helped clarify a set of underlying coproduction of health goals and prerequisites (See Table 9.5).

Each coproduction of health goal addresses a complex challenge facing the nation's health sector. They include transitions to an all-population approach, accountability for stakeholders, cross-sector coordinated care requirements, and a commitment to sustainable community initiatives for maximum collective impact. The suggested coproduction of health prerequisites, a collation of emerging health sector organizational strategies, reflect the essential components

Drivers of Change

Concerning Quality and Safety Issues	Unacceptable Health Inequities/ and Disparities (SDOH)	Common System Delivery and Care Coordination Gaps	Unsustainable Costs/Burden to Consumer
*Unacceptable health outcomes *Patient safety/issues *Variations in quality *Unsustainable interventions	*Pervasive health inequities * Limited access to Care *Short term community approaches	*Delivery Systems inefficiencies *Uncoordinated care *Workforce shortages *Intra-sector loose linka	*Unsustainable Costs *Transactional model *Clinician-led coordination

Health Sector Responses, Achievements, and Innovations

National Health Policy	Technological Achievements – Digital/ Clinical	Health Organizational Transformations/ Innovative ACO Model	Shifts in Cultural Expectations – Consumerism/ Multi-Sector Collaboration
*Standards/ Incentives *Shared Risk for all Stakeholders *Value over Volume *Targeted Community initiatives	*Digital Care Strategies *Personalized Medicine *Interoperability for cross-sector relationships	*Dissolution of medical model paradigm *Lifespan Care Coordination *Shared Investments	*Consumer Focus *Decentralization of healthcare delivery *Quality of life Returns *Patient guided care

Co-Production of Health Framework

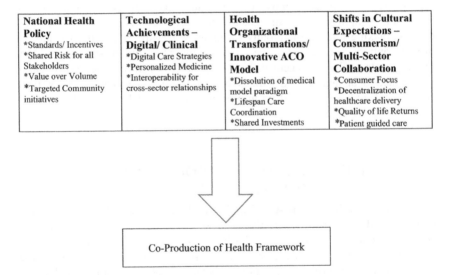

Fig. 9.1.   Health Sector Pathway to the Coproduction of Health.

of the coproduction of health framework and are preconditions that describe the transitional activities to attain the outlined coproduction goals. Collectively, they offer strategies for expanding and enhancing care, implementing organizational missions that require social contract accountability, alleviating operational shortcomings in the current healthcare system and developing appropriate and innovative multi-sector arrangements that align cross-sector stakeholders to

Table 9.5. Coproduction of Health: Goals and Prerequisites Examples.

Goals	Prerequisites
Facilitates the transition from medical model to an all-population-based approach and addresses the underlying social issues	Adoption of a population health focus Social accountability for community vision
Provides specific expectations and accountability alignment designed to maximize outcomes via standardization and the adoption of innovative alternative payment models that emphasize shared risk	Alignment of quality outcomes and cost containment strategies Payer/Provider/Patient Incentives
Requires a multi-sector coordinated care approach that spans the entire lifespan and emphasizes patient-guided and personalized care	Patient-centricity/consumer friendly embedded health delivery Patient Experience Pathway
Supports, long-term, sustainable initiatives involving integrating organizational frameworks with community and other nontraditional stakeholders to facilitate maximum collective impact.	Investment in sustainable cross-sector relationships and initiatives Implementation of a coproduction of health operational framework

improve quality of life. Ultimately, the coproduction of health framework seeks to enable value cocreation.

IMPLEMENTING THE COPRODUCTION OF HEALTH FRAMEWORK

For a coproduction of health approach to achieve collective impact, necessary organizational transitions include development of a common agenda, a centralized infrastructure, informed stakeholders, and a structured process that leads to shared measurement, along with mutually reinforcing activities among all entities (Kania & Kramer, 2011). Nies (2014) suggests that a coproduction of care approach involves the integration of local communities, with patients as primary contributors in the codesign and delivery of healthcare services. A learning health system perspective describes the coproduction of health role as "the interdependent work of users and professionals who are creating, designing, producing, delivering, assessing, and evaluating the relationships and actions that contribute to the health of individuals and populations" (Gremyr et al., 2021). Of primary concern to healthcare management will be the systems integrations of organizational structural and working relationships required to manage cross-sector connections capable of aligning health systems with community organizations, clinicians, social service, government and public health agencies, nonhealth sector partners and patients/consumers (Caron & Hewitt, In Press).

For any complex enterprise, the implementation of organizational structure and governance decisions remain crucial. For health initiatives capable of reducing or solving contemporary health problems, the amount of investment needed is not only significant but should be leveraged across participating organizations over time (Nielsen et al., 2021). To achieve the collective goals of a network of organizations, individual institutions and agencies may also need to voluntarily relinquish part of their autonomy to achieve a balance between the initiative's mission, autonomy, and interdependence (Hearld & Westra, 2022). Implementing these suggested strategies will require transformative organizational models and actions that may not be in common use today.

Currently, three operational strategies, integrator, convener, and aggregator, have emerged and appear feasible for implementing a coproduction of health framework.

(1) The integrator model, already adopted by health systems collaborating with community organizations and/or local or regional health coalitions in less formal relationships, relies on a leadership position. An integrator's role can be filled by either an organization or an individual employee and focuses on combining integration of effort and specialization of activities (Lawrence & Lorsch, 1967). Serving as a facilitator, the integrator must be capable of aligning all multi-sector stakeholders to deliver the essential functions that will achieve positive outcomes in health and well-being for a defined population (Nemours, 2012). Integrators help organizations collaborate to solve specific social problems that no one entity could address alone (Nemours Childrens Health, 2023). System integration activities range from partnership development and redesign of care to population health activities and financial management (Chang et al., 2020; Wagner & Hewitt, 2022). System integrators fulfill the organizational role for aligning processes across diverse sectors and coordinating stakeholder outputs. Any community could have more than one integrator to perform these system level functions and engage partners such as Health Maintenance Organizations (HMOs), ACOs, public health departments, health systems, and community based nonprofit groups.

(2) The convener model relies on a third-party agent that facilitates healthcare provider support of community-based initiatives that do not require participating stakeholders to make direct investments in individual social needs service agencies or engage in formal partnerships (Cheney, 2020). The purpose of the convener organization is to be a "trusted broker" and intermediary to establish a network of social service providers capable of completing referrals among payers and community social service agencies, synchronizing payment models, and providing a payer alternative to making direct investments in community-based organizations (Raths, 2021). HealthPartners, an integrated not-for-profit member-governed health system in the upper Midwest, convened a large coalition of more than 130 stakeholders from 13 different sectors to successfully complete a 10-year commitment addressing the underlying drivers of childhood obesity. As a convener, HealthPartners successfully leveraged all stakeholder competencies (Pronk, 2018). Conveners contribute an external service role for the health system and other stakeholders.

(3) The third implementation option utilizes an aggregator position that recruits cross-sector companies interested in well-researched, sustainable community investments that typically impact social determinants of health risk factors (Nielsen et al., 2021). Aggregators serve an essential function in identifying multi-sector stakeholder groups that can collectively finance key investment areas to improve quality of life (Nichols & Taylor, 2018). The aggregator model differs from both the integrator and convener as the stakeholder recruitment strategy requires a willingness to collaboratively invest and be contractually obligated in targeted community interventions with the recognition that the return on investment (benefit) will spread across several stakeholders (Nielsen et al., 2021). Potential investors may include for-profit and nonprofit providers of care, competing organizations, and philanthropic organizations not located within the community. The product or service provided is referred to as an aggregated precision investment (API). Examples include social determinants of health intervention opportunities such as construction of community housing for those in need or development of a behavioral health services network to meet local demand (Hawryluk, 2019; Reed, 2021). The aggregator assumes the complex responsibility for calculating the benefit level for each stakeholder based on appropriate price points for needed services or investment, recruiting the investors, and contracting with the service providers. For communities that struggle with barriers to collaboration, the aggregator model requires a convener of stature that cannot only successfully align investor alliance but also provide the management, technology infrastructure and contracting pricing skills to aggregate a sustained targeted investment (Nielsen et al., 2021).

As coproduction of health initiatives emerge, evidence of accountability and positive health outcomes as well as justification of investment and fiscal models will require study and evidence to determine optimal organizational and relationship structures.

ORGANIZATIONAL SCIENCE THEORIES UNDERLYING THE COPRODUCTION OF HEALTH FRAMEWORK

To determine the viability of the coproduction of health framework as a valid organizational strategy requires research focusing on theoretical frameworks and organizational processes. A study examining both organizational science theories and healthcare research from the last decade found evidence of distinct perspective differences between both disciplines' research (Mayo et al., 2021). Other scholars have suggested research efforts assessing effectiveness across various organizational dimensions (Nowell & Milward, 2022), such as analyzing conceptualization, theoretical application, and sustainment of cross-sector and investment alliances (Murray & Lewis, 2022; Nielsen et al., 2021). Hearld and Westra (2022) refined their study focus to evaluate capabilities of an organization's network independence, management, and governance. The consensus from these studies appears to be a clear perspective on the elements of production whether a product, service, or idea.

Within general organization science theoretical perspectives, the author selected four theories/models (institutional, socioeconomic, network theory/ network analysis theory, and resource dependency theory), to briefly review and assess their relevance for clarifying and improving coproduction of health organizational structures and processes. Criteria for selection included importance to innovative organizational development, contemporary healthcare delivery transformations, and relationship alignments affecting the health sector. Table 9.6 introduces the selected theories/models, definitions, and their relationship to the coproduction of health framework.

Table 9.6. Selected Organization Science Theories/Models, Definitions, and Relevance to the Coproduction of Health.

Model/Theory:	Definition:	Relevance:
Institutional	Institutional theory proposes that organizations within a field become increasingly similar (isomorphic) as the result of different external pressures (Scott et al., 2000).	All-population health approach
Socioeconomic Model	The Socioeconomic model's main premise states that factors at one level influence factors at another level via relationships (CDC, 2022)	Social Accountability
Network Theory/ Network Analysis Theory	Network theory examines social relationships and their coordination efforts across three different levels – micro, meso, and macro while network analysis theory focuses on the structure of the organizational relationship ties and the content of the ties (Burns et al., 2021).	Multi-sector coordination of healthcare service delivery and patient centrality
Resource Dependency Theory	Resource dependency theory posits that an organization must engage in transactions with other actors and organizations in its environment to acquire resources (Hilman et al., 2009)	Sustainable cross-sector initiatives Collective Impact

Institutional Theory

Organizational science postulates that organizations are motivated to establish linkages with other organizations to effectively accomplish tasks (Parmigiani & Rivera-Santos, 2011). New coproduction models offer effective population health strategies to better serve their community, reduce the burden of disease, and potentially lower cost of care which aligns with this perspective (Gray, 2017). Institutional theory also suggests that organizations may form cross-sector alliances based on the assumption of becoming popular in the community. Current evidence shows coproduction of health arrangements are becoming more institutionalized across the country (Murray & Lewis, 2022; Scott et al., 2000). But complex management and systems integration challenges also require strong organizational design and internal infrastructure strengths as multistakeholder alliances are vulnerable to disruption if key stakeholders leave (D'Aunno et al., 2019). Both health and nonhealth sector organizations need to make substantial changes in how they approach health and allocate resources (Kindig & Isham, 2014). Other researchers have suggested a coproduction decision-making pathway but not addressed the partnership development decisions and choices available to current health systems today (Wagner & Hewitt, 2022). These types of critical decisions impact the successful transformation of the health system to a coproduction of health approach.

An organizational science theory exhibiting the strongest alignment with the development and adoption of the coproduction of health framework is institutional theory. Institutional theory proposes that organizations within a field become increasingly similar (isomorphic) as the result of different external pressures (Scott et al., 2000). Leeman et al. (2022) suggest that three types of external pressures (mimetic, normative or coercive) are applicable to the health sector, and coercive pressure exerts the greatest forces when organizations transact with agencies of the state and depend on a single or several similar sources of support for vital resources. The healthcare industry is clearly dependent on major government entities and proprietary insurance payers for sustainable funding, and health providers for service delivery. Contemporary health systems are reflecting the impact from mimetic pressures which happens when organizations copy the approaches of others. The recent rapid rise of private equity into healthcare and the encroachment of large nonsector industry corporations serve as two relevant examples of coercive pressure. The formation of multi-sector alliances necessary for the coproduction of health aligns with the institutional theory proposition that suggests that these organizational relationships may be forming to gain stature, reputation or to attain opportunities for other resources (Scott et al., 2000).

Institutional theory studies have focused on analyzing hospital responses to external demands for finance and quality (Burnett et al., 2015), identifying ways social welfare systems responded to policymaker demands for evidence-based solutions (Birken et al., 2017), and factors associated with the implementation of a health promotion smoking cessation model (Martinez et al., 2017). A final and relevant aspect of institutional theory is the inherent proposition that normative pressure increases for highly professionalized fields such as healthcare (Birken et al., 2017; Novotna et al., 2012).

Socioeconomic Model

Given the boundary spanning issues inherent in the coproduction of health framework, multi-disciplinary theories of organizational transactions and relationships should be considered essential components for review. Theories and frameworks derived from the socio-eco-model describe the potential for macro relationships between individuals, communities, and society (ATSDR, 2015;

CDC, 2022; Dahlberg & Krug, 2002; WHO, 1947). The socioeconomic model's main premise states that factors at one level influence factors at another level via relationships. To facilitate this type of social change, a collective impact perspective suggests that combining influence factors from multiple levels and change agents from within levels will produce a greater social product than any single entity could manage alone (Kania & Kramer, 2011). The idea that large-scale social change comes from better cross-sector coordination rather than from the isolated intervention of individual organizations relates to the health sector's pathway from a fragmented silo approach focusing on acute care to a lifetime continuum of care improving quality of life. This shift is not merely a matter of encouraging more collaboration or public–private partnerships as it requires a systemic approach to social impact that focuses on the relationships and the progress toward shared objectives (Kania & Kramer, 2011).

Network Collaborations and Network Theory

Organizational decision strategies will need to analyze network collaborations appropriate for complex and sustainable relationships. Both business and community researchers have identified network relationship typologies. Business perspectives focus on closed and hierarchical networks, open and hierarchical networks (innovation mall), open and flat networks (innovation community), or closed and flat networks (a consortium) (Pisano & Verganti, 2008). The community approach emphasizes four relationship levels in the continuum of collaboration framework: networking, coordinating, cooperating, and collaborating (ASPHN, 2017; Himmelman, 2002). Mashek (2015) has suggested the continuum be expanded by adding "integrating" as a final level. Both examples present relationship alignments among diverse health stakeholders that preface network development. Current health sector examples of relevant network types include multi-stakeholder alliance, cross-sectoral partnerships, patient referral networks, and collaboration efforts between care professionals (Peteers et al., 2022). As coproduction of health networks become more commonplace, relationship, and integration theory can offer useful perspectives on their success.

Network theory, a complex organizational perspective, examines social relationships and their coordination efforts across three different levels – micro, meso, and macro (Burns et al., 2021). Because the coproduction of health involves complex arrangements with multiple partners, categorizing these types of integration (coordination) within networks (structural, functional, normative, interpersonal, and process) can lead to identification of organizational quality and cost impact factors (Singer et al., 2020). A coproduction of health organization fits the classification of a purpose-oriented network (Nowell & Kenis, 2019; Nowell & Milward, 2022) which includes at least three or more autonomous organizations working together to achieve a common goal (Borgatti & Halgin, 2011; Carboni et al., 2019; Hearld & Westra, 2022).

Network analysis theory's focal point is not only network type but also the structure of the organizational relationship ties and the content (work activity) of the ties (Burns et al., 2021). The value of network analysis is the capability to examine coproduction of health networks at multiple levels (patient to multi-sector), the dimensions of the relational collaborations, and both process flow and decision-making capacity (Peeters et al., 2022; Turini et al., 2010). Previous research examined collaboration among HIV agencies, not multi-sector alliances, using social network theory and relational correlation factors and found shared goals and mutual respect indicated high rates for success (Khosla et al., 2016). Gittell and Ali (2022) suggest that research on relational coordination within networks should continue to focus on purpose, dimensional impact comparisons, and types of interventions needed to strengthen networks.

RESOURCE DEPENDENCY THEORY

An alternative framework theory, aligned with the relational coordination perspective, would be a resource dependency approach. Hearld and Westra (2022) suggest that resource dependence "as an extension of the relational view" and can be used to manage network participation. Resource dependency theory posits that organizations, such as a business firm, must engage in transactions with other actors and organizations in its environment to acquire resources (Hilman et al., 2009). Today, environmental pressures targeting healthcare service delivery improvements and quality and population health outcomes, serve as significant external forces on coproduction of health stakeholders. The potential for these forces to influence organizational partnerships' decisions and selection of cross-sector stakeholders would be significant. Operational strategies to minimize environmental dependencies include (a) mergers/vertical integration, (b) joint ventures and other interorganizational relationships, (c) boards of directors, (d) political action, and (e) executive succession (Hilman et al., 2009; Pfeffer & Salancik, 1978). Health systems have adopted mergers/vertical integration and joint ventures and other interorganizational relationships in recent years, and the passage of the 2010 PPACA illustrates political action change designed to reduce external pressure for improvement. Resource dependency theory also focuses on the impact of organizational strategies for scenarios with scarce resources and/or high demands (Ansmann et al., 2021). Health systems' responses to nursing shortages and burnout (scarce resources), and their innovative strategies in addressing surge capacity during the COVID-19 pandemic, would be strategic examples appropriate for resource dependence analysis (Bonciani et al., 2022). Today's healthscape exhibits low munificence and high dynamism and complexity and supports the use of resource dependency theory as extremely relevant for coproduction of health initiatives.

COPRODUCTION OF HEALTH RESEARCH DIRECTIONS

The health system innovations that coalesced to create the coproduction of health framework has enabled the sector to shift forward from previous less-formal health system and single community organization collaborations to sophisticated inter-sector alliances and advanced cross-sector relationships that feature both social and fiscal outcome accountability. These developing organizational frameworks represent diverse stakeholder perspectives and strategies to address contemporary grand challenges. Will the redesign of current healthcare systems allow the coproduction of health approaches to be successful? Or will the necessity for intersectoral relationships require the development of newer frameworks?

These major organizational behavior theories and models, Institutional Theory, Social-Economic Model, Network Theory/Network Analysis Theory, and Resource Dependency Theory, form an initial basis for examining the management complexities and system integration goals inherent in the coproduction of health framework. All these frameworks suggest organizational characteristics and/or dimensions deserve review within broad categories:

- Directional strategy choices and outcomes;
- Stakeholder selection, characteristics, and relationships;
- Context of operational and network models chosen, including intervention type, location, and duration;
- Accountability, sustainability, and return on investment results;
- Effectiveness and health outcomes at individual, organizational, network, community, and social levels.

Specific study should be undertaken for each of the initially identified prerequisites to determine their contributions to the overall success of any coproduction initiative or activity.

Previous health researchers have suggested the need for a stronger research alliance between organizational science and healthcare (Mayo et al., 2021). The next coproduction of health research iteration could build on an approach that incorporates the socioeconomic model to recognize an additional layer of relationship impact factors not currently included in organization science. For example, an initial focus could concentrate on assessing both the value and utility of the integrator, convener, and aggregator alternatives from each stakeholder's perspective including the population in need. Another line of inquiry could focus on the governance and decision-making complexities unique to the coproduction of health framework. Heaton et al. (2016) suggest that the coproduction of health provides useful insights about the "qualities of collaborative working that inspire the requisite mechanisms for generating knowledge that is translated into practice."

A recent commentary on changing the future of healthcare delivery in the United States suggested that value-based care may be "stuck in neutral" (Hagland & Wider, 2023). The impetus for organizational research that assesses transformative system changes, such as the coproduction of health framework, will inform and accelerate improved health sector management strategies for the future.

CONCLUSION

In Kuhn's postscript, written seven years after the publication of *The Structure of Scientific Revolutions*, two assertions appear relevant to the current coproduction of health search for theoretical explanations. First, "a paradigm governs, not a subject matter, but rather a group of practitioners (p. 180), and scientific knowledge is embedded in theory and rules; problems are supplied to gain facility in their application." Today's grand health challenges will only respond to significant and sustained collaborations of scale. They offer daily opportunities to test the proposed coproduction of health framework (cross-sector network alliance initiatives), and to assess its utility and strength to produce a paradigm change. As suggested above, a targeted review of the coproduction of health framework's prerequisites should provide evidence for future enhancement and refinement.

This chapter describes a population health management pathway leading to a coproduction of health framework. Given the continuing complexities of healthcare management and delivery, the healthscape should expect continuing grand challenges and wicked problems to reflect the socially embedded health disparities and operational fragmentations of today. The coproduction of health framework is primarily an organizational model designed to address contemporary challenges. Institutional socioeconomic, network/network analysis, and resource dependency theories/models, and offer research directions for examining the various constructs of the framework.

Will the coproduction of health framework become one of the new norms for health care as suggested by health experts? Or will the penultimate question become – Does the co-production of health framework lead to value co-creation for the primary stakeholders, the patient/consumer? And the conclusive question, Will the coproduction of health approach accomplish the needed health sector paradigm conversion?

REFERENCES

Abbott, B. (2022, August 4). How the Covid-19 pandemic changed American's health for the worse. *Wall Street Journal*, A6. https://www.wsj.com/articles/how-the-covid-19-pandemic-changed-americans-health-for-the-worse-11659260165

Absher, H. (2022, November 30). Tripled pay is great for travel nurses – Not for hospitals. https://www.wfyi.org/news/articles/tripled-pay-is-great-for-travel-nurses–not-for-hospitals

Agency for Toxic Substance and Disease Registry (ATSDR). (2015). Models and frameworks for the practice of community engagement. https://www.atsdr.cdc.gov/communityengagement/pce_models.html

AHA. (2020). Investment strategy for community health: Investing in community health: A toolkit for hospitals. https://centerforcommunityinvestment.org/sites/default/files/Investment%20Strategy%20for%20Community%20Health.pdf

AHA. (2021). Precision medicine and population health. https://www.aha.org/sponsored-executive-dialogues/2021-03-22-precision-medicine-and-population-health

AHA. (2023). Population health management. What is population health management. https://www.aha.org/center/population-health-management

AHA. (2023, March). Fact sheet: Hospital mergers and acquisitions can expand and preserve access to care. https://www.aha.org/fact-sheets/2023-03-16-fact-sheet-hospital-mergers-and-acquisitions-can-expand-and-preserve-access-care

Ansmann, L., Vennedey, V., Hillen, H., Stock, S., Kuntz, L., Pfaff, H., Mannion, R., & Hower, K. (2021). Resource dependency and strategy in healthcare organizations during a time of scarce resources: Evidence from the metropolitan area of cologne. *Journal of Health, Organisation and Management, 35*(9), 211–227. https://doi.org/10.1108/JHOM-12-2020-0478

ASPE. (2022a, May 3). Impact of the COVID-19 pandemic on the hospital and outpatient clinician workforce challenges and policy responses. Office of Health Policy. https://aspe.hhs.gov/sites/default/files/documents/9cc72124abd9ea25d58a22c7692dccb6/aspe-covid-workforce-report.pdf

ASPE. (2022b, March 18). The Affordable Care Act and its accomplishments. Office of the Assistant Secretary for Planning and Evaluation. https://aspe.hhs.gov/reports/aca-accomplishments

Association of State Public Health Nutritionists (ASPHN). (2017, November 16). ASPHN collaboration primer. https://asphn.org/wp-content/uploads/2017/10/collaboration-primer.pdf

Bakshi, S. (2021). The essential role of population health during and beyond COVID-19. *American Journal of Managed Care, 27*(3), 123–128. https://doi.org/10.37765/ajmc.2021.88511. https://www.ajmc.com/view/the-essential-role-of-population-health-during-and-beyond-covid-19

Balser, J., Ryu, J., Hood, M., Kaplan, G., Perlin, J., & Siegel, B. (2021, April 7). Care systems COVID-19 impact assessment: Lessons learned and compelling needs. https://nam.edu/care-systems-covid-19-impact-assessment-lessons-learned-and-compellingneeds

Batalden, M., Sabadosa, K., Myers, S., Bass, J., Hicks, J., & Gunther-Murphy, C. (2016). The new world of coproducing-in-health and health care. Audio/Video. https://www.ihi.org/resources/Pages/AudioandVideo/WIHI-The-New-World-of-Coproducing-in-Health-and-Health-Care.aspx

Beresford, P., Farr, M., Hickey, G., Kaur, M., Ocloo, J., Tembo, D., & Williams, O. (2021). *COVID-19 and co-production in health and social care research, policy, and practice: Volume 1: The challenges and necessity of co-production*. Bristol University Press. https://www.jstor.org/stable/j.ctv1p6hqjs

Berwick, D. M., Nolan, T. W., & Whittington, J. (2008). The triple aim: Care, health, and cost. *Health Affairs, 27*(3), 759–769.

Bestsennyy, O., Chmielewski, M., Koffel, A., & Shah, A. (2022, February 1). *From facility to home: How healthcare could shift by 2025*. McKinsey. https://www.mckinsey.com/industries/healthcare-systems-and-services/our-insights/from-facility-to-home-how-healthcare-could-shift-by-2025

Bialek, R., Moran, J., Amos, K., & Lamers, L. (2020). *Cross-sector collaboration: Making partnerships work for your community Public Health Foundation* (p. 36). Public Health Foundation. http://www.phf.org/events/Pages/Cross_Sector_Collaboration_Making_Partnerships_Work_for_Your_Community.aspx#:~:text=Cross-sectorcollaborationisa,toacommunitytheyserve.&text=Resourcestohelpyouaddresscommoncommunityhealthchallenges

Birk, S. (2023, January/February). The question of private equity: Arguments in favor of private equity investment in healthcare make sense. *Healthcare Executive, 38*(1), 16–22.

Birken, S., Bunger, A., Powell, B., Turner, K., Clary, A., Klaman, S., Yu, Y., Whitaker, D., Self, S., Rostad, W., Shenley Chatham, J., Kirk, M., Shea, C., Haines, E., & Weiner, B. (2017). Organizational theory for dissemination and implementation research. *Implementation Science, 12*, 62. https://doi.org/10.1186/s13012-017-0592-x

Bodenheimer, T., & Sinsky, C. (2014). From triple to Quadruple Aim: Care of the patient requires care of the provider. *The Annals of Family Medicine, 12*, 573–576. https://doi.org/10.1370/afm.1713

Bonciani, M., Corazza, I., & De Rosis, S. (2022). The COVID-19 emergency as an opportunity to co-produce an innovative approach to health services provision: The women's antenatal classes move on the web. *Italian Journal of Marketing, 2022*, 59–85. https://doi.org/10.1007/s43039-021-00045-6. https://link.springer.com/article/10.1007/s43039-021-00045-6

Borgatti, S. P., & Halgin, D. S. (2011). On network theory. *Organization Science, 22*(5), 1168–1181.

Bovaird, T. (2007, September/October). Beyond engagement and participation: User and community coproduction of public services. *Public Administration Review*, 846–860. https://www.cbs.dk/files/cbs.dk/bovaird_final_version_pdf_1.pdf

Brandsen, T., & Honingh, M. (2018). Distinguishing different types of coproduction: A conceptual analysis based on the classical definitions. *Public Administration Review, 76*, 427–435. https://interlink-project.eu/wp-content/uploads/2021/03/Distinguishing-different-types-of-coproduction.pdf

Brandsen, T., Steen, T., & Verschuere, B. (Eds.). (2018). *Co-production and co-creation: Engaging citizens in public services.* Taylor-Francis.

Bresnick, J. (2017, July 19). How do population health, public health, community health differ? What's the difference between population health, public health, and community health? https://healthitanalytics.com/news/how-do-population-health-public-health-community-health-differ

Brown, G. D., Pasupathy, K. S., & Patrick, T. B. (2019). *Health informatics: A systems perspective* (2nd ed.). Health Administration Press (HAP); Association of University Programs in Health Administration (AUPHA).

Bruce, G., & Twenter, P. (2022, December 19). *Can health systems compete with disruption from CVS, Walgreens?* https://www.beckershospitalreview.com/disruptors/can-health-systems-compete-with-disruption-from-cvs-walgreens.html?origin=BHRE&utm_source=BHRE&utm_medium=email&utm_content=newsletter&oly_enc_id=145015993723C6U

Bruch, J., Nair-Desai, S., Oray, E., & Tsai, T. (2022, September). Private equity private equity acquisitions of ambulatory surgical centers were not associated with quality, cost, or volume changes. *Health Affairs, 41*(9). https://doi.org/10.1377/hlthaff.2021.01904https://www.healthaffairs.org/doi/full/10.1377/hlthaff.2021.01904

Buehler, J., Snyder, R., Freeman, S., Carson, S., & Ortega, A. (2018, January–February). It's not just insurance: The Affordable Care Act and population health. *Public Health Reports, 133*(1), 34–38. https://doi.org/10.1177/0033354917743499

Burnett, S., Mendel, P., Nunes, F., Wigg, S., Van den Bovenkamp, H., Karltun, A., Robert, G., Anderson, J., Vincent, C., & Fulop, N. (2015). Using institutional theory to analyse hospital responses to external demands for finance and quality in five European countries. *Journal of Health Services Research & Policy, 21*, 109–117. https://doi.org/10.1177/1355819615622655

Burns, L. R., Nembhard, I. M., & Shortell, S. M. (2021). Integrating network theory into study of integrated healthcare. *Social Science & Medicine, 296.* https://doi.org/10.1016/j.socscimed.2021.114664

Byrne, M. D. (2020, October). Telehealth and the COVID-19 pandemic. *Journal of PeriAnesthesia Nursing, 35*(5), 548–551. https://doi.org/10.1016/j.jopan.2020.06.023

Carboni, J. L., Saz-Carranza, A., Raab, J., & Isett, K. R. (2019). Taking dimensions of purpose-oriented networks seriously. *Perspectives on Public Management and Governance, 2*(3), 187–201.

Caron, R., & Hewitt, A. (In Press). Population health: An integrating approach for aligning public health and healthcare systems. *Journal of Health Administration Education.*

Castrucci, B., & Auerbach, J. (2019, January 16). Meeting individual social needs falls short of addressing social determinants of health. *Health Affairs Forefront.* https://www.healthaffairs.org/do/10.1377/forefront.20190115.234942/

CDC. (2022, January 18). The social-ecological model: A framework for prevention. https://www.cdc.gov/violenceprevention/about/social-ecologicalmodel.html#:~:text=This%20model%20considers%20the%20complex,from%20experiencing%20or%20perpetrating%20violence

Chalhoub, M. (2007). A framework in strategy and competition using alliances: Application to the automotive industry. *International Journal of Organization Theory and Behavior, 10*(2).

Chandra, A., Acosta, J., Carman, K. G., Dubowitz, T., Leviton, L., Martin, L. T., Miller, C., Nelson, C., Orleans, T., Tait, M., Trujillo, M., Towe, V., Yeung, D., & Plough, A. L. (2017, January). Building a national Culture of Health: Background, action framework, measures, and next steps. *Rand Health Quarterly, 6*(2), 3.

Chang, D. I., Gertel-Rosenberg, A., Blackburn, K., & Taylor, B. (2020, March). Notes from the field. https://www.movinghealthcareupstream.org/wp-content/uploads/2020/03/HealthCareRolesInPopulationHealthNetworks.pdf

Cheney, C. (2020, February 5). *Convener model helps healthcare providers address social determinants of health.* HealthLeaders Media. https://www.healthleadersmedia.com/clinical-care/convener-model-helps-healthcare-providers-address-social-determinants-health

Christensen, C., Raynor, M., & McDonald, R. (2015, December). What is disruptive innovation? Twenty years after the introduction of the theory, we revisit what it does—and doesn't—explain. https://hbr.org/2015/12/what-is-disruptive-innovation

CMS. (2010, July 13). CMS and ONC final regulations define meaningful use and set standards for electronic health record incentive program. https://www.cms.gov/newsroom/fact-sheets/cms-and-onc-final-regulations-define-meaningful-use-and-set-standards-electronic-health-record

CMS. (2022, January 26). Medicare shared savings program continues to grow and deliver high-quality, person-centered care through accountable care organizations. https://www.cms.gov/newsroom/press-releases/medicare-shared-savings-program-continues-grow-and-deliver-high-quality-person-centered-care-through#:~:text=This%20brings%20the%20total%20number,Program%20to%20483%20in%202022

Coburn, D., Denny, K., Mykhalovskiy, E., McDonough, P., Robertson, A., & Love, R. (2003, March). Population health in Canada: A brief critique. *American Journal of Public Health*, *93*(3), 392–396. https://doi.org/10.2105/ajph.93.3.392

Collins, F., & Varmus, H. (2015). A new initiative on precision medicine. *New England Journal of Medicine*, *372*, 793–795.

Colquitt, J., & George, G. (2011). Publishing in AMJ–Part 1: Topic choice. *Academy of Management Journal*, *54*, 432–435. https://doi.org/10.5465/AMJ.2011.61965960

Cordani, D. (2020, February 29). Healthcare is on an unsustainable trajectory, requiring a renewed push for transformation. *Modern Healthcare*. https://www.modernhealthcare.com/opinion/healthcare-unsustainable-trajectory

Culture of Health Framework. (n.d.). Robert Wood Johnson Foundation. https://www.evidenceforaction.org/about-us/what-culture-health#:~:text=A%20Culture%20of%20Health%20is,that%20lead%20to%20healthy%20lifestyles

D'Aunno, T., Hearld, L., & Alexander, J. A. (2019, April/June). Sustaining multistakeholder alliances. *Health Care Management Review*, *44*(2), 183–194. https://doi.org/10.1097/HMR.0000000000000175

Dahlberg, L. L., & Krug, E. G. (2002). Violence: A global public health problem. In E. Krug, L. L. Dahlberg, J. A. Mercy, A. B. Zwi, & R. Lozano (Eds.), *World report on violence and health* (pp. 1–21). World Health Organization.

Delaronde, S. (2019, February 6). The iron triangle of health care: Access, cost, and quality. https://insideangle.3m.com/his/blog-post/the-iron-triangle-of-health-care-access-cost-and-quality/

Dunn, R. (2021a). Emerging influences in healthcare. In R. Dunn (Ed.), *Dunn and Haimann's healthcare management* (11th ed., p. 171). HAP/AUPHA Publishing.

Dunn, R. (2021b). Process and quality improvement. In R. Dunn (Ed.), *Dunn and Haimann's healthcare management* (11th ed., pp. 416–419). HAP/AUPHA Publishing.

Dunn, R. (2021c). Managerial planning. In R. Dunn (Ed.), *Dunn and Haimann's healthcare management* (11th ed., p. 204). HAP/AUPHA Publishing.

Farmanova, E., Baker, G. R., & Cohen, D. (2019, April). Combining integration of care and a population health approach: A scoping review of redesign strategies and interventions, and their impact. *International Journal of Integrated Care*, *19*(2), 5. https://doi.org/10.5334/ijic.4197

Feeley, D. (2017, November 28). The Triple Aim or the Quadruple Aim? Four points to help set your strategy. https://www.ihi.org/communities/blogs/the-triple-aim-or-the-quadruple-aim-four-points-to-help-set-your-strategy

Ferraro, F., Etzion, D., & Gehman, J. (2015). Tackling grand challenges pragmatically: Robust action revisited. *Organization Studies*, *36*(3), 363–390. *PAHM* vol 20.

Filipe, A., Renedo, A., & Marston, C. (2017). The co-production of what? Knowledge, values, and social relations in health care. *PLoS Biology*, *15*(5), e2001403. https://doi.org/10.1371/journal.pbio.2001403; https://journals.plos.org/plosbiology/article?id=10.1371/journal.pbio.2001403

Findlay, S. (2017). Implementing Medicare Access and CHIP Reauthorization Act of 2015 (MACRA). *Health Affairs*.

Fiorio, C. V., Gorli, M., & Verzillo, S. (2018, February 8). Evaluating organizational change in health care: The patient-centered hospital model. *BMC Health Services Research*, *18*(1), 95. https://doi.org/10.1186/s12913-018-2877-4

Friedman, D. J., & Starfield, B. (2003, March). Models of population health: Their value for US public health practice, policy, and research. *American Journal of Public Health, 93*(3), 366–369. https://doi.org/10.2105/ajph.93.3.366

Gawande, A. (2019). *Haven.* Haven Healthcare. https://havenhealthcare.com/

Gaynor, M. (2020, March). *The Hamilton project. What to do about health-care markets? Policies to make health-care markets work.* https://www.brookings.edu/wp-content/uploads/2020/03/Gaynor_PP_FINAL.pdf

George, J. M. (2014). Compassion and capitalism: Implications for organizational studies. *Journal of Management, 40*(1), 5–15.

George, G., Howard-Grenville, J., Joshi, A., & Tihanyi, L. (2016). Understanding and tackling societal grand challenges through management research. *Academy of Management Journal, 59,* 1880–1895.

George, N., Radman, R., Zomahoun, H., Boivin, A., & Ahmed, S. (2022). Linkages between health systems and communities for chronic care: A scoping review protocol. *BMJ Open,* e06043. https://doi.org/10.1136/bmjopen-2021-060430

Gittell, U., & Ali, H. (2022). Strengthening networks for healthcare integration: A commentary. *Social Science & Medicine, 305,* 1–8.

Goldstein, F., Shephard, V., & Duda, S. (2016). Policy implications for population health: Health promotion and wellness in population health: Creating a culture of wellness. In D. Nash, R. Fabius, A. Skoufalos, J. Clarke, & M. Horowitz (Eds.), *Population health* (2nd ed.). Jones & Bartlett Publishing.

Gordon, D. (2021, December 22). Is the era of healthcare consumerism finally here? New survey says yes. https://www.forbes.com/sites/debgordon/2021/12/02/is-the-era-of-healthcare-consumerism-finally-here-new-survey-says-yes/?sh=6e5e13133840

Gray, M. (2017). Value based healthcare. *BMJ (Online).* https://doi.org/10.1136/bmj.j437

Gremyr, A., Andersson, G. B., Thor, J., Elwyn, G., Batalden, P., & Andersson, A. C. (2021, November). The role of co-production in learning health systems. *International Journal for Quality in Health Care, 33*(Suppl. 2), ii26–ii32. https://doi.org/10.1093/intqhc/mzab072

Grieve, P. (2022, November 14). The lifetime cost of healthcare averages $700,000 for many insured Americans. https://money.com/health-care-costs-lifetime/?utm_medium=rss_synd&utm_source=applenews&xid=applenews

Gronroos, C. (2011). Value co-creation in service logic: A critical analysis. *Marketing Theory, 11*(3), 279–301. https://doi.org/10.1177/1470593111408177

Hagland, M., & Wider, H. (2023, January 17). Change, opportunities, and threats: Our state of the industry survey. https://www.hcinnovationgroup.com/policy-value-based-care/article/21290180/change-opportunities-and-threats-our-state-of-the-industry-survey?utm_source=HI+Daily+NL&utm_medium=email&utm_campaign=CPS230125115&o_eid=6978A6266356F5Z&rdx.ident[pull]=omeda|6978A6266356F5Z&oly_enc_id=6978A6266356F5Z

Hardcastle, L., Record, K., Jacobson, P., & Gostin, L. (2011). Improving the population's health: The Affordable Care Act and the importance of integration. *Journal of Law Medicine & Ethics, 39,* 317–327.

Hawryluk, M. (2019, October 4). *Why hospitals are getting into the housing business.* KHN. https://khn.org/news/why-hospitals-are-getting-into-the-housing-business/

Head, B. W., & Alford, J. (2015). Wicked problems: Implications for public policy and management. *Administration & Society, 47*(6), 711–739.

Health Information and Portability and Accountability Act of 1996. (HIPAA). (1996, August 20). Public law 104-191. https://aspe.hhs.gov/reports/health-insurance-portability-accountability-act-1996

Hearld, L., & Westra, D. (2022). Charting a course: A research agenda for studying the governance of health care networks. In S. Shortell, L. Burns, & J. Hefner (Eds.), *Advances in health care management. Vol 21. Responding to the grand challenges in health care via organizational innovation: Volume 21. Needed advances in management research. Advances in health care management* (pp. 111–132).

Heaton, J., Day, J., & Britten. (2016). Collaborative research and the co-production of knowledge for practice: An illustrative case study. *Implementation Science, 11*. https://doi.org/10.1186/s13012-016-0383-9

Hefner, J., & Nembhard, I. (2022). Preface. In *The contributions of health care management to grand health care challenges* (Vol. 20). Emerald Publishing Limited.

Hewitt, A. (2022). Population health management: A framework for the health sector. In A. Hewitt, J. Mascari, & S. Wagner (Eds.), *Population health management: Strategies, tools, applications and outcomes* (p. 7). Springer Publishing.

Hewitt, A. (In Press). *Population health: Practical skills for future health professionals*. Cognella Publishing.

Hewitt, A., & Dykstra, D. (2022). Assessing population health: Community health needs assessments. In A. Hewitt, J. Mascari, & S. Wagner (Eds.), *Population health management: Strategies, tools, applications and outcomes*. Springer Publishing.

Hilman, A., Withers, M., & Collins, R. (2009). Resource dependence theory: A review. *Journal of Management, 35*, 1404–1427 https://doi.org/10.1177/0149206309343469. http://www.iot.ntnu.no/innovation/norsi-pims-courses/harrison/Hillman,%20Withers%20&%20Collins%20(2009).PDF

Hilts, K., Yeager, V., Gibson, P., Halverson, P., Blackburn, J., & Menachemi, N. (2021, May/June). Hospital partnerships for population health: A systematic review of the literature. *Journal of Healthcare Management, 66*(3), 170–198. https://doi.org/10.1097/JHM-D-20-00172

Himmelman, A. T. (2002, January). *Collaboration for a change: Definitions. Decision making model, roles, and collaboration process guide*. Himmelman Consulting.

HIPAA Journal. (2020). What is the HITECH Act? *HIPAA Journal*. https://www.hipaajournal.com/what-is-the-hitech-act/

Holst, L. (2015, January 30). The precision medicine initiative: Data-driven treatments as unique as your own body. https://obamawhitehouse.archives.gov/blog/2015/01/30/precision-medicine-initiative-data-driven-treatments-unique-your-own-body

Hostetter, M., & Klein, S. (2022, November 9). Making health care consolidation work for patients: An interview with commonwealth fund president David Blumenthal. The Commonwealth Fund. https://www.commonwealthfund.org/publications/2022/nov/making-health-care-consolidation-work-for-patients-interview-david-blumenthal

Hughes, S. (2022, August 26). Industry voices—Facing unprecedented challenges, America's. hospitals and health systems need help now. https://www.fiercehealthcare.com/hospitals/industry-voices-facing-unprecedented-challenges-americas-hospitals-and-health-systems

Institute of Medicine (US) Committee on assuring the health of the public in the 21st century. (2002). In *The future of the public's health in the 21st century* (Vol. 2). National Academies Press (US). Understanding Population Health and Its Determinants. https://www.ncbi.nlm.nih.gov/books/NBK221225/

Institute for Health Improvement (IHI). (2022). The IHI triple aim. http://www.ihi.org/Engage/Initiatives/TripleAim/Pages/default.aspx

Internal Revenue Service (IRS). (2020). Community health needs assessment for charitable hospital organizations – Section 501(r)(3). https://www.irs.gov/charities-non-profits/community-health-needs-assessment-for-charitable-hospital-organizations-section-501r3

Jacobson, P., & Parmet, W. (2018). Public health and health care: Integration, disintegration, or eclipse. *Journal of Law Medicine & Ethics, 46*(4), 940–951. https://doi.org/10.1177/1073110518821994

Johri, N. (2022). Health data analytics for population health management. In A. Hewitt, J. Mascari, & S. Wagner (Eds.), *Population health management: Strategies, tools, applications and outcomes*. Springer Publishing.

Kabasawa, H. (2022, March 1). MR imaging in the 21st century: Technical innovation over the first two decades. *Magnetic Resonance in Medical Sciences, 21*(1), 71–82. https://doi.org/1 0.2463/mrms.rev.2021-0011

Kacik, A. (2023, January 18). Hospital M & A volume reaches decade -plus low. *Modern Healthcare*. https://www.modernhealthcare.com/mergers-acquisitions/hospital-ma-2022-ponder-atrium-health-deaconess-health?utm_source=modern-healthcare-am-thursday&utm_medium=email&utm_campaign=20230118&utm_content=article1-readmore

Kania, J., & Kramer, M. (2011, Winter). Collective impact. *Stanford Social Innovation Review*. https://ssir.org/articles/entry/collective_impact

Kaplan, M. (2016, April 1). Co-production: A new lens on patient-centered care. https://www.ihi.org/communities/blogs/co-production-a-new-lens-on-patient-centered-care

Khademhosseini, A., & Langer, R. (2019). A decade of progress in tissue engineering. *Nature Protocols, 11*(10), 1775–1782. https://tissueeng.net/lab/papers/A%20decade%20of%20progress%20in%20tissue%20engineering.pdf

Khosla, N., Marsteller, J., Hsu, Y., & Elliott, D. (2016). Analysing collaboration among HIVs agencies through combining network theory and relational coordination. *Social Science & Medicine, 150*, 85–94.

Kindig, D., & Isham, G. (2014). Population health improvement: A community health business model that engages partners in all sectors. *Frontiers of Health Services Management, 30*(4), 3–20.

Kindig, D., & Stoddart. (2003). What is population health? *American Journal of Public Health, 93*(3), 380–383. https://doi.org/10.2105/AJPH.93.3.380

Kivunjal, C., & Kuyini, A. (2017, September 1). Understanding and applying research paradigms in educational contexts. *International Journal of Education, 6*(5), 26–41. https://doi.org/10.5430/ijhe.v6n5p26

Kohli, J., & De Biasi, A. (2017, August 2). *Supporting healthy communities.* Deloitte Insights. https://www2.deloitte.com/insights/us/en/industry/health-care/building-and-funding-healthy-communities.html

Kuhn, T. S. (1962). *The structure of scientific revolutions* (2nd ed.). The University of Chicago Press.

Kumar, R., & Chattu, V. K. (2018, May–June). What is in the name? Understanding terminologies of patient-centered, person-centered, and patient-directed care! *Journal of Family Medicine and Primary Care, 7*(3), 487–488. https://doi.org/10.4103/jfmpc.jfmpc_61_18. https://www.ncbi.nlm.nih.gov/pmc/articles/PMC6069658/

LaMonica, P. (2021). *Haven – the joint health care venture by Amazon, Berkshire and JPMorgan – is shutting down.* CNN Business. https://www.cnn.com/2021/01/04/investing/haven-shutting-down-amazon-jpmorgan-berkshire/index.html

Lawrence, P., & Lorsch, J. (1967, November). New management job: The integrator. *Harvard Business Review.* https://hbr.org/1967/11/new-management-job-the-integrator

Leeman, J., Wangen, M., Kegler, M., Lee, M., O'Leary, M., Ko, L., Fernandez, M., & Birken, S. (2022). Applying theory to explain the influence of factors external to an organization on the implementation of an evidence-based intervention. *Frontiers in Health Services, 3*, 1–8. https://doi.org/10.3389/frhs.2022.889786

Lehoux, P., Miller, F., & Daudelin, G. (2016). How does venture capital operate in medical? Innovation? *BMJ Innov, 2*, 111–117. https://doi.org/1136/bmjinnov-2015-000079

LeTourneau, B. (2004). Co-opetition: An alternative to competition. *Journal of Healthcare Management, 49*(2), 81. American College of Healthcare Executives.

Martinez, C., Castellano, Y., Andres, A., Fu, M., Anton, L., Ballbe, M., Fernandez, P., Carera, S., Riccobene, A., Gavilan, E., Feliu, A., Baena, A., Margalef, M., & Fernandez, E. (2017). Factors associated with implementation of the 5As smoking cessation model. *Tobacco Induced Diseases, 15*, 41. https://doi.org/10.1186/s12971-017-0146-7

Martin, A., Hartman, M., Benson, J., Catlin, A., & The National Health Expenditure Accounts Team. (2022, December 14). National health care spending in 2021: Decline in federal spending outweighs greater use of health care. *Health Affairs.* https://doi.org/10.1377/hlthaff.2022.01397

Mashek, D. (2015, June). Capacities and institution support needed along the collaboration. Continuum In *A presentation to the Academic Dean's Committee of Claremont College.*

Mayo, A., Myers, C., & Sutcliffe, K. (2021). Organizational science and health care. *Academy of Management Annals, 15*(2), 537–576.

Medical Model. (2012). Farlex partner medical dictionary. https://medical-dictionary.thefreedictionary.com/medical+model

Medline Plus: National Library of Medicine. (2022, May 22). What is precision medicine. https://medlineplus.gov/genetics/understanding/precisionmedicine/definition/

Millar, A. (2022, September 26). Robotic-powered prostheses – State of play. Medical Device Network. https://www.medicaldevice-network.com/features/robotic-powered-prostheses-state-of-play/#:~:text=Increasingly%2C%20prosthetics%20are%20being%20integrated,under%20development%20are%20mind%2Dcontrolled

Miller, A. (2022). Population health models – Part 1. In A. Hewitt, J. Mascari, & S. Wagner (Eds.), *Population health management: Strategy, tools, applications and outcomes.* Springer Publishing Company.

Murphy, B. (2017, June 26). Going beyond clinic's 4 walls to address health's social roots. https://www.ama-assn.org/education/accelerating-change-medical-education/going-beyond-clinic-s-4-walls-address-health-s

Murphy, K., Davis, J., Waddill, K., LaPointe, J., Heath, S., Wicklund, E., & Sokol, E. (2019, December 20). Decade-defining moments in healthcare innovation, reform. https://ehrintelligence.com/news/decade-defining-moments-in-healthcare-innovation-reform

Murray, G., & Lewis, V. (2022). Cross-sector alliances between healthcare organizations and community based organizations: Marrying theory and practice. *Advances in Health Care Management, 21,* 89–110. Responding to the Grand Challenges in Health Care via Organizational Innovation.

National Academy of Medicine (NAM). (2000). *To err is human: Building a safer health system.* National Academy Press.

National Academy of Medicine (NAM). (2001). *Crossing the quality chasm: A new health system for the 21ˢᵗ century.* National Academy Press.

National Priorities Partnership (NPP). (2008). *National priorities and goals: Aligning our efforts to transform America's healthcare.* National Quality Forum. Available via email at.info@qualityforum.org. http://www.qualityforum.org/Setting_Priorities/National_Priorities_Partnership_-_Call_for_Organizational_Nominations.aspx

Needham, C., & Carr, S. (2009). *SCIE research briefing 31: Co-Production: An emerging evidence base for adult social care transformation.* Social Care Institute for Excellence. www.scie.org.uk

Nembhard, I., Burns, L., & Shortell, S. (2020, April 17). *Responding to Covid-19: Lessons from management research.* https://catalyst.nejm.org/doi/full/10.1056/CAT.20.0111

Nemours. (2012). Integrator role and functions in population health improvement initiatives. https://www.networksofopportunity.org/resources/Integrator-Role-and-Functions-in-Population-Health-Improvement-Initiatives

Nemours Childrens Health. (2023). Moving health upstream. https://www.movinghealthcareupstream.org/population-health-integrators/#:~:text=Population%20Health%20Integrators%20from%20a,one%20entity%20can%20address%20alone

New York Times. (2023, January 14). Coronavirus in the U.S.: Latest map and case count. https://www.nytimes.com/interactive/2021/us/covid-cases.html

Nichols, L. & Taylor, L. (2018). Social determinants as a public goods: A new approach to financing key investments in healthy communities. *Health Affairs Blog.* https://doi.org/10.1377/hlthaff.2018.003

Nielsen, R., Muhlestein, D., & Leavitt, M. (2021, June 14). Social determinants of health: Aggregated precision investment. *Health Affairs Forefront.* https://doi.org/1 0.1377/hblg20210610.928520

Nies, H. (2014, April–June). Communities as co-producers in integrated care. *International Journal of Integrated Care, 14,* e022. https://www.ncbi.nlm.nih.gov/pmc/articles/PMC4079094/

NIHCM Foundations. (2020, November 3). Hospital consolidation: Trends, impacts & outlook. https://nihcm.org/publications/hospital-consolidation-trends-impacts-outlook

Novotna, G., Dobbins, M., & Henderson, J. (2012). Institutionalization of evidence-informed practices in healthcare settings. *Implementation Science, 7,* 112. https://doi.org/10.1186/1748-5908-7-112

Nowell, B., & Kenis, P. (2019, September). Purpose-oriented networks: The architecture of complexity. *Perspectives on Public Management and Governance, 3*(2), 169–173. https://doi.org/10.1093/ppmgov/gvz012

Nowell, B., & Milward, H. B. (2022). *Apples to apples: A taxonomy of networks in public management and policy.* Cambridge University Press.

Office of the Associate Director for Policy and Strategy (OADPS). (2016). Health in all policies. https://www.cdc.gov/policy/hiap/index.html

Office of the National Coordinator for Health Information Technology (ONC). (2023). Electronic health record: Frequently asked questions. https://www.healthit.gov/faq/what-electronic-health-record-ehr

Ostrom, E. (1996). Crossing the great divide: Coproduction, synergy, and development. *World Development, 24,* 1073–1087.

Parmigiani, A., & Rivera-Santos, M. (2011). Clearing a path through the forest: A meta – Review of interorganizational relationships. *Journal of Management, 37*. https://doi.org/10.1177/0149206311407507

Patient Protection and Affordable Care Act (PPACA). (2010). Patient Protection and Affordable Care Act. HealthCare.gov. https://www.healthcare.gov/glossary/patient-protection-and-affordable-care-act/

Peeters, R., Westra, D., van Raak, A., & Ruwaard, D. (2022). So happy togethers; a review of the literature on the determinants of effectiveness of purpose-oriented networks in health care. *Medical Care Research and Review*, 1–17. https://doi.org/10.1177/10775587221118156

Pfeffer, J., & Salancik, G. R. (1978). *The external control of organizations: A resource dependence perspective*. Harper & Row.

Pisano, G., & Verganti, R. (2008, December). Which kind of collaboration is right for you? *Harvard Business Review*. https://hbr.org/2008/12/which-kind-of-collaboration-is-right-for-you

Population Health Alliance (PHA). (n.d.). The premier organization for improving population health. https://populationhealthalliance.org/

Population Health Alliance (PHA). (2018). Population health management: Our framework for optimizing senior health across the continuum. https://populationhealthalliance.org/wp-content/uploads/2018/02/pha_phm_frameworkseniorhealthbriefreleaseoct2017fnl.pdf

Pronk, N. (2018). The role of a trusted convener in building corporate engagement in community health initiatives. *ACSM's Health & Fitness Journal, 22*(1), 44–46. https://doi.org/10.1249/FIT.0000000000000358

PWC. (2023). Health services US deals: 2023 outline. https://www.pwc.com/us/en/industries/health-industries/library/health-services-deals-outlook.html

Qualifacts and National Council of Behavioral Health (NCBH). (2020). *The new role of virtual care in behavioral healthcare*. Qualifacts and National Council of Behavioral Health. https://naccme.s3.amazonaws.com/Qualifacts+August+2020+WP/The_New_Role_Of_Virtual_Care_In_Behavioral_Healthcare__Qualifacts.pdf?__hstc=233546881.9eaa5e568f758a79e21a1a75923e4184.1603991852815.1603991852815.1603991852815.1&__hssc=233546881.1.1603991852816&__hsfp=3055432663. https://www.rwjf.org/en/library/research/2010/10/health-starts-where-we-learn.html

Raths, D. (2021, November 30). Healthy alliance IPA expanding SDOH network across N.Y. State. https://www.hcinnovationgroup.com/population-health-management/social-determinants-of-health/news/21248429/healthy-alliance-ipa-expanding-sdoh-network-across-ny-state

Rattel, H. W., & Webber, M. M. (1973). Dilemmas in a general theory of planning. *Policy Sciences, 4*(2), 155–169.

Realpe, A., & Wallace, L. (2010). *What is co-production*. The Health Foundation.

Reed, T. (2021, February 22). The money behind mental health: How the pandemic increased innovation, investment in behavioral health care. https://www.fiercehealthcare.com/hospitals/money-behind-mental-health

Riley, R. (2010, October 19). *Health starts where we learn*. Robert Wood Johnson Foundation. https://www.rwjf.org/en/library/research/2010/10/health-starts-where-we-learn.html

Samuel. (2022, September 23). *The impact of patient care technologies on the quality and cost of healthcare*. https://www.excel-medical.com/the-impact-of-patient-care-technologies-on-the-quality-and-cost-of-healthcare/

Schulte, F. (2022, November 14). *Sick profit: Investigating private equity's stealthy takeover of health care across cities and specialties*. KHN. https://www.ncbi.nlm.nih.gov/pmc/articles/PMC7042846/

Schwartz, S., Lopez, E., Rae, M., & Newman, T. (2020, September 2). What we know about provider consolidation. https://www.kff.org/health-costs/issue-brief/what-we-know-about-provider-consolidation/

Scott, W., Ruef, M., Caronna, C., & Mendel, P. (2000). *Institutional change and healthcare organizations: From professional dominance to managed care* (1st ed.). University of Chicago Press.

Shah, S., Rooke-Ley, H., & Brown, E. (2023, January 23, 12). Corporate investors in primary care — Profits, progress, and pitfalls. *New England Journal of Medicine*. https://doi.org/10.1056/NEJMp2212841.388-00-101

Shahzad, M., Upshur, R., Donnelly, P., Bharmal, A., Wei, X., Feng, P., & Brown, A. D. (2019, June 17). A population-based approach to integrated healthcare delivery: A scoping review of clinical care and public health collaboration. *BMC Public Health, 19*(1), 708. https://doi.org/10.1186/s12889-019-7002-z

Shashank, A. (2017, June 21). Healthcare's Triple Aim: Beyond the four walls of hospitals. https://innovaccer.com/resources/blogs/healthcares-triple-aim-beyond-the-four-walls-of-hospitals

Singer, S., Kerrissey, M., Friedberg, M., & Phillips, R. (2020). A comprehensive theory of integration. *Medical Care Research and Review, 77*, 196–207. PMID: 29606036. https://doi.org/10.1177/1077558718767000

Singh, Y., Song, Z., Polsky, D., Bruch, J. D., & Zhu, J. M. (2022). Association of private equity acquisition of physician practices with changes in health care spending and utilization. *JAMA Health Forum, 3*(9), e222886. https://doi.org/10.1001/jamahealthforum.2022.2886

Sweeney, A. (2022, August 11). The future of healthcare: Digitally streamlined workflows. https://medcitynews.com/2022/08/the-future-of-healthcare-digitally-streamlined-workflows/

Thornton, R. L. J., & Yang, T. J. (2023). Addressing population health inequities: Investing in the social determinants of health for children and families to advance child health equity. *Current Opinion in Pediatrics, 35*(1), 8–13. https://doi.org/10.1097/MOP.0000000000001189

Tikkanen, R., & Abrams (2020, January 30). U.S. Health care from a global perspective, 2019: Higher spending, worse outcomes? Issue brief: The commonwealth fund. https://www.commonwealthfund.org/publications/issue-briefs/2020/jan/us-health-care-global-perspective-2019

Tolbert, J., Orgera, K., & Dammico, A. (2020, November 6). *Key facts about the uninsured population.* Kaiser Family Foundation. https://www.kff.org/uninsured/issue-brief/key-facts-about-the-uninsured-population/

Tozzi, J. (2019). *Amazon-JPMorgan-Berkshire health-care venture to be called haven.* Bloomberg. https://www.bloomberg.com/news/articles/2019-03-06/amazon-jpmorgan-berkshire-health-care-venture-to-be-called-haven

Turini, A., Cristofoli, D., Forisni, F., & Nasi, G. (2010). Networking literature about determinants of network effectiveness. *Public Administration, 88*(2), 528–550. https://doi.org/10.1111/j.1467-9299.2009.0179.x

United Health Foundation. (2022). 2021 annual report. International comparison – Infant mortality. America's health rankings. https://www.americashealthrankings.org/learn/reports/2021-annual-report/international-comparison

U.S. Centers for Medicare & Medicaid Services (US-CMMS). (n.d.). Patient Protection and Affordable Care Act. https://www.healthcare.gov/glossary/patient-protection-and-affordable-care-act/ USDHHSU.S

U.S. DHHS. (2017). HIPAA for professionals. https://www.hhs.gov/hipaa/for-professionals/index.html

Van Oorschot, K., Nujen, B., Solli-Saether, H., & Mwesiumo, D. (2022, July 1). The complexity of post-mergers and acquisitions reorganization: Integration and differentiation. *Global Strategy Journal.* https://doi.org/10.1002/gsj.1454

Vasquez Reyes, M. (2020, December). The disproportional impact of COVID-19 on African Americans. *Health Hum Rights, 22*(2), 299–307. PMID: 33390715; PMCID: PMC7762908. https://www.ncbi.nlm.nih.gov/pmc/articles/PMC7762908/

Wagner, & Hewitt. (2022). Collaborations and coproduction of health. In A. Hewitt, J. Mascari, & S. Wagner (Eds.), *Population health management: Strategies, tools, applications and outcomes* (pp. 240). Springer Publishing.

Wernau, J., & Kamp, J. (2022, December 22). U.S. Life expectancy fell to lowest level since 1996. *The Wall Street Journal,* A3. https://www.wsj.com/articles/u-s-life-expectancy-fell-to-lowest-level-since-1996-11671667059

Whittington, J. W., Nolan, K., Lewis, N., & Torres, T. (2015). Pursuing the triple aim: The first 7 years. *The Milbank Quarterly, 93*(2), 263–300.

World Health Organization. (1947). *Constitution.* WHO.

Zhu, J. M., Hua, L. M., & Polsky, D. (2020, February 18). Private equity acquisitions of physician medical groups across specialties, 2013–2016. *JAMA, 323*(7), 663–665. https://doi.org/10.1001/jama.2019.21844

CHAPTER 10

PERCEIVED VALUE OF THE INCLUSION OF PARENT-TO-PARENT SUPPORT IN CASE CONFERENCES AND CARE PLANNING FOR CHILDREN WITH SPECIAL HEALTHCARE NEEDS

Valerie A. Yeager[a], Jyotsna Gutta[a], Lisa Kutschera[b] and Sarah M. Stelzner[b]

[a]Indiana University Richard M. Fairbanks School of Public Health, USA
[b]Indiana University School of Medicine, USA

ABSTRACT

This chapter qualitatively explored the impact of including parent liaisons (i.e., parents with lived experience caring for a child with complex needs, who support other caregivers in navigating child and family needs) in a case conferencing model for children with complex medical/social needs. Case conferences are used to address fragmented care, shared decision-making, and set patient-centered goals. Seventeen semi-structured interviews were conducted with clinicians and parent liaisons to assess the involvement of parent liaisons in case conferencing. Two main themes included benefits of parent liaison involvement (10 subthemes) and challenges to parent liaison involvement (5 subthemes). Clinicians reported that liaison participation and support of patients reduced stress for clinicians as well as family members. Challenges to liaison involvement included clinical team/parent liaison communication delays, which were further exacerbated by the COVID-19 pandemic. Parent liaison involvement in case conferences is perceived to be beneficial to children

Research and Theory to Foster Change in the Face of Grand Health Care Challenges
Advances in Health Care Management, Volume 22, 211–229
Copyright © 2024 Valerie A. Yeager, Jyotsna Gutta, Lisa Kutschera and Sarah M Stelzner
Published under exclusive licence by Emerald Publishing Limited
ISSN: 1474-8231/doi:10.1108/S1474-823120240000022010

with complex needs, their families, and the clinical team. Integration of liaisons ensures the familial perspective is included in clinical goal setting.

Keywords: Case conferencing; care coordination; social determinants of health; children with special healthcare needs; care planning; parent-to-parent support

INTRODUCTION

One in five American families have a child with special healthcare needs or medical care needs beyond those of typical children (Council on Children with Disabilities and Medical Home Implementation Project Advisory Committee, 2014; McPherson et al., 1998). Children with medical complexity (i.e., complex chronic health conditions associated with significant functional status limitations) account for less than 1% of the entire pediatric population but represent a significant portion of children with chronic conditions (Cohen et al., 2012), and care for these children can require significant clinical time investments (Kuo et al., 2011). Caring for these children involves the medical complexity of treating multi-organ systems, rare/unfamiliar diagnoses, numerous medications, and often involves caregivers or home environments impacted by barriers related to social determinants of health (SDOH). Further complicating care for children with special healthcare needs, primary care providers in the US healthcare environment have limited time and resources to share with patients and their caregivers. The fragmentation of existing healthcare systems frequently makes it difficult for these families to get the services they need. Families spend considerable time communicating among providers and across systems, assimilating recommendations, coordinating appointments, addressing insurance and financial issues, managing education needs, performing therapeutic activities, and seeking appropriate and supportive recreation opportunities (Data Resource Center for Child & Adolescent Health, 2018).

Care coordination helps improve outcomes related to the medical and social needs of these patients (Cooley et al., 2009; Palfrey et al., 2004; Turchi et al., 2009). These services can be enhanced when the family perspective is routinely included in care. Engaging patients and their families has shown improved health outcomes, quality and safety measures, and decreased healthcare costs, underscoring the benefits of including a family perspective (Carman et al., 2013), but such integration is rare (Adams et al., 2013; Wells & Partridge, 2011). This is particularly true in primary care for children with complex medical care needs (Berry, 2015; Bodenheimer, 2008; Turowetz, 2015). Care coordination, as it stands, often lacks integrated approaches to multidisciplinary communication and collaboration (Bodenheimer, 2008).

Case conferencing, an interdisciplinary team-based care coordination model that incorporates a patient-centered and goal-oriented care plan, offers a mechanism to address the fragmented care that children with special healthcare needs and their families encounter. Case conferences have been shown to foster multidisciplinary collaboration, and improve performance among healthcare teams (Schmutz et al., 2019; Tuso et al., 2014; Vest et al., 2018; Yeager et al., 2021). Additionally, a recent study found that primary care case conferencing was associated with reduced probability of emergency department visits and inpatient admissions (Vest et al., 2021). One design consideration that may help explain the impact of these conference sessions is whether external community-based partners participate alongside the clinical care team. These partners may help center and address patient and family needs. Despite the multidisciplinary nature of case conferences, to date, no studies have examined the role of external partners as members of case conference teams. Because of this, we do not know providers' perspectives on how incorporating external partners can address a patient's nonmedical needs. Given the increasing emphasis on the family perspective's role in quality health care, understanding the contributions of these partners is important.

This current study qualitatively examines the role of parent-to-parent support or "parent liaisons" as an external community-based partner in case conferencing. In this context, parent liaisons are staff members of a parent-to-parent organization who have lived experience as a caregiver to a child or children with complex healthcare needs. Parent liaisons are trained to provide support to families of children with complex healthcare needs, to train family members or caregivers to anticipate child needs, identify resources, access community systems, and navigate the healthcare system (Indiana Family to Family, 2023). To understand the role of parent liaisons as members of the case conferencing teams, interviews were conducted with case conference clinical team members and parent liaisons. Clinical team members and parent liaisons were asked about the perceived benefits and challenges to parent liaison participation in case conferences. This study was conducted within an existing pediatric case conference program within a safety net healthcare system predominantly serving vulnerable children and their families. Additionally, this work was conducted during the COVID-19 pandemic, which impacted access to care and exacerbated social and economic inequities for children with special healthcare needs and their caregivers.

Perspectives about the role and value of parent liaisons in case conferencing, both in routine care and pandemic times, are presented. The aim of this study was to understand providers' perspectives on incorporating external partners to address patients' nonmedical needs (i.e., social determinants of health). Increasingly, healthcare systems seek to address patients' nonmedical needs. Understanding the facilitators and barriers associated with different interventions are key to ensuring that these interventions are sustainable. Findings will be of interest to organizational leaders and clinicians serving children with special healthcare needs as well as health systems serving children who are disproportionately impacted by factors such as loss of health insurance, housing instability, food insecurity, language barriers, and educational disparities.

BACKGROUND

Eskenazi Health

Eskenazi Health is a safety-net hospital located in Indianapolis, Indiana. The Eskenazi Health system also includes seven Federally Qualified Community Health Center (FQHC) primary care clinics serving approximately 60,000 patients annually. As a safety-net provider, Eskenazi Health has a history of serving low-income, ethnically diverse, and medically underserved populations. More than 8 out of 10 Eskenazi patients are Black, Indigenous, and People of Color (BIPOC), 17% are Hispanic, and 24% seek care on a sliding fee scale (i.e., they are uninsured or underinsured). Since 2016, pediatric health teams at Eskenazi Health FQHCs have worked to implement case conferences to provide enhanced care to children with chronic conditions and complex social and healthcare needs. Case conferencing provides a structured clinical context for case conferencing teams to move beyond the scope of traditional 15-minute clinic visit limitations. It empowers them to work together to identify solutions to SDOH challenges, connects children and families to appropriate social supports, and provides a long-term follow-up plan for each patient.

Case Conference Model

Patients are added to a provider's case conferencing schedule if a physician/nurse practitioner, nurse, or medical assistant feels the patient would benefit from a team-based approach. Providers determine the amount of time their team will convene and the frequency of case conference meetings. Individual provider case conferences average 3–6 hours per month across 1–2 meetings. The time spent discussing a single patient varies depending on the complexity of a patient's needs as well as whether the patient is new to case conference or whether the discussion is a follow-up to a prior meeting. Team members may spend the majority of a case conference discussing one complex case or may discuss several less complex patient cases. Typical patients that have been included in the case conference model have complex medical and/or social situations that cannot easily be addressed during a routine clinic appointment or if the child, or their caregivers, could benefit from a collective approach to setting goals and developing a care plan. During the COVID-19 pandemic, case conferences were temporarily suspended or moved to a teleconferencing model depending on the provider.

Eskenazi Health case conferences incorporate a variety of clinical disciplines including the primary care team (physician/nurse practitioner, nurse, and/or medical assistant), behavioral health providers, social workers/case management, and occasional external partners as needed such as school nurses or subspecialists. Most pediatric case conferences include a parent liaison from About Special Kids (ASK), a local parent-to-parent organization focused on children with special healthcare needs. During the case conference, parent liaisons provide a parental perspective and assist in meeting a patient's unmet social, educational, recreational, or healthcare financing needs. A patient may formally be referred to ASK before, during, or after the case conference, depending on when a provider recognizes the need for ASK's support. To refer a patient to ASK, the provider completes a referral form, which is either provided in person during a conference or faxed to the ASK office. Patient caregivers must sign a waiver providing consent for ASK to contact them. If the waiver is not completed, ASK's involvement is limited to the case conference setting.

If the waiver is completed, the parent liaison will speak with a family at least three times. Each call will focus on identifying appropriate resources for the patient's needs and family's needs. As needed, parent liaisons also provide emotional support to the family members and send caregivers relevant resources (via mail or email) for the child's or the family's needs. Parent liaisons check in with caregivers about their progress in meeting their goals. Although they sometimes assist parents in filling out paperwork, the primary focus is to teach and train caregivers on these processes. Parent liaisons will routinely communicate patient/family progress and recommendations for next steps or other referrals back to the case conference team via secure email or during a follow-up case conference. Parent liaisons may also facilitate meetings with other nonclinical partners in a child's care (e.g., schools) to assist parents in ensuring their child has a multi-sectoral support system to meet their needs.

METHODS

Study Design and Population

We qualitatively explored parent liaison involvement in case conferences within Eskenazi Health's FQHC primary care settings. All members of the case conference teams were eligible for inclusion in this study. These included physicians, nurse practitioners, nurses, medical assistants, social workers, and parent liaisons. Additionally, to understand the role of parent liaisons, key members of the parent liaison organization (ASK) were also invited to participate in an interview.

All clinicians who are routinely involved in pediatric case conferencing at Eskenazi Health's FQHCs were invited to participate in an interview. ASK leadership provided contact information for the ASK parent liaisons involved in case conferencing. A total of 21 individual health team members who participate in pediatric case conferences or ASK leaders or parent liaisons were invited via email to participate in an interview. Individuals were eligible to participate if they were either a parent liaison or clinical team member who routinely participated in pediatric care conferencing in the Eskenazi Health system. Individual, semi-structured telephone or Zoom teleconference interviews were conducted by (blinded for review) with members of case conference teams as well as parent liaisons and leaders within ASK. Qualitative interviews were conducted until thematic saturation was achieved (i.e., no new insights were being shared by participants). Interviews took place during June and July of 2021. Interviews were recorded with permission and transcribed.

Interview Guide

Two interview guides (see Appendix) were developed for this study after observing case conference sessions (conducted over Zoom). One interview guide was designed for clinical members of the case conferencing teams, while the other was designed for ASK representatives/parent liaisons. Using a combination of open-ended questions (e.g., "In your opinion, what has been the impact of ASK liaisons attending the case conferences?") and probes (e.g., "Have the ASK liaisons been able to increase your awareness of unmet social needs?"), the guides were designed to capture interviewees' perceptions of value from including ASK parent liaisons in case conferencing. Additionally, related perceptions and experiences regarding workflow and information sharing were discussed. Questions also asked about experiences with case conferences and parent liaisons during the COVID-19 pandemic. Though these interview guides were distinct, the topics discussed were complementary.

Analysis

Transcriptions were reviewed, and thematic analysis was employed to identify key themes and subthemes (Vaismoradi et al., 2013) using Dedoose (v 9.0). Using inductive coding (Vaismoradi et al., 2013), a subset of transcripts was reviewed by VAY and JG to create a codebook. Though we used two interview guides (one for clinical team members and the other for ASK liaisons), we used one codebook for both types of interviews. The codes were then applied to the remaining transcripts by JG, with any further emerging themes/subthemes incorporated into the codebook and prior transcripts revised (if appropriate). Completed coding was reviewed and discussed, and discrepancies were resolved using discussion and consensus. The study was approved by the Institutional Review Board at the university of the first author.

FINDINGS

Qualitative interviews were conducted with 17 of the 21 individuals invited to participate (81% response rate). Participants from the clinical team included physicians ($n = 5$), a nurse practitioner ($n = 1$), and social workers ($n = 3$). Participants from ASK included parent liaisons ($n = 5$) and members of organizational leadership ($n = 3$). Before COVID-19 necessitated the shift to a virtual format, clinical leaders (physicians or nurse practitioners) reported holding case conferences at 4/5 FQHC locations with varying frequency. However, each clinician held at least 1 case conference per month.

Two primary themes were identified: perceived benefits of parent liaison participation in case conferences and challenges to parent liaison involvement. Among perceived benefits reported by participants, 10 subthemes were identified (Table 10.1). These include process-related benefits and outcome-related benefits. Process-related benefits included increasing clinician awareness of resources, patient/caregiver linkages to essential resources, supporting educational needs,

Table 10.1. Perceived Benefits of About Special Kids (ASK) Participation in Case Conferences.

Theme	Description	Exemplifying Quote
Process-Related Benefits		
Clinician awareness of resources	ASK liaisons provide clinicians improved awareness/knowledge of resources available to both parents and patients. ASK also created educational resources (e.g., webinars, trainings, resource directory) for clinicians.	"And then having [ASK liaisons], they just help provide more services I didn't even know I wasn't aware existed beforehand." – Clinical Team Member "[If] we didn't have the liaison it would be a lot of stuff that I would be doing on my own, so taking twice as long to do it or even longer than that, not knowing the resources to help direct the families." – Clinical Team Member
Patient/Caregiver linkage to essential resources	ASK liaisons assisted families and linked them to resources that most families were not aware of, such as medical waivers, resulting in increased engagement/connection in support networks.	"Having About Special Kids as a part of the team enabled me...for the first time in 22 years to be able to get my [patients] with families who have limited English proficiency into the waiver programs. The only reason I could do it was because ASK was a part of my case conferencing". – Clinical Team Member "I felt awful that I could never quite negotiate that [medical waiver] system for my families, and now I can." – Clinical Team Member
Supporting educational needs	ASK liaisons can provide assistance to clinicians and parents in working with schools to support a patient's educational needs, such as individual educational plans, school policies and processes, and state educational policies.	"[The ASK liaison] has a little more fine detail knowledge of the IEP [Individual Educational Plan] process and the behavior improvement plans that can be put in place for students to protect them from suspensions and expulsions, and child educational right. I feel like [the liaison] is kind of our expert in those areas and I feel like we've become more expert, but because of her contributions to our understanding." – Clinical Team Member "[ASK Liaisons] have also taught our nurses and medical assistants a tremendous amount about resources and navigating, not only our very complicated healthcare system, but a lot about school." – Clinical Team Member
Advocacy for patient priorities	ASK liaisons ensured that the parental perspective is heard during case conferences. They provide additional input about specific patient challenges, which may not have been disclosed to the medical team, and ensure that patient goals (as determined by	"Their ability to give a parent perspective, because many of our families, especially from other cultures have this deferential thing for physicians...Really, [ASK liaisons] don't have an MD after their names, but they are the experts in all of the

Table 10.1. *(Continued)*

Theme	Description	Exemplifying Quote
	families) are being prioritized. If ASK has worked with the client's family prior to the case conference, priorities may have been disclosed to an ASK liaison. Challenges often include nonmedical barriers such as transportation concerns or assistance with medical waiver programs.	things for [the] child and I think [parents] appreciate that". – Clinical Team Member "I think [ASK liaisons] always just continuously interject the family perspective and the shared decision-making. And they're kind of always just pushing us [clinicians] in that direction in a very gentle way teaching both us and the families, how to do that better." – Clinical Team Member
Creative solutions for children's needs	ASK liaisons are able to create nonmedical solutions to meet child needs. ASK liaisons were able to help meet needs brought on by/exacerbated by the COVID-19 pandemic and were able to share about COVID-19 policies that affected patients and their families with the care team.	"[Liaisons] can offer ideas that the physicians probably just aren't going to think of, and they aren't medically founded, little things like, 'Have you ever thought about putting a ball pit in your house? Here's a really cheap way to do it. Here's what it looks like, here's what I used, it was the jogging trampoline. Here's what I did with a yoga mat', and just give them ideas that can provide a little bit of [sensory] input to the kid that isn't necessarily all medically founded." – Parent Liaison "Sometimes we have to be pretty creative with the things we can do to help these families. A lot of my families are undocumented and that starts a long process. There's a lot of groups or organizations we like to lean on, but they only accept folks that are documented, and we do a lot of thinking outside the box... so [the parent liaison's] been awesome." – Clinical Team Member
Building a peer support network	ASK provides awareness of peer support opportunities between parents/guardians, as well as children, for parent caregivers to interact and create support networks, and for children to have recreational/socialization opportunities for children. ASK liaisons also organize social events for patients/families.	"They have 'parent cafes' at churches...for parents of children with different types of special needs or mental health diagnosis. They have different groups where they can share...different childcare options and things." – ASK Administrator "Another important thing that ASK provides is recreation. I think it's important for these kids to know that they can do things outside of just doctors' appointments and all of that. [ASK] helps families with finding activities that these kids can do and have fun with and socialize with their peers and surprise themselves with their

Table 10.1. *(Continued)*

Theme	Description	Exemplifying Quote
		actual ability and the things that they can do." – Parent Liaison
Outcome-Related Benefits		
Holistic approach to care	ASK liaisons reduce barriers to care and the overall success of the care plan, including nonmedical factors. Liaisons provided information and connection to resources that addressed patient needs that were not purely medical in nature but could greatly improve a client's quality of life.	"[The ASK Liaison] knows of some of these things that may not be at the top on our list of known resources within the community… then the family might be able to have a place to stay, or things that I would not know details wise. I think it's that thinking, outside of the box thinking, outside of our siloed world in terms of what's available". – Clinical Team Member
		"I find that the ASK representatives are just full of knowledge. They are very helpful in brainstorming about patients. They bring things up that normally I might not be privy to. I just see things from my medical purview and that's how I've been trained. So, I've gotten a lot better at several things when it comes to social determinants of health, or asking about other things that are outside of the clinic." – Clinical Team Member
Reduced familial stress	ASK liaisons reduced the stress of the patient's family members. ASK liaisons recognized that caregiving for a child with complex needs could be overwhelming for family members.	"[Patient's mom] felt really guilty for feeling depressed and she's said, 'I still love my child, but I do feel really, really sad and I feel poorly supported right now'. And I was able to connect her with [an ASK liaison] whose son had many, many surgeries as well and kind of has probably had similar experience in the past, and so that mom in particular found the connection helpful to kind of validate that she's not the only person who's felt that way about a child who has a lot of extra needs." – Clinical Team Member
		"To have a behavioral specialist for your child with autism go to the school and help navigate that, come to your home in the summer and be able to take them out, and do socialization and activities and volunteer work and give the families respite… I mean that has just been life changing for them." – Clinical Team Member
Parental education/ skill building	ASK liaisons assist parents/caregivers in finding and applying for resources but empower them/build skills so parents can continue on their own. By	"I want to take somebody's hand and help them get to a point of being able to stand…Not only am I going to get control of my life, but I'm going to

Table 10.1. *(Continued)*

Theme	Description	Exemplifying Quote
	providing caregivers with the skills to seek out resources, ASK liaisons empower parents and caregivers.	allow that person to then turn around to somebody who is behind them and be able to walk them through the same path". – Parent Liaison
Reduced clinical team stress/burnout	ASK liaison integration into case conference allowed clinical team to address more needs and reduced provider stress.	"I think [the social workers] didn't have the time [to navigate the waiver system] because they knew they could say 'this is something you should do' but that wasn't something that our social workers had the bandwidth to do. ASK is able to really guide these families that much to help them." – Clinical Team Member

Note: Themes are listed by frequency of occurrence with more common themes at the top of the table.

advocacy for patient priorities, creative solutions for children's needs, and building a peer support network. Outcome-related benefits included a holistic approach to care, reduced familial stress, parental education and skill building, and reduced clinical team stress and burnout.

In general, clinicians spoke about the shared decision model as being beneficial. One clinician stated,

I think the thing I really liked about the case conference thing we've been doing, it's very team based... It does not matter that I'm the physician, does not matter that [the social worker] is a social worker, or who's the nurse or whatever, because we just are trying to figure out what we need to do. And whoever is the one that knows about the thing is the one that's going to talk about it, or help us with the next steps.

Participants emphasized the role of ASK liaisons in addressing multifaceted social needs for children with complex needs. For example, one clinician said,

[ASK Liaisons] were really helpful in helping me understand what some of the schools were doing during hybrid, because they had someone in the school system that they knew personally, [who] would give them more information... that inside scoop really helped me know and kind of better understand what the schools were doing to help students, and so that then helped us help the patients the families navigate things a little bit better.

Participants felt that the support provided by ASK liaisons enabled parents to advocate for their child's needs and increased social support for the entire family (parents, siblings, and children with complex needs). Participants reported that this translated to reduced stress for both families and clinicians who are unable to address these needs during a clinical visit or a case conference.

Participants identified a total of five perceived challenges related to parent liaison participation in case conferencing (Table 10.2). Perceived challenges include: COVID-19, patient communication (i.e., communication between patients and providers, or patients and ASK), workflow challenges, telehealth/teleconferencing

Table 10.2. Perceived Challenges Related to Parent Liaison Participation in Case Conferencing.

Theme	Description	Exemplifying Quote
COVID-19 disruptions and issues	COVID-19 created unforeseen challenges for parent liaison support of families and children with special healthcare needs. COVID-19 required ASK liaisons to adapt their own workflows as well as address challenges faced by parents/caregivers of children with complex needs.	"Initially [parent liaisons'] caseloads went down. That's what was interesting, our number of cases were down, but our length of cases went up. When COVID first hit is when we decided to add an additional follow-up call [to caregivers] and what also was taking a little bit longer is because resources were changing. Parent liaisons were having to learn about telehealth, and they were having to learn things like how special education law was impacted based upon at home learning, and so things that were just second nature to them before, they were having to spend more time just training and learning and researching." – ASK Administrator
Patient communication	Parent liaisons can encounter challenges when attempting to contact or communicate with patients, patient caregivers, or patient families (e.g., language barriers or nonresponse).	"When [someone] calls from the clinic, they tend to get a better response [from caregivers]. I bet their unable to reach numbers are much lower than [ASK]'s... Sometimes when [parent liaisons] call, I don't think they recognize the phone number, or they don't recognize the name that's coming across, so I think there's a little more hesitation in answering the phone". – Parent Liaison
Workflow	This theme speaks to challenges encountered by parent liaisons regarding workflow, processes, or procedures that affected their participation in case conferencing.	"I actually had a little snafu with that situation at one point because the social worker shared some information from Epic with me via email. I didn't even know what Epic was at that time, and then there were some concerns about you know, do we have the rights to do that, and all of that, [so] it would be nice if we had a shared system." – Parent Liaison
Telehealth/ teleconferencing	ASK liaisons reported technology-related challenges arising when utilizing teleconferencing software, such as Zoom, when participating in case conferences.	"So really, the challenge with virtual is that we can't always hear some of that information." – Parent Liaison
General communication	Communication challenges exist between parent liaisons and the clinic teams. For example, if a case conference is canceled, the parent liaison may not be informed and then they spend travel time and time figuring out that the conference is canceled. Communication issues also occurred within the parent liaison organization as a result of pandemic changes related to working from home.	"Conferences get cancelled and we would have driven over there...and then there was no case conference. So, we'd sit there for a little bit and wait to find somebody who could figure it out, and then we leave. And so it was a lot of our time...They thought they had talked to everybody, but hadn't, so really having good communication with just scheduling and consistency." – Parent Liaison

Table 10.2. *(Continued)*

Theme	Description	Exemplifying Quote
		"[Liaisons] were not getting feedback from each other and then we had to figure out a way to communicate with each other, those little things that normally we hear from each other, because we were surrounded by each other." – Parent Liaison

Note: Themes are listed by frequency of occurrence with more common themes at the top of the table.

(i.e., problems associated with using web-based platforms for case conferencing), and general communication (e.g., problems associated with communication between organizations or within an organization). The primary challenge that participants spoke about was the impact of COVID-19, which exacerbated already existing challenges. For example, as a result of the COVID-19 pandemic, parents had to learn about and begin using telehealth to meet with their child's clinicians. Parent liaisons recognized that parents may need support in navigating these new tools and layered an additional follow-up call into their workflow to support parents in these changes.

Some workflow insights were made during the interviews with liaisons. Respondents often provided suggestions or workarounds to their perceived challenges of general communication in effective case conferencing. For example, it was suggested that it would be helpful to:

> ...get a list of who [the clinic teams is] going to discuss in case conference a day ahead of time... If I get it ahead of time, then I can check in our [tracking] system, to see if it's a family we've actually talked to before, to be able to share additional information I may know, too.

While communication challenges existed prior to the pandemic (e.g., a liaison not learning that a case conference was canceled until driving over to be there in person), new challenges arose as a result of the COVID-19 pandemic requiring that ASK employees work from home. As a liaison explained,

> ...we had to change the way we were reporting back and forth to each other...when we were all in an office together, not only could I hear what the conversations were, they could all hear each other as well.

Due to the COVID-19 pandemic, many of the case conferences were either paused or moved to a virtual teleconferencing setting. When asked about the impact of COVID-19, many respondents indicated that the integration of tele-communication allowed for more efficient use of the ASK liaison's time. One healthcare team member stated that,

> I think [meeting virtually] allows for a little bit more flexibility in terms of utilization of time and not making [liaisons] feel like they are wasting their time when they come because before...

[liaisons had to] drive across town to get here, so I felt so much pressure, and I think this sort of allows for the best of both worlds, we can utilize them efficiently.

Participants acknowledged that there were some "issues" with acclimatizing to the technology, such as difficulty hearing all participants, but suggested a more permanent transition to teleconferencing in order to best utilize ASK resources (e.g., time) and solve workflow concerns.

Both providers and ASK liaisons stated that there were some barriers related to communicating with patients. One of these barriers related to communication with families who primarily spoke non-English languages. Though some providers and liaisons are multilingual, one liaison stated,

We do talk to a fair number of families that are Spanish speaking, and I am not Spanish speaking. So when they're having the conversation I can hear it, but then, I have to have it translated in a paraphrase.

Another patient communication barrier was the inability to reach patients consistently. A clinical team member explained that, "Sometimes, my referral gets closed because the family never answers... likely their phone service was off, or we didn't have the right phone number for them."

DISCUSSION

Prior studies of case conferences have shown that these multidisciplinary team-based models improve collaboration and performance among healthcare teams; however, this is the first study to specifically examine the role of external partners as members of case conference teams (Schmutz et al., 2019; Tuso et al., 2014; Vest et al., 2018; Yeager et al., 2021). Given the call for an increased emphasis on the patient and family perspective toward improved outcomes and healthcare quality, findings from this study may inform similar models and expanded case conferencing with external support partners including parent liaisons.

Findings from this study indicated that parent liaison participation in case conferences is perceived to be beneficial for both the care provider team and for patients and their caregivers. The integration of parent-to-parent organizations in case conferences is also perceived to address issues of fragmented health care, unmet social needs for children with special healthcare needs and their families, and reduce clinician and provider stress. Parent liaisons contribute parental perspectives and voices to the case conferencing team and ensure that care planning includes patient and family goals and shared decision-making, which aligns with the recommendations for quality health care (Adams et al., 2013; Wells & Partridge, 2011) and prior related work (Bodenheimer, 2008; Golden & Nageswaran, 2012). In addition to providing the parental perspective, parent liaisons' knowledge of available resources was shared with clinicians, alerting them to resources of which they were often not aware. Although not discussed in interviews, it is possible that clinicians may also leverage these resources for their patients who are not formally included in case conferences.

Interviewees emphasized the unique knowledge provided by the ASK liaisons, indicating that they provide linkages to services that differ from those provided by a social worker. Liaisons provided knowledge of external resources and opportunities that clinical team members would not be aware of and would not have the time to research. For example, the patient population served by this safety-net hospital includes many families for whom English was a second language and individuals of low socioeconomic status. It was reported that liaisons suggested appropriate services and connections for these families and taught caregivers how to request services, increasing their ability to navigate both the medical and social support systems.

Healthcare organizations considering case conferencing and parent liaison involvement should explore reimbursement policies that can support these models. For example, Medicare billing and payment for care coordination requires that a minimum of three individuals be in attendance for case conferences in order to bill for these services (Yeager et al., 2018). As such, it can be financially beneficial to the healthcare organization to include parent liaisons in case conferencing as they can serve as the third member required to bill for care coordination, facilitating healthcare reimbursement for this essential service for patients. However, healthcare organizations should consider ways to share reimbursement with parent-to-parent family organizations providing the parent liaisons, especially given the perceived value to clinicians and patients. Communication workflows between clinic teams and parent liaisons will also need to be considered. Some of the communication issues documented in this study were discussed in the context of the lack of HIPAA-compliant messaging systems between the parent-to-parent organization and the clinic. Health systems that are considering a similar arrangement with a parent-to-parent organization should explore options to avoid communication delays and barriers. Similar recommendations have been made in a prior case conference study focused on partnering with public health agencies (Vest et al., 2021).

PRACTICE IMPLICATIONS

Research is needed to identify best practices for case conferencing, including developing and supporting care plans, especially for children with special healthcare needs (Berry, 2015). Based on findings from this study, including parent liaisons is a valuable aspect of these programs as they ensure familial perspectives are included in goal setting and decision-making. The decision to utilize team-based case conferencing models that incorporate patient advocates and wrap around service representatives should be informed by clinician and patient needs. Such experiences/needs may not be common in all types of clinical settings or among all types of providers and may be more likely in settings that have a higher proportion of patients who have complex medical and social needs.

Given the organizational changes and investments necessary for this intervention, it should be led by clinicians who are challenged to meet patient needs in routine visits and motivated to undertake the initiative. In terms of implementation insights, piloting the team-based case conferencing model is recommended. This will facilitate continuous quality improvement, the development of standardized processes, and successful integration within additional organizational settings over time.

STRENGTHS AND LIMITATIONS

To date, no studies have examined the role of external partners in case conferencing and clinicians' perceptions of the impact of those external members. However, there are limitations to note. Though interviews were conducted until thematic saturation was reached, the sample size was limited due to the number of clinical members and ASK liaisons involved in case conferencing who could participate in interviews. Potential biases include social desirability bias and selection bias. To limit social desirability bias, participants were assured their responses would be de-identified and data would only be reported in the aggregate. Input from providers who elected not to participate in case conferences was not available. Additionally, although a few parent liaisons had supported case conferences in another health system, most participants had participated in case conferences within a single hospital system, thereby limiting the generalizability of study findings to other locations and clinical settings. This research focused on the perceived value of parent liaison inclusion within pediatric care conferencing settings. Parents and caregivers were not included in this study. While parents and caregivers were aware that their child's needs may be discussed by the clinical team and ASK parent liaisons, parents/caregivers may not understand the setting in which these discussions occurred. Future work could examine the role of parent liaisons participation in case conferencing on caregiver satisfaction with healthcare services and well as health outcomes among children with special healthcare needs. Future work could also examine parent or caregiver knowledge, understanding, and perceptions of pediatric care conferences, and how parents/caregivers perceived the value added by parent liaisons in representing the family voice to clinical team members.

REFERENCES

Adams, S., Cohen, E., Mahant, S., Friedman, J. N., MacCulloch, R., & Nicholas, D. B. (2013). Exploring the usefulness of comprehensive care plans for children with medical complexity (CMC): A qualitative study. *BMC Pediatrics, 13*(1), 10.

Berry, J. G. (2015). What children with medical complexity, their families, and healthcare providers deserve from an ideal healthcare system. *System, 3*(8).

Bodenheimer, T. (2008). Coordinating care-a perilous journey through the health care system. *New England Journal of Medicine, 358*(10), 1064.

Carman, K. L., Dardess, P., Maurer, M., Sofaer, S., Adams, K., Bechtel, C., & Sweeney, J. (2013). Patient and family engagement: A framework for understanding the elements and developing interventions and policies. *Health Affairs, 32*(2), 223–231. https://doi.org/10.1377/hlthaff.2012.1133

Cohen, E., Berry, J. G., Camacho, X., Anderson, G., Wodchis, W., & Guttmann, A. (2012). Patterns and costs of health care use of children with medical complexity. *Pediatrics, 130*(6), e1463–e1470. https://doi.org/10.1542/peds.2012-0175

Cooley, W. C., McAllister, J. W., Sherrieb, K., & Kuhlthau, K. (2009). Improved outcomes associated with medical home implementation in pediatric primary care. *Pediatrics, 124*(1), 358–364. https://doi.org/10.1542/peds.2008-2600

Council on Children with Disabilities and Medical Home Implementation Project Advisory Committee. (2014). Patient- and family-centered care coordination: A framework for integrating care for children and youth across multiple systems. *Pediatrics, 133*(5), e1451–e1460. https://doi.org/10.1542/peds.2014-0318

Data Resource Center for Child & Adolescent Health. (2018). *National survey of children's health and national survey of children with special healthcare needs.* http://www.childhealthdata.org

Golden, S., & Nageswaran, S. (2012). Caregiver voices: Coordinating care for children with complex chronic conditions. *Clinical Pediatrics, 51*, 723–729. https://doi.org/10.1177/0009922812445920

Indiana Family to Family. (2023). Parent-to-parent support services. https://www.findhelp.org/indiana-family-to-family–indianapolis-in–parent-to-parent-support-services/6476407470555136?postal=47006

Kuo, D. Z., Cohen, E., Agrawal, R., Berry, J. G., & Casey, P. H. (2011). A national profile of caregiver challenges among more medically complex children with special health care needs. *Archives of Pediatrics and Adolescent Medicine, 165*(11), 1020–1026. https://doi.org/10.1001/archpediatrics.2011.172

McPherson, M., Arango, P., Fox, H., Lauver, C., McManus, M., Newacheck, P. W., & Strickland, B. (1998). A new definition of children with special health care needs. *Pediatrics, 102*(1), 137–139.

Palfrey, J. S., Sofis, L. A., Davidson, E. J., Liu, J., Freeman, L., & Ganz, M. L. (2004). The pediatric alliance for coordinated care: Evaluation of a medical home model. *Pediatrics, 113*(5 Suppl. l), 1507–1516.

Schmutz, J. B., Meier, L. L., & Manser, T. (2019). How effective is teamwork really? The relationship between teamwork and performance in healthcare teams: A systematic review and meta-analysis. *BMJ Open, 9*(9), e028280.

Turchi, R. M., Berhane, Z., Bethell, C., Pomponio, A., Antonelli, R., & Minkovitz, C. S. (2009). Care coordination for CSHCN: Associations with family-provider relations and family/child outcomes. *Pediatrics, 124*(Suppl. 4), S428–S434. https://doi.org/10.1542/peds.2009-1255O

Turowetz, J. (2015). Citing conduct, individualizing symptoms: Accomplishing autism diagnosis in clinical case conferences. *Social Science & Medicine, 142*, 214–222. https://doi.org/10.1016/j.socscimed.2015.08.022

Tuso, P., Watson, H. L., Garofalo-Wright, L., Lindsay, G., Jackson, A., Taitano, M., Koyama, S., & Kanter, M. (2014). Complex case conferences associated with reduced hospital admissions for high-risk patients with multiple comorbidities. *The Permanente Journal, 18*(1), 38–42. https://doi.org/10.7812/tpp/13-062

Vaismoradi, M., Turunen, H., & Bondas, T. (2013). Qualitative descriptive study. *Nursing and Health Sciences, 15*, 398–405. https://doi.org/10.1111/nhs.12048

Vest, J. R., Blackburn, J., Yeager, V. A., Haut, D. P., & Halverson, P. K. (2021). Primary care-based case conferences and reductions in health care utilization. *Journal of Health Care for the Poor and Underserved, 32*(3), 1288–1300. https://doi.org/10.1353/hpu.2021.0132

Vest, J. R., Caine, V., Harris, L. E., Watson, D. P., Menachemi, N., & Halverson, P. (2018). Fostering local health department and health system collaboration through case conferences for at-risk and vulnerable populations. *American Journal of Public Health, 108*(5), 649–651. https://doi.org/10.2105/ajph.2018.304345

Wells, N., & Partridge, L. (2011). Families are key in improving quality. *Academic Pediatrics, 11*(3), S85–S86.

Yeager, V. A., Taylor, H. L., Menachemi, N., Haut, D. P., Halverson, P. K., & Vest, J. R. (2021). Primary care case conferences to mitigate social determinants of health: A case study from one FQHC system. *American Journal of Accountable Care, 9*, 4–11. https://www.ajmc.com/view/primary-care-case-conferences-to-mitigate-social-determinants-of-health-a-case-study-from-one-fqhc-system

Yeager, V. A., Wharton, M. K., Monnette, A., Price-Haywood, E., Nauman, B., Angove, R. S. M., & Shi, L. (2018). Non-face-to-face chronic care management: A qualitative study assessing the implementation of a new CMS reimbursement strategy. *Population Health Management, 21*(6), 454–461. PMID: 29658847.

APPENDIX

CARE CONFERENCE INTERVIEW
GUIDE – PARENT LIAISON

Background

Can you start by telling me a little about which locations you attend/have attended care conferences and for how long? Are these all pediatric care conferences? How often do these meet, and, on average, what percent of these are you able to attend?

- How long have you been involved as an ASK liaison in the care conference model?
- Tell us a little about the goals of a care conference.
- What is your role during a care conference?
- During a typical care conference, what kinds of information do you gather about your clients? *(Probe: health, community information, history, etc.)*
- Do you typically have all the required information you need to participate in a meaningful way to a care conferences? What is missing/what are the gaps?
- What happens after the care conference?
- How do you approach patients' families, and can you describe a typical introduction?
- When you, as a liaison, collect information about what a patient's family needs, what happens next?
- Is the information you collect from families shared during future case conferences? Is it used in care conference team decisions?
- How do you typically communicate with parents/families?
- In what kind of ways have the ASK liaisons been able to support care conferences?
  - *(Probe: social context? Awareness of unmet social needs?)*
- In your opinion, what has been the *impact* of liaisons attending the care conferences?
- Do you have any feedback from parents about their child's quality of care before care conferences? Any insight about their perceptions of working with ASK liaisons as a part of care conferences?
- Do you have any particular success stories you would like to share?
- How do you think the care conferences have been valuable in providing care to patients and their families?
- What are the biggest barriers you face in your work as a liaison during care conferences? What factors help you in the most?
- What would you change about care conferences in an ideal world? What should continue?

I'd like to ask you some questions about how COVID-19 has impacted this work.

- How has COVID-19 changed how care conferences are conducted? Any challenges? Less participation?

- Any insights you can share about how COVID-19 has impacted the patients and their families? (probe: financially? Insurance? Social needs?)
- Are there particular services that patients/their families are struggling to access due to COVID-19?
- Have there been any benefits that you're aware of due to COVID-19? (for example, easier access to telehealth, etc.)
- Is there anything I (we) missed, or should have asked, that we didn't? Is there any other information that would be beneficial for us to know?
- Is there anyone who you think we should talk to in order to better understand the roles of ASK liaisons in care conferences?

CARE CONFERENCE INTERVIEW GUIDE – CLINICIAN/ PROVIDER

Background

Can you start by telling me a little about which locations you attend/have attended care conferences and for how long? Are these all pediatric care conferences? How often do these meet, and, on average, what percent of these do you attend?

- What is your role during a care conference?
- What do you perceive as the goal of a care conference?
- Thinking about a typical care conference, what kinds of information is required for your decision-making?
  (Probe: health, community information, history, etc.)
- Generally, is all the information you need provided during the care conferences? If not, what pieces of information are missing?
- What kind of information do the external parties, like the ASK liaisons, provide?
- How is that information used in the care conferences?
- How have the ASK liaisons been able to support care conferences?
  (Probe: social context? Awareness of unmet social needs?)
- Is information about unmet social needs usually available to you without the ASK liaisons? If so, how can you access it? How often do you access it?
- In your opinion, what has been the *impact* of ASK liaisons attending the care conferences?
- Do you have any feedback from parents about their child's quality of care before versus after the integration of ASK liaisons into care conferences?
- Do you have any particular success stories you would like to share?
- Has being a part of care conferences alerted you to or increased your awareness of new problems faced by families caring for children with special healthcare needs?
- Has your organization explored adopting any new programs or policies in response to the care conferences or working with ASK?

- Do you think the care conferences have been valuable in providing care to your patients and their families?
- What would you change about care conferences in an ideal world? What should continue?

COVID-19

I'd like to ask you some questions about how COVID-19 has impacted this work.

- How has COVID-19 changed how care conferences are conducted? Any challenges? Less participation?
- Any insights you can share about how COVID-19 has impacted the patients and their families? (probe: financially? Insurance? Social needs?)
- Are there particular services that patients/their families are struggling to access due to COVID-19?
- Have there been any benefits that you're aware of due to COVID-19? (for example, easier access to telehealth, etc.)
- Is there anything I (we) missed, or should have asked, that we didn't? Is there any other information that would be beneficial for us to know?
- Is there anyone who you think we should talk to in order to better understand the roles of ASK liaisons in care conferences?

CHAPTER 11

ORGANIZATIONAL AND POLICY CHALLENGES AND PRIORITIES FOR INTEGRATING FAMILY CARE PARTNERS INTO THE HEALTHCARE TEAM

Minakshi Raj

University of Illinois Urbana Champaign, USA

ABSTRACT

Family care partners are significantly involved in healthcare tasks in order to support adult relatives. Yet, unlike pediatric models of care where caregivers of children are formally integrated into healthcare teams, care partners of adults are rarely engaged in a formal, structured, or consistent manner. Their inclusion in the healthcare team is critical to their capacity to continue supporting their relative. A meaningful dialogue between policy and healthcare management is required to identify feasible and effective ways of engaging family care partners in healthcare teams.

Keywords: Family caregivers; policy; team-based care; technology; trust; quality

INTRODUCTION

Family care partners – i.e., unpaid individuals supporting a spouse/partner, sibling, child, parent, or other relative – have always been critical to patient care. Prior to the late 1800s, when the American Medical Association (AMA) published its first code of ethics and quality standards to ensure optimal patient safety enhanced through care delivered in hospital environments (American

Research and Theory to Foster Change in the Face of Grand Health Care Challenges
Advances in Health Care Management, Volume 22, 231–237
Copyright © 2024 Minakshi Raj
Published under exclusive licence by Emerald Publishing Limited
ISSN: 1474-8231/doi:10.1108/S1474-823120240000022011

Medical Association, 2023), patients were cared for in the home by family members with house calls from doctors as needed (Puglionesi, 2018). In these instances, presumably, family members provided the doctor with key information about their relative's condition and needs so that the doctor could develop a treatment plan. They likely carried out those recommendations to support their relative's recovery and healing.

Family care partners continue to uphold critical healthcare responsibilities such as communicating with healthcare providers, coordinating care, managing medications, and even navigating sociocultural aspects of medical care (Raj, Feldman, et al., 2021; Raj, Zhou, et al., 2021; Wolff et al., 2016; Wolff, Mulcahy, et al., 2018). Care partners were initially recognized informally for their importance to patients' well-being through the Family Caregiver Alliance (now, National Alliance for Caregiving) in 1977 (National Alliance for Caregiving, 2023). And yet, they are still considered distinct from the rest of the healthcare team unit. Still, organizations face increasing pressures to integrate family care partners (IPFCC, 2021), particularly since the COVID-19 pandemic highlighted the role family care partners have upheld in ensuring continuity of care for adult patients (Robertson, 2020) and the challenges associated with restricting family members' access to patients. With new channels of care delivery including asynchronous and synchronous uses of health information technology (Adler-Milstein et al., 2015; ONC, 2020) and incentives for care coordination to improve healthcare quality and health outcomes (Long et al., 2017), organizations are increasingly urged to integrate distinct aspects of care delivery at both individual and population levels (National Academies Press, 2019).

The notion of integrating family care partners into the healthcare team in a formal and standardized way is multifaceted. Professional norms of teams and teamwork have been maintained for decades with the goal of achieving consistent and optimal quality of care (Mickan & Rodger, 2009; Taplin et al., 2013). Family care partners do not necessarily obtain professional training, and policies for compensating family members for their work vary by state (Feinberg, 2019; Kaye & Teshale, 2020). Further, there is no existing mechanism for navigating the boundaries between patient privacy and the information needs family members require to proactively support their relative. This commentary will discuss these challenges through the lens of healthcare management. It will also provide emerging evidence and opportunities for researchers to examine a) the potential for formally integrating family care partners of adult patients into healthcare teams at multiple system levels and b) the optimal nature of their integration such that care partners are involved in care teams in an effective, efficient, and meaningful way.

Team: Greater Than the Sum of Its Parts

Cross-disciplinary teams are fundamental to provision of quality health care due to evolving knowledge and specialization and interdependence of professionals (Nembhard & Edmondson, 2006) with clearly defined roles and goals (Cassidy & Stanley, 2019; Kozlowski & Ilgen, 2006). But they are also subject to communication failures (Tucker & Edmondson, 2003) and a strict hierarchy wherein "higher status" team members may not communicate and collaborate effectively with "lower status" team members (Nembhard & Edmondson, 2006). Problematically, these status-based hierarchies are maintained among teams comprised of professionally trained and paid healthcare workers. Thus, the inclusion of an unpaid, informally trained caregiver – regardless of their knowledge of the patient – presents a barrier to the norms of teamwork in health care and creates additional hierarchical nuances.

Given the well-established importance of trust in communication and collaboration in healthcare teams (Mechanic, 1998; Thom et al., 2004; Wilk & Platt, 2016), we explored trust between physicians and family care partners and found that in some instances, physicians may actually trust family care partners for certain types of information (e.g., daily observations, perceptions of patient's fatigue or emotional state) more than they trust another physician (Rao & Raj, 2022). Still, over half of a national sample of care partners never spoke with their older relative's clinicians in the prior year (Wolff et al., 2020). Notably, over 80% of care partners in this study were responsible for carrying out the logistics of coordinating care, inferring that communicating with clinicians would likely have been helpful for them to carry out this important responsibility. In the case that clinicians do, indeed, perceive value in communicating with a family care partner (i.e., anticipating that the care partner can provide reliable support and information about the patient's care needs even without professional training) and trust care partners, perhaps healthcare teams are in fact willing to bend their existing norms of hierarchy. Accordingly, the more pressing barrier may be that there is no consistent and reliable mechanism to allow healthcare teams to integrate care partners.

Fragmented Policy Landscape

Policies to support family care partners in the healthcare context are limited and fragmented. Medicaid waivers such as those providing compensation or respite and training services to family care partners are concerned with supporting care partners in the home but do not address demands in the healthcare context (Kaye & Teshale, 2020; Raj & Singer, 2021). Policies such as the Caregiver Advise, Record, Enable (CARE) Act (Coleman, 2016) and initiatives to increase transparency of health information during office visits (Wolff et al., 2017) reflect excellent first steps in alleviating information asymmetries between healthcare teams and family care partners. However, even these efforts are limited by the absence of policies explicitly governing the nature and amount of information, and the channel of communication between the healthcare team and care partner. First, inconsistent identification and documentation of family caregivers (and whether there are multiple) in medical records presents barriers to a common understanding of who to contact and under what circumstances, within healthcare teams (Friedman & Tong, 2020). Second, inconsistent practices and the absence of policies around allowing care partners access to their relative's online medical records leads to exclusion of care partners from accessing information enabling them to provide effective support to their relative (Iott et al., 2020).

A lack of policy regarding health information sharing with care partners complicates matters further, with organizations and individual clinicians demonstrating variability in their practices and permissions to care partners (Raj et al., 2020). Although the Health Insurance Portability and Accountability Act (HIPAA) grants "personal representatives" access to patients' health information when they have been granted state authority to make decisions for the patient, this policy does not extend neatly to the context of family caregivers who may informally (i.e., without state authority) support relatives. For these caregivers, HIPAA does not offer an opportunity to access information beyond informal contracts between patients (care recipients), clinicians, and family caregivers (HHS, 2023). Additionally, clinicians and healthcare organizations face competing priorities and incentives – and perceive little to no incentive to engage with family caregivers, especially in the context of increasing workloads with limited time per patient (Friedman & Tong, 2020). And yet, the potential for engaging with family caregivers to improve health outcomes such as disease management and functional status are compelling reasons to further explore incentives for caregiver integration within the healthcare team.

Future of the Healthcare Team

Effectively and meaningfully integrating family care partners into the healthcare team requires first, the development of standardized policies that support consistent organizational and clinician practices. For instance, even with health information exchange promising the interconnectedness of health information across organizations (Thune et al., 2015), persistent variability in the type of information clinicians document about designated family care partners presents barriers to fully realizing the value of interoperability. Second, further inquiry is needed to understand the relationship between care partners and clinical members of the healthcare team. Our exploratory work suggests that clinicians may trust family care partners who demonstrate dependability and beneficence toward their care recipient (Rao & Raj, 2022). But the preferences of care partners and clinicians should be examined further – for instance, what types of information care partners want to have about their relative's condition and needs, and how clinicians want to communicate with care partners.

Organizations and policymakers could use extant models of family caregiver integration in the pediatric setting to guide models of integration among caregivers of adults. For example, proxy patient portal access (Wolff, Kim, et al., 2018), and parent-partnered care delivery models for newborns and infants (Franck & O'Brien, 2019) could serve as models for integrating caregivers of adults into healthcare teams. Moreover, there is a need to better understand how patients prefer for their family caregiver(s) to be involved in their healthcare team in contexts where caregivers are not considered surrogates (e.g., dementia). For instance, some patients may want their caregiver to be highly engaged with the care team through all parts of the care continuum, while others may have concerns about the privacy of their health information or whether their caregiver is acting in their best interest.

Third, conceptual advancement is needed to understand the intersection and interconnectedness of policy and healthcare management. Despite being coupled in educational settings, healthcare management and health policy remain siloed disciplines. Policy encourages – and sometimes, incentivizes – change within healthcare organizations and organizational leaders are tasked with carrying out or advocating for policy, and yet dialogue between the two remains absent. One area for conceptual development might explore the influence of policy on organizational change and the conditions under which organizations are ready to implement policies effectively, consistently, and sustainably such as those integrating care partners into care teams. Developing policies to include family care partners in the care team requires understanding how teams and organizations which are practicing care partner inclusion adapt to this new approach to teamwork.

CONCLUSION

Integrating care partners into healthcare team reflects a long-term investment in improving the quality of care for patients who receive support from relatives as well as the quality of life for care partners (Raj et al., 2022). Healthcare organizations and policies are adapting to new technologies and practices that emerged from the pandemic such as the expanded use of telehealth (CDC, 2020; LaRosa, 2020; Shachar et al., 2020), and need to also account for and define the role of care partners who are increasingly recognized as more than "visitors" within the health system (IPFCC, 2021). Care partners' responsibilities within the health system are likely to grow, and organizations must proactively integrate them into care teams to ensure the sustainability of caregiving and the well-being of care partners.

REFERENCES

Adler-Milstein, J., DesRoches, C. M., Kralovec, P., Foster, G., Worzala, C., Charles, D., Searcy, T., & Jha, A. K. (2015). Electronic health record adoption in US hospitals: Progress continues, but challenges persist. *Health Affairs*, *34*(12). https://doi.org/10.1377/hlthaff.2015.0992

American Medical Association. (2023). *AMA history*. AMA.

Cassidy, S. A., & Stanley, D. J. (2019). Getting from 'me' to 'we': Role clarity, team process, and the transition from individual knowledge to shared mental models in employee dyads. *Canadian Journal of Administrative Sciences – Revue Canadienne des Sciences de l Administration*, *36*(2), 208–220.

CDC. (2020). *Using telehealth to expand access to essential health services during the COVID-19 pandemic*. Centers for Disease Control and Prevention. https://www.cdc.gov/coronavirus/2019-ncov/hcp/telehealth.html

Coleman, E. A. (2016). Family caregivers as partners in care transitions: The caregiver advise record and enable act. *Journal of Hospital Medicine*, *11*, 883–885.

Feinberg, L. F. (2019). Paid family leave: An emerging benefit for employed family caregivers of older adults. *Journal of the American Geriatrics Society*. https://doi.org/10.1111/jgs.15869

Franck, L. S., & O'Brien, K. (2019). The evolution of family-centered care: From supporting parent-delivered interventions to a model of family integrated care. *Birth Defects Research, 111*, 1044–1059.

Friedman, E. M., & Tong, P. K. (2020). *A framework for integrating family caregivers into the health care team*. https://www.rand.org/pubs/research_reports/RRA105-1.html

HHS. (2023). *Individuals' Right under HIPAA to access their Health Information 45 CFR § 164.524*. HHS.

Iott, B., Raj, M., Platt, J., & Anthony, D. (2020). Family caregiver access of online medical records: Findings from the Health Information National Trends Survey. *Journal of General Internal Medicine, 35*(11).

IPFCC. (2021). *Institute for patient- and family-centered care*. https://www.ipfcc.org/

Kaye, N., & Teshale, S. (2020). *Medicaid supports for family caregivers*. National Academy for State Health Policy. https://www.nashp.org/medicaid-supports-for-family-caregivers/#toggle-id-8

Kozlowski, S. W., & Ilgen, D. R. (2006). Enhancing the effectiveness of work groups and teams. *Psychological Science in the Public Interest, 7*(3), 77–124.

LaRosa, J. (2020). *The benefits of telehealth during a pandemic — And beyond*. The Commonwealth Fund. https://www.commonwealthfund.org/blog/2020/benefits-telehealth-during-pandemic-and-beyond

Long, P., Abrams, M., & Milstein, A. (2017). *Effective care for high-need patients: Opportunities for improving outcomes, value, and health*. National Academy of Medicine. https://nam.edu/wp-content/uploads/2017/06/Effective-Care-for-High-Need-Patients.pdf

Mechanic, D. (1998). The functions and limitations of trust in the provision of medical care. *Journal of Health Politics, Policy, and Law, 23*(4), 661–686.

Mickan, S. M., & Rodger, S. A. (2009). Effective Health Care Teams: A model of six characteristics developed from shared perceptions. *Journal of Interprofessional Care, 19*(4), 358–370. https://doi.org/10.1080/13561820500165142

National Academies Press. (2019). *Integrating social care into the delivery of health care: Moving upstream to improve the nation's health*. National Academies Press.

National Alliance for Caregiving. (2023). *History*. NAC.

Nembhard, I. M., & Edmondson, A. C. (2006). Making it safe: The effects of leader inclusiveness and professional status on psychological safety and improvement efforts in health care teams. *Journal of Organizational Behavior, 27*, 941–966.

ONC. (2020). *Telemedicine and telehealth*. Office of the National Coordinator for Health Information Technology (ONC). https://www.healthit.gov/topic/health-it-health-care-settings/telemedicine-and-telehealth

Puglionesi, A. (2018). Americans once avoided the hospital at all costs—Until ERs changed that. *History*.

Raj, M., Feldman, S., Platt, J. E., & Chang, T. (2021). "If it needs to be done, it needs to be done": National survey of youth experiences and perspectives on caregiving. *Journal of Adolescent Health, 69*(4).

Raj, M., Iott, B., Anthony, D., & Platt, J. (2020). Family caregivers' experiences with telehealth during COVID-19: Insights from Michigan. *The Annals of Family Medicine, 20*(1), 69–71.

Raj, M., & Singer, P. M. (2021). Redefining caregiving as an imperative for supporting caregivers: Challenges and opportunities. *Journal of General Internal Medicine. 36*, 3844–3846.

Raj, M., Stephenson, A. L., DePuccio, M. J., Sullivan, E. E., Tarver, W., Fleuren, B., Thomas, S. C., & McAlearney, A. S. (2022). Conceptual framework for integrating family caregivers into the health care team: A scoping review. *Medical Care Research and Review*. https://doi.org/10.1177/10775587221118435

Raj, M., Zhou, S., Yi, S. S., & Kwon, S. (2021). Caregiving across cultures: Priority areas for research, policy, and practice to support family caregivers of older Asian immigrants. *American Journal of Public Health*. https://doi.org/10.2105/AJPH.2021.306494

Rao, R., & Raj, M. (2022). Trust between physicians and family caregivers: Qualitative insights from three family-centered academic medical centers. *Journal of Elder Policy, 2*(2).

Robertson, L. (2020). ACL supports family caregiving during the COVID-19 pandemic response. *Health and Human Services*. https://www.hhs.gov/blog/2020/05/01/acl-supports-family-caregiving-during-the-covid-19-pandemic-response.html

Shachar, C., Engel, J., & Elwyn, G. (2020). Implications for telehealth in a postpandemic future: Regulatory and privacy issues. *JAMA*. https://doi.org/10.1001/jama.2020.7943

Taplin, S. H., Foster, M. K., & Shortell, S. M. (2013). Organizational leadership for building effective health care teams. *The Annals of Family Medicine*, *11*(3).

Thom, D. H., Hall, M. A., & Pawlson, G. (2004). Measuring patients' trust in physicians when assessing quality of care. *Health Affairs*, *23*(4).

Thune, J., Alexander, L., & Roberts, P. (2015). Where is HITECH's $35 billion dollar investment going? *Health Affairs Blog*.

Tucker, A. L., & Edmondson, A. C. (2003). Why hospitals don't learn from failures: Organizational and psychological dynamics that inhibit system change. *California Management Review*, *45*, 55–72.

Wilk, A. S., & Platt, J. E. (2016). Measuring physicians' trust: A scoping review with implications for public policy. *Social Science and Medicine*, *165*, 75–81. https://doi.org/10.1016/j.socscimed.2016.07.039

Wolff, J. L., Darer, J. D., Berger, A., Clarke, D., Green, J. A., Stametz, R. A., Delbanco, T., & Walker, J. (2017). Inviting patients and care partners to read doctors' notes: OpenNotes and shared access to electronic medical records. *Journal of the American Medical Informatics Association*, *24*(e1), e166–e172.

Wolff, J. L., Freedman, V. A., Mulcahy, J. F., & Kasper, J. D. (2020). Family caregivers' experiences with health care workers in the care of older adults with activity limitations. *JAMA Network Open*, *3*(1).

Wolff, J. L., Kim, V. S., Mintz, S., Stametz, R., & Griffin, J. M. (2018). An environmental scan of shared access to patient portals. *Journal of the American Medical Informatics Association*, *25*(4), 408–412.

Wolff, J. L., Mulcahy, J., Huang, J., Roth, D. L., Covinsky, K., & Kasper, J. D. (2018). Family caregivers of older adults, 1999–2015: Trends in characteristics, circumstances, and role-related appraisal. *The Gerontologist*, *58*(6), 1021–1032.

Wolff, J. L., Spillman, B. C., Freedman, V. A., & Kasper, J. D. (2016). A national profile of family and unpaid caregivers who assist older adults with health care activities. *JAMA Internal Medicine*, *176*(3), 372–379.

INDEX

Printed and bound by CPI Group (UK) Ltd, Croydon, CR0 4YY

12/02/2024

08235457-0001